I0819330

THE RAILROAD PHOTOGRAPHY OF
PHIL HASTINGS

RAILROADS PAST AND PRESENT

H. Roger Grant and Thomas Hoback, editors

Recent Titles in the *Railroads Past and Present* series

The Station Agent and the American Railroad Experience
H. Roger Grant

The Diesel That Did It
Wallace W. Abbey

Crossroads of a Continent
Peter A. Hansen, Don L. Hofsommer, and Carlos Arnaldo Schwantes

Narrow Gauge in the Tropics
Augustus J. Veenendaal, Jr.

Amtrak, America's Railroad
Geoffrey H. Doughty, Jeffrey T. Darbee, and Eugene Harmon

The Panama Railroad
Peter Pyne

Last Train to Texas
Fred W. Frailey

Transportation and the American People
H. Roger Grant

American Steam Locomotives
William L. Withuhn

My Life with Trains
Jim McClellan

The Railroad Photography of Lucius Beebe and Charles Clegg
Tony Reevy

Chicago Union Station
Fred Ash

John W. Barriger III
H. Roger Grant

Riding the Rails
Robert D. Krebs

Wallace W. Abbey
Scott Lothes and Kevin P. Keefe

Branch Line Empires
Michael Bezilla with Luther Gette

Indianapolis Union and Belt Railroads
Jeffrey Darbee

Railroads and the American People
H. Roger Grant

Derailed by Bankruptcy
Howard H. Lewis

Electric Interurbans and the American People
H. Roger Grant

The Iron Road in the Prairie State
Simon Cordery

The Lake Shore Electric Railway Story
Herbert H. Harwood, Jr. and Robert S. Korach

The Railroad That Never Was
Herbert H. Harwood, Jr.

James J. Hill's Legacy to Railway Operations
Earl J. Currie

Railroaders without Borders
H. Roger Grant

The Iowa Route
Don L. Hofsommer

The Railroad Photography of Jack Delano
Tony Reevy

THE RAILROAD PHOTOGRAPHY OF
PHIL HASTINGS

TONY REEVY

INDIANA UNIVERSITY PRESS

This book is a publication of

Indiana University Press
Office of Scholarly Publishing
Herman B Wells Library 350
1320 East 10th Street
Bloomington, Indiana 47405 USA

iupress.org

This book is printed on acid-free paper.

Manufactured in China

Second printing 2023

Library of Congress Cataloging-in-Publication Data

Names: Reevy, Tony, author.
Title: The railroad photography of Phil Hastings / Tony Reevy.
Description: Bloomington, Indiana : Indiana University Press, [2023]
Series: Railroads past and present | Includes bibliographical references and index.
Identifiers: LCCN 2022052173 (print) | LCCN 2022052174 (ebook) | ISBN 9780253066497 (hardback) | ISBN 9780253066503 (ebook)
Subjects: LCSH: Hastings, Philip R., 1925-1987. | Photography of railroads—United States. | Railroads—North America. | Photographers—United States—Biography. | Physicians—United States—Biography. | BISAC: TRANSPORTATION / Railroads / Pictorial | PHOTOGRAPHY / Subjects & Themes / Historical
Classification: LCC TR715 .R444 2023 (print) | LCC TR715 (ebook) | DDC 779/.9385—dc23/eng/20230119
LC record available at https://lccn.loc.gov/2022052173
LC ebook record available at https://lccn.loc.gov/2022052174

Dedicated to,

JIM WRINN

1961–2022

CONTENTS

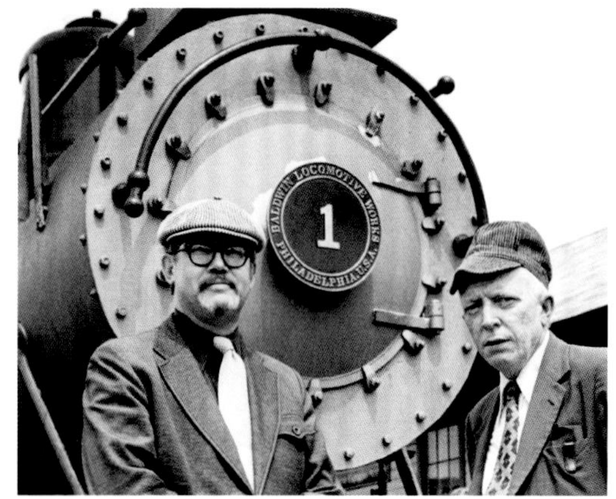

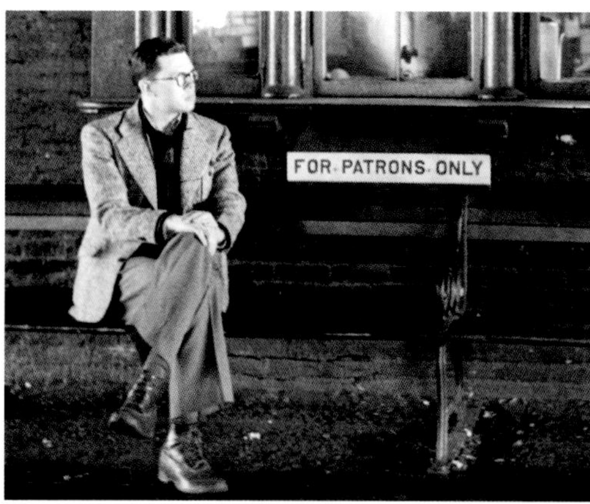

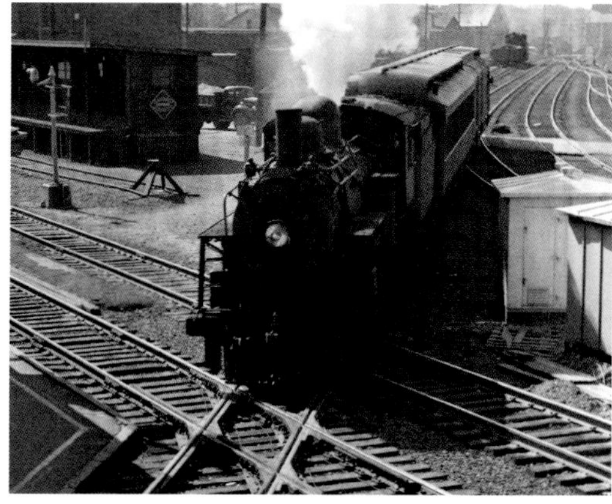

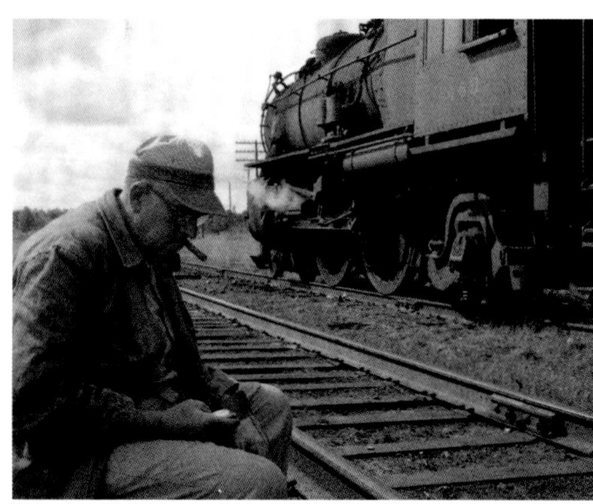

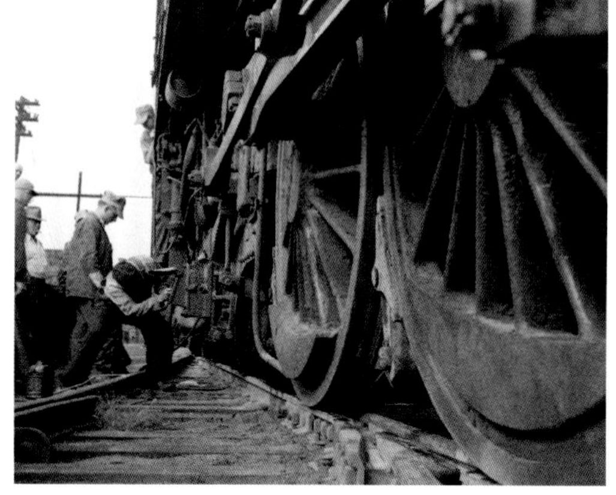

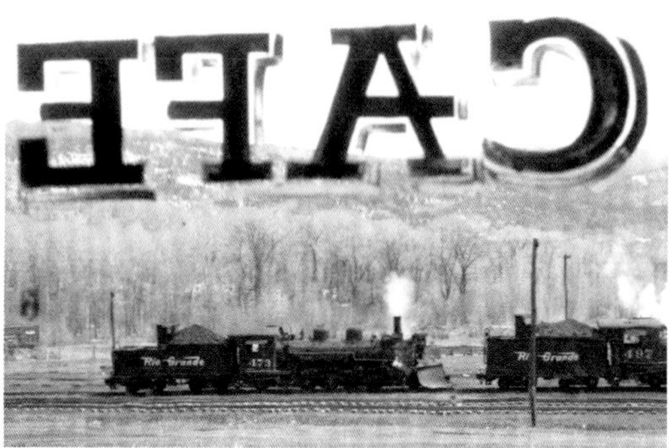

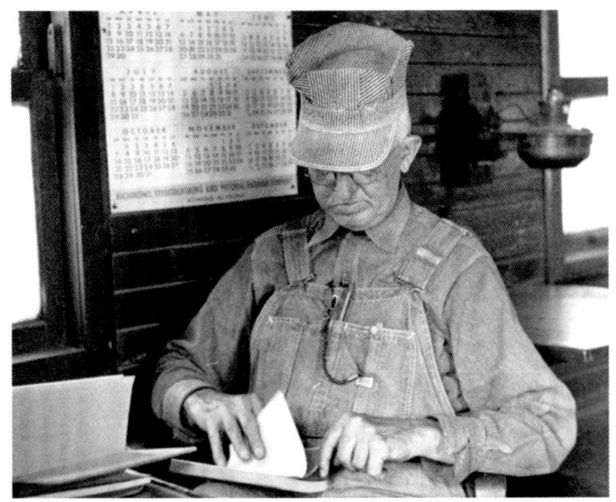

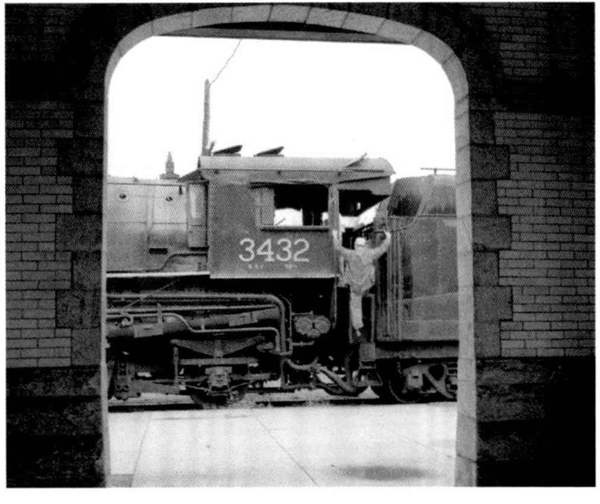
3432

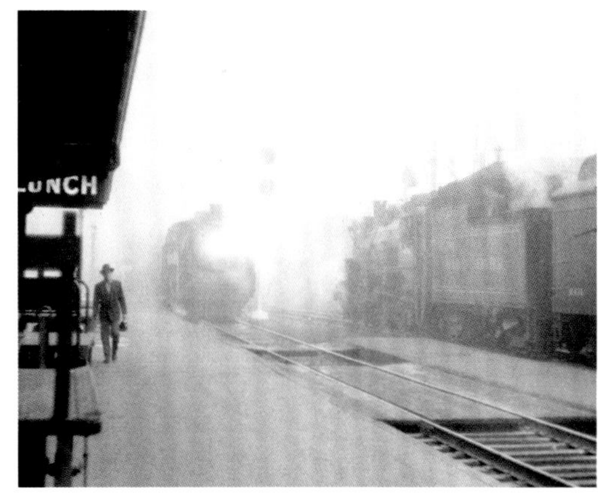
LUNCH

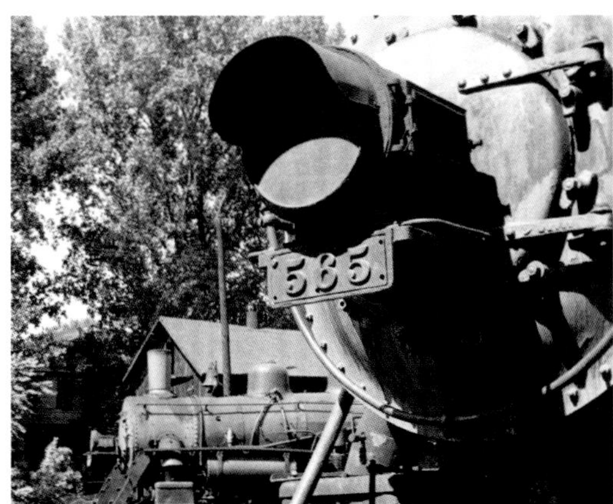
565

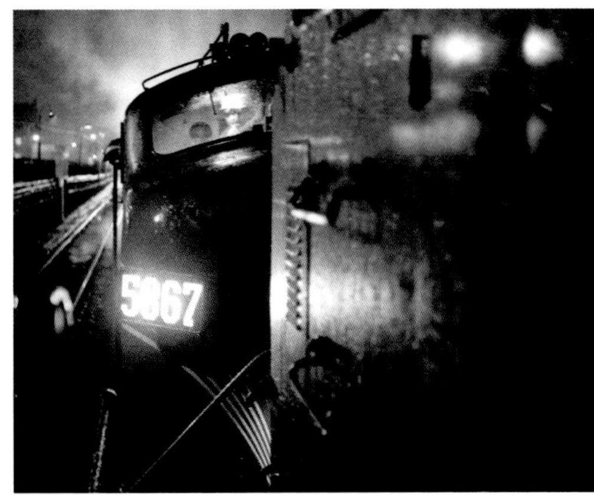
5067

FOREWORD

THE PHIL HASTINGS I KNEW

I was fourteen years old when the name Philip R. Hastings first caught my attention. As an early Christmas present, my parents had signed me up for a subscription to a magazine I'd only recently discovered, and now the November 1965 issue of *Trains* was sitting there amid the pile of the day's mail on our living room coffee table. It was an auspicious way to start a lifelong association: that edition celebrated the magazine's twenty-fifth anniversary and included some of the finest brief essays ever written by the celebrated editor in chief David P. Morgan.

The issue also featured images from a who's who of railroad photographers, names I would come to know as well as the baseball players I followed or the rock and roll bands I heard on the radio. I memorized all the credit lines: Richard Steinheimer, J. Parker Lamb, Don Wood, Jim Shaughnessy, Stan Kistler, Robert Hale, and many more. Some made stunning action images of trains at speed; others showed railroading in quieter, sometimes bittersweet moments. Having just entered this exciting world as depicted in *Trains*, I wanted to know more about all of them.

One name stuck with me, and that was Philip R. Hastings. There were only two contributions by him in the issue—small shots included in a montage supporting Morgan's essay "The Limiteds We Lost"—but the pictures stayed with me. One showed a Maine Central passenger diesel posed beside the depot in Bangor, Maine; the other showed an overhead view of the steam-powered Missouri-Kansas-Texas passenger train *Bluebonnet* somewhere in Texas. Both hinted at Hastings's greatness as an artist who always portrayed something besides the obvious.

As author Tony Reevy's excellent introduction explains, Phil Hastings led an extraordinary life as a physician and a photographer, as well as a husband and a father. A New Englander by birth and, later, a midwesterner by choice, he followed his wide-ranging instincts—and some good luck in his relationship with Morgan—to create a photographic body of work that transcended specifics of regions, railroad companies, and technology.

His standing in the pantheon of railroad photographers was secured the moment Morgan included him in a special photo section in the November 1955 issue of *Trains*, in which the editor showcased a dozen photographers deemed critical to the magazine's success. Morgan wrote: "The circulation and the longevity of the magazine have been due in no mean measure to the photographers who've hauled their gear to trackside, there to record the ever-changing mode of the flanged wheel. In a demanding yet specialized field of illustration the standards have been high and the rewards necessarily meager."

That certainly applied to Hastings. Of his own work, Phil had this to say: "When the steam locomotives are all gone and it is no longer any fun to take pictures, I intend to devote my life to the study of why people like trains." For his part in that 1955 issue,

Phil contributed a fine backlit portrait of a Boston & Maine 4-6-2 made at Bradford, Vermont, in 1946. Up to that point, Hastings had called it "his favorite unpublished shot."

As an eager teenager in November 1965, I never would have dreamed of meeting Phil Hastings. But life is impossible to predict, and barely ten years later a string of unusual circumstances led me to a position as an ad copywriter for *Trains* magazine's parent company, Kalmbach Publishing, in downtown Milwaukee, Wisconsin. Not long after arriving on the job, I discovered that one of my first assignments would be to devise a promotional campaign for an exciting new book compiling all the *Trains* articles Morgan and Hastings produced in the mid-1950s as they tracked down some of the last steam locomotives in America.

Often referred to as the "Steam in Indian Summer" series (a moniker Morgan had affixed to one specific group of stories), the articles had an outsized effect on their audience. The book's title came from one of their more memorable episodes: *The Mohawk That Refused to Abdicate, and Other Tales*. As writer-and-photographer collaborations go, this was a dream team, such was the interplay between Morgan's words and Hastings' photographs. I don't think it's an exaggeration to compare their efforts with those of writer James Agee and photographer Walker Evans, whose monumental 1941 book *Let Us Now Praise Famous Men* made vivid the struggle of Depression era tenant farmers. In a similar vein, Morgan and Hastings created a valedictory for an entire way of life.

I decided that to do a good job on the book promotion—and to write the dust jacket copy—getting to know Phil would be a priority. Gathering impressions from Morgan would be easy; his office was just down the hall on the fifth floor. But Phil lived 260 miles away in Waterloo, Iowa. I called and left a message with his wife, Marian.

It wasn't long before my phone rang. "Hi, Kevin, this is Phil Hastings." His measured baritone was soothing, his manner quite relaxing—evidence, no doubt, of a long career in psychiatry. What I remember is that we talked like we'd been friends for years. He put this green ad writer utterly at ease. After that, my work on promoting *Mohawk* came together easily. It was the highlight of my brief stint in Kalmbach's sales department.

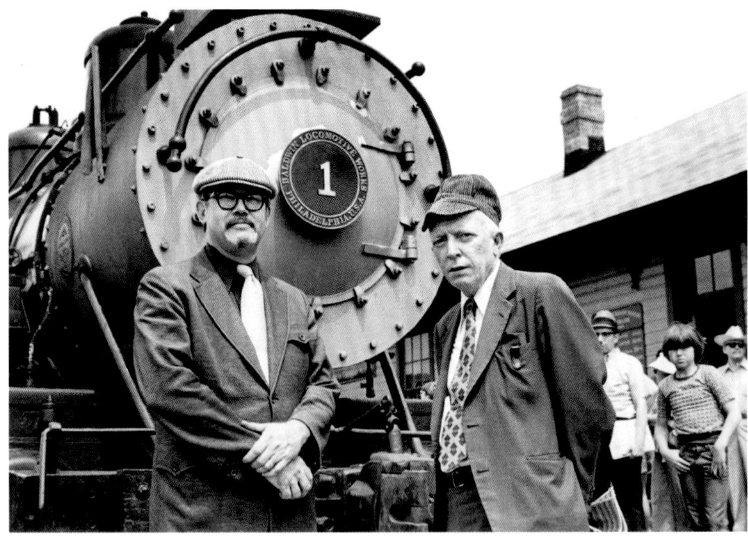

Figure 0a.1. Hastings (left) and David P. Morgan (he was not yet fifty when this photo was taken) reunite at the Mid-Continent Railway Museum in 1975. Colon cancer claimed Hastings in 1987; Morgan died in 1990.

Photo by Kevin P. Keefe

Having a small role in the book was an honor. I cannot think of a body of work in railroad publishing that is more beloved. Its influence has persisted way beyond those first appearances of their stories in *Trains* between 1953 and 1957. First there was 1975's *Mohawk* book, in which Kalmbach enshrined Phil's images in rich duo-tone black reproduction and wrapped them in an elegant foil cover. Nearly thirty years later, the entire series was reissued again under the rubric "In Search of Steam," this time in the form of three separate stand-alone magazines published in 2007, 2009, and 2011 by *Classic Trains* magazine and distributed on newsstands throughout North America. Today, many of those same Hastings photographs populate the book you hold in your hands.

I left Kalmbach not long after the publication of *Mohawk*. Luckily for me, my direct involvement with Phil wasn't over. In the spring of 1976, I returned to a daily newspaper career in Michigan. I also was fortunate to land a side job editing *Passenger Train Journal*, a small upstart magazine launched in 1968 by my friend Kevin McKinney, who in those days was working for the state of Michigan's passenger train program. We were producing *PTJ* on a shoestring but doing our best to compete with the big boys of rail-enthusiast magazines, *Trains* and *Railfan*. One of our biggest challenges was persuading some of the better-known writers and photographers to do some work for us.

One day in late 1976, a letter arrived from Waterloo. It was from Phil, and he had a proposal for us. Despite what he'd once said about giving up railroad photography "when steam locomotives are all gone," Phil spent a lot of time in the 1960s photographing passenger trains—the kind pulled by diesels. As he did in the 1950s with steam locomotives, Phil recognized that the American passenger train was running on borrowed time, so he set about photographing "the vanishing varnish" as much as he could.

As was his wont, Phil concentrated not on the glamour trains still around—the *Super Chief* or the *California Zephyr* or the *Panama Limited*—but instead on lesser-known secondary trains, the kind that mainly plied quieter main lines and served quieter places. Thus, he rode Kansas City Southern's *Flying Crow* down through the Ozarks, Erie's *Lake Cities* from Chicago to Hoboken, and Milwaukee Road's *Copper Country Limited* from Chicago to Michigan's Upper Peninsula, along with several more. Because he was aboard the trains, he couldn't get the kinds of dramatic action shots that quicken railfans' pulses, but he plumbed something richer: life aboard the trains. For him, the joy came in recording the telling moment, the revelatory detail. His were stories told in images of conductors punching tickets, Dutch door glimpses of small towns blurring past, passengers standing on lonely station platforms, and a simple dining car menu tucked behind a carnation in a bud vase.

Phil had originally submitted the idea for a series on these forgotten trains to David P. Morgan, but, inexplicably, DPM rejected it. I'm still puzzled by the great editor's decision, but *Trains'* lost opportunity was a huge boost for little *Passenger Train Journal*, and we eagerly said yes to Phil. We decided to call the series "Once in a Timetable" and soon had it up and running over several issues. Not surprisingly, the photo stories were a hit with readers, and Kevin and I took great pride in putting the name Philip R. Hastings on the cover. Most of all, though, I loved working with Phil again. He was the ideal collaborator, full of his own good ideas but generous in his acceptance of ours.

Phil Hastings died in 1987 at sixty-one, a shockingly young age when you ponder what he had yet to accomplish both as a physician and a photographer. It's our good fortune he chose photography as his great avocation, because what he left behind tells us as much about the artist as it does his subjects. In his pitch-perfect obituary in the May 1987 issue of *Trains*, Dave Morgan offered that "none of us who knew Phil Hastings personally knew him any better than anyone who simply saw, or will see, his photography. His imagination, intelligence, and compassion are invested and remain in his negatives for the common good." That will be abundantly evident here in the photographs chosen by Tony Reevy. For some it will be a fresh journey, for others a blessed rediscovery. Ultimately, Phil Hastings reveals himself to all of us.

Kevin P. Keefe
Milwaukee, Wisconsin
June 2022

ACKNOWLEDGMENTS

Phil Hastings was a modest man and not well known beyond the rail-enthusiast community. He died relatively young more than thirty-five years ago. For all of these reasons, this book could not have been written without a great deal of help from collaborators and colleagues.

Let me start by thanking those who helped me with the 2008 *Railroad History* article "Artist of the Rail: Phil Hastings." The article was shepherded by then *Railroad History* editor Pete Hansen. Pete passed away several years ago and is much missed. I interviewed the late Jim Shaughnessy for the article; he is also much missed. Then and now, I thank Bob Cohen for assistance with back issues of railroad-subject magazines. Ellen Halteman of the California State Railroad Museum Library and Archives, now retired, provided expert assistance for the article, as did the staff of the Mid-Continent Railway Historical Society.

This book would not have happened without a publisher, and I have benefited so much, for the third time, from my association with Indiana University Press. This book was acquired by Ashely Runyon, now head of the University Press of Kentucky. David Hulsey, of the press, took this project over, and then Dan Crissman carried it through. Thank you also to Eileen Allen, Samantha Heffner, Dave Miller, Megan Schindele, and Stephen Williams.

This project also would not have happened if Marian Hastings and her family had not donated Phil Hastings's photographs and papers to a sound repository. Thank you, Mrs. Hastings—from a remove of more than twenty-five years—for donating the Hastings collection to the California State Railroad Museum Library and Archives, where it is well curated and available to researchers.

Photo books are expensive, with the author being responsible for photo scans and reproduction fees. This book also required a research visit to the California State Railroad Museum Library and Archives. Many thanks to Tom Hoback for his support of this book. Thank you also to the Railway & Locomotive Historical Society, who awarded a 2019 John H. White Research Fellowship Award to help fund my visit to the California State Railroad Museum Library and Archives. The Lexington Group in Transportation History awarded a 2020 Richard C. Overton Prize in support of this book.

Speaking of the California State Railroad Museum Library and Archives, I spent a week in July 2021 there, researching Phil Hastings. I extend great thanks to Chris Rockwell, Claire Phillips, and volunteer Jeff Asay.

Several folks gave their time generously to help with this book. I interviewed Greg McDonnell and Kevin Keefe for the book, and both Greg and now retired *Classic Trains* editor Rob McGonigal helped me identify locations for the Hastings photos featured in the book. There are a few locations we have not been able to identify—if you recognize them, please contact me through Indiana University Press. New information will be included in any future edition of *The Railroad Photography of Phil Hastings*.

Many thanks also to Kevin Keefe for his insightful foreword.

This book is dedicated to the memory of Jim Wrinn, who passed away in 2022 after a valiant struggle with cancer. Jim was going to write the foreword but didn't have a chance to complete it before his passing. I first met Jim when my wife, Caroline, and I lived around the corner from him in the historic area of Concord, North Carolina, in the early 1990s. Jim, we lost you too soon—rest in peace. And sympathies to Cate Kratville-Wrinn and all those who knew and loved Jim.

Finally, our children are now away at graduate school and college, but the biggest round of thanks goes to my wife, Caroline Weaver—always patient and always my first reader. Thank you, Caroline, with love!

If I have missed thanking anyone for a work that spans at least fifteen years and that was interrupted by the COVID-19 pandemic, I apologize. And, of course, errors and omissions are the fault of this author alone.

THE RAILROAD PHOTOGRAPHY OF
PHIL HASTINGS

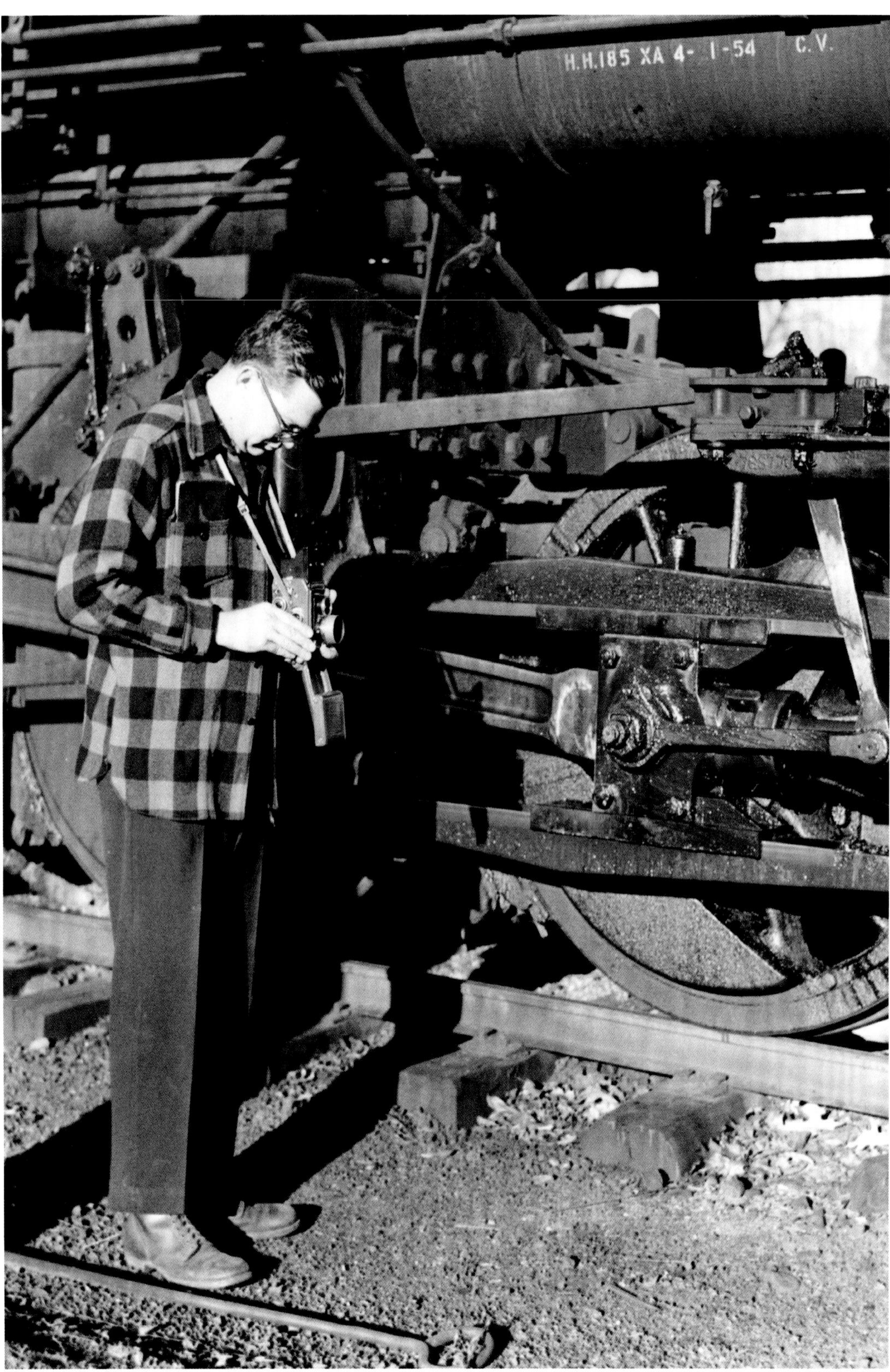

Figure 0b.1. Phil Hastings in the field.

Courtesy of California State Railroad Museum. Philip Ross Hastings, MD, Collection, [Negative 10470].

INTRODUCTION

Dr. Philip R. "Phil" Hastings (1925–1987) was one of a small group of photographers of the North American railroad who, under the influence of the photojournalistic movement that developed during their childhoods, expanded their work from the traditional locomotive roster and action shots into a holistic view of the railroad environment. These men—Hastings, his close friend Jim Shaughnessy, Dick Steinheimer, O. Winston Link, David Plowden, and others—found an outlet on the pages of *Trains* magazine under the editorship of David P. Morgan and in the railroad photo books of Lucius Beebe and Charles Clegg. Collectively, and in tandem with Morgan, Beebe, and US Farm Security Administration photographers such as Walker Evans and Jack Delano, they changed the way we look at the North American railroad—even as the railroad environment was evolving in a less visually interesting way. This change accelerated Hastings's work, and that of his contemporaries, and was exemplified by the replacement of steam locomotives with diesels, the decline of the intercity passenger train, and the closing of most local staffed railroad stations. Their commitment to building a record of this scene came just in time to preserve it for posterity.

THE LIFE

Phil Hastings was born on April 26, 1925, in the village of Bradford, Vermont, located on the north–south Connecticut River line of the Boston & Maine Railroad. His parents were Hugh and Jessie Stevenson Hastings.[1] Hastings's mother was from Quebec, Canada, which may explain the feel for Canadian society and landscape that can be seen in Hastings's photos of that country.[2]

Just a year before his death, Hastings wrote movingly about his boyhood there and its influence on his photography:

> Dad enjoyed taking his sons for a Sunday afternoon walk down to the Boston & Maine Railroad depot to watch the southbound Canadian Pacific (CPR) freight roar by. . . . As I grew more interested, Mr. Hooker [the B&M agent/operator at Bradford] gave me tasks around the depot—sweeping the floors, scraping snow off the platform, selling tickets, passing out timetables. . . . Somewhere along the line, I started taking photos of trains with the family's 120 Kodak box camera. I photographed the B&M 2-6-0 and 4-6-2 engines as they stopped at Bradford on passenger trains. . . . I treasure and enjoy the legacy of my father and Mr. Hooker.[3]

Hastings's father, Hugh W. Hastings, was an attorney and, according to *Railroad* editor Freeman Hubbard, a "dedicated railroad buff" whose interest rubbed off on his young son. Hubbard profiled Hastings in *Railroad* magazine in 1970, noting that he grew up in "a big, old-fashioned, frame house" that gave Hastings a "clear view of Boston & Maine trains."[4]

Hastings took his first railroad photo, a blurry side shot of a Boston & Maine 4-4-0 "American" steam locomotive at Concord, New Hampshire, in 1937.[5] He soon graduated to using a 616 Kodak box camera, followed by a Kodak Vigilant folding camera, which was presented to him in 1939 by an older friend who admired his photography. The Vigilant could shoot at 1/200th of a second, allowing Hastings to begin taking action shots.[6] Hastings would use a Rolleiflex ("Rollei") roll film camera for the majority of his significant work.[7]

The earliest influences on Hastings's railroad photography were the photos appearing in *Railroad* magazine and its earlier incarnations, which he first discovered at the town dump in Bradford. He soon became a member of the magazine's "Engine Picture Club." In 1941, while visiting his older brother, he discovered *Trains* magazine on a Boston newsstand.[8] As early as 1940, Hastings had stepped back from Lucius Beebe–style action shots to capture a brakeman opening a siding switch, a craggy-faced engineer peering from the cab, and a section crew unloading ties. These images were milestones in a then developing "environmental" view of American railroad-subject photography.[9]

Hastings went off to Tufts College after his high school graduation in 1942.[10] Enlisting in the army in 1943, during World War II, Hastings also attended Fordham University and New York University. He had intended to earn an engineering degree and work in the railroad industry, but he decided to pursue a medical career. While in the army, he also worked for the Jersey Central on Sundays at the Jersey City terminal.[11] In 1945, he returned to Vermont to study premedicine and then medicine at the University of Vermont in Burlington. He graduated from the University of Vermont with an MD degree in 1950, interned in Spokane, Washington, and then served in the army during the Korean Conflict.[12] After his second army stint, Hastings completed a residency in psychiatry at Albany Medical Center (1953–1956) and joined the US Veterans Administration (1956–1959), which maintains a network of hospitals for American veterans.[13]

In 1942, Hastings met a young woman from Glover, Vermont—Marian Bickford, who was a close friend of one of his cousins.[14] They married in 1945.[15] Marian and Phil Hastings stayed together for forty-five years, until his death in 1987, and had five children: Pamela, Steven, Hugh, Douglas, and David.

Marian Hastings did not, according to accounts published both by her and by *Trains* editor David P. Morgan, share her husband's passion for railroad photography, but she tolerated it for forty-five years. As she wrote in an obituary for her husband, "his 'extreme interest' in railroads continued to grow, becoming an obsession. Phil used every free moment and family vacation trip to visit and photograph his favorite railroads. Many times, the family chafed impatiently while Phil waited beside the tracks for the one last chance to record a special event in the annals of railroading."[16] Morgan, in his obituary for the photographer, noted that Hastings was "indebted to wife Marion [*sic*] and family for forbearance and support while on the trail."[17]

Hastings transformed his railroad photography from an avocation to a part-time vocation during his years as a medical student at the University of Vermont. His first railroad-subject photo publication was in 1946, and his first article publication was a piece in *Trains* on the 120-mile-long St. Johnsbury & Lake Champlain Railroad, a classic New England short line.[18] Years later, Hastings wrote, "The $64 payment was big money to us and reinforced my pattern of submitting material to the rail magazines. Meanwhile, I took on some other photography to help finance medical college."[19] The article, titled simply "St. Johnsbury & Lake Champlain," appeared on pages 50 to 59 of the May 1947 issue.[20] It does not seem a freshman effort at all but rather the work of an experienced magazine author. Its prose, an extended piece of writing by Hastings, is excellent, and the photos—especially the opening spread, showing an ill-maintained stretch of track and a switch stand against a panorama of Vermont hills and sky—are extraordinarily innovative for 1947, presaging O. Winston Link's daytime photos of the Norfolk & Western Railway's rural Abingdon (Virginia to North Carolina) Branch taken a decade later.

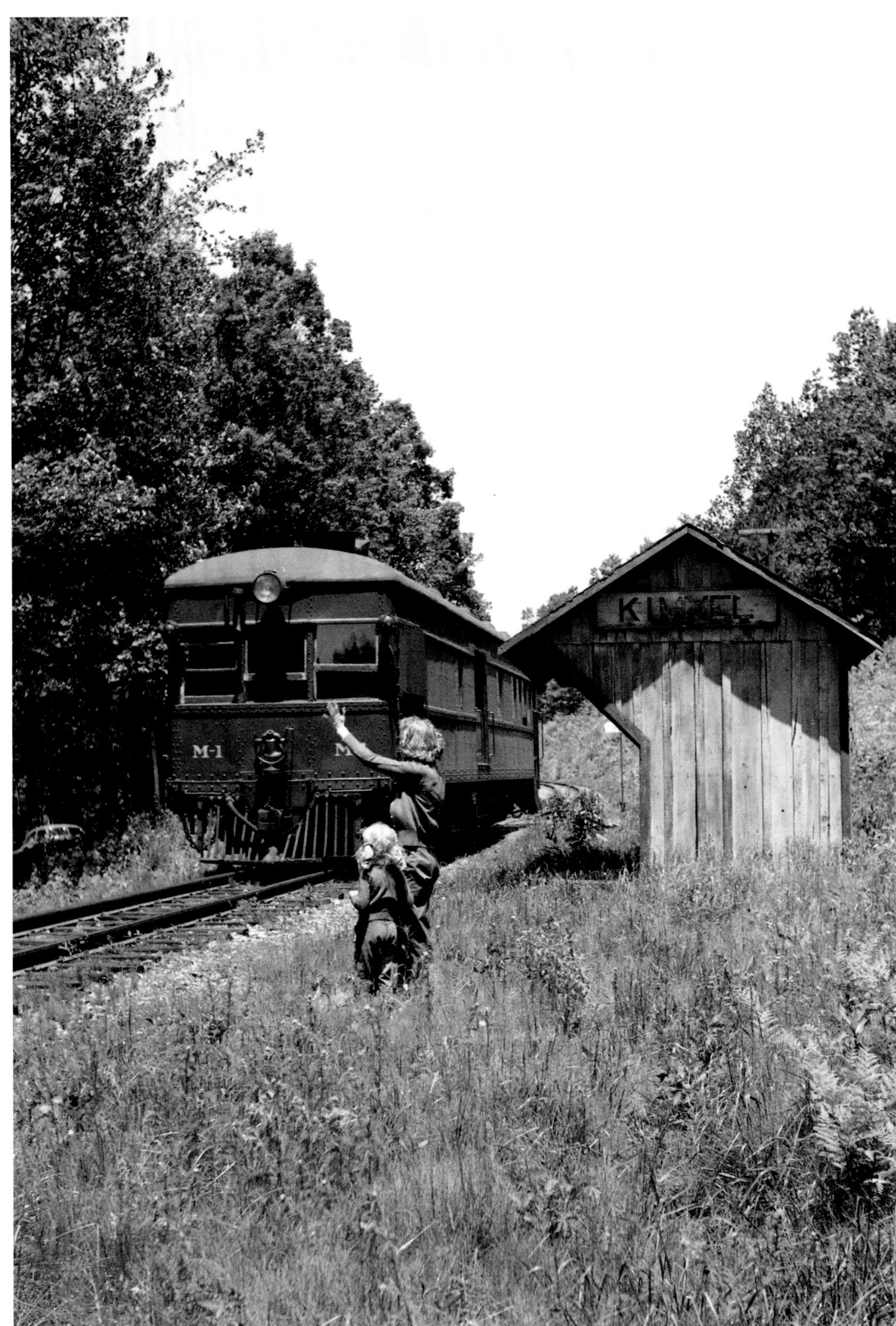

Figure 0b.2. East Broad Top "doodlebug" M-1 passes the line's passenger shelter at Kimmel, Pennsylvania. Hastings's wife, Marian, waves in the foreground, and their daughter, Pamela, stands with her mother.

Courtesy of California State Railroad Museum. Philip Ross Hastings, MD, Collection, [Negative 7640].

In the article's introductory comments, Hastings wrote, "Especially in the fall, when hills glory in the red and gold of retiring foliage's one last fling, a ride on the StJ&LC is an experience of natural beauty unsurpassed. 'Unspoiled Vermont' lacks, perhaps, the grandeur of a Mt. Rainier; but certainly it is endowed with purple mountain majesties, the loveliness of crystal lakes, and the soothing velvet of emerald meadows. Sunlight trickles through roofs of leaves arched overhead; rail clicks are sharp in the murmur of a fresh countryside; the cool breath of a rocky cut is bathed by icy springs."[21]

In his obituary for Hastings, Morgan wrote, "The StJ could have served as the valedictory of a lesser man, but Phil had miles to go, and 50,000 black-and-white and 10,000 color slides to compose, before he slept. Tirelessly, imaginatively, he roamed the U. S. and Canada, particularly during his second term in the Army (1950–1953) and thereafter with the Veterans Administration."[22]

Hastings's focus on his photography also emerges through his vigorous efforts to protect his copyrights and to be paid for his work. In one letter, Hastings says, "I should be compensated for my material. Therefor [*sic*] I enclose my statement for $270, representing a nominal charge of $5 for each of 54 8X10 B&W prints reproduced."[23]

Hastings's style was affected by the feedback he received from then prominent photographers and editors. H. W. "Jack" Pontin, of Rail Photo Service, said in a 1949 letter to Hastings, "As an Art School graduate, I might point out that your shot at Montpelier Junction in the rain, might well have been a Salon Subject worth many hundreds of dollars, IF, there had been two figures coming toward you shrouded in raincoats or umbrellas, hence producing the all-necessary Human Interest angle in such works of art. To me, the shot remains one of the finest I have seen for many moons. This I hope would be incentive enough for you to try more of these night compositions."[24]

In 1954, after taking back the editorship of *Railroad*, Freeman Hubbard wrote to Hastings,

> While I admire the quality of your photography, personally, I feel that there was much too much similarity in the photos which my predecessor selected for use with "Mogul Country Farewell" . . . If I were ordering a picture-story, I would ask for a wide variety in subjects—instead of practically nothing but distance shots of engines and trains, excellent though the latter may be. I would want some close-ups of people doing things, some distance shots of engines and trains in scenic backgrounds, preferably one or more oddities, some unusually-shaped shots (i.e., tall and thin, designed to fill one column of the magazine). Maybe a pretty girl or an animal thrown in if she or it would logically belong there, etc.[25]

Hubbard, in a postscript to this letter, also asked Hastings to undertake a standard freelance writing practice by querying him about articles before submitting them.

Hastings, like Jim Shaughnessy and O. Winston Link, gained notability for his night photography. He described his night-photography technique for Freeman Hubbard this way:

> I am most proud of my night shots of railroad scenes. I have been taking night shots for the past 25 or more years and feel I have developed a pretty good technique. Nowadays [in 1969] I rarely use supplemental flash, but rely on judicious use of available light. I am particularly proud of my color night shots on High Speed Ektachrome film, which I expose either on a tripod or hand-held by leaning against existing structures an [*sic*] an exposure of ½ or 1 second at f/2. Night shots satisfy me more because they are technically more difficult and therefor [*sic*] more challenging.[26]

Hastings's night photography was receiving very positive reviews as early as 1947, while he was a student at the University of Vermont. In a letter from noted railroad author Frank P Donovan Jr., then a research editor at *Trains*, Donovan said, "Your letter of August 18 stating you are sending us a 'batch of photographs of railroad scenes at night . . . a somewhat unusual set' is a gross understatement. Every one of those pictures are ringers and we have slated the group to run as a photo story. To

***Facing*, Figure ob.3.** A night self-portrait by Phil Hastings at the Central Vermont's Essex Junction, Vermont station. Hastings was an innovator in night railroad-subject photography.

Courtesy of California State Railroad Museum. Beebe and Clegg Photo Collection, [Negative 4022].

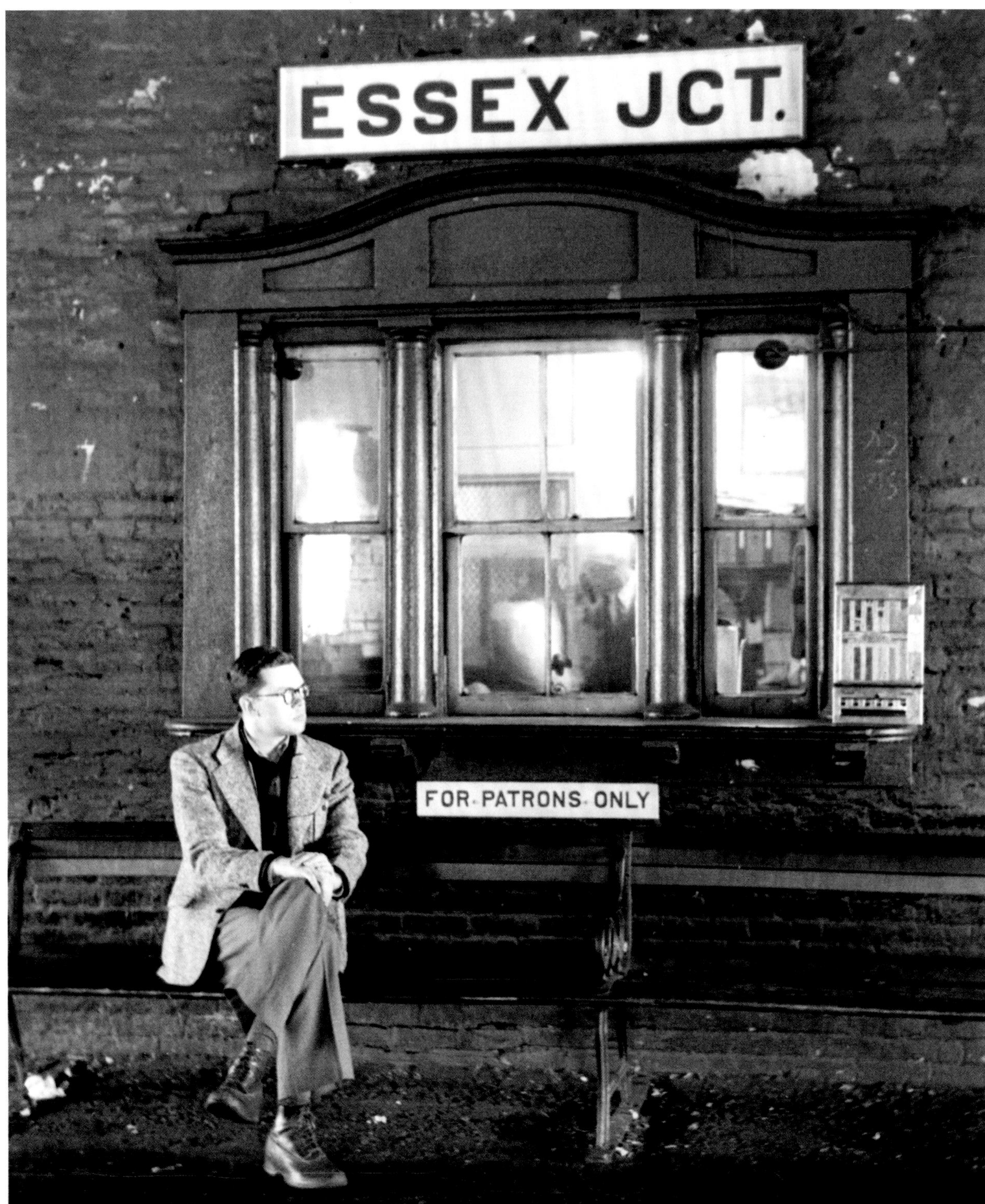
ESSEX JCT.
FOR PATRONS ONLY

my way of thinking it is one of the most unusual features on night photography I have ever seen."[27]

A series of articles in *Trains* and *Railroad* followed.[28] In *Trains,* Hastings first teamed up with David P. Morgan to illustrate an article on Missouri Pacific Railroad's Kingsville Division in the June 1949 issue. Also notable are solo *Trains* articles on the Western Maryland Railway's passenger trains (July 1953), the Pennsylvania Railroad's Enola (Pennsylvania) Yard (September 1953), and the East Broad Top (November 1953). Hastings also cracked *Railroad* magazine with notable articles, including "Railroad Town," about Hagerstown, Maryland, and "Mogul Country Farewell," about Boston & Maine 2-6-0 locomotives.[29]

In addition to selling articles to *Trains, Railroad,* and other magazines, Hastings sold prints of his railroad photos and historic photos. As a student at the University of Vermont, he, with his wife's help, photographed weddings and did other freelance jobs.[30] He tried to sell other types of nonfiction articles, with subjects such as fishing in Quebec and maple sugaring time, but struggled to publish articles not focused on railroading. For a time, he participated in H. W. Pontin's Rail Photo Service. In the mid-1950s, he placed photos in railroad trade publisher Simmons-Boardman's 1956 guide, *The Handbook of American Railroads* by Robert G. Lewis. In later life, he licensed slide sets to Blackhawk Films, sold prints through Rails Unlimited, and contributed to railroad-subject calendars. Hastings planned to expand his photography business in retirement, but this was not to be—he died before he reached retirement age.[31]

The stage was now set for Hastings's renowned partnership with *Trains* editor David P. Morgan to document, in more than thirty articles appearing in the magazine during the years 1954–1958, the end of steam power on US and Canadian railroads. Except for a few pieces, these appeared in three series, titled "In Search of Steam," "Smoke over the Prairies," and "Steam in Indian Summer." Hastings's affinity for small locomotives and short lines—undoubtedly a legacy from his exposure to Boston & Maine "Moguls" and the rusty branches plied by its trains, as well as those of the Rutland and St. Johnsbury & Lake Champlain—is reflected in this body of work. Standout photographic portfolios, other than the New England and Canada features within these articles, include his works on Wabash "Moguls"; the

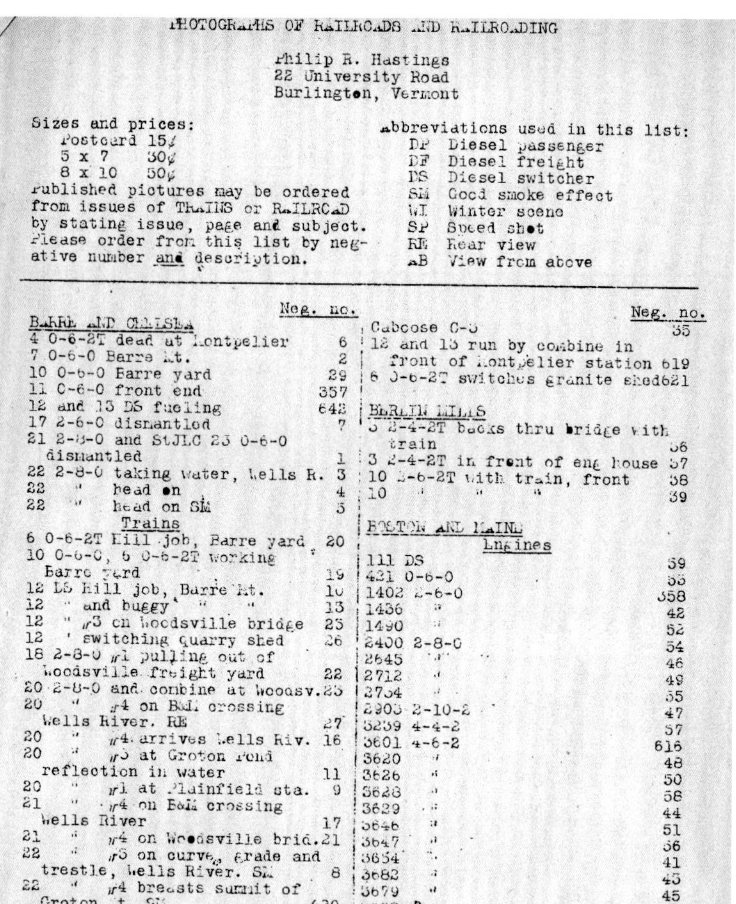

PHOTOGRAPHS OF RAILROADS AND RAILROADING

Philip R. Hastings
22 University Road
Burlington, Vermont

Sizes and prices:
Postcard 15¢
5 x 7 30¢
8 x 10 50¢
Published pictures may be ordered from issues of TRAINS or RAILROAD by stating issue, page and subject. Please order from this list by negative number and description.

Abbreviations used in this list:
DP Diesel passenger
DF Diesel freight
DS Diesel switcher
SM Good smoke effect
WI Winter scene
SP Speed shot
RE Rear view
AB View from above

BARRE AND CHELSEA	Neg. no.
4 0-6-2T dead at Montpelier	6
7 0-6-0 Barre Mt.	2
10 0-6-0 Barre yard	29
11 0-6-0 front end	357
12 and 13 DS fueling	642
17 2-6-0 dismantled	7
21 2-8-0 and StJLC 23 0-6-0 dismantled	1
22 2-8-0 taking water, Wells R.	3
22 " head on	4
22 " head on SM	5
Trains	
6 0-6-2T Hill job, Barre yard	20
10 0-6-0, 6 0-6-2T working Barre yard	19
12 DS Hill job, Barre Mt.	10
12 " and buggy " "	13
12 " #3 on Woodsville bridge	25
12 " switching quarry shed	26
18 2-8-0 #1 pulling out of Woodsville freight yard	22
20 2-8-0 and combine at Woodsv.	23
20 " #4 on B&M crossing Wells River. RE	27
20 " #4 arrives Wells Riv.	16
20 " #3 at Groton Pond reflection in water	11
20 " #1 at Plainfield sta.	9
21 " #4 on B&M crossing Wells River	17
21 " #4 on Woodsville brid.	21
22 " #3 on curve, grade and trestle, Wells River. SM	8
22 " #4 breasts summit of Groton Mt. SM	620

	Neg. no.
Caboose C-3	35
12 and 13 run by combine in front of Montpelier station	619
6 0-6-2T switches granite shed	621
BERLIN MILLS	
3 2-4-2T backs thru bridge with train	36
3 2-4-2T in front of eng house	37
10 2-6-2T with train, front	38
10 " " "	39
BOSTON AND MAINE	
Engines	
111 DS	59
421 0-6-0	53
1402 2-6-0	358
1436 "	42
1490 "	52
2400 2-8-0	54
2645 "	46
2712 "	49
2734 "	55
2903 2-10-2	47
3239 4-4-2	57
3601 4-6-2	616
3620 "	48
3626 "	50
3628 "	58
3629 "	44
3646 "	51
3647 "	56
3654 "	41
3682 "	43
3679 "	45
3698 "	40

Figure ob.4. An early catalog of Phil Hastings's photos for sale. At this point in his career, he sold his images himself.

Courtesy of California State Railroad Museum. Philip Ross Hastings, MD, Collection.

***Facing,* Figure ob.5.** A portrait of *Trains* editor David P. Morgan, by Phil Hastings, during one of their searches for steam in the 1950s. The photo was probably taken during their trip that included crossing the Bay of Fundy on the Canadian Pacific's *Princess Helene.*

Courtesy of California State Railroad Museum. Philip Ross Hastings, MD, Collection, [Negative 9505].

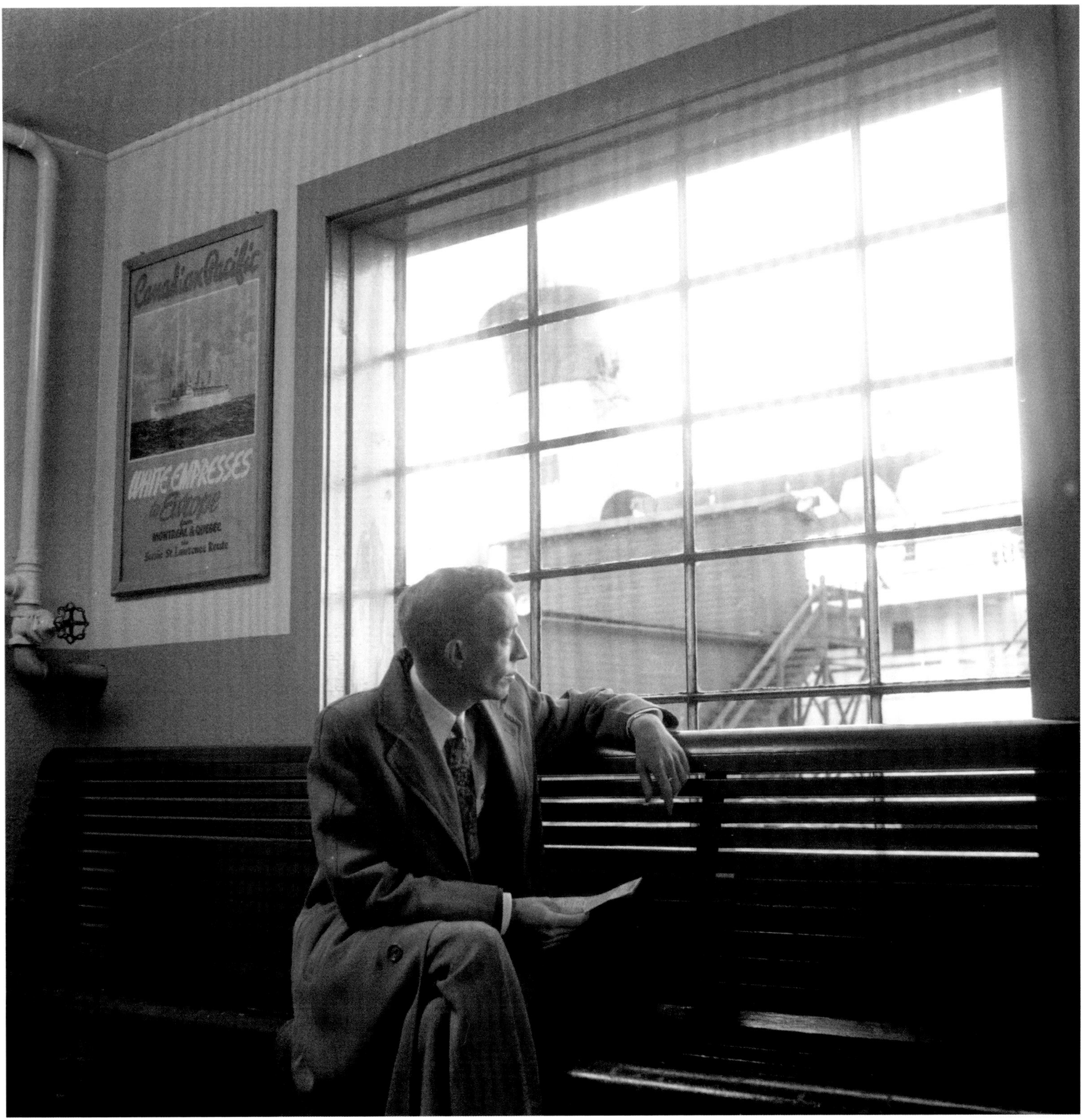
Canadian Pacific
WHITE EMPRESSES
to Europe
from
MONTREAL & QUEBEC
Scenic St. Lawrence Route

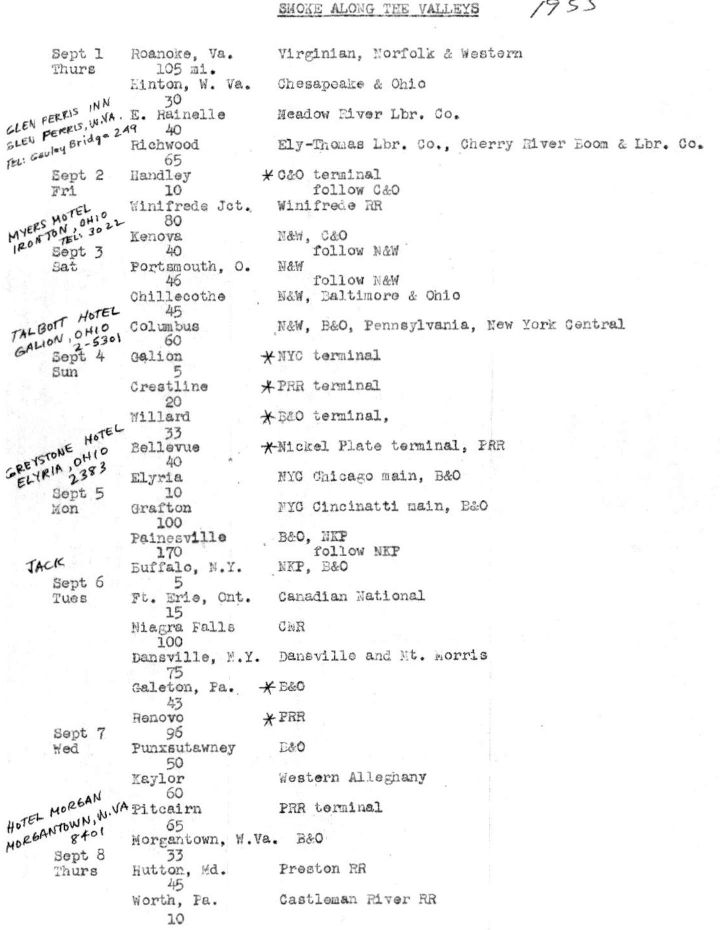

SMOKE ALONG THE VALLEYS 1955

Sept 1 Thurs — Roanoke, Va. — Virginian, Norfolk & Western
105 mi.
Hinton, W. Va. — Chesapeake & Ohio
30
GLEN FERRIS INN / GLEN FERRIS, W.VA. / TEL: Gauley Bridge 249 — E. Rainelle — Meadow River Lbr. Co.
40
Richwood — Ely-Thomas Lbr. Co., Cherry River Boom & Lbr. Co.
65
Sept 2 Fri — Handley — *C&O terminal, follow C&O
10
Winifrede Jct. — Winifrede RR
80
MYERS HOTEL / IRONTON, OHIO / TEL: 3022 — Kenova — N&W, C&O, follow N&W
40
Sept 3 Sat — Portsmouth, O. — N&W, follow N&W
46
Chillecothe — N&W, Baltimore & Ohio
45
TALBOTT HOTEL / GALION, OHIO / 2-5301 — Columbus — N&W, B&O, Pennsylvania, New York Central
60
Sept 4 Sun — Galion — *NYC terminal
5
Crestline — *PRR terminal
20
Willard — *B&O terminal,
33
GREYSTONE HOTEL / ELYRIA, OHIO / 2383 — Bellevue — *Nickel Plate terminal, PRR
40
Elyria — NYC Chicago main, B&O
10
Sept 5 Mon — Grafton — NYC Cincinatti main, B&O
100
Painesville — B&O, NKP, follow NKP
170
JACK — Buffalo, N.Y. — NKP, B&O
5
Sept 6 Tues — Ft. Erie, Ont. — Canadian National
15
Niagra Falls — CNR
100
Dansville, N.Y. — Dansville and Mt. Morris
75
Galeton, Pa. — *B&O
43
Renovo — *PRR
96
Sept 7 Wed — Punxsutawney — B&O
50
Kaylor — Western Allegheny
60
HOTEL MORGAN / MORGANTOWN, W.VA / 8401 — Pitcairn — PRR terminal
65
Morgantown, W.Va. — B&O
33
Sept 8 Thurs — Hutton, Md. — Preston RR
45
Worth, Pa. — Castleman River RR
10

Figure ob.6. Page one of the itinerary "Smoke along the Valleys" from the David P. Morgan–Phil Hastings trip that resulted in *Trains* articles and the "Steam in Indian Summer" section of *The Mohawk That Refused to Abdicate, and Other Tales.*

Courtesy of California State Railroad Museum. Philip Ross Hastings, MD, Collection.

closing of the Oneida & Western Railroad in Tennessee; Jersey Central "Camelback" steam engines; West Virginia short lines; the tour de force photography and writing (by Morgan) of "The Mohawk That Refused to Abdicate, and Other Tales"; Pennsylvania "Decapods"; and Union Pacific "Big Boys."

In describing why he undertook these quests, Morgan wrote, "Phil Hastings and I took to the field in those changing, wrenching 1950's. Because change in those years was spelled d-i-e-s-e-l, and the diesel had come to supplant and not simply to supplement, no matter what the coal-haulers said to pacify their customers. So, with the forbearance of Marion [*sic*] Hastings, who sensed and responded to the urgency of our plan, and with the money of a hard-pressed publisher who really couldn't afford such an investment for his smallest, weakest magazine, we set forth to chronicle that change."[32]

The articles were researched during one- or two-week journeys in 1953, 1954, 1955, 1956, and 1957.[33] Hastings called this work "the absolute, all-time pinnacle of my life-long avocational preoccupation with railroading."[34]

Both men seemed to view Hastings as the junior partner in these efforts. On the twentieth and thirtieth anniversaries of the beginning of these trips, Hastings would beseech Morgan to revisit their steam safaris. In response to Hastings's interest in a twentieth-anniversary safari, Morgan begged off the project by citing a lack of time—but he went on to note what was probably his real reason: "The philosophical objection is that I don't think in this instance that we can go back and recreate the spirit of the earlier searches. You and I are older . . . steam is largely missing . . . I think, as a writer that I would be trespassing upon diesel territory best left to a younger, Extra 2200 South generation."[35]

In a 1982 letter to Morgan on the eve of the thirtieth anniversary of their steam safaris, Hastings said, "Wouldn't a trip down east for the last stand of the Alcos be as noble in 1983 as a Steam Safari in 1953?"[36] Morgan must have declined this suggested trip as well because it did not happen.

Hastings was one of the twelve men Morgan featured in his first pantheon of noted *Trains* photographers, along with Bill Middleton, Steinheimer, Shaughnessy, J. Parker Lamb, Bob Hale, Hank Griffiths, H. Reid, and others. In the blurb about himself, Hastings says, reflecting the soon-to-be psychiatrist, "When the steam locomotives are all gone and it is no longer any fun to take pictures, I intend to devote my life to the study of why people like trains."[37]

During these critical and creative years, Hastings formed another important friendship. While he was serving his residency in Albany, New York, during the summer of 1954, he called a young man from nearby Troy, Jim Shaughnessy. Almost ten years Hastings's junior, Shaughnessy had been publishing photos in *Trains* since his 1952 debut. In the "Interesting Railfan Questionnaire," which he completed for Freeman Hubbard at *Railroad*, Hastings notes, "While taking my residency in psychiatry at Albany, New York, in 1954 I first met Jim Shaughnessy, who lives in Troy. Since then, we have done a lot of rail fanning together. I take some pride in the impression that I had something to do with developing Jim's talent and skill in taking night photos of railroads, which has been a special interest of mine for many years."[38]

In his "Remembering Phil Hastings," the afterword to the book *Philip R. Hastings: Portrait of the Pennsylvania Railroad*, Shaughnessy wrote, "We had seen each other's work in various places, and he invited me to come to his Cedar Hill apartment, near Albany, to discuss railroad photography. This led to many junkets to photograph trains together. . . . Finally, in 1958, he found a medical group in Waterloo, Iowa, and moved one last time. I visited him there once on the way to Colorado, and occasionally we would meet in Albany for a meal while he and his family were enroute to Vermont for the holidays. My association with Phil was a memorable period in my life."[39]

If Hastings felt like Morgan's junior partner, his relationship with Shaughnessy was as a senior partner in their efforts. Hastings mentioned teaching Shaughnessy night photography, and his papers include a number of postcards from Shaughnessy suggesting, even imploring, Hastings to go on photographic trips with him.[40] Today, it is clear that Shaughnessy's night photography at least equals Hastings's, and as author of *The Rutland Road* and *Delaware & Hudson*, Shaughnessy's authorial output exceeded Hastings's. Of course, photography, not writing, was always Hastings's focus; Shaughnessy worked in both genres.

Marian Hastings, and Hastings's family, tolerated a passion for railroad-subject photography that, as it often does, bordered on obsession. Hastings, in his questionnaire to Freeman Hubbard at *Railroad*, recounted one such travail:

> The time my wife and our two oldest children, who were then pre-schoolers, drove from Spokane, Wash., where I was interning, down to the Camas Prairie R. R. in northern Idaho—I parked our car on the prairie and climbed down into Lapwai Canyon, some 1500 vertical feet to photograph an N. P. 2-8-2 on the 4% grade—it took a lot longer to make the climb than I had expected and about 4 hours elapsed before I got back—when I arrived exhausted at the car I found the ground covered by a snow storm that had not penetrated the canyon, and my wife about frantic with concern that I had fallen or had been bitten by one of the many rattlesnakes which infest the area.[41]

Phil Hastings's career with the army, and then the Veterans Administration (VA), finally ended in the late 1950s. He emerged from the VA as a psychiatrist, was certified as such in 1959, and moved one more time—to take a position with a medical practice in Waterloo, Iowa.[42] He was a member of the Northeast Psychiatric Clinic and served in private practice. In addition to railroading and photography, he was interested in classical music.[43]

The Midwest seems a surprising terminal for this small-town New England boy, but he stayed in Waterloo the rest of his life. During the 1960s and 1970s, he did a great deal of work on the Chicago, Rock Island & Pacific Railroad, the Chicago Great Western Railway (CGW), and CGW's merger successor, the Chicago & North Western Railway. Hastings's quantity of work decreased during this period. As anyone with a professional life and a family will understand, the demands of a psychiatry career, combined with the responsibility of supporting a wife and five children, undoubtedly played a role.

Hastings's published output during this period was a small number of articles and photos, until the books featuring his photography—to be described below—began to appear in the mid-1970s. During the late 1970s, he also provided a series of photo essays, "Once in a Timetable," for *Passenger Train Journal* magazine when it was under the editorship of Kevin Keefe, who later became editor and then publisher of *Trains*. These pieces documented Hastings's 1960s forays recording the last days of lesser-known intercity passenger trains, such as the *Flying Crow*, the *Mainstreeter*, and the *Lake Cities*.[44] While they were well received at the time, this series has not been issued in book form.[45]

Hastings described the genesis of this series of photos in a letter to Keefe: "After some years had passed, and I had partially recovered from the demise of steam, I started, in 1966, going on weekend or longer trips on various passenger trains, recording the experience photographically as I went. From 1966 until May,

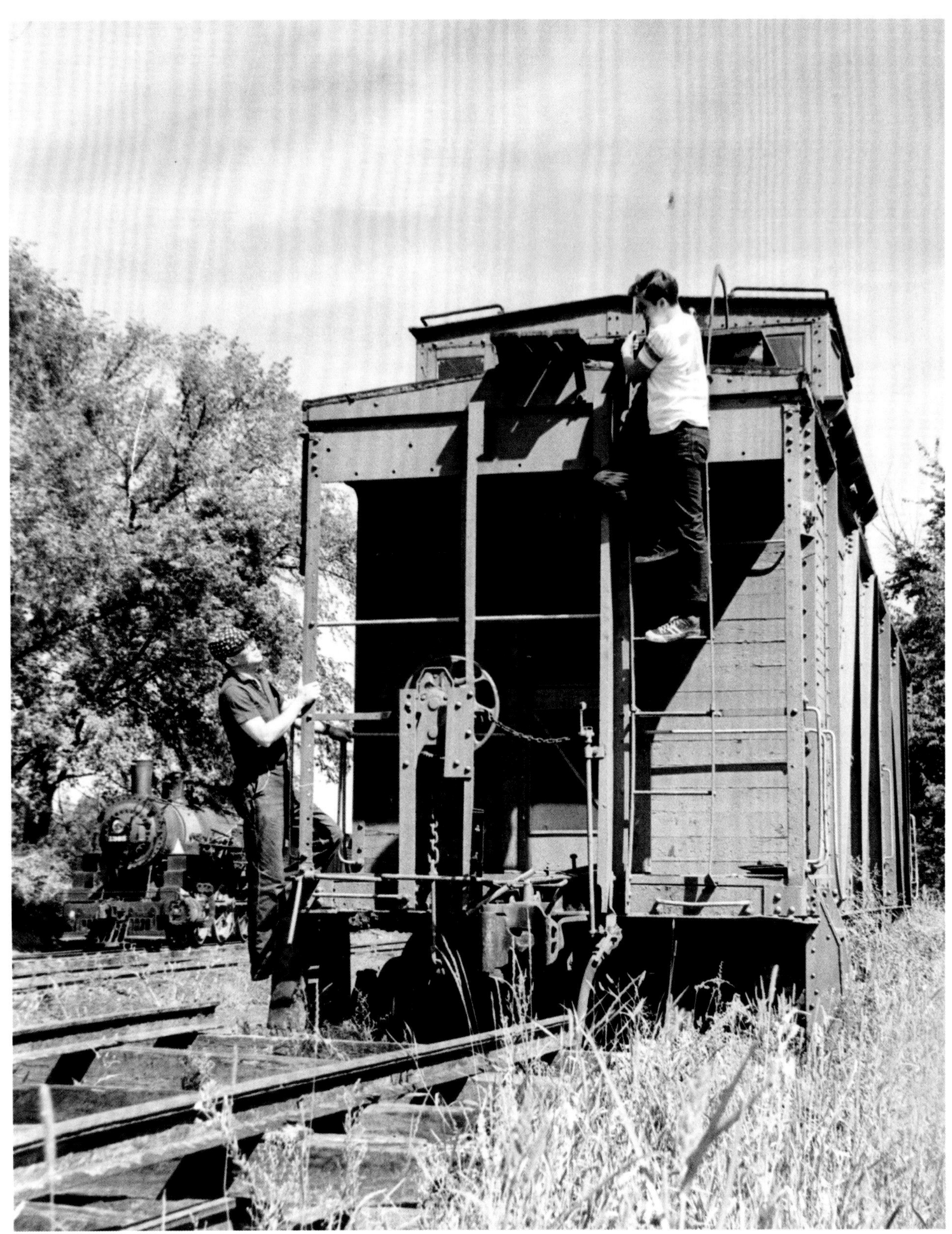

1971, I recorded 19 different such trips, some involving as many as nine different passenger trains in one trip. These varied from the 'Copper Country Ltd' to the 'Yampa Valley Mail' to the 'New England States' to the 'Flying Crow' to the 'Century' and the 'Super Chief' . . . My own euphemism for this venture was 'Vanishing Varnish.'"[46]

Hastings became involved with the Mid-Continent Railway Historical Society and its museum in North Freedom, Wisconsin, in the early 1960s and began devoting more and more of his avocational railroading interest and time to it. He served as vice president of operations for the museum from 1972–1984 and as president from 1984–1986.[47] He purchased Chicago, Rock Island & Pacific caboose No. 17772 in 1967 and moved it to the museum.[48] Because the Mid-Continent Railway Museum is situated more than a hundred miles from Waterloo, many of Hastings's avocational hours must have been taken up in travel.

In a letter, Hastings described his life at this time and its effect on his photography: "I usually put in 55–60 hours/week at my livelihood, try to adequately meet the needs of one wife and five kids, take seriously my responsibilities as a Director and Vice-President, Operations, of the Mid-Continent Railway Museum at North Freedom, WI, and in my spare time serve in some civic and professional organizations, and print railroad photos for some of the many persons who request some for various publications—oh yes, I also do a little current railroad photography (plus have a garden)."[49]

The lore of the train always drew Hastings. In a biographic statement in the collection held by the California State Railroad Museum, he says, "My office window in downtown Waterloo overlooks (from the 6th floor) the bridge of the former CGW RR over the Cedar River, and as I gaze pensively past my patient's head during the psychiatric interview, I can see former CGW F-units now painted C&NW yellow going across the bridge."

In 1985, the Railway & Locomotive Historical Society awarded Hastings its annual photography award. The citation stated, in part, "His hallmark is scene and context; Hastings photographs tell a story, set a scene, or place the action in relationship to adjoining architecture or natural environment." The citation was one of the first published essays to recognize Hastings's style as "photojournalistic" and identified him as a one-man influence on railroad-subject photography, stating, "The modern style of railroad photography is the 'Phil Hastings style.'" It went on to acknowledge the book *The Mohawk That Refused to Abdicate* as the work "of which Phil is most proud" and to recognize his leadership at the Mid-Continent Railway Museum.[50] The award came just in time. Less than two years later, Hastings's career, family life, and railroading avocation ended with his untimely death from colon cancer in February 1987. As he contemplated his mortality, Hastings was still making plans. He noted in a letter to *Railfan and Railroad* editor Jim Boyd just before his death that he wanted to "use my remaining time to get some more railroad things published, as my main goal over the years was to share my photographs with others."[51]

Eight years later, in 1995, Hastings's widow, Marian, donated Hastings's collection, fifty-five boxes of photos, negatives, and paper materials, to the California State Railroad Museum Library and Archive, ensuring that Hastings's photos and papers would be available to scholars of railroad-subject photography. In a letter to the museum staff, Marian Hastings said, "As the boxes were carried to the U. P. S. truck I was overcome with the feeling that Phil's spirit was going with them. (But that is only my own personal grief.)"[52]

Among the photographers this author has studied closely, Hastings is the hardest to know. His fame did not rise to the level of O. Winston Link's or Lucius Beebe's, so his life is relatively undocumented. And, unlike Jack Delano and Lucius Beebe, Hastings did not write a great deal about his own life.

Greg McDonnell, who knew Hastings well, said this about the man behind the camera: "I felt like I knew Phil Hastings long before I did—and he was exactly who I imagined he was. That's because I grew up aware of Phil Hastings—the very first

***Facing*, Figure ob.7.** After moving to Waterloo, Iowa, Phil Hastings became very involved with the Mid-Continent Railway Museum / Mid-Continent Railway Historical Society in North Freedom, Wisconsin. This image shows Hastings and his son Hugh on their Chicago, Rock Island & Pacific Railroad caboose 17772. The caboose was rebuilt from a boxcar in the early 1940s. The caboose is still at the museum. A well-known locomotive from the museum's collection, Chicago & North Western 4-6-0 1385, is in the background.

Courtesy of California State Railroad Museum. Philip Ross Hastings, MD, Collection, [Negative 9210].

photographs I saw were his. We met in the early 1980s and I made a major trip with him in 1985. I visited with him just before he died. I also went with him when he took his last photograph, of the Chicago Central. Phil Hastings was one of the gentlest people I knew, and he was also a 'gentleman.' He was extraordinarily pleasant, contemplative, and conversational."[53]

Retired Kalmbach Media executive and noted author, preservationist, and photographer Kevin Keefe also knew Hastings well. Keefe worked on the book *The Mohawk That Refused to Abdicate, and Other Tales* and also as editor of *Passenger Train Journal*. He had the wisdom to run Hastings's series of articles on vanishing passenger trains; work David P. Morgan had rejected. "I was aware of Hastings's work before I met him," Keefe said, "and we have enshrined him for all the right reasons. I discovered his series of articles with David P. Morgan in back issues of *Trains* when I was in college." He continued:

> When I first talked with Hastings, it was by phone, and he intrigued me. He was easy to talk to; he spoke in slow, soothing, reassuring cadences. I met him in person in June 1975 at the launch party for *The Mohawk That Refused to Abdicate*; it was a reunion for him with Dave Morgan. I got to know Phil quickly. He had no ego. He looked professorial and elegant. He seemed like an easygoing midwesterner. I think his profession [psychiatry] and his personality interacted. I soon felt like I had known him for twenty years. He had a commanding presence, but Phil also made you feel like a pal. I was struck with his generosity, and how he always asked about others. Working with him was a lot of fun. The tragedy of Phil's life is that he left us so young; he was gone from the scene so suddenly.[54]

THE LEGACY

Just what is Hastings's legacy? In an interview for the author's *Railroad History* article, which preceded this book, the late Jim Shaughnessy said,

> He influenced people to look at the total picture. There are a lot of great pictures out there now—it has become the standard now because everybody does that. Really, it is hard to say where what you [interviewer Reevy] called "environmental railroad photography" started. But, certainly, Phil Hastings was a major influence.
>
> He was interested in the total picture of the railroad. It was a case of either taking a picture or capturing a moment. Phil wanted to capture a moment, at a time when just taking a picture was what was typical. Now, people can go back to his photos and see what things were like at the time. The railroad scene has diminished a great deal in terms of its colorfulness—in addition to the loss of steam, agency stations and engine terminals have vanished, and a lot of surviving track is lost inside a vegetative tunnel. Phil, and others like him, recorded what was there before these changes.[55]

Hastings's talented contemporary, photographer Richard "Dick" Steinheimer, described Hastings's work this way: "His educated and considered approach created beautiful visual explorations of the stately and the humble, the inanimate and the vital. Concentrating on the human side of the photographic equation, these studies . . . are some of the most genuine and unobtrusive glimpses into the world of railroading that have come down to us."[56]

It is extravagant to claim, as many have, that Hastings was the first to take photos of the entire American railroad environment—Charles Clegg, for example, was there before him—but he certainly was the most influential member of the generation of photographers following Clegg and his partner, Lucius Beebe, in popularizing this important change.[57] He and his closest peers soon raised their work, perhaps unconsciously, to the level of art. When O. Winston Link and David Plowden—both of them partially inspired by what they saw in *Trains*—entered the movement with conscious artistic intent in the mid-1950s, the level of discourse moved yet another step forward.[58]

David P. Morgan, who perhaps knew Hastings's work better than any other observer, said, "Initially, some objected to his unorthodoxy, but as his work expanded in volume it became apparent that he was supplementing, not supplanting, his predecessors, pushing back the old parameters of angle and subject, trying to fill film with ever more of a patently enormous panorama. . . . in a sense, none of us who knew Phil Hastings personally knew him any better than anyone who simply saw, or will see, his photography. His imagination, intelligence, and compassion are invested and remain in his negatives for the common good."[59]

The dialogue focusing on Hastings's work representing a "one-man breakthrough in rail photography technique"—Morgan's words—appears to have been created by Morgan himself, especially in his epilogue to the book *The Mohawk That Refused to Abdicate, and Other Tales*. In the epilogue, Morgan wrote, "He was a fundamental, identifiable influence upon his generation and upon the next. He placed the train in the context of the overall railroad scene."[60]

Heady words to apply to the work of one man—and also words that may lead to future misunderstandings with regard to the contemporaneous work being done by Jim Shaughnessy, Dick Steinheimer, Bill Middleton, and others. Shaughnessy often teased Hastings, saying that he must have hypnotized Morgan into taking him on all of those mid-1950s steam safaris. Later, *Locomotive & Railway Preservation* editor Mark Smith was to champion Hastings and his work as well.

Hastings himself said of his photography, "I look for photos which tie in train action with locale, local scenery plus trackside railroad impedimenta. I rarely take straight engine photos, unless it is to record some unusual piece of equipment. I like some people in the photo, doing something appropriate to the scene to add interest. When I take trackside structure photos, I prefer to have a train or locomotive in the scene to add snap. I still err in not taking quite enough close-ups to add variety to a photo story."[61]

Locomotive & Railway Preservation editor Smith, a primary late-career proponent of Hastings's work, described his photography this way: "I find in your pictures a different perspective—you have a special sense of relationships that make your pictures for me unusual and thus outstanding. They illustrate an aspect of railroading not immediately seen. I also like the way that you capture the human elements—the interaction of people and the trains."[62]

Many years earlier, the publisher of *Trains* and founder of what is now Kalmbach Media, A. C. Kalmbach, extolled Hastings's photography in a letter to Hastings: "I love your photography, Mr. Hastings, especially those beautiful panoramic shots of the rolling Vermont hills. I don't think I've ever seen anything like it amongst the material which comes into our office. I still remember that exceptionally striking shot framed by the rails and the switch stand, which we used with the title block of the St. Johnsbury & Lake Champlain."[63]

Is the dialogue about Phil Hastings being the first environmental railroad photographer justified? Certainly he was one of the first to step back from roster and action shots, and even shots—such as Beebe's—focusing on railroaders, to take in the entire scene of American railroading.[64] By doing so, he was one of the first photographers working within the railfan subculture to take the photojournalistic precepts that had been popularized by magazines such as *Life* and given social content by photographers working for the Farm Security Administration (FSA) and its successors and apply them to photographing American railroading. And, with his first such photos taken in about 1940, Hastings came on the scene before contemporaries such as Steinheimer, Shaughnessy, Link, and Plowden.

McDonnell, who knew Hastings personally, said of Hastings's photography:

> I don't want to give singular credit to someone in the development of railroad-subject photography at the time. Hastings was one of the influencers, but J. Parker Lamb, Jim Shaughnessy, and Dick Steinheimer were also within that circle of influence. All of these photographers did work that was more contextual—they brought in the people of railroading. And none of this existed in a vacuum.
>
> Hastings's photography is characterized by soul; it has soul. A Hastings image is far more than a photograph—it can put you "there"—it brings you in through an "unseen element." In short, his photographs make such an impression that you almost feel you were there.[65]

McDonnell would reinforce and continue Hastings's influence by editing the *Trains* articles that were the basis for *The Mohawk That Refused to Abdicate, and Other Tales* for a contemporary audience in special issues of the magazine *Classic Trains* in 2007, 2009, and 2011.

Keefe also singles out Hastings, Lamb, Shaughnessy, and Steinheimer as primary influences on the railroad-subject

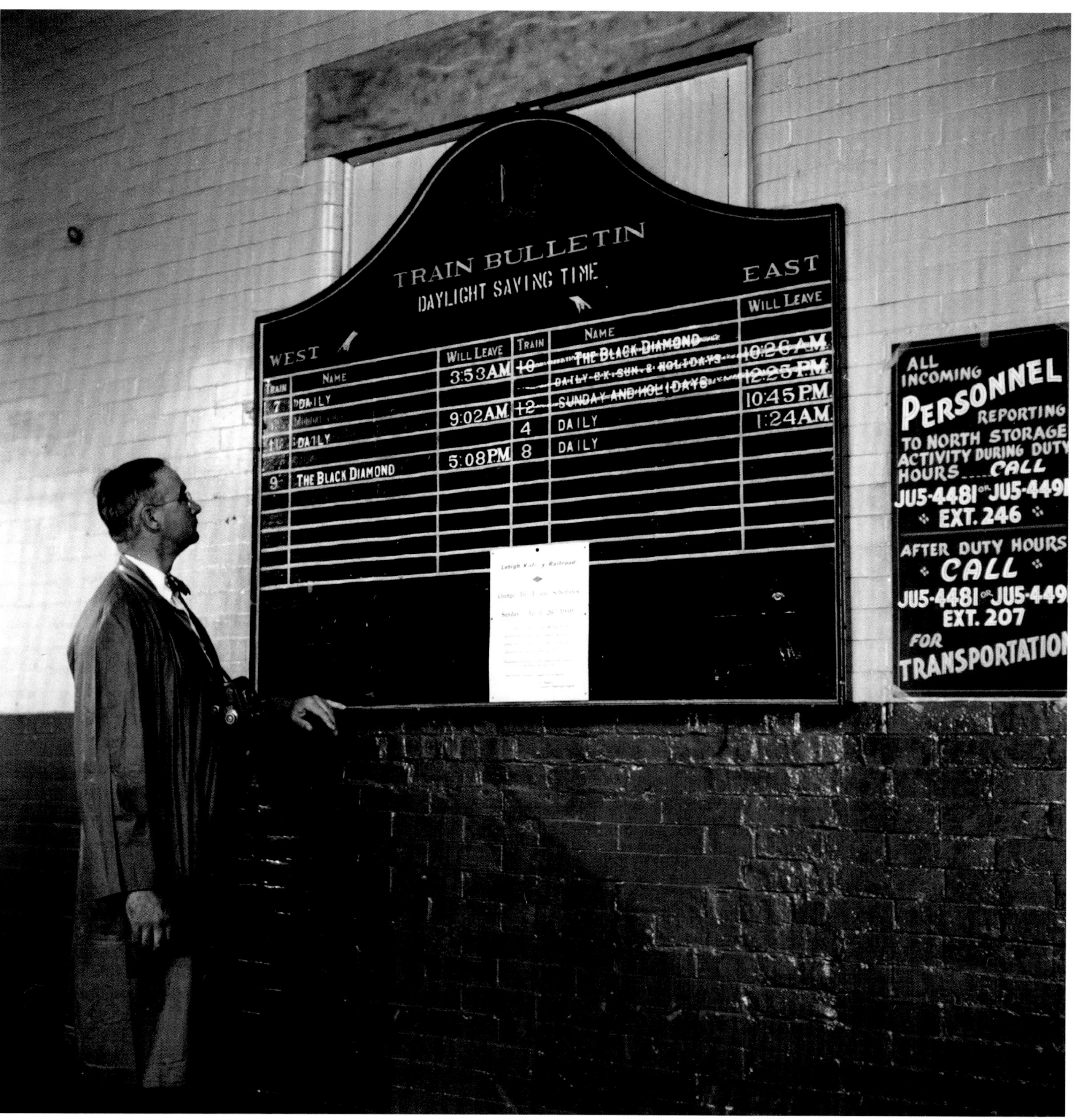
TRAIN BULLETIN
DAYLIGHT SAVING TIME
WEST
EAST
TRAIN
NAME
WILL LEAVE
7 DAILY
9 THE BLACK DIAMOND
3:53AM
9:02AM
5:08PM
10 THE BLACK DIAMOND 10:26AM
DAILY EX. SUN. & HOLIDAYS 12:25PM
12 SUNDAY AND HOLIDAYS 10:45PM
4 DAILY 1:24AM
8 DAILY
ALL INCOMING
PERSONNEL
REPORTING
TO NORTH STORAGE
ACTIVITY DURING DUTY
HOURS ... CALL
JU5-4481 OR JU5-4491
EXT. 246
AFTER DUTY HOURS
CALL
JU5-4481 OR JU5-4491
EXT. 207
FOR
TRANSPORTATION

photography of their time, calling them "pivotal photographers." "Phil Hastings is in the pantheon for a reason," Keefe said. "He focused on what railroading is about. His photography was about breaking rules, shattering rules; he moved away from the wedge shot. He realized that railroading is a wonderful world for a photographer to work in.

"Hastings's compositions are transcendent. And he took photographs at all kinds of times—twilight, dawn, night shots, shots from all kinds of angles. He worked with people in his photos. And he was disarming when he talked with people. In fact, Phil's chosen profession was an influence on what he shot."[66]

Hastings's influence on others of his generation and beyond is strong—largely because of the bittersweet popularity of the mid-1950s Morgan/Hastings field trips in search of the last American and Canadian steam locomotives for *Trains*. Those articles inspired a generation of writers and photographers focusing on the American railroad. Hastings's photos were also frequently featured in books, beginning with Beebe and Clegg's *The Age of Steam* and were easily available to interested photographers in those works.[67]

So Hastings's photos, along with Clegg's from the mid- and late-1940s, were the first "environmental" views of American railroading that most railfan contemporaries had ever seen. But they were not really firsts—they were, if firsts at all, only such in the subculture that gathered around *Railroad* and *Trains* magazines and the Beebe/Clegg books of the day. They were preceded by views taken by photojournalistic photographers, many of them working for the FSA, beginning in the mid-1930s. For example, the railroad-subject views by FSA / Office of War Information photographer Jack Delano—images in the photojournalistic style taken from 1940 to 1943—first came to wide notice in the late 1970s, and Delano's reputation has been rising ever since. Most of the other FSA/OWI photographers took similar railroad-subject views, images that are yet to be surveyed in one volume.

Facing, Figure ob.8. The 1950s was a time of great change for American railroading. In addition to the end of steam on US railroads, railroad passenger service was dwindling rapidly. This Phil Hastings photo of a Lehigh Valley Railroad train bulletin tells a stark story.

Courtesy of California State Railroad Museum. Philip Ross Hastings, MD, Collection, [Negative 3669].

The change to more creative railroad photography was a movement, it should be added, that was also driven by a contemporary revolution in the quality and affordability of photographic equipment and film and in the availability—following more than a decade of economic depression—of personal income with which to buy such things.

It should also be noted that Hastings is known for black-and-white photographs, but he took many color images as well. These remain fairly unexplored today. Hastings described his color work in a letter to author and photographer Don Ball this way: "My first color effort was a 12-pack of 2½ by 3½ Ektachrome, shortly after the RUT 4-8-2's arrived in 1946, which I tried to develop myself. I took 2½ by 3½ color sparingly during the next few years, and started 35mm for color in 1953. Have a few fairly choice oldies and scads of more recent stuff."[68]

We do not have any direct evidence of the nature of Hastings's early influences, save for his comments about *Railroad* and *Trains* magazines.[69] We do know, however, that *Trains* editor Morgan and his tastes in photography were strongly influenced by *Life*. The late photographer and writer John Gruber, in his monograph *Focus on Rails*, mentions the influence on Hastings, Morgan, and their contemporaries of FSA photographers. In the monograph, Gruber also recognizes the crucial influence of photojournalism as typified by *Life* (first published in its classic form in 1936), *Look*, and other magazines.[70] These people, publications, and organizations must have exerted an influence on Hastings.

THE PUBLICATIONS

Where does Hastings, and his published legacy, stand today? Unfortunately, in the past, one of the major challenges facing those who seek to understand his work and influence was the lack of a comprehensive volume that gathers the best of his images, regardless of subject, in one place. Prior to the publication of this work, six books have featured Hastings's photography, but none of those surveyed his entire photographic oeuvre.

Hastings is known best for his mid-1950s photographic work on the end of steam power, carried out in tandem with *Trains* author and editor Morgan. It is not surprising, then, that the

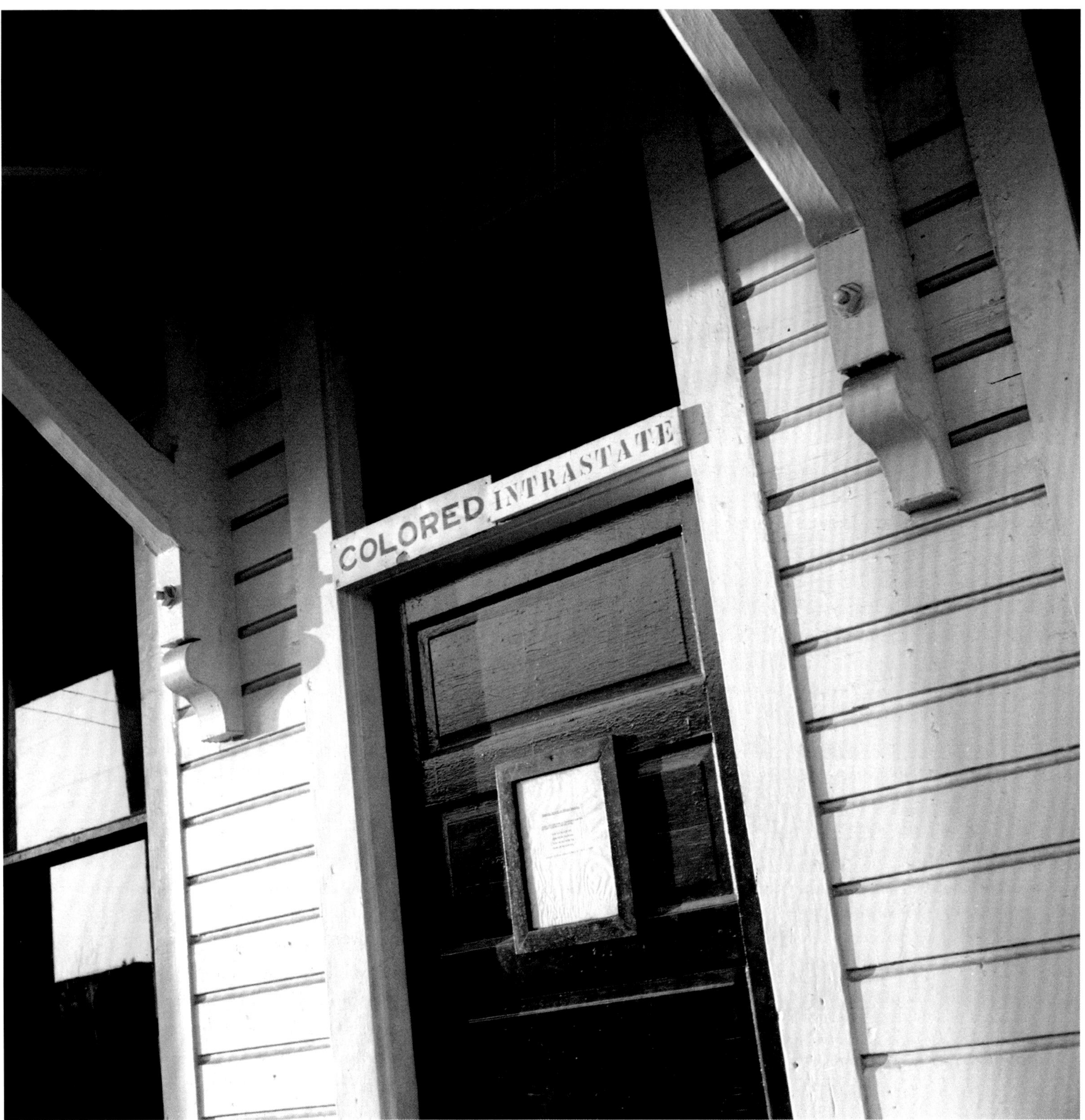
COLORED
INTRASTATE

first book of Hastings photographs to be published, in 1975, was a compendium of these articles, *The Mohawk That Refused to Abdicate, and Other Tales*. The book was produced by *Trains* publisher Kalmbach. The volume is out of print but is easily available on the used-book market. As a showcase for Hastings's work, it suffers because, like all of the books featuring Hastings's photography in the past, it is not a comprehensive look at his work—it includes only photos taken for the articles written by Morgan for *Trains* during the mid-1950s.[71]

Despite this limitation, *The Mohawk That Refused to Abdicate, and Other Tales,* which predated art photography railroad-subject books such as *Steam, Steel & Stars* and *A Time of Trains* by more than a decade, was successful when it was released. Three books based on Hastings's photographic coverage of individual railroads were soon to follow. All of them were published in the horizontal 8½ × 11–inch staple-bound format, which was popularized in the North American railfan market by Carstens. These works are paperbacks that suffer from a lack of durability, and the staple binding limits the length of such works.

The first of this trio, *Grand Trunk Heritage: Steam in New England,* edited and designed by John Krause and Edward Crist, was released by Railroad Heritage in 1978. As noted earlier, Hastings's New England work is generally very strong, and these outstanding photos of the Grand Trunk Railway's operations are no exception. The next Hastings release in this format was *Chicago Great Western Railway,* a sampling of Hastings's Chicago Great Western and ex–Chicago Great Western work that was compiled by John Krause, Fred Kramer, and Edward Crist, circa 1980. The book is particularly interesting in that it gives readers a glimpse into Hastings's lesser-known work of the 1960s and 1970s.

Figure ob.9. The 1950s was also a pivotal time for American society. The end of the McCarthy Era, the beginning of the interstate highway system, and the Brown v. Board of Education case were just some of the epochal changes underway as Morgan and Hastings searched for the last of steam. This Hastings image also tells a story of the times. According to *Railroad* editor Freeman Hubbard, who profiled Hastings as an "interesting railfan," interracial summer camps were an important influence on Hastings, and he and his wife, Marian, belonged to an interracial dialogue group.

Courtesy of California State Railroad Museum. Philip Ross Hastings, MD, Collection, [Negative 5618].

Hastings's final outing in this form, and the last book that was edited with his assistance, was *Remember the Rock,* which was published soon after his death in 1987. Walt Lankenau edited the volume, which features 1960s and 1970s photos of the Chicago, Rock Island & Pacific Railroad, an intriguing but financially weak midwestern carrier that became a "fallen flag" when it shut down in 1980.

Hastings's photos of the Boston & Maine Railroad and the Rutland Railroad/Railway are arguably his best.[72] The next Hastings book, also posthumous, was Locomotive & Railway Preservation's *The Boston & Maine: A Photographic Essay,* issued in 1989 with text by Frank Kyper and an introduction by William B. Stewart. This volume, a labor of love for *Locomotive & Railway Preservation* then editor and publisher Mark Smith, benefits from excellent photo selection, good organization, and an appealing layout obviously influenced by art photography books. The design bears a noticeable resemblance to the first survey of O. Winston Link's work, *Steam Steel & Stars: America's Last Steam Railroad,* published by Harry N. Abrams in 1987. Many readers have complained that the images in the book were printed too dark, and while this does affect some of the reproductions, especially the front-end details of a number of the steam locomotives, it is still a handsome volume, easily the best of the six monographs featuring Hastings's photos. The book, now out of print, was issued in a small-press run and can be purchased on the used-book market—but, because of its scarcity and popularity, it commands a fairly high price. Smith had planned to do a number of book-length surveys of Hastings's work, but financial problems intervened, and he was not able to realize this vision.[73]

The latest Hastings volume, and the third to be issued posthumously, was *Philip R. Hastings: Portrait of the Pennsylvania Railroad,* by Douglas M. Nelson with a foreword by Kevin P. Keefe and an afterword by Jim Shaughnessy. Since Hastings's photos are now in the *Philip Ross Hastings, MD Collection* at the California State Railroad Library, Nelson was able to draw on this curated material to select images for the volume issued by Pine Tree in 2002. It is a handsome, hardbound book, nicely produced, albeit in a somewhat awkward horizontal 9¾ × 11–inch format.

The present book is, in many ways, the culmination of a project Hastings pursued but never realized during his lifetime. Early on, Hastings worked with friend John (Johnny) Krause on a series of books, but, as Krause's personal demons destroyed him, Hastings turned to David P. Morgan, proposing a book or books featuring his work—to no avail.[74] In a letter a few years later to *Locomotive and Railway Preservation* editor Mark Smith, Hastings suggested "designing a book (or books) to depict my first fifty years of railroad photography." Hastings had three plans for this work: a "chronological presentation"; a "geographical presentation," which is largely realized with this book; or "a series of books, one for each geographical area, starting with northern New England."[75] This interchange resulted in the book published by Smith focusing on Hastings's Boston & Maine work, which was unfortunately posthumous. Smith's financial situation after this did not allow him to produce further Hastings books as he had planned. Indeed, Hastings's oeuvre is so extensive that, for example, his excellent photos of the Pacific Northwest, and perhaps of Canada, could easily be featured in full books.[76]

Smith responded to Hastings and noted, "Consider this: the first chapter could be written in narrative/description form presenting your years of experience in photographing trains. The narrative could be written by somebody else and of course incorporate some key photographs that best reflect your work and ideas about trains and photography. . . . Then I would see the book working through a series of chapters devoted to regions. Each chapter would have an introduction describing railroading in the region and then move into the actual photographs which would be heavily captioned."[77]

David P. Morgan and Phil Hastings also spent years discussing a book of Hastings's work. Their original discussion posited a survey of Hastings's work, rather than the "steam safari" wrap-up that eventually emerged, *The Mohawk That Refused to Abdicate, and Other Tales*. Morgan's vision for this book, as he outlined it to Hastings in a 1957 letter, was described this way: "I think it should be slanted toward the general reading public with the illustration covering various phases of railroading with the steam locomotive included but not necessarily dominating. In other words, it should cover such things as train dispatching, flagging, engine servicing, conductor working over waybills in caboose, section gang, engineer, station scenes, etc. I think we'd need about 100 prints to submit to a publisher but of course we can draw on your work in our files for many of these."[78]

The quality of Phil Hastings's work, its extent, and its popular topic during the mid-1950s—the end of American and Canadian steam—led most photographers of American railroading in Hastings's generation, and in the generation that followed, to view him as the leader of his field. Hastings himself wanted to be remembered for his children, his patients, his development of mental health resources in his area, and, finally, his photographs.[79] However, with most working photographers of American railroading now being in the second, third, or even fourth generation following Hastings, his influence is waning. But Hastings's photos—because of a generous and forward-thinking gift by his wife, Marian B. Hastings, in 1995, including forty-six thousand black-and-white negatives, four thousand prints, and thirty-two thousand 35mm color transparencies—are safely ensconced in the California State Railroad Museum Library and Archives.[80] As the images collected in this book show, Phil Hastings still has much to teach others interested in the full span of American railroading and its depiction on film.

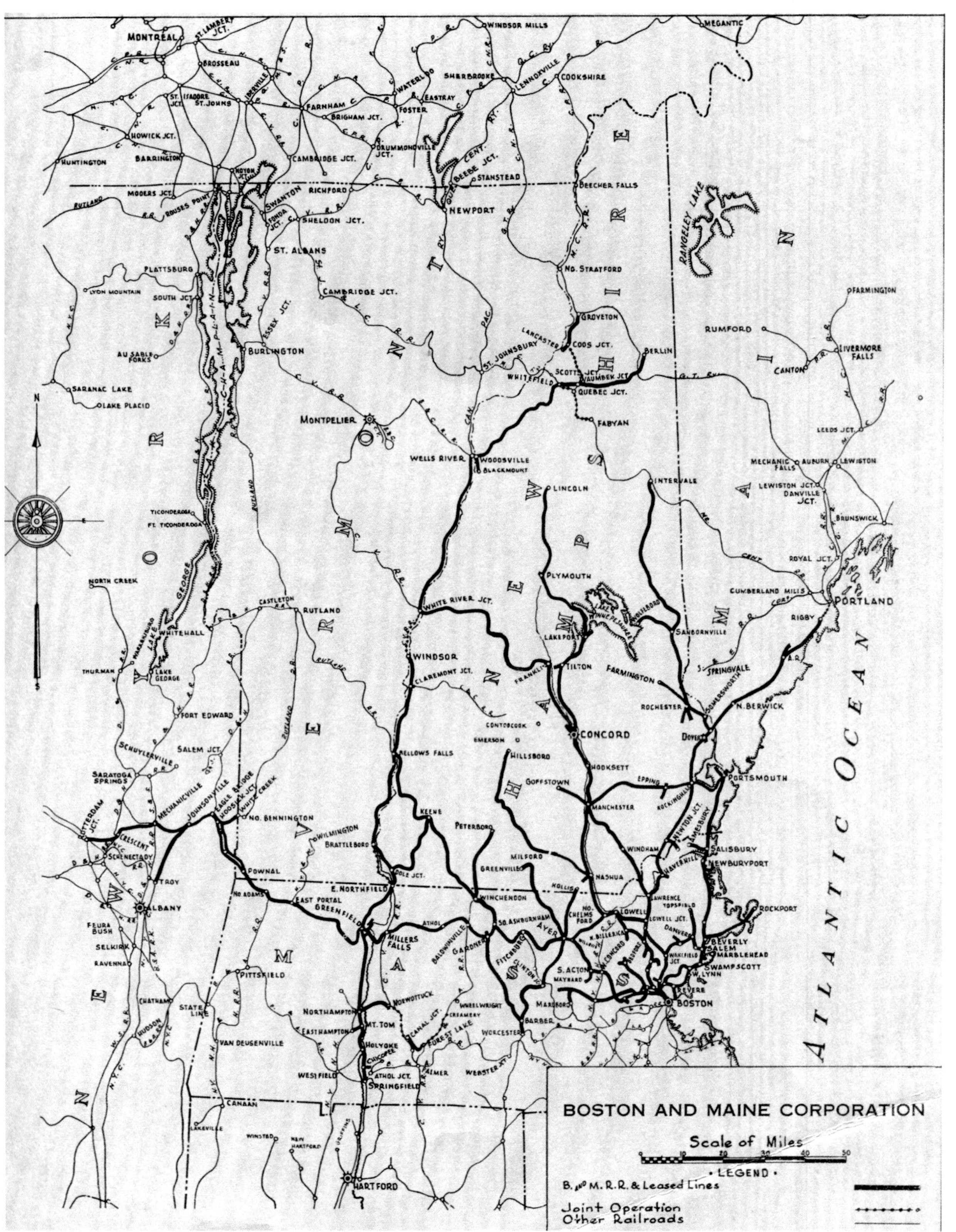

Figure 1.1. Map of the Boston & Maine, 1966.

Courtesy of Tony Reevy Collection.

PORTFOLIO ONE

THE BOSTON AND MAINE

Phil Hastings grew up in Bradford, Vermont, and so the Boston & Maine was his hometown railroad. The B&M was an old-line New England carrier with a dense network covering upper New England—mostly in New Hampshire and Massachusetts. The B&M route through Bradford ran along the Connecticut River on the Vermont side of the state's border with New Hampshire.

The Boston & Maine was a very early American railroad, founded in 1835. Originally formed to link Boston, Massachusetts with Portland, Maine, it grew through acquisitions into a more than two-thousand-mile system centered on Boston.[1] Its dense network of lightly trafficked New England branch lines could not survive the Great Depression, the coming of interstate highways, and the end of mail contracts. Today, about half of the former system survives.

The history of the B&M in recent years is checkered. Bankrupt by 1970, the railroad declined to be included in Conrail and rebuilt itself as a profit-making enterprise on its own—an astounding feat.

The last four decades of the railroad's history are controversial. The B&M emerged from bankruptcy in 1983, when it was purchased by Timothy Mellon. The railroad company still exists as a corporate shell, but Mellon, who is viewed by some as a twentieth-century robber baron, forged a complex structure, including Guilford Rail System, Springfield Terminal, and Guilford's successor, Pan Am Railways.[2] Beyond marketing considerations, the purpose of this structure is to use Springfield Terminal's favorable labor rules.

As this book goes to press, CSX, one of North America's six megarailroads, has just purchased Pan Am Railways. This transaction places both of New England's major east–west main lines—the former B&M Hoosac Tunnel route and the former Boston & Albany, both running mostly through Massachusetts—under the same owner.

Plates 1 and 2 depict the B&M in Bradford, Vermont, Hastings's hometown. Plate 1 shows the Bradford station in 1949, and plate 2, taken in 1940 or 1941, shows a Canadian Pacific train passing the Bradford station. Plate 3 shows the B&M's *Alouette* near the railroad's station in Woodsville, New Hampshire, just across the Connecticut River from Wells River, Vermont.

Plates 4, 5, and 6 depict the B&M's Peterboro Branch, one of Hastings's favorite locations on the railroad. Plate 4, one of Hastings's best-known images, shows a Peterboro Branch train crossing the "diamonds" of the railroad's east–west main line in Gardner, Massachusetts. Plate 5, an innovative and unusual view, shows a B&M fireman transferring his gear from one B&M "Mogul" to another at Peterboro, New Hampshire.[3] The railroader is framed by the locomotives, especially their cylinders, which dominate the foreground of the photo. Finally, plate 6 shows B&M Conductor Mike Downey on a Peterboro Branch train.

Plates 7 and 8 depict another location frequently depicted in Hastings's photos of the B&M, the Hillsboro Branch. Plate 7 shows a B&M train approaching a road crossing at South Lyndeboro, New Hampshire, and plate 8 shows a B&M locomotive at the turntable at Hillsboro, New Hampshire, the end of the line.

Plates 9 and 10 show the B&M in Concord, New Hampshire, a scene that was dominated by a classic railroad station built in 1885 and designed by Bradford L. Gilbert. The station was demolished in 1959 and served the B&M and the Suncook Valley Railroad.[4]

Plate 11 closes our look at the B&M in New Hampshire with a view of the road's "Mogul" 1490 framed by the well-known covered railroad bridge in Contoocook, New Hampshire. The bridge survives.

In plates 12–14, we turn to the Boston & Maine's home state of Massachusetts. Plate 12 shows a notable locomotive, B&M BL-2 1551, an early diesel. The BL-2 is framed within an unusual train station, the B&M station in Salem, Massachusetts, demolished in 1954. Plates 13 and 14 depict the B&M's Central Massachusetts branch, formerly an independent railroad.

Finally, this Boston & Maine portfolio closes with the interloper, and eventual victor over steam, the diesel. In plate 15, a trainman "bends the iron" at a switch for B&M diesel E-7 4208.

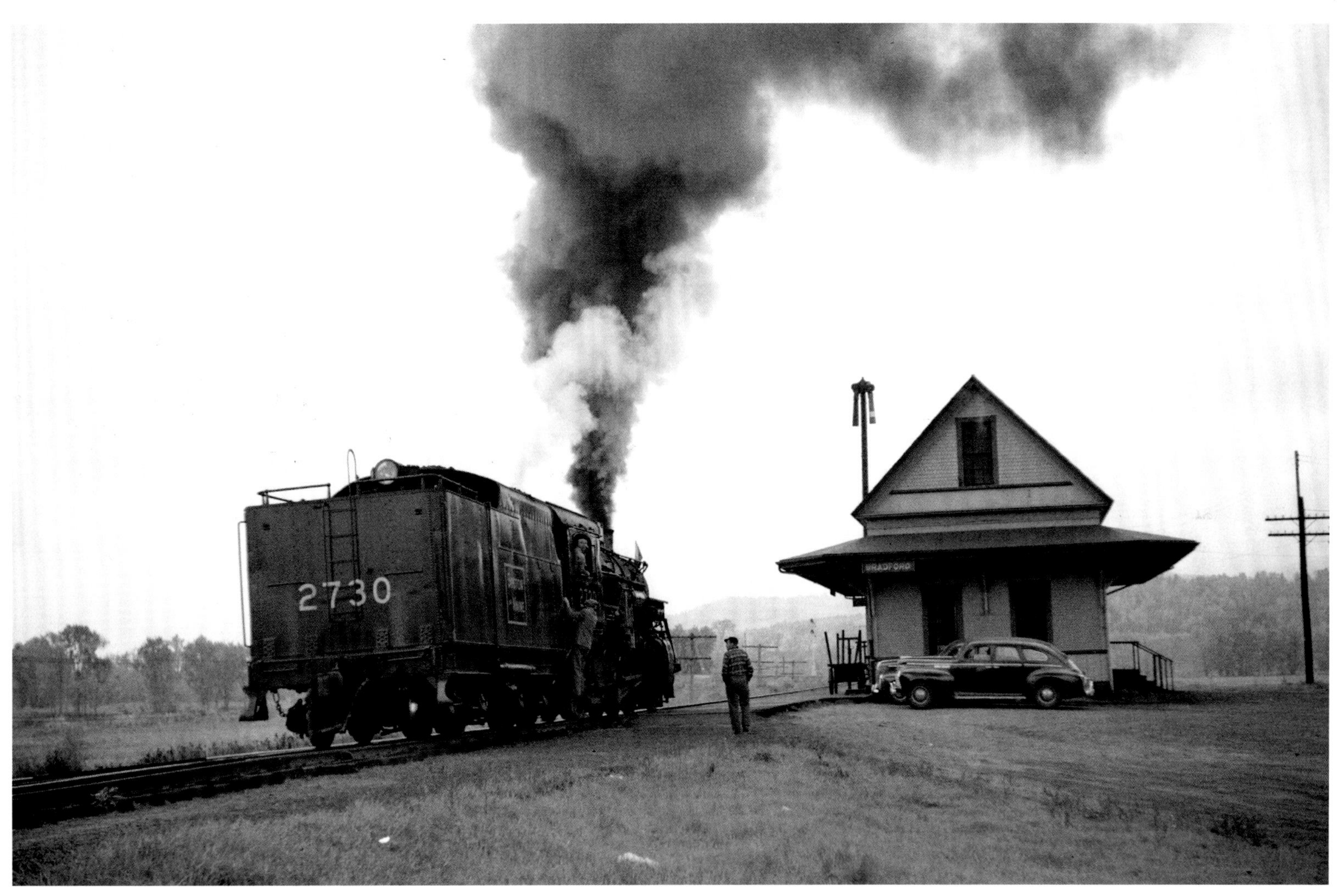

Plate 1. The Boston & Maine station in Bradford, Vermont, 1949. The locomotive is Boston & Maine 2-8-0 2730. Phil Hastings grew up in Bradford and learned to love railroading while he visited his local railroad station.

Courtesy of California State Railroad Museum.
Philip Ross Hastings, MD, Collection, [Negative 1188].

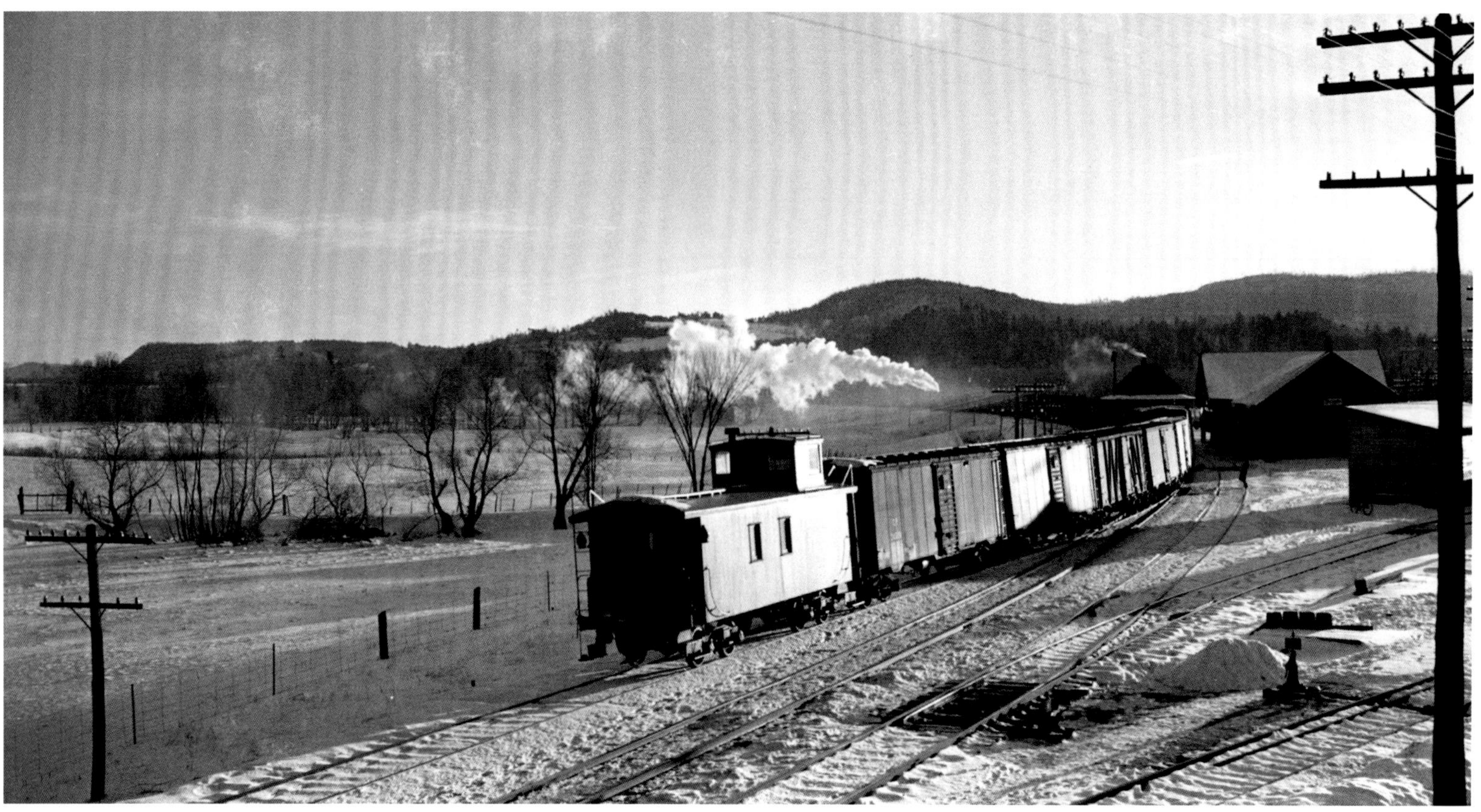

Plate 2. In a very early photo, taken in the winter of 1940–1941 at Bradford, a Canadian Pacific 4-6-0 fills the chill winter air with steam following a meet with a Boston & Maine passenger train at Bradford, Vermont. The Canadian Pacific engine, van (caboose), and crew ran through from Newport to White River Junction, Vermont. The buildings to the right of the train are the Boston & Maine freight house and a feedstore.

Courtesy of California State Railroad Museum. Philip Ross Hastings, MD, Collection, [Negative 679].

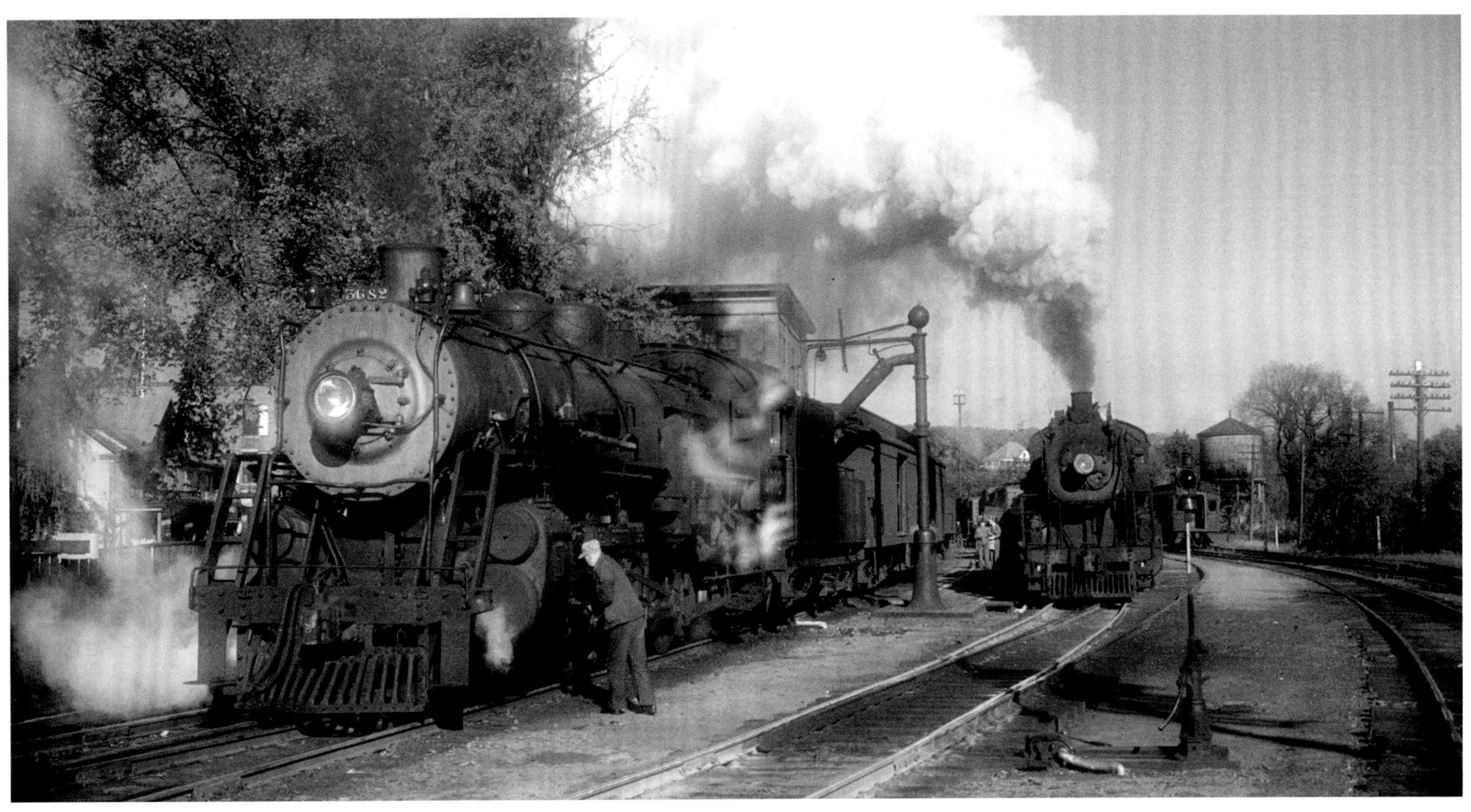

Plate 3. The Boston & Maine's southbound *Alouette,* east of the station in Woodsville, New Hampshire.

Courtesy of California State Railroad Museum. Philip Ross Hastings, MD, Collection, [Negative 320].

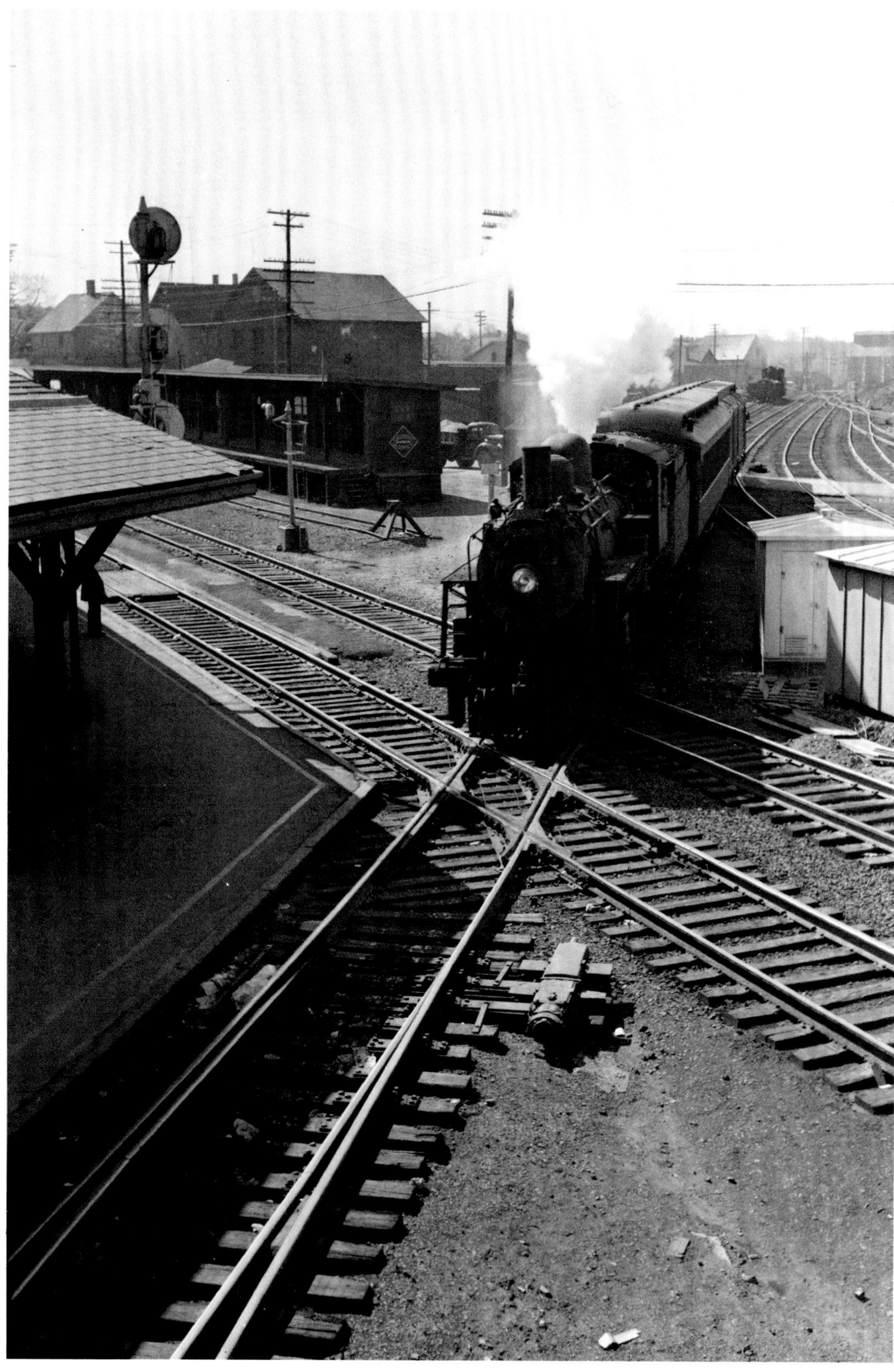

Plate 4. The Boston & Maine was Hastings's first love as a photography subject and is featured in many of his best photos. In this classic view, a short B&M train clatters across the diamonds at Gardner, Massachusetts. The train is on the Peterboro Branch and is crossing the B&M's Fitchburg division. Many of Hastings's B&M photos are collected in the 1989 book *The Boston & Maine: A Photographic Essay.*

Courtesy of California State Railroad Museum. Philip Ross Hastings, MD, Collection, [Negative 182].

Plate 5. In this unusual view, a Boston & Maine passenger fireman transfers his gear from "Mogul" (2-6-0) 1448 to "Mogul" 1468 on the Peterboro branch at Peterboro (Peterborough), New Hampshire.

Courtesy of California State Railroad Museum. Philip Ross Hastings, MD, Collection, [Negative 185].

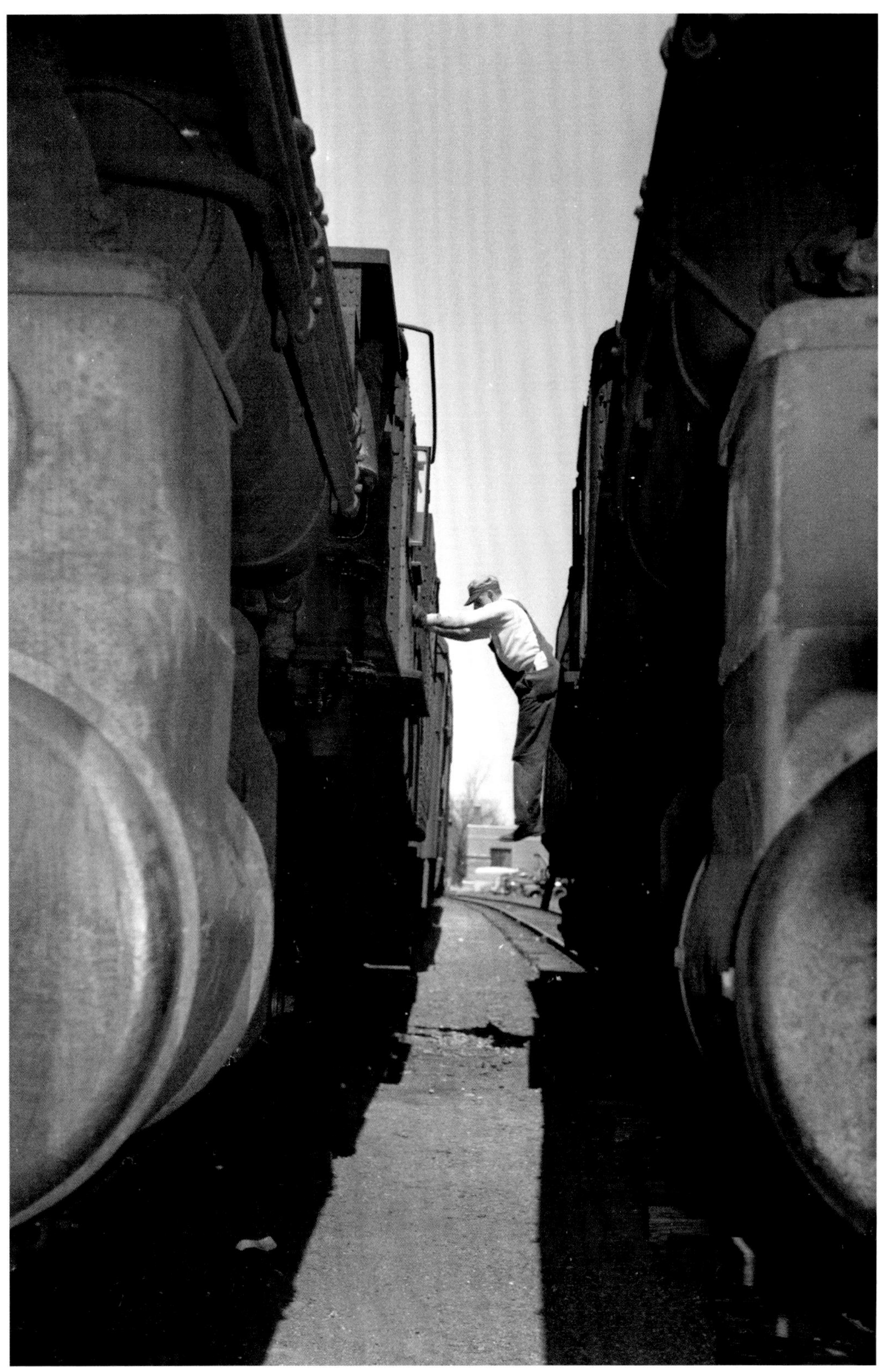

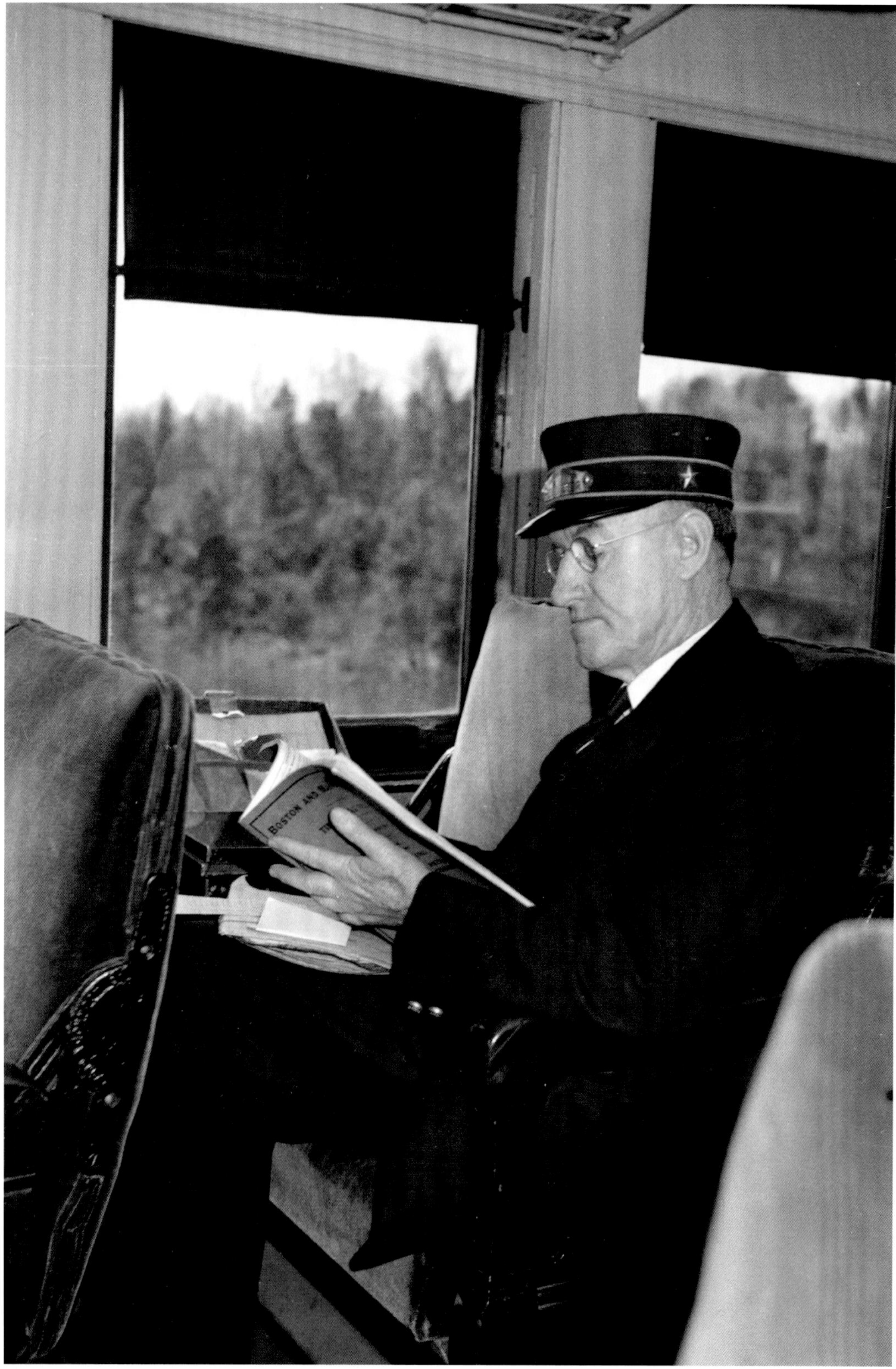

Plate 6. Boston & Maine conductor Mike Downey on a train on the Peterboro branch, 1952.

Courtesy of California State Railroad Museum. Philip Ross Hastings, MD, Collection, [Negative 386].

Plate 7. Boston & Maine 1455 whistles for the Route 31 crossing at South Lyndeboro (Lyndeborough), New Hampshire, on the railroad's Hillsboro branch.

Courtesy of California State Railroad Museum. Philip Ross Hastings, MD, Collection, [Negative 352].

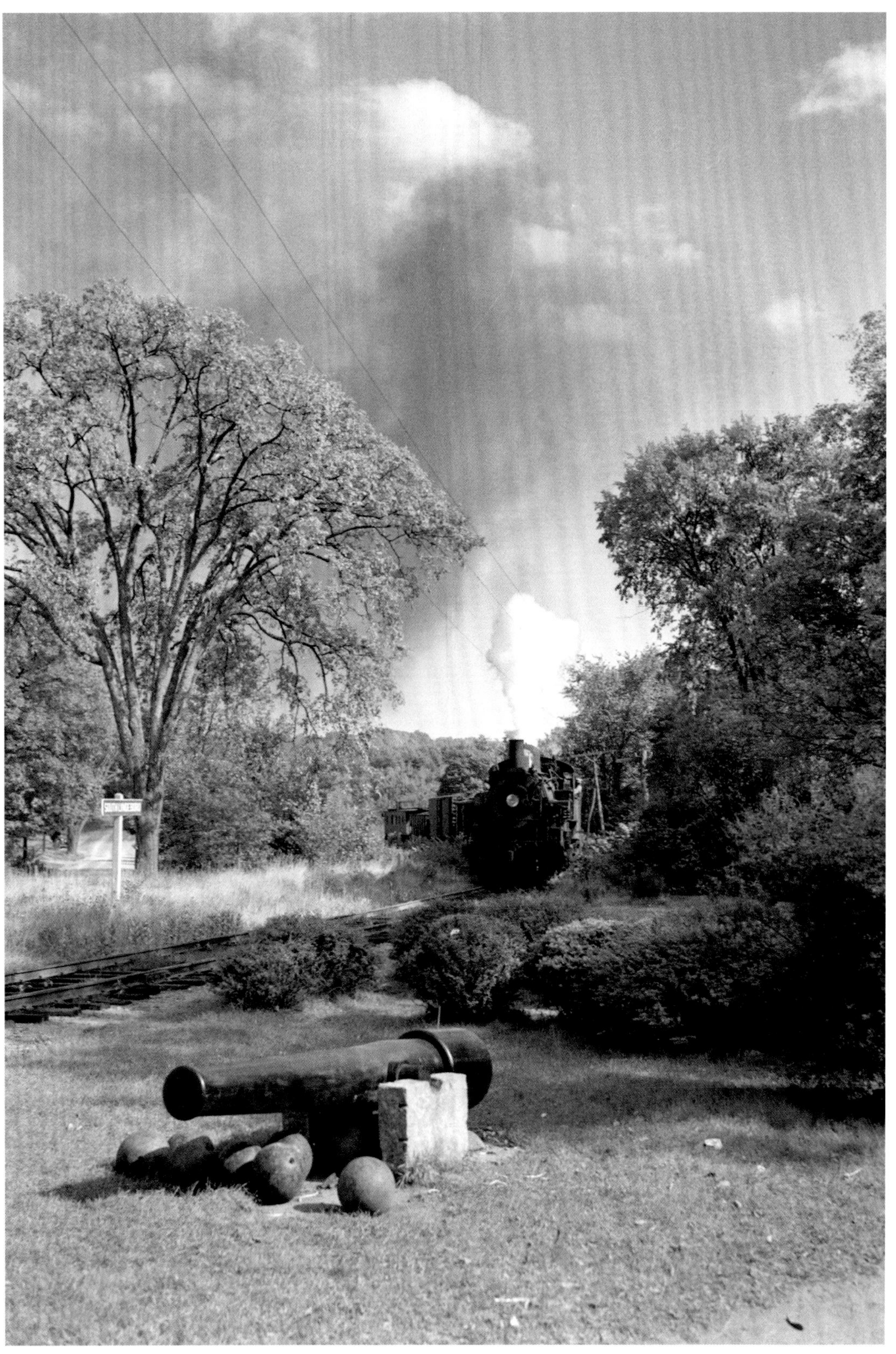

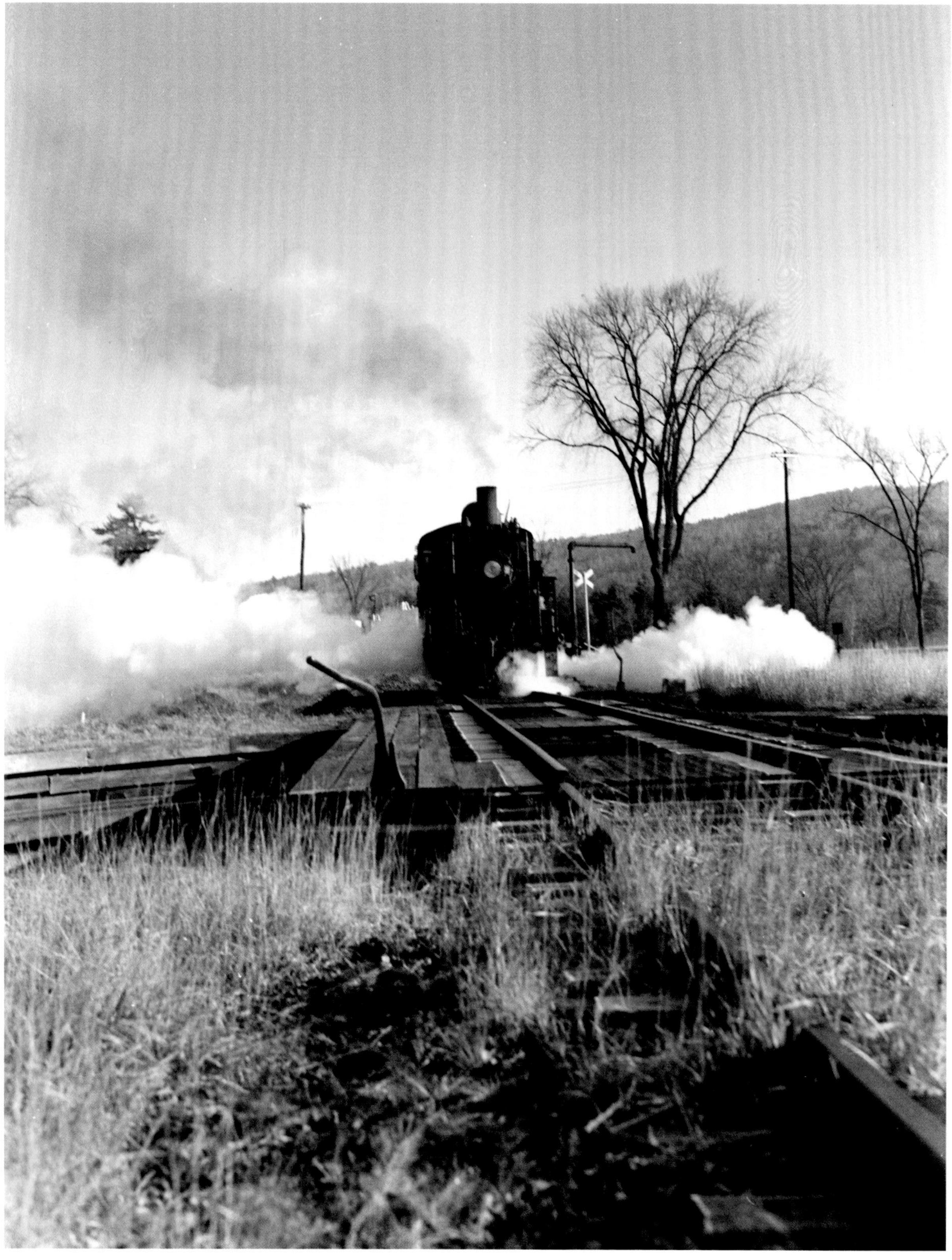

Plate 8. A Boston & Maine locomotive approaches the turntable at Hillsboro (Hillsborough), New Hampshire.

Courtesy of California State Railroad Museum. Philip Ross Hastings, MD, Collection, [Negative 1257].

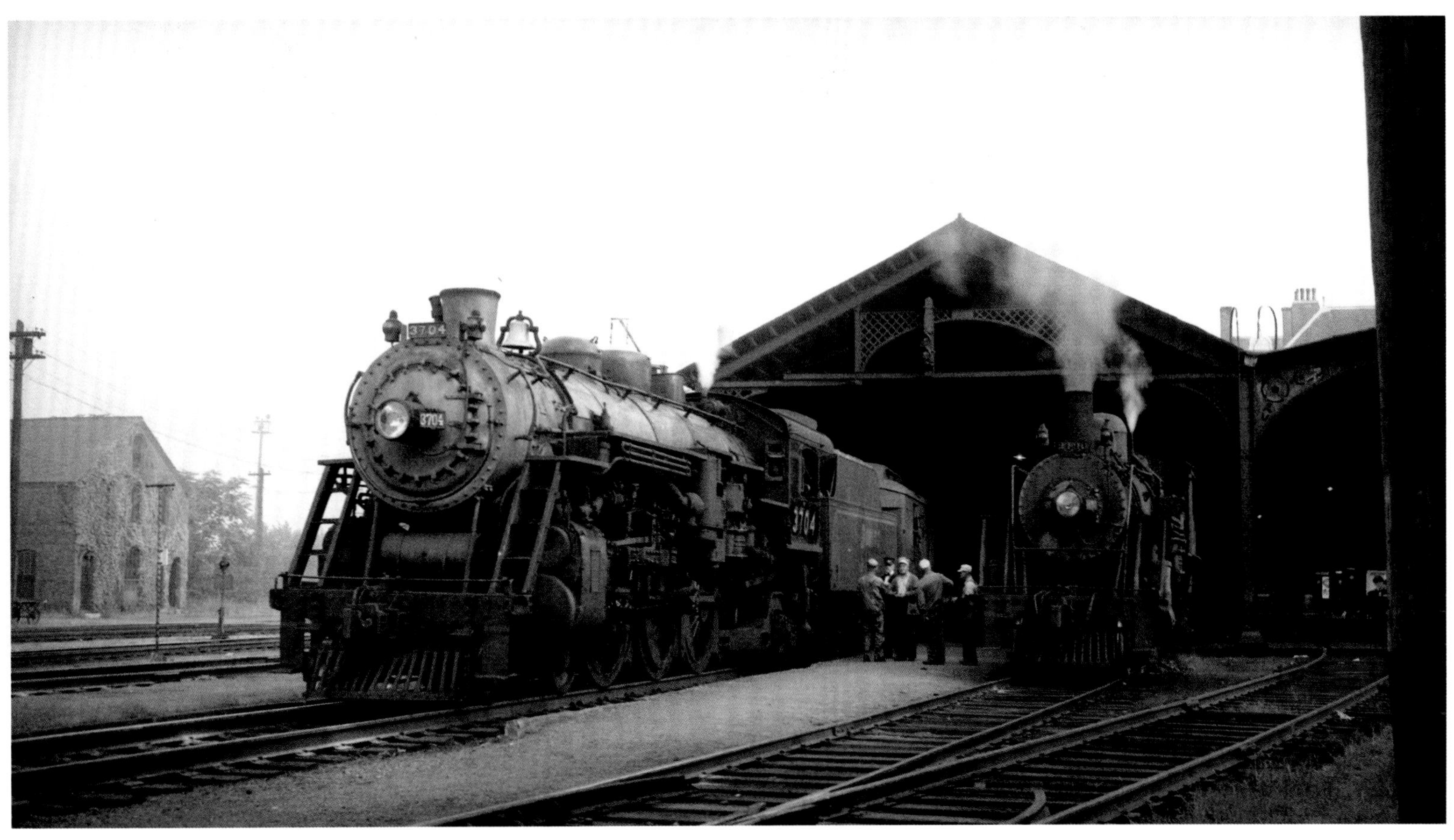

Plate 9. The crew of "Mogul" 1490 compares notes with the crew of P-3 "Pacific" 3704. Both engines are in front of the impressive station in Concord, New Hampshire. The "Mogul's" train is bound for Claremont Junction and the "Pacific" is pulling train 313 bound for White River Junction, Vermont.

Courtesy of California State Railroad Museum. Philip Ross Hastings, MD, Collection, [Negative 1145].

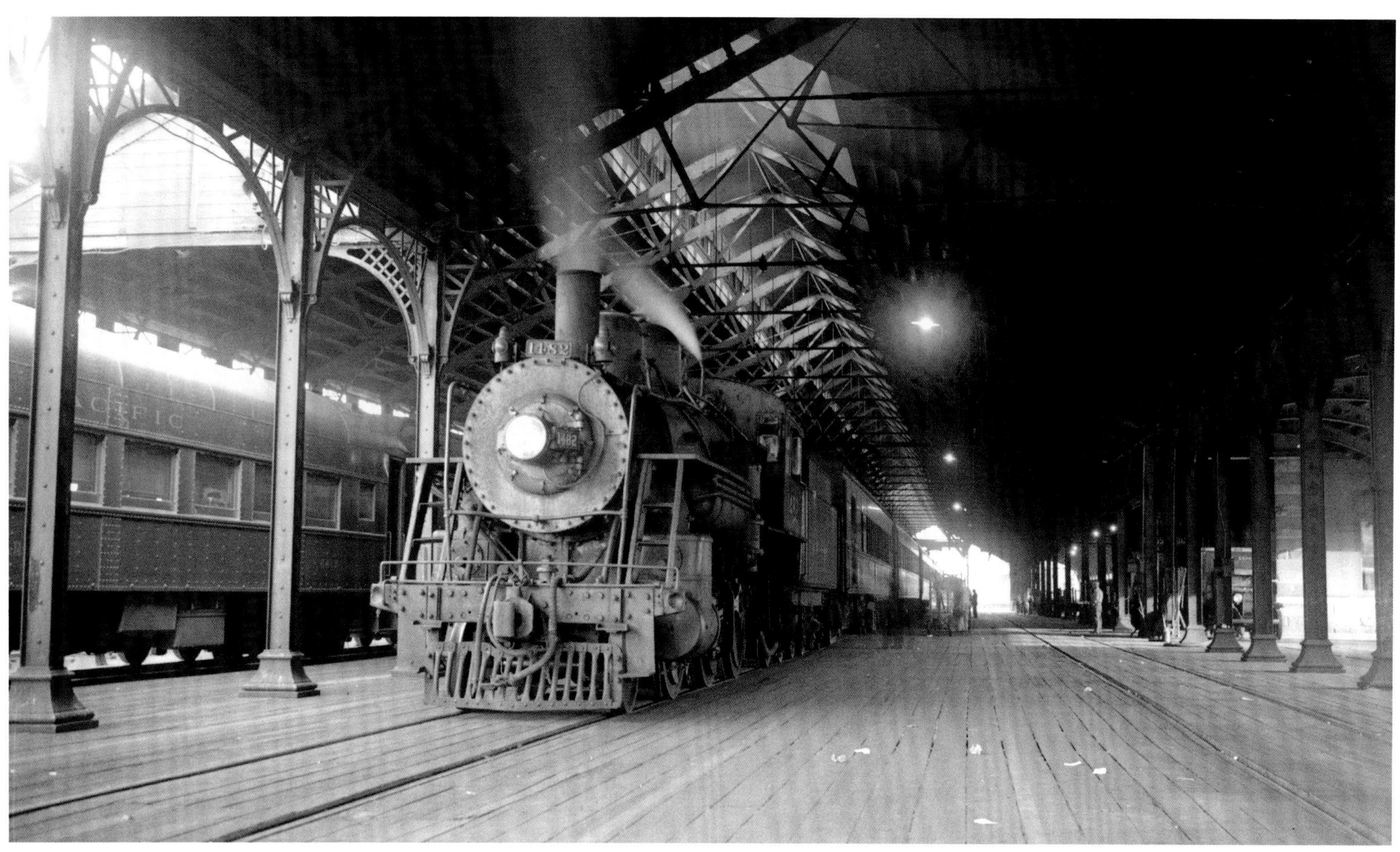

Plate 10. A local to White River Junction, Vermont, with Boston & Maine "Mogul" 1482 sits inside the Concord, New Hampshire, station's train shed.

Courtesy of California State Railroad Museum. Philip Ross Hastings, MD, Collection, [Negative 403].

Plate 11. The Boston & Maine covered bridge at Contoocook, New Hampshire, with a local to Henniker, New Hampshire, in 1952. The B&M station is to the right. The engine is B&M "Mogul" 1490. The bridge survives today.

Courtesy of California State Railroad Museum. Philip Ross Hastings, MD, Collection, [Negative 350].

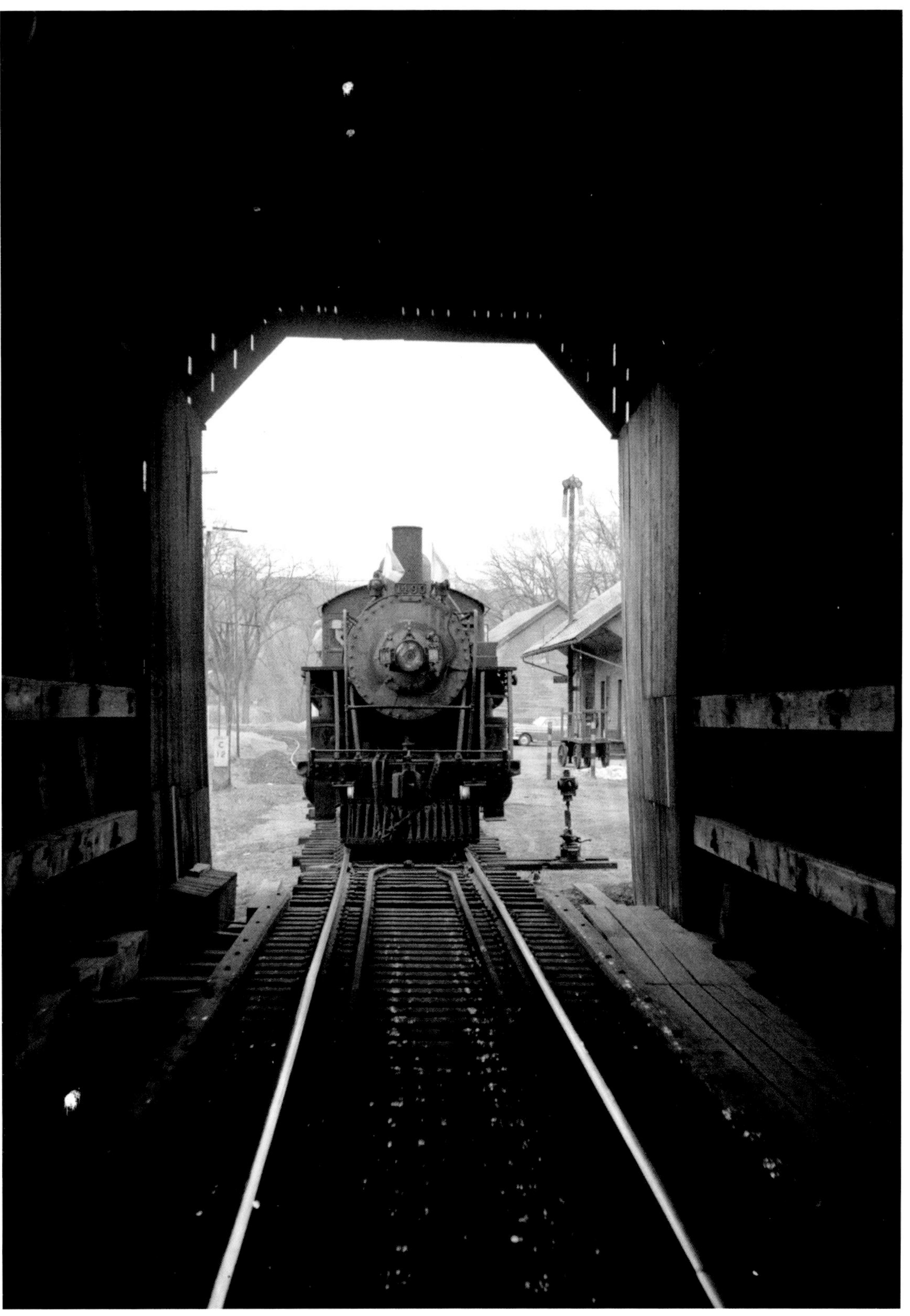

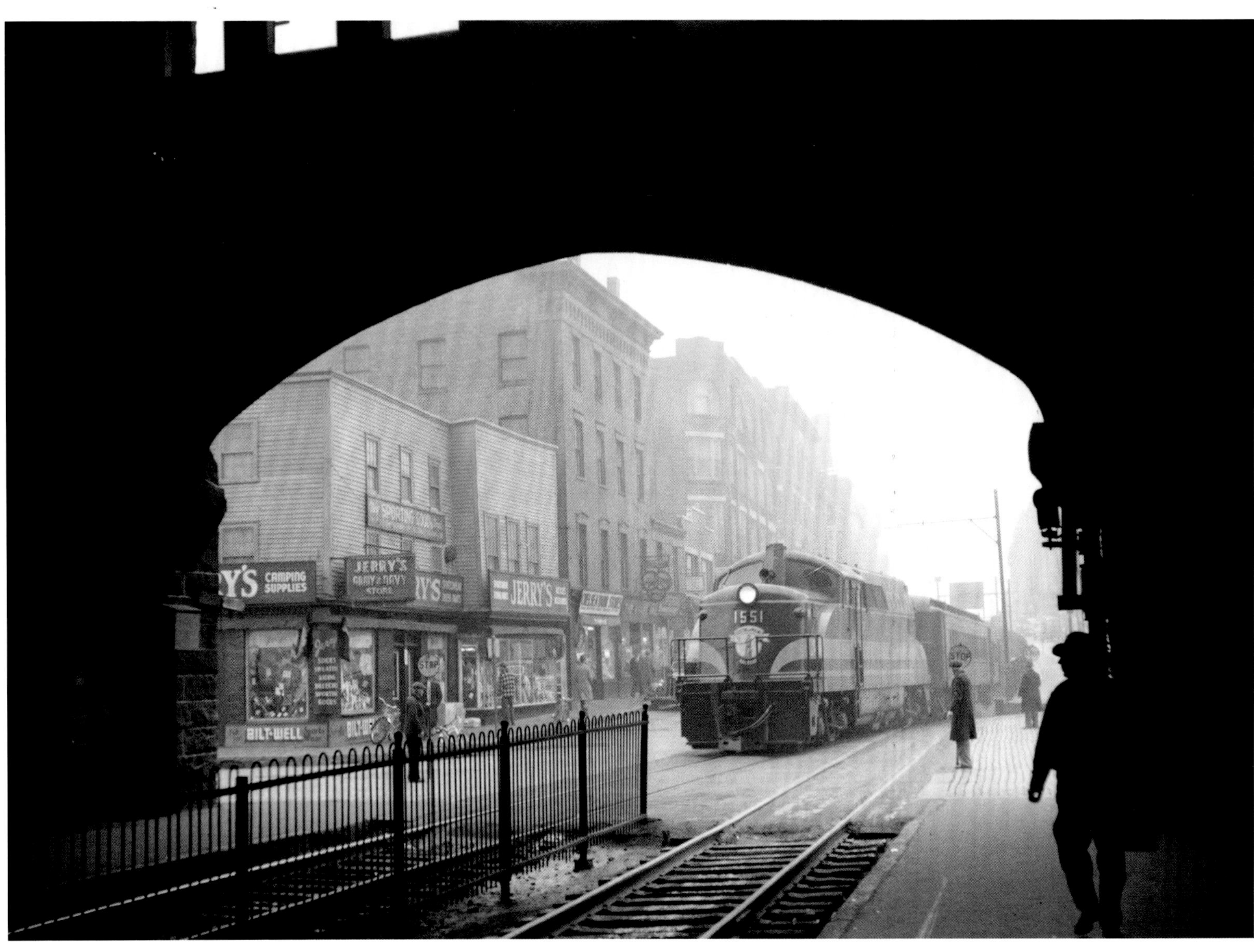

Plate 12. This is the unusual Boston & Maine station in the famed witch trials town of Salem, Massachusetts. The train in the photo is led by a diesel, a BL-2, 1551.

Courtesy of California State Railroad Museum. Philip Ross Hastings, MD, Collection, [Negative 188].

Plate 13. A Boston-bound commuter train on the Boston & Maine's Central Massachusetts branch exits a tunnel near Clinton, Massachusetts, July 1954.

Courtesy of California State Railroad Museum. Philip Ross Hastings, MD, Collection, [Negative 161].

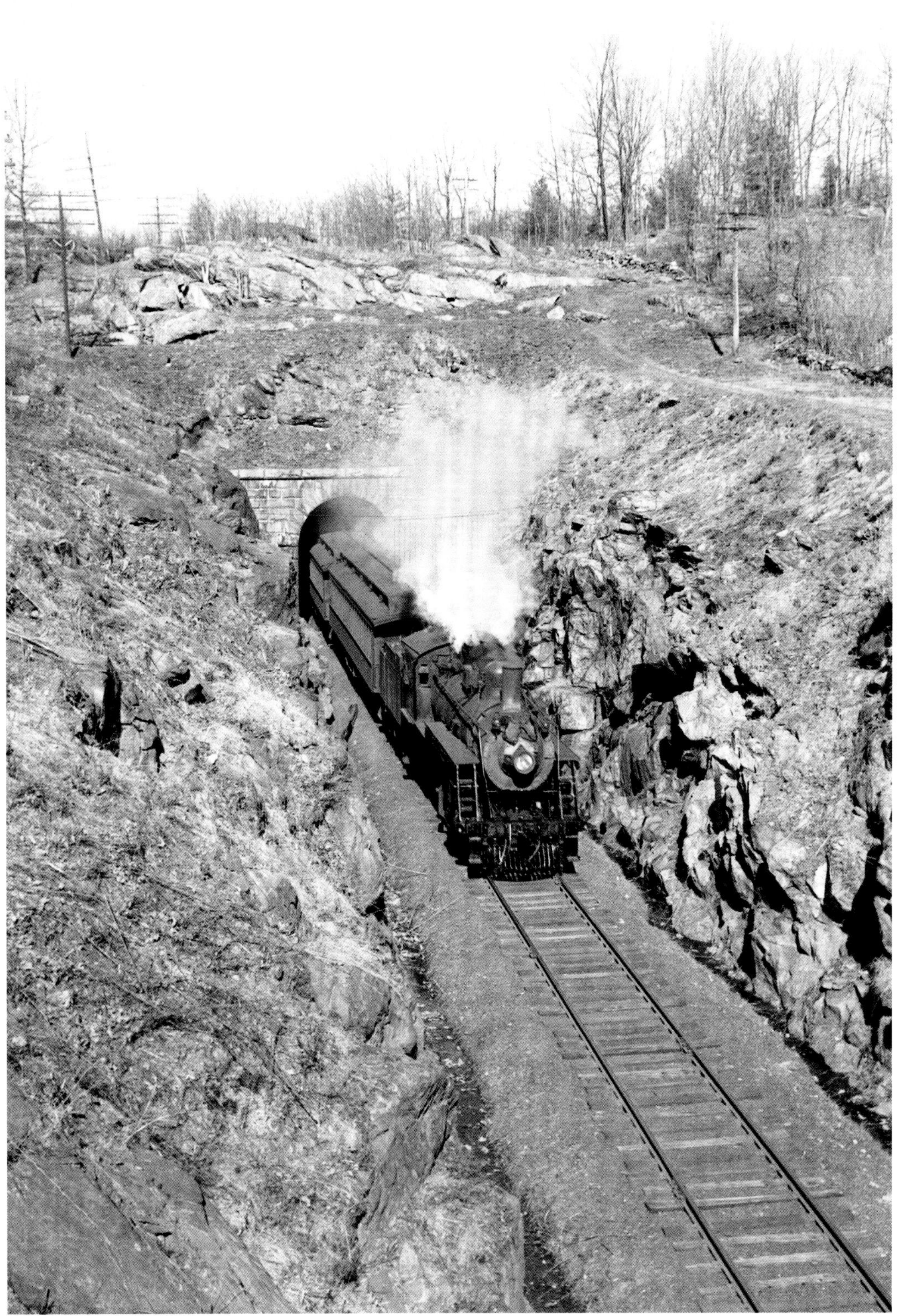

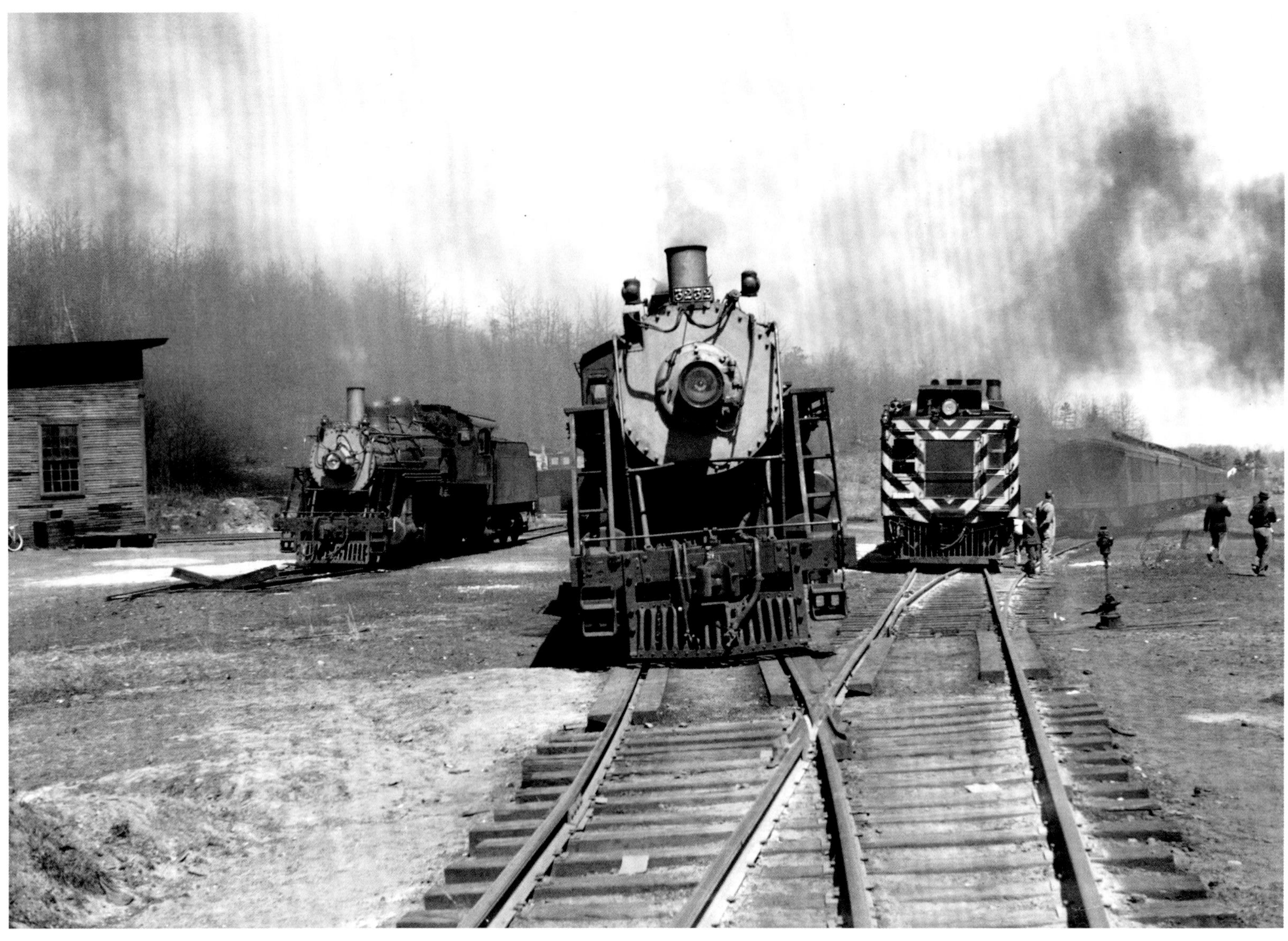

Plate 14. B-15 "Mogul" 1388, J-1-b "Atlantic" 3232, and a gas-electric car are gathered for a Railroad Enthusiasts excursion over the Central Massachusetts branch, April 1948.

Courtesy of California State Railroad Museum. Philip Ross Hastings, MD, Collection, [Negative 166].

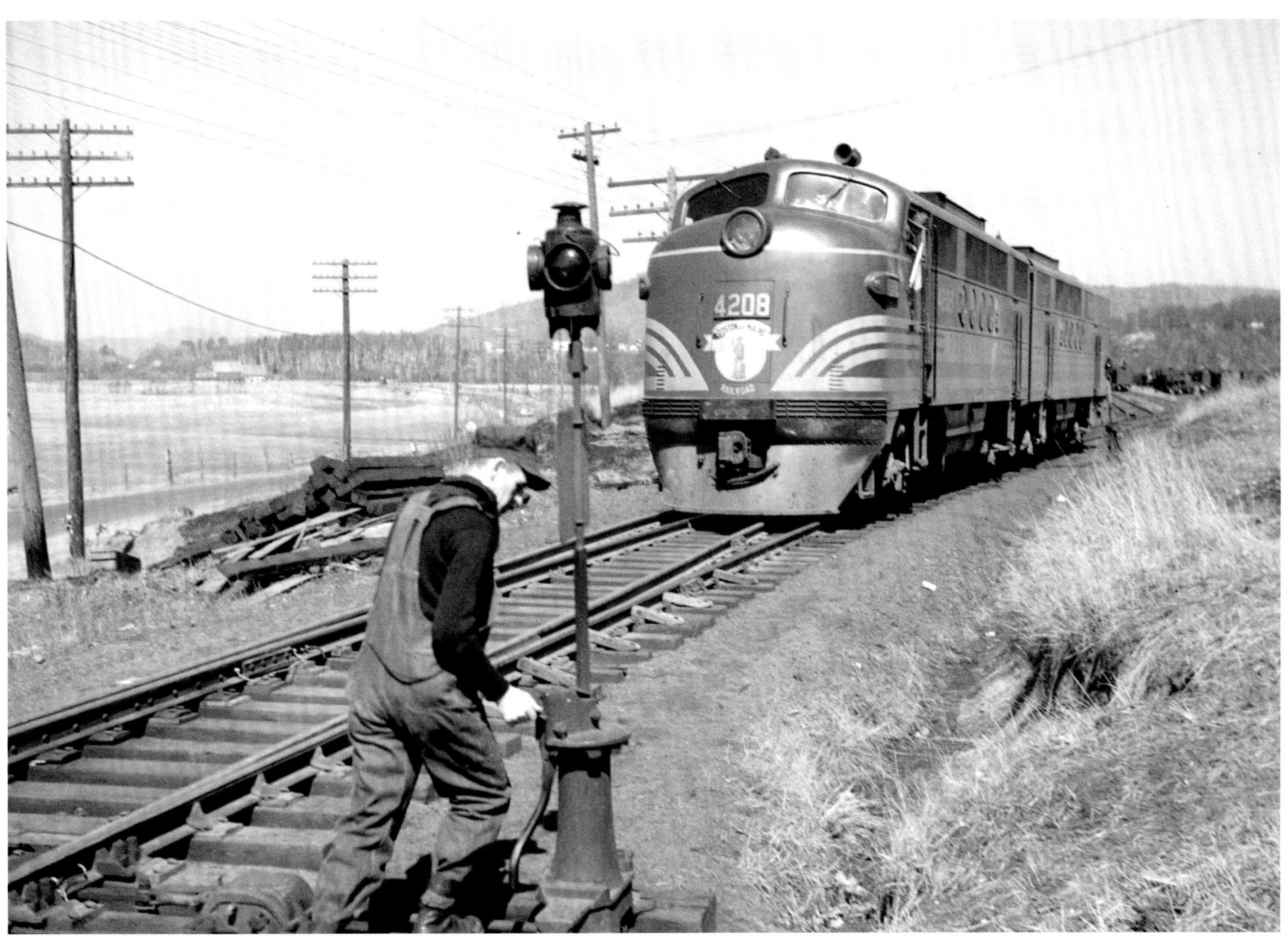

Plate 15. A Boston & Maine crewman "bends the iron" for diesel 4208. This is an FT A-and-B unit coupled together.

Courtesy of California State Railroad Museum. Philip Ross Hastings, MD, Collection, [Negative 1093].

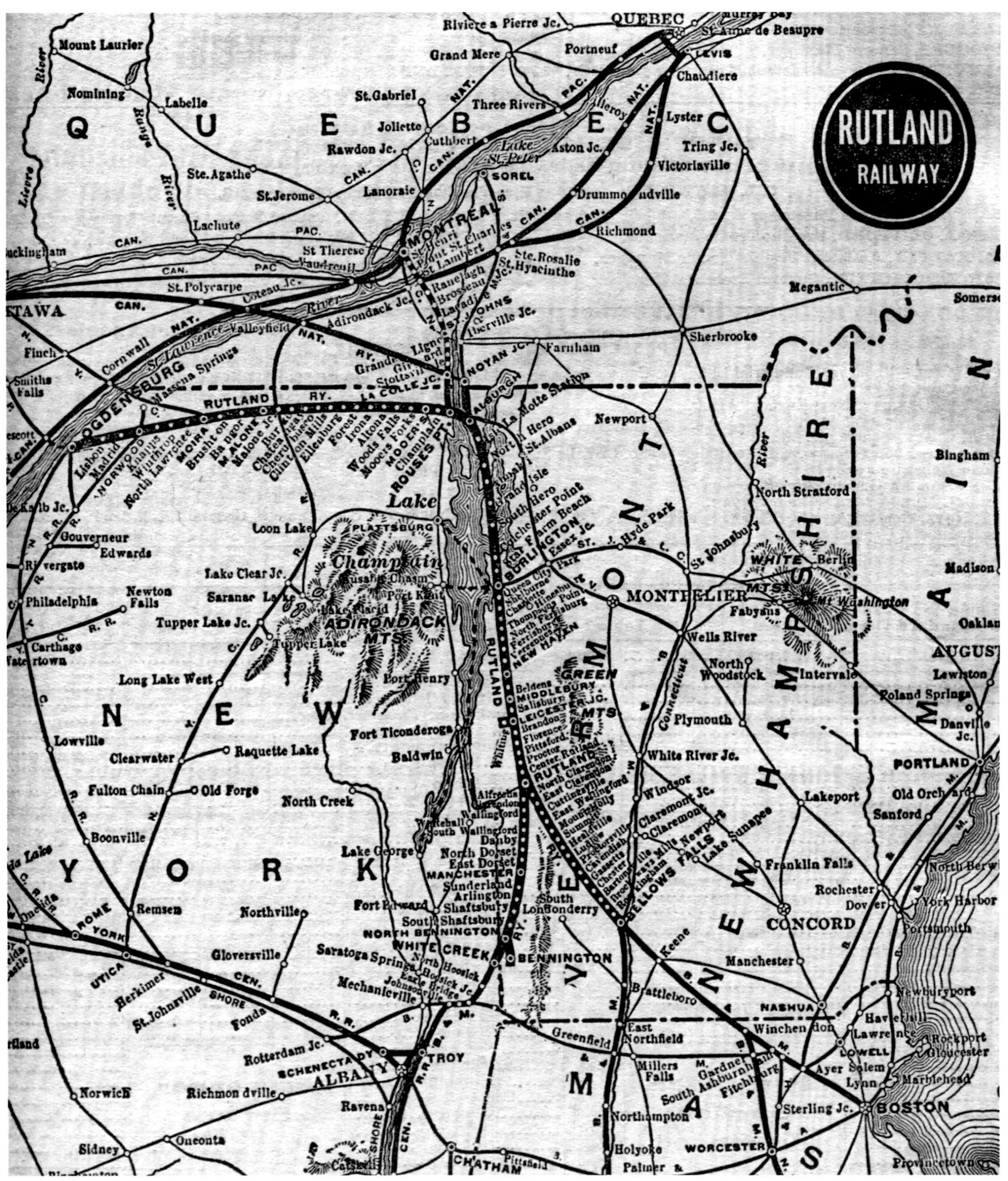

RUTLAND
RAILWAY
QUEBEC
LEVIS
Chaudiere
Lyster
Tring Jc.
Victoriaville
Drummondville
Richmond
Megantic
Sherbrooke
Newport
Farnham
Three Rivers
Grand Mere
Portneuf
St.Gabriel
Joliette
Rawdon Jc.
Lanoraie
SOREL
Aston Jc.
Mount Laurier
Nominingue
Labelle
Ste.Agathe
St.Jerome
Lachute
MONTREAL
St.Polycarpe
Coteau Jc.
Valleyfield
Adirondack Jc.
Iberville Jc.
Ste.Rosalie
St.Hyacinthe
Finch
Cornwall
Smiths Falls
OGDENSBURG
Massena Springs
RUTLAND RY.
NORWOOD
MOIRA
MALONE
ROUSES PT.
Champlain
Mooers
ALBURGH
NOYAN JC.
LA COLLE JC.
North Hero
St.Albans
Grand Isle
South Hero
Essex Jc.
BURLINGTON
PLATTSBURG
Lake Champlain
Loon Lake
Lake Clear Jc.
Saranac Lake
Lake Placid
Tupper Lake Jc.
Tupper Lake
ADIRONDACK MTS.
Port Kent
Port Henry
Fort Ticonderoga
Baldwin
De Kalb Jc.
Gouverneur
Edwards
Rivergate
Philadelphia
Newton Falls
Carthage
Watertown
Long Lake West
Lowville
Clearwater
Raquette Lake
Fulton Chain
Old Forge
North Creek
Boonville
Lake George
Fort Edward
Remsen
Northville
Gloversville
NEW YORK
ROME
UTICA
Herkimer
St.Johnsville
Fonda
Oneida
Rotterdam Jc.
SCHENECTADY
ALBANY
TROY
Mechanicville
Saratoga Springs
WHITE CREEK
NORTH BENNINGTON
BENNINGTON
Norwich
Richmondville
Ravena
Oneonta
Sidney
Catskill
CHATHAM
Pittsfield
RUTLAND
NEW HAVEN
MIDDLEBURY
Leicester Jc.
Brandon
Pittsford
Proctor
RUTLAND
Wallingford
Danby
Dorset
MANCHESTER
Sunderland
Arlington
Shaftsbury
South Londonderry
BELLOWS FALLS
GREEN MTS.
VERMONT
MONTPELIER
St. Johnsbury
Wells River
White River Jc.
Windsor
Claremont Jc.
Claremont
Newport
Lake Sunapee
Brattleboro
Keene
East Northfield
Greenfield
Millers Falls
Northampton
Holyoke
Palmer
MASS.
South Ashburnham
Gardner
Fitchburg
Winchendon
WORCESTER
NEW HAMPSHIRE
North Stratford
Berlin
WHITE MTS.
Mt. Washington
Fabyans
North Woodstock
Plymouth
Intervale
Lakeport
Franklin Falls
CONCORD
Manchester
NASHUA
Rochester
Dover
York Harbor
Portsmouth
Newburyport
Haverhill
Lawrence
LOWELL
Ayer
Salem
Lynn
Marblehead
Rockport
Gloucester
Sterling Jc.
BOSTON
Provincetown
MAINE
Bingham
Madison
Oakland
AUGUSTA
Lewiston
Poland Springs
Danville Jc.
PORTLAND
Old Orchard
Sanford
North Berwick
Somerset

PORTFOLIO TWO

THE RUTLAND

The Rutland Railroad was a New England regional railroad with extensive trackage in New York.[1] It was shaped like an upside-down Y with a tail—the southern points were Chatham, New York, and Bellows Falls, Vermont; the tail turned away at Alburgh, Vermont, and ran across northern New York to reach the Great Lakes at Ogdensburg.

Phil Hastings did not grow up along the Rutland Railroad, but he spent a lot of time in Burlington, Vermont, while attending the University of Vermont. Burlington, then as now, was the largest town in Vermont—and it was also the most important town on the Rutland. Hastings developed a special affinity for the Rutland and took many images of the railroad. He later said that the Rutland "reawakened my interest in railroading" after World War II.[2] Many of Hastings's images of the Rutland illustrate Jim Shaughnessy's fine history of the railroad, *The Rutland Road*.

The Rutland is also seen as a poster child for the US railroad industry in its decline. Like the New York, Ontario & Western Railway, abandoned in 1957, the Rutland closed in 1963. This was just five years before the Penn Central was formed in 1968, and seven years before that railroad's spectacular failure in 1970.

Unlike the New York, Ontario & Western, much of the Rutland was saved, largely due to the innovative and progressive actions of the state of Vermont. The Burlington to Bennington portion of the railroad became the Vermont Railway, today a successful regional railroad, and the Bellows Falls to Rutland segment became the Green Mountain Railroad.[3] Due to Phil Hastings's outstanding and plentiful photography, we have an excellent view of the Rutland in the fifteen or so years before its closing.

Plate 16 opens this portfolio with a scene of Rutland railroaders chatting; a switch engine smokes up the landscape in the background. The Rutland formed an important passenger connection between the United States and Canada, and plate 17 depicts a US Customs and Immigration inspector waiting to board a southbound Rutland passenger train at St. Johns, Quebec, Canada. This view probably had significant meaning for Hastings, as his father worked as a Customs and Immigration inspector for four years in the early 1900s.[4]

The Rutland's rails ran through many miles of bucolic Vermont scenery, especially on the lines to Bennington and Bellows

***Facing*, Figure 2.1.** Map of the Rutland Railway, 1954.

Courtesy of Tony Reevy Collection.

Falls south and southeast of Rutland. Plate 18 shows Rutland steam engine 76 whistling for a crossing at North Clarendon, Vermont, just southeast of Rutland.

One of the iconic Rutland photo locations is where the Bellows Falls line joins the Bennington to Burlington line at what was then the Howe Scale Company in Rutland, Vermont. Plate 19 shows one of the railroad's classic trains, the New York section of the *Green Mountain Flyer*, coming into Rutland from Bennington and points south.

Plate 20, a classic Hastings image, shows Rutland switch engine 101 and a crew at the Rutland yard. A brass hat—railroad supervisor/executive—appears at the right edge of the photo. In plate 21, another iconic view, a Rutland freight conductor goes through paperwork at his desk in the caboose.

Thanks to Hastings's work, we have a number of fine views of section gangs during late steam–era US railroading. Hastings liked views of section gangs with their "speeders"—several of Hastings's best images are of this type. Plate 22 shows the Rutland's Colchester, Vermont, section gang leaving their section house on their speeder as a workday in 1950 begins.

One of the vanished sections of the Rutland, not saved by the state of Vermont in the early 1960s, was its fascinating route up Lake Champlain on Vermont's Lake Champlain Islands. The interior part of this line was not that scenic, but its Lake Champlain crossings were magnificent. Plate 23 shows a Rutland milk train—milk was a large part of the railroad's traffic—on the three-mile-long fill from mainland Vermont to South Hero.

Plate 24 shows a Rutland milk train at Shelburne, Vermont, with mail and express being handled. The sour-faced trainman tossing mail sacks clearly does not believe in "safety first."

The Rutland's line up Lake Champlain essentially started with the fill shown in plate 23 and ended with a trestle spanning the Richelieu River between Alburgh, Vermont, and Rouses Point, New York. Plate 25 depicts this trestle. Once across the trestle, the Rutland ran across northern New York from Rouses Point to Ogdensburg. Plate 26 shows a westbound Rutland freight on this line at Champlain, New York.

At its heart, though, the Rutland was a Vermont railroad. Plate 27 shows a double-headed Rutland freight in central Vermont on the line from Bellows Falls to Rutland at East Clarendon.

One of the Rutland's end points was Bellows Falls, where it connected with the Boston & Maine. Plate 28, an innovative Hastings view, shot from inside the Bellows Falls roundhouse, shows Rutland steam locomotive 76 taking on water.

Our Rutland portfolio closes with a last run and an interloper. Plate 29 shows the crew of Rutland train 43 on the occasion of its last run, March 15, 1948. All Rutland Railway passenger service would end as the result of a strike in 1953.

In an effort to economize, the Rutland dieselized early. It became well-known for its green-and-yellow Alco road switchers, RS-1s and RS-3s. This Rutland portfolio closes with Rutland RS-3 208 leading a freight train across a rural road protected by a sign reading "Railroad Crossing—Look Out for the Cars."

Plate 16. Two young Rutland trainmen talk business.

Courtesy of California State Railroad Museum. Philip Ross Hastings, MD, Collection, [Negative 2113].

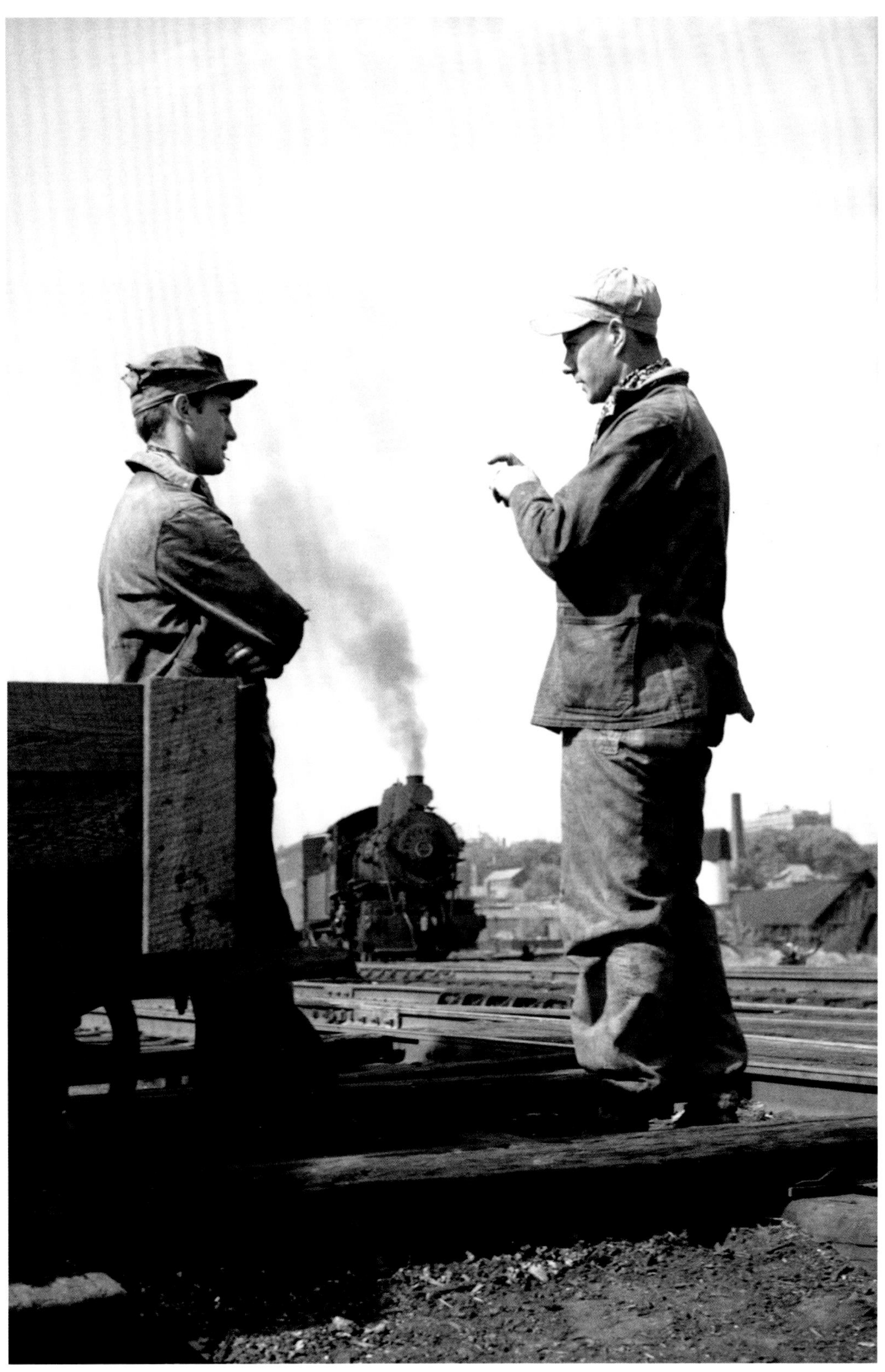

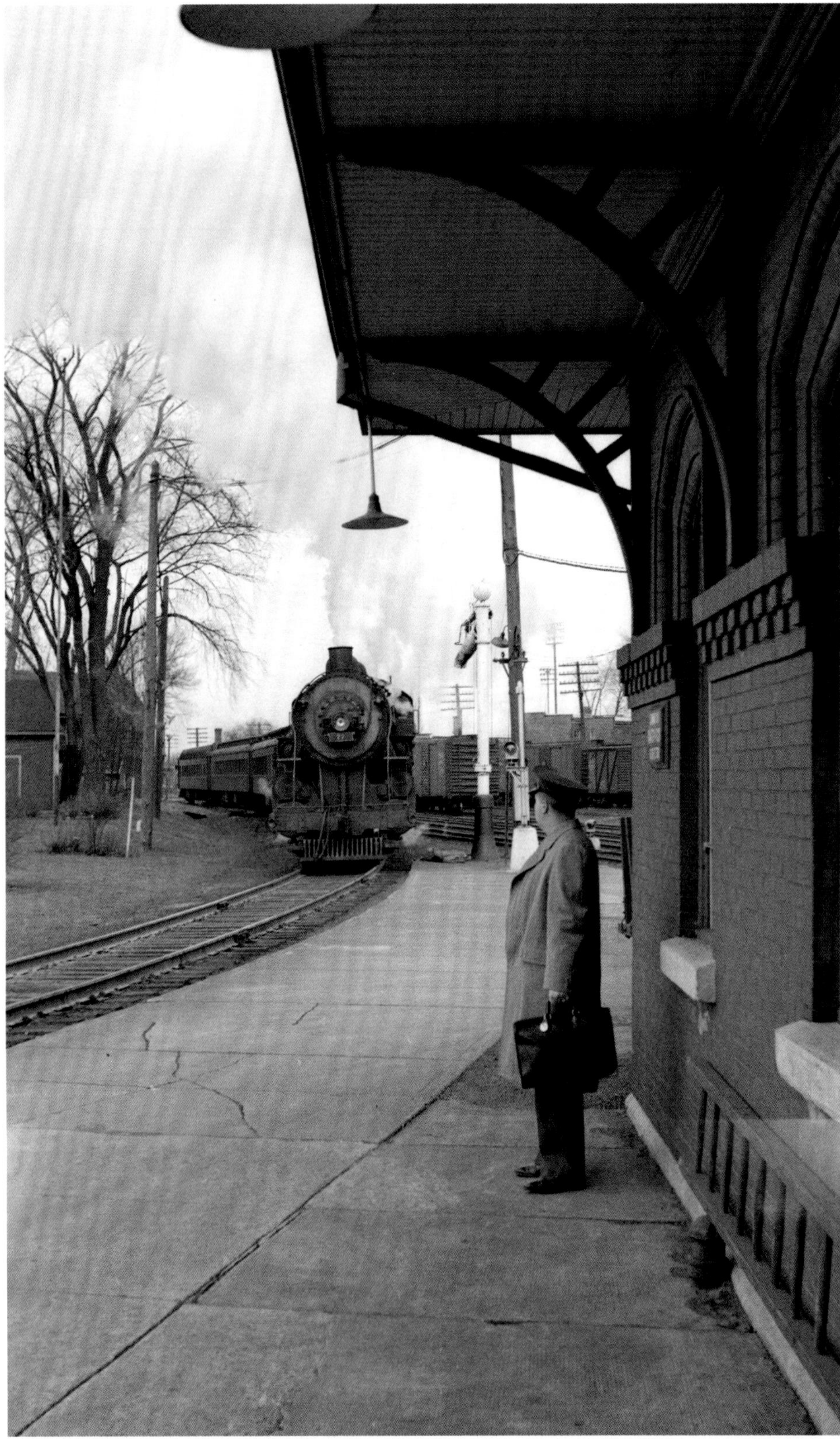

Plate 17. A US Customs inspector waits to board a southbound *Green Mountain Flyer* as it stops at St. Johns, Quebec.

Courtesy of California State Railroad Museum. Philip Ross Hastings, MD, Collection, [Negative 2228].

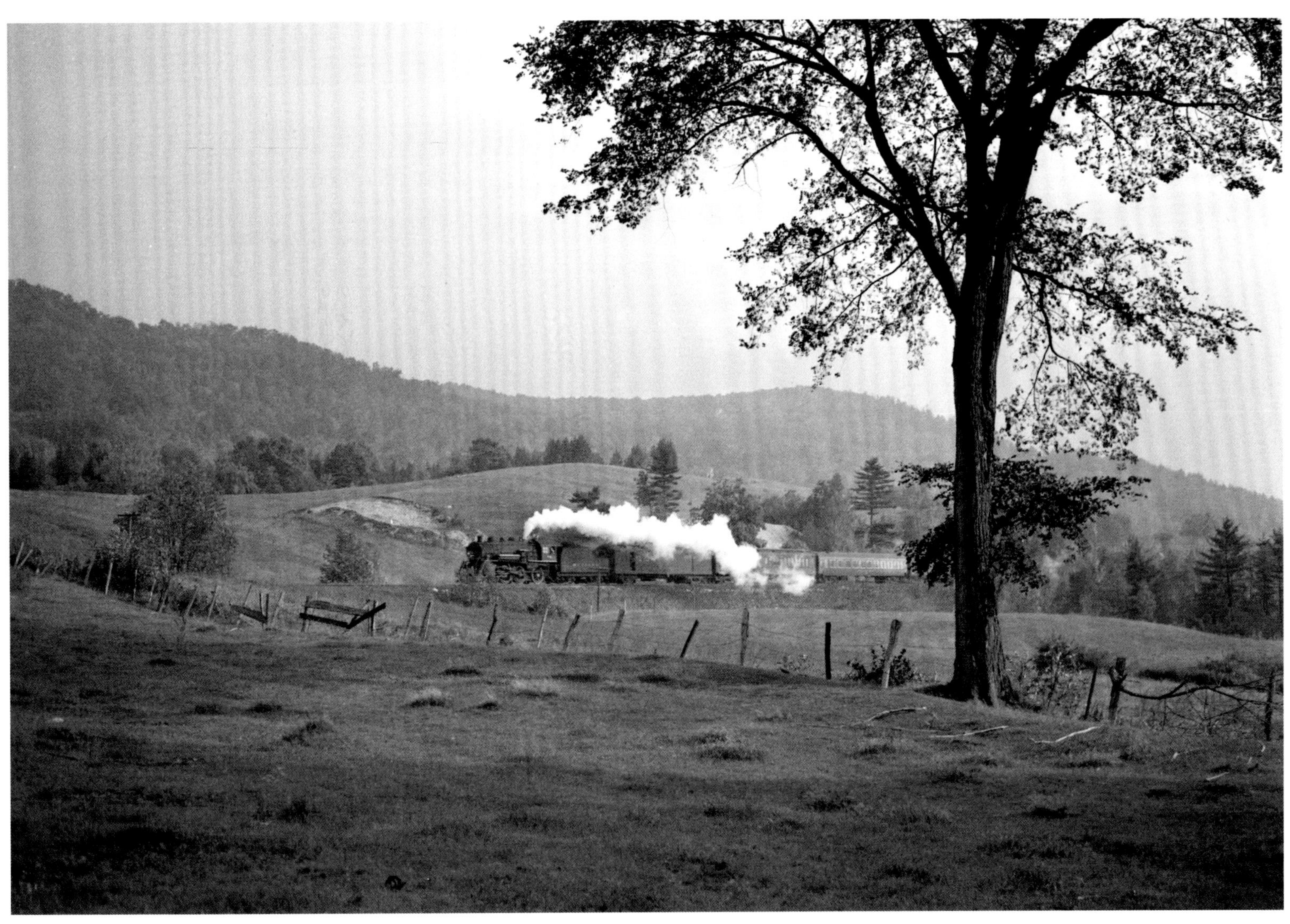

Plate 18. Hastings used a number of photo techniques expertly and repeatedly. One of these was catching a locomotive, often in winter, trailing steam from a whistle. In this image, "Ten-Wheeler" 76 whistles for a road crossing as she brings the Boston section of the *Green Mountain Flyer* into Rutland. The location is North Clarendon, Vermont.

Courtesy of California State Railroad Museum. Philip Ross Hastings, MD, Collection, [Negative 2155].

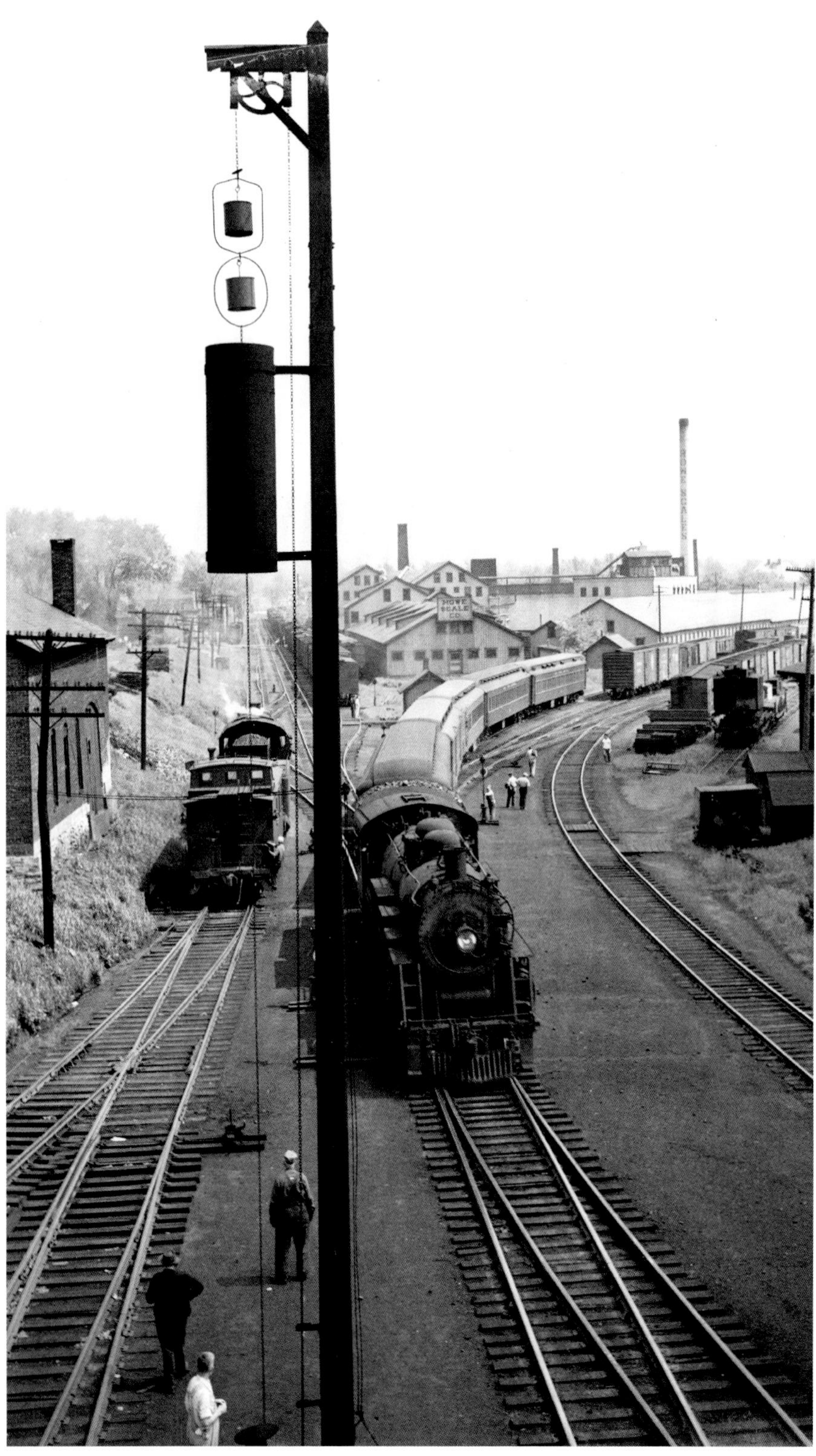

Plate 19. Another classic photo location on the Rutland Railroad/Railway was at the Howe Scale Company in Rutland, Vermont. The line from Burlington to Bennington meets the route from Rutland to Bellows Falls here. In this image, the New York section of the *Green Mountain Flyer* comes into Rutland from Bennington, Vermont, behind Boston & Maine "Pacific" 3656. A ball signal looms over the train—Howe Scale is behind it—and another engine and caboose are to the left.

Courtesy of California State Railroad Museum. Philip Ross Hastings, MD, Collection, [Negative 2177].

Plate 20. A Rutland trainman with switch engine 101 waits while a colleague talks with another employee wearing the traditional uniform of a railroad executive ("brass hat"): a fedora and a jacket. Switch engine 101 was an 0-6-0 built in 1907.

Courtesy of California State Railroad Museum. Philip Ross Hastings, MD, Collection, [Negative 2176].

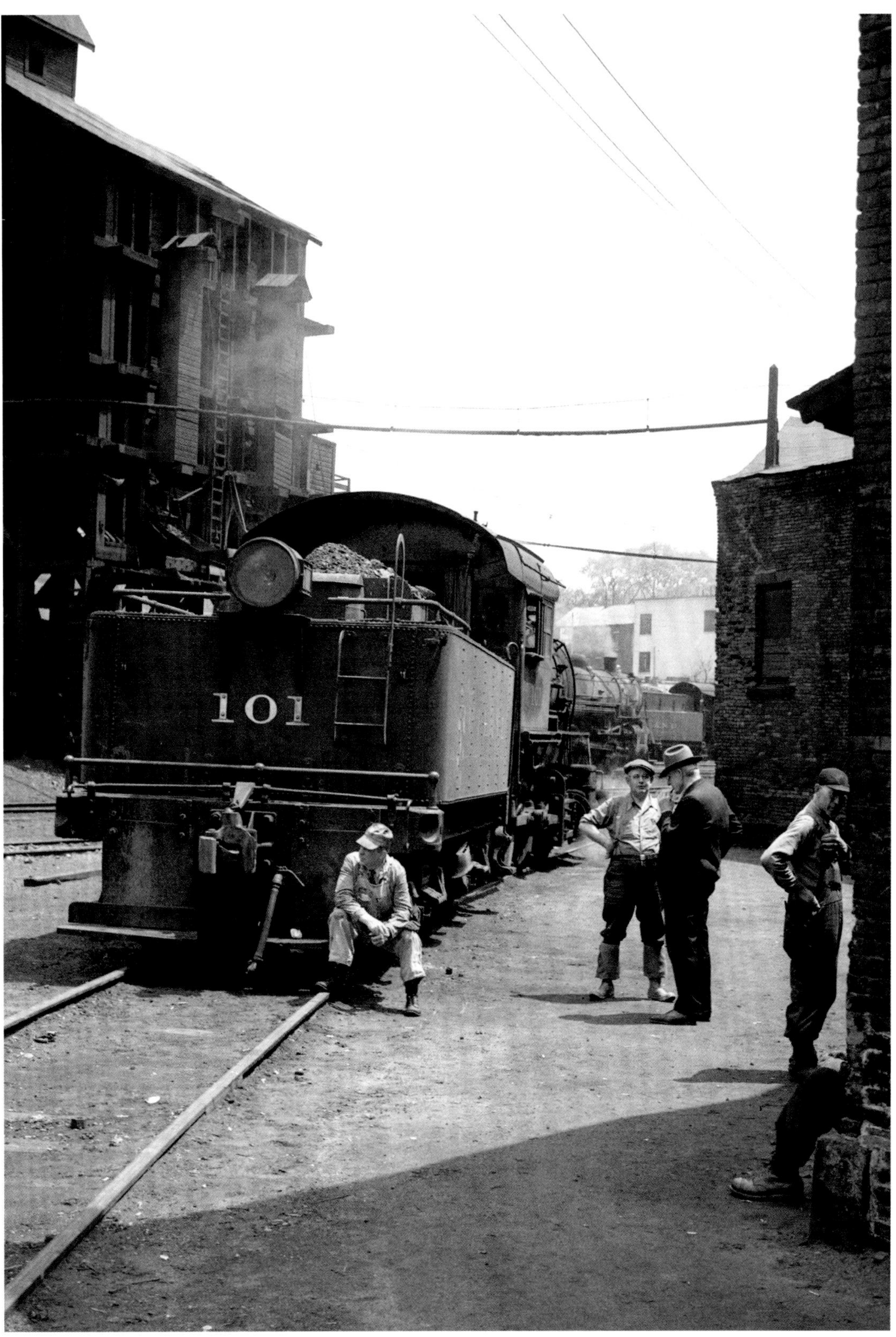

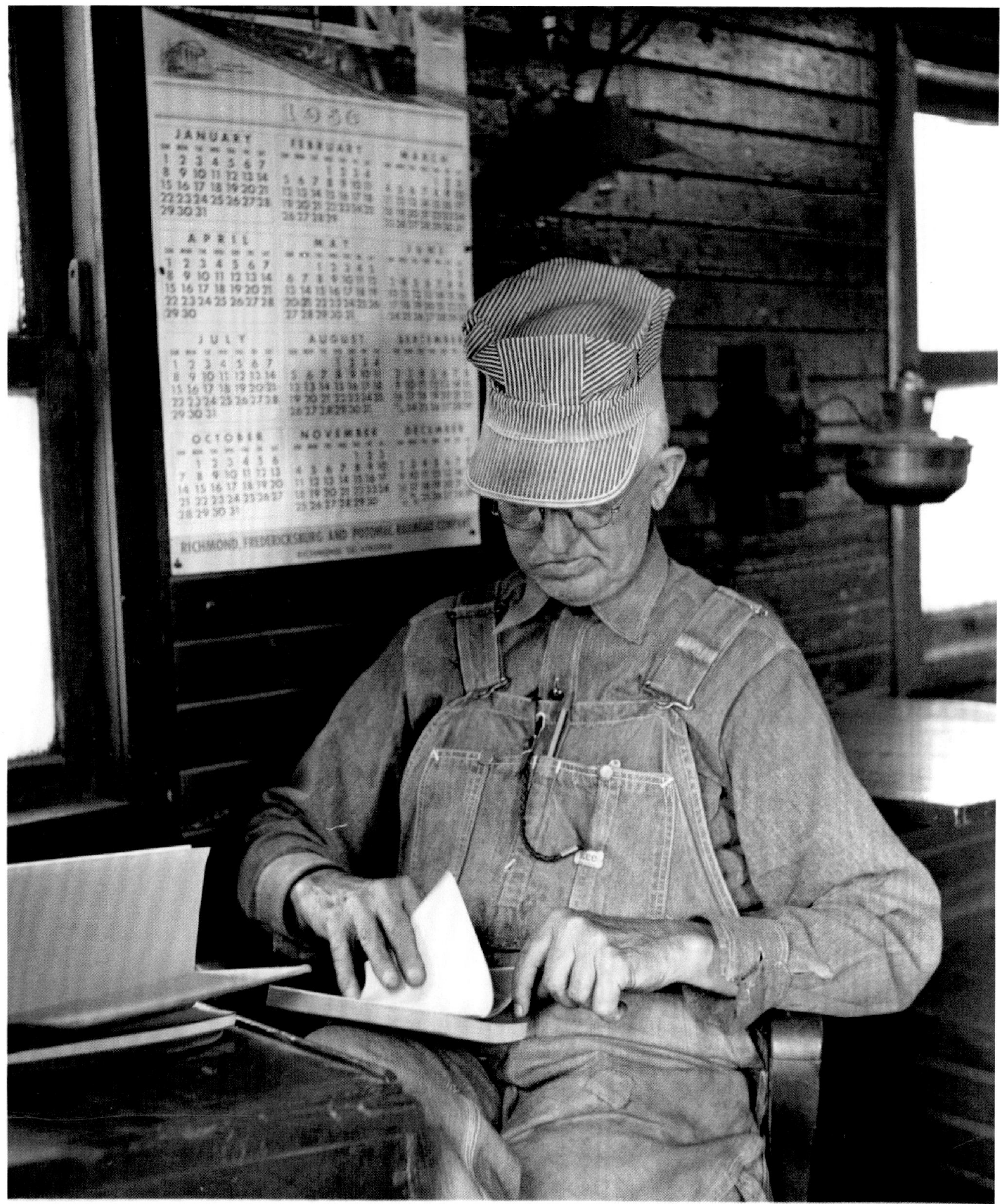
1956
JANUARY
FEBRUARY
MARCH
APRIL
MAY
JUNE
JULY
AUGUST
SEPTEMBER
OCTOBER
NOVEMBER
DECEMBER
RICHMOND, FREDERICKSBURG AND POTOMAC RAILROAD COMPANY

***Facing,* Plate 21.** A Rutland conductor checks over his paperwork in the caboose. If the calendar on the caboose wall is up-to-date, this was taken in 1956.

Courtesy of California State Railroad Museum. Philip Ross Hastings, MD, Collection, [Negative 10509].

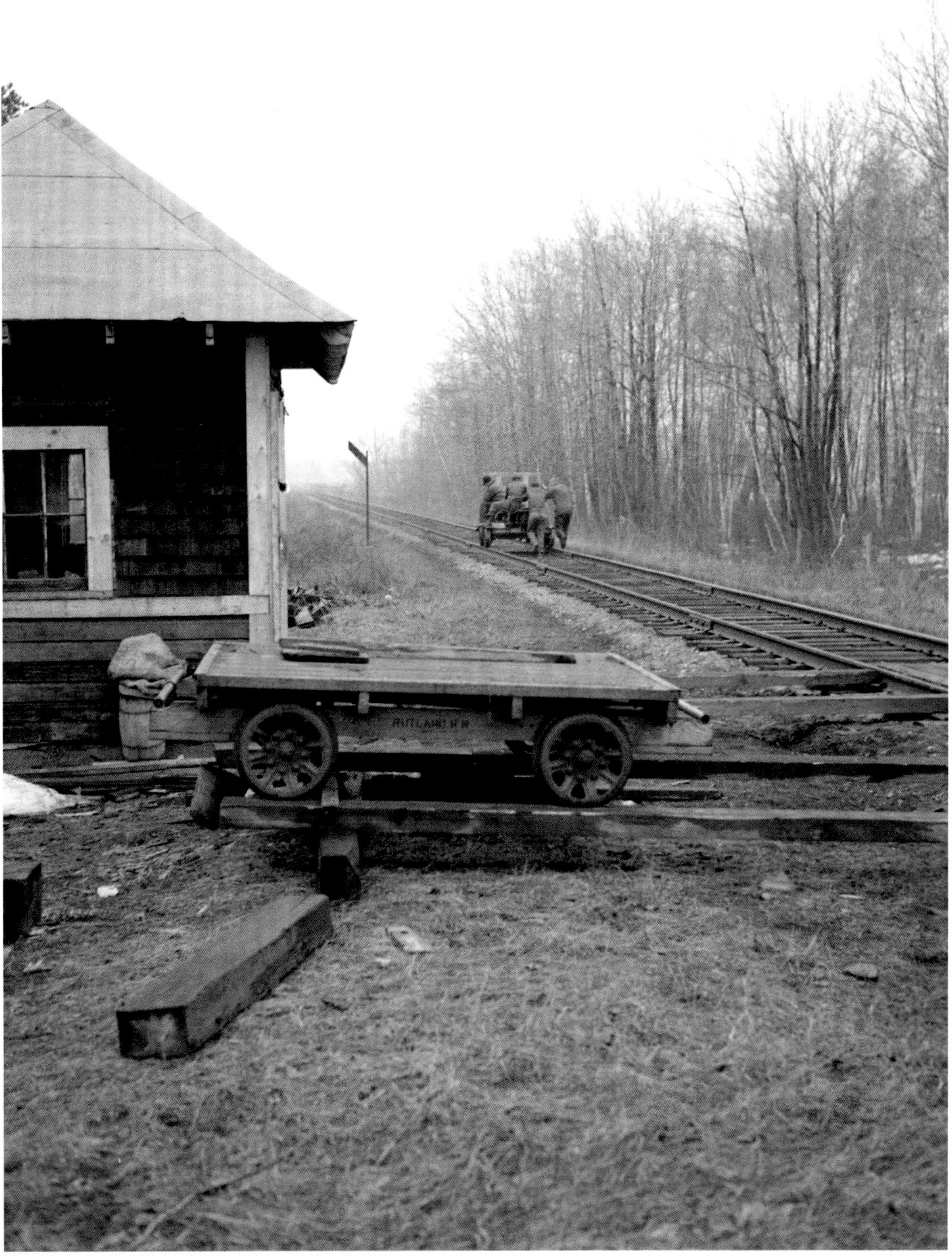

Plate 22. The Colchester, Vermont, section gang heads out on the line under a shroud of fog in 1950.

Courtesy of California State Railroad Museum. Philip Ross Hastings, MD, Collection, [Negative 2138].

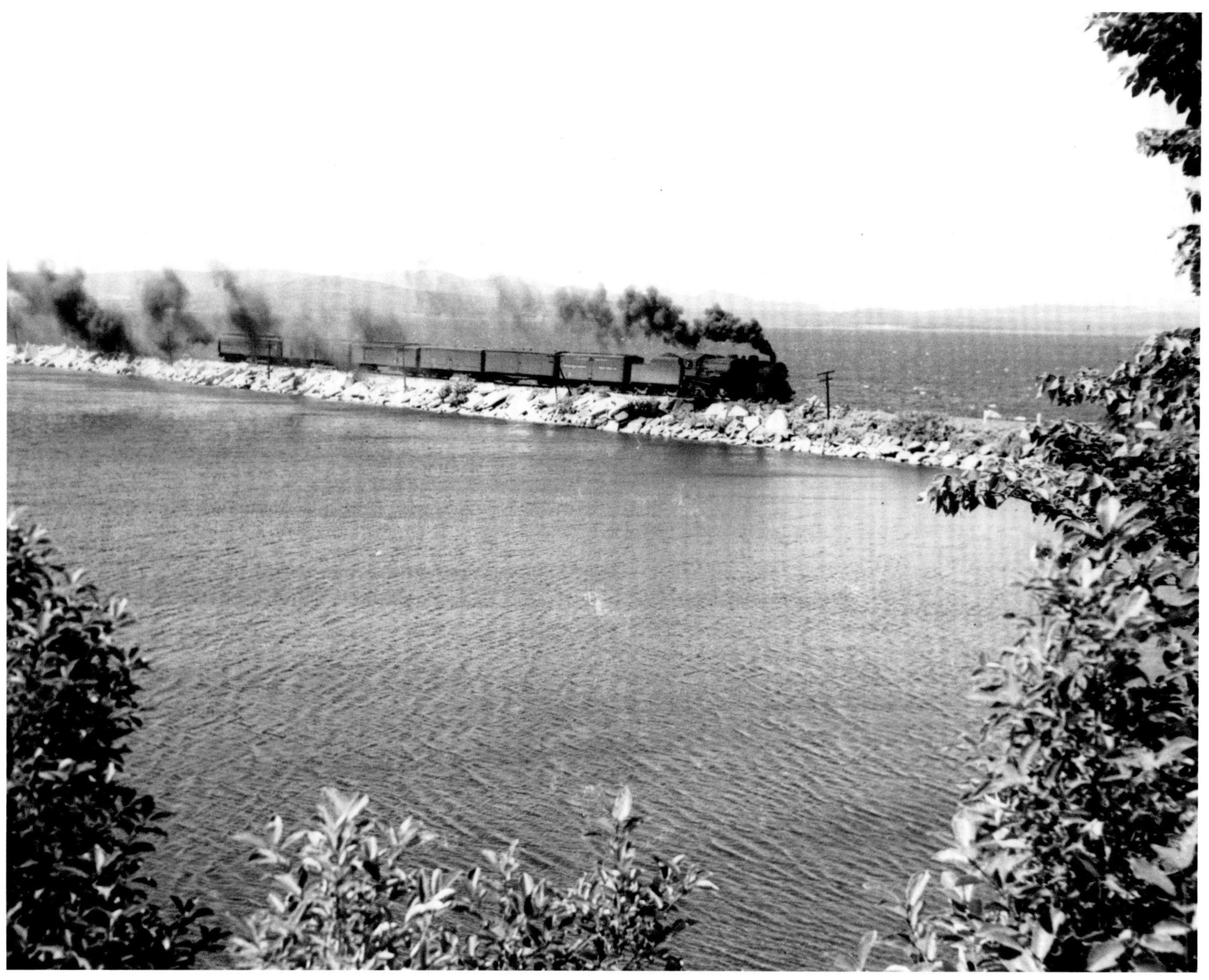

Plate 23. In addition to its well-known Bellows Falls-Rutland and Burlington-Rutland-Bennington lines, the Rutland had routes from Bennington to Chatham, New York; a line from Rouses Point to Ogdensburg, New York; and an amazing route north from Burlington straight through the Lake Champlain Islands to Alburgh, Vermont, and then across the Richelieu River to Rouses Point. In this photo, Phil Hastings caught "Pacific" 80 with a milk train on the three-mile fill from mainland Vermont to South Hero Island, Vermont. Lake Champlain dominates the scene.

Courtesy of California State Railroad Museum. Philip Ross Hastings, MD, Collection, [Negative 10506].

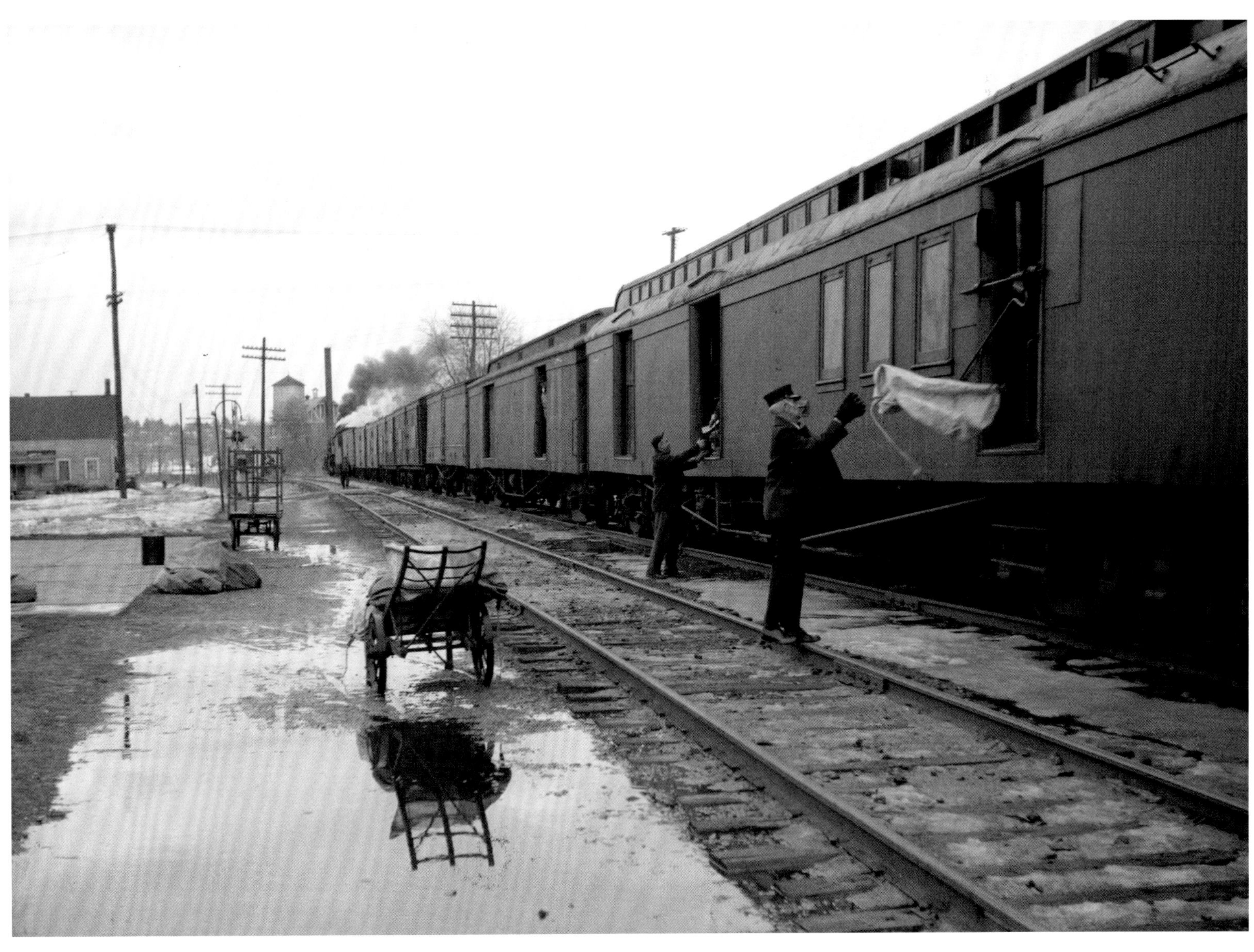

Plate 24. In one of the author's favorite Rutland images, a sour-faced trainman stands on the rail as he tosses a mail sack onto a northbound milk train at Shelburne, Vermont. This pose would not meet today's safety standards! As can be seen from Hastings's images, milk was an important part of the Rutland's traffic "diet." Today, the Shelburne station is a beautifully restored part of the Shelburne Museum.

Courtesy of California State Railroad Museum. Philip Ross Hastings, MD, Collection, [Negative 2170].

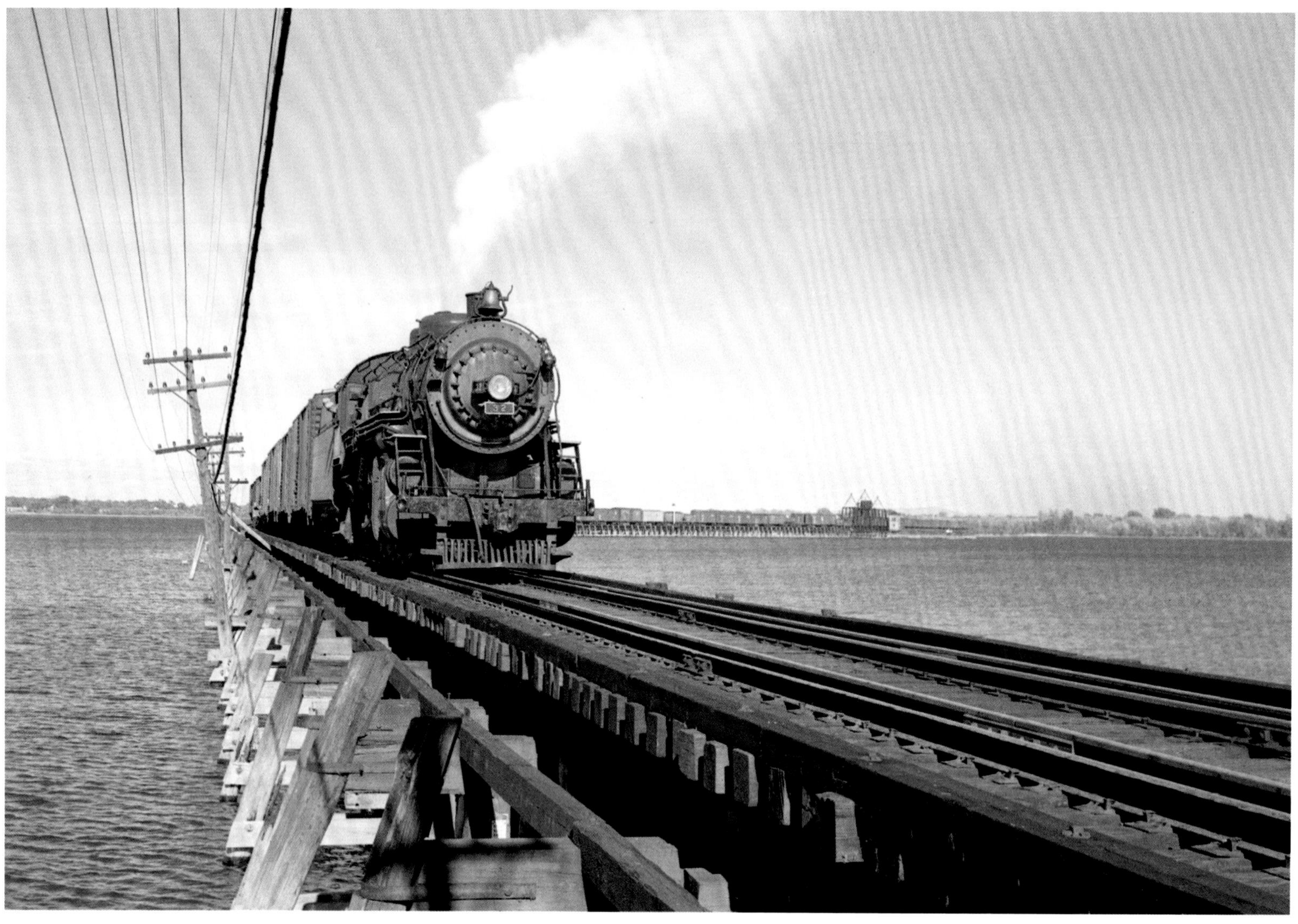

Plate 25. The Rutland's trackage north of Burlington included a shaky trestle across the Richelieu River connecting Alburgh, Vermont, with Rouses Point, New York. Here, Hastings caught "Mikado" 32 with a westbound freight train. This bridge was shared with the Central Vermont.

Courtesy of California State Railroad Museum. Philip Ross Hastings, MD, Collection, [Negative 2197].

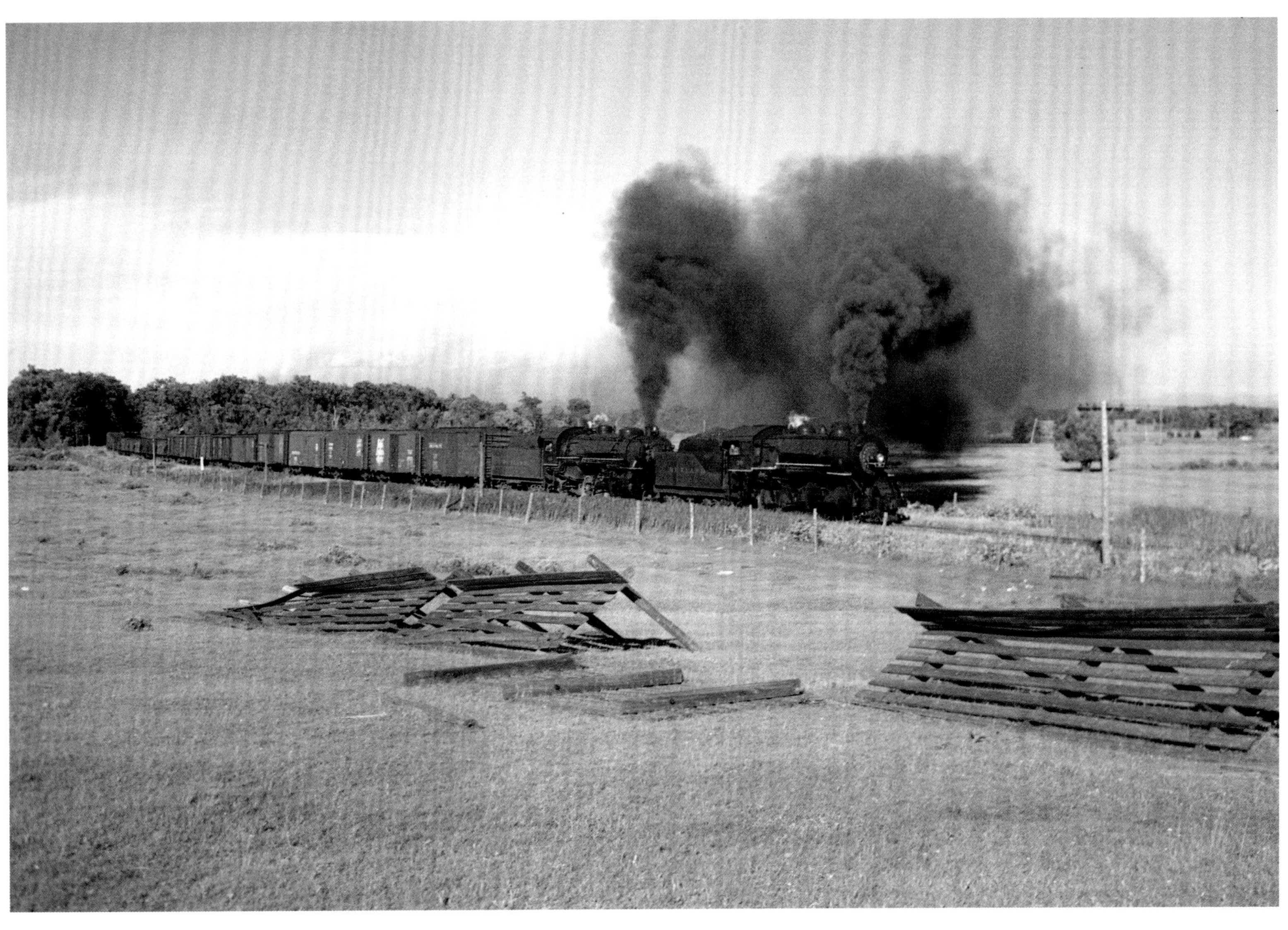

Plate 26. A westbound freight on the Rouses Point to Ogdensburg, New York, portion of the Rutland climbs away from Lake Champlain. The location is Champlain, New York.

Courtesy of California State Railroad Museum. Philip Ross Hastings, MD, Collection, [Negative 2230].

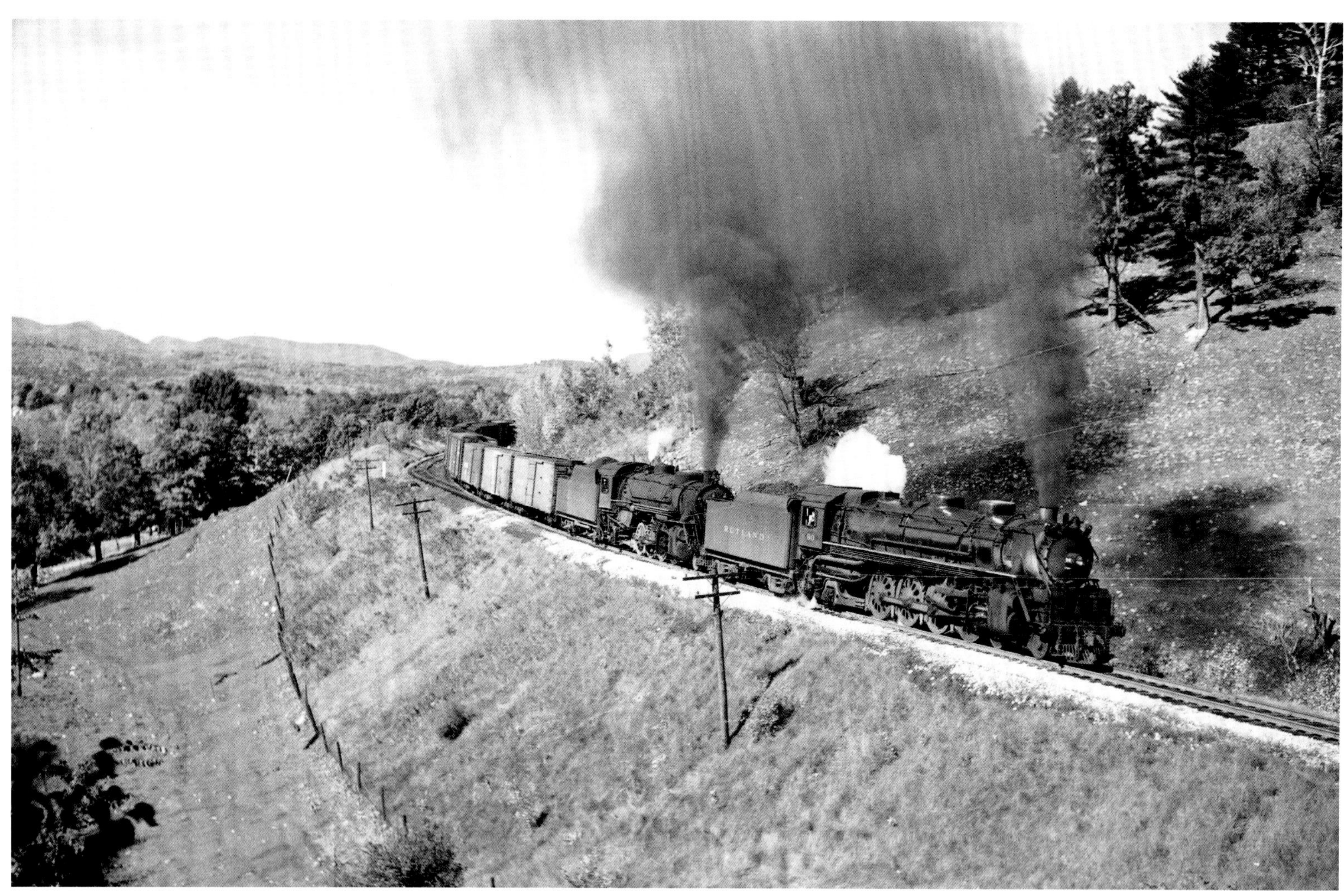

Plate 27. A double-headed Rutland freight on the line from Rutland to Bellows Falls, Vermont, in October 1949. The location is East Clarendon, Vermont.

Courtesy of California State Railroad Museum. Philip Ross Hastings, MD, Collection, [Negative 2157].

Plate 28. For this image, Phil Hastings stood inside the Bellows Falls roundhouse and shot "Ten-Wheeler" 76 as it took on water outside. The 76 will take a northbound train out of Bellows Falls after that train arrives from Boston on the Boston & Maine.

Courtesy of California State Railroad Museum. Philip Ross Hastings, MD, Collection, [Negative 2226].

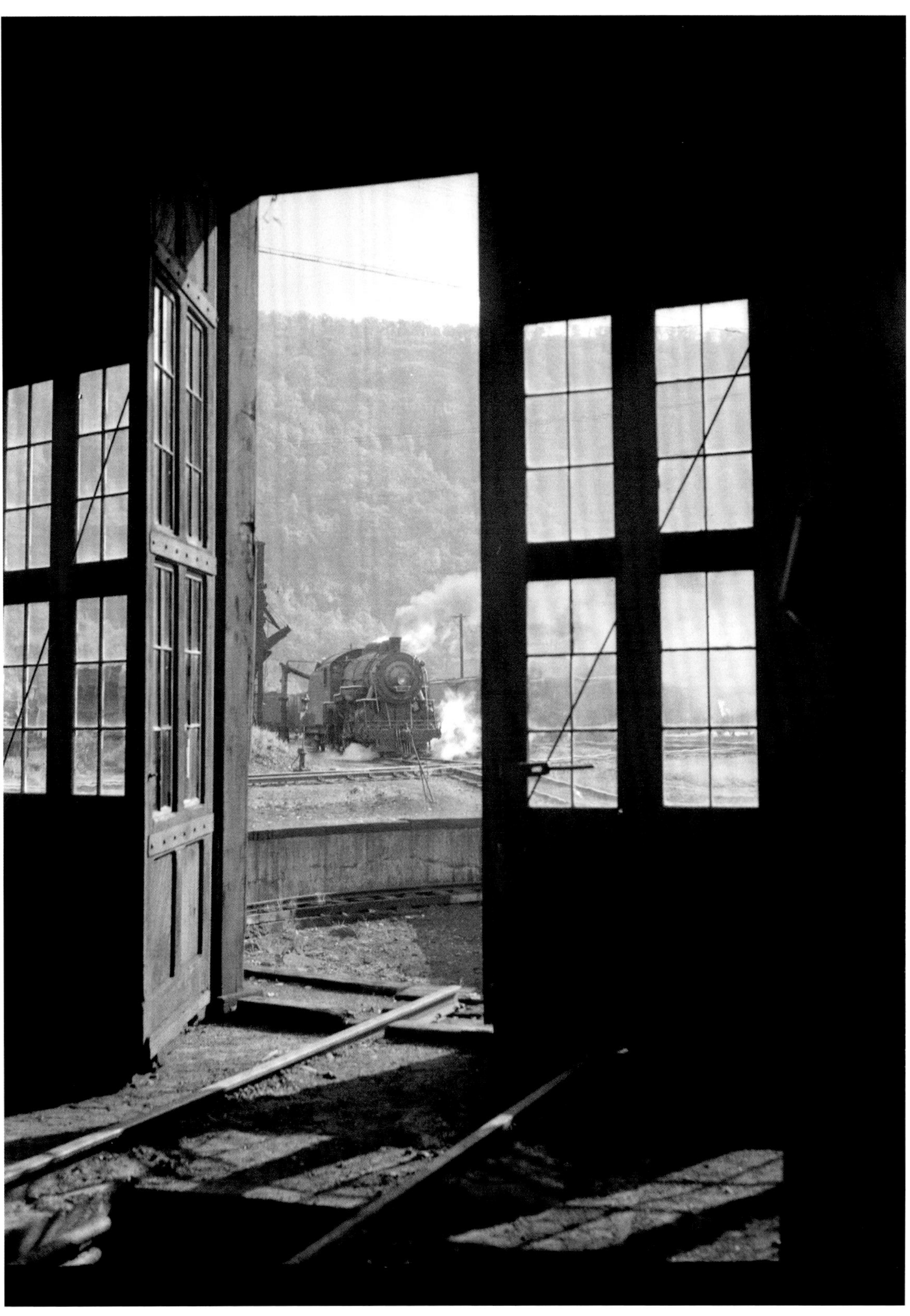

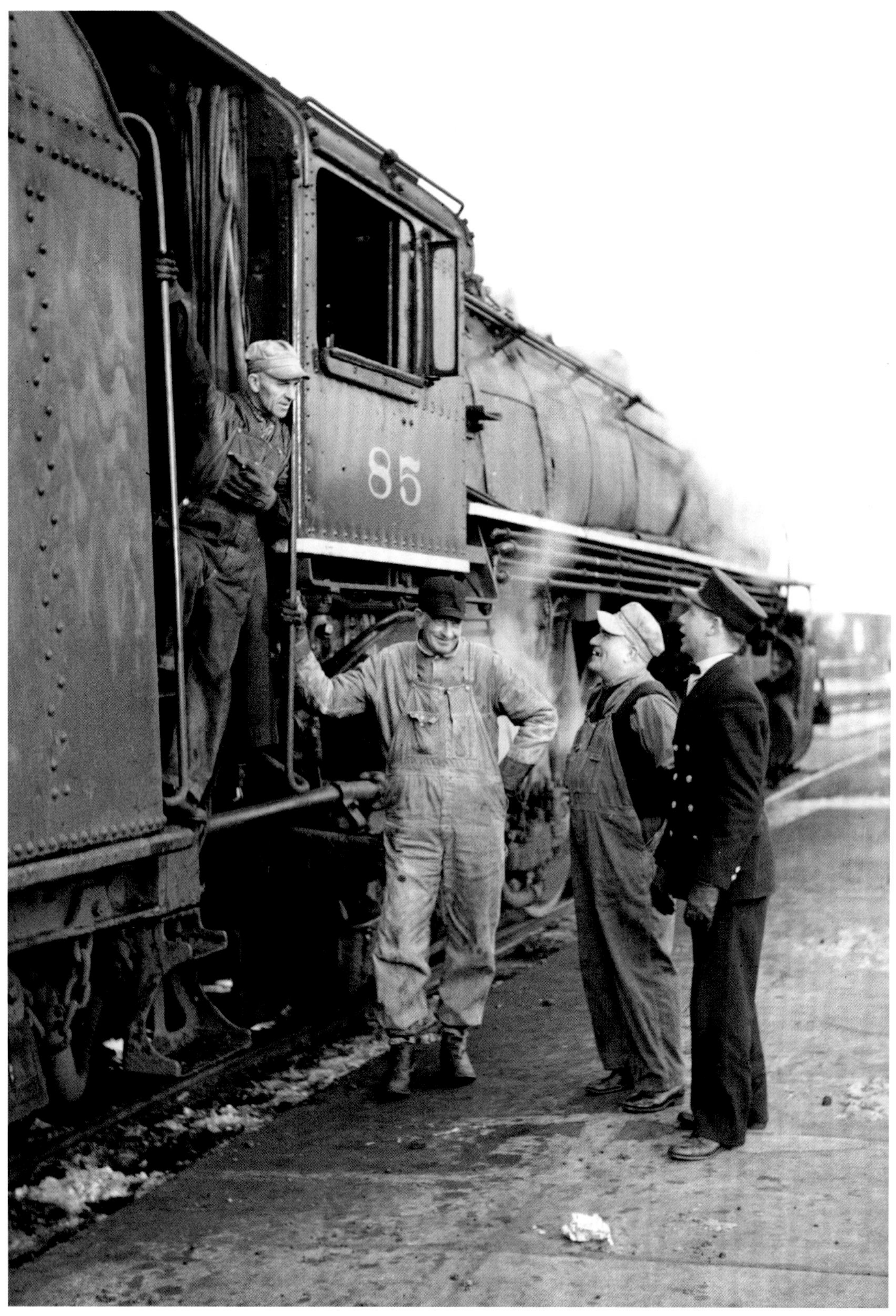

Plate 29. The location is Burlington, Vermont; the date is March 15, 1948; and the occasion is the last run of Rutland train 43. The engine is 4-6-2 85, and the crew is (left to right) fireman Dick Davis, engineer Bill Cannon, baggageman Earl Moody, and an unidentified flagman.

Courtesy of California State Railroad Museum. Philip Ross Hastings, MD, Collection, [Negative 2114].

***Facing*, Plate 30.** The Rutland dieselized in the early 1950s. A major strike in 1953 led to the end of the Rutland's passenger service and another strike led to the abandonment of the railroad, with all service ending in 1961. Significant portions survived as the Vermont Railway and the Green Mountain Railroad. Trackage at the far western end of the Rutland, from Norwood to Ogdensburg, New York, also survived. In this image, Hastings captures a new diesel, Rutland RS-3 208, crossing a road protected by an ancient "look out for the cars" sign. The engine is a diesel, but the scene cries out New England.

Courtesy of California State Railroad Museum. Philip Ross Hastings, MD, Collection, [Negative 2240].

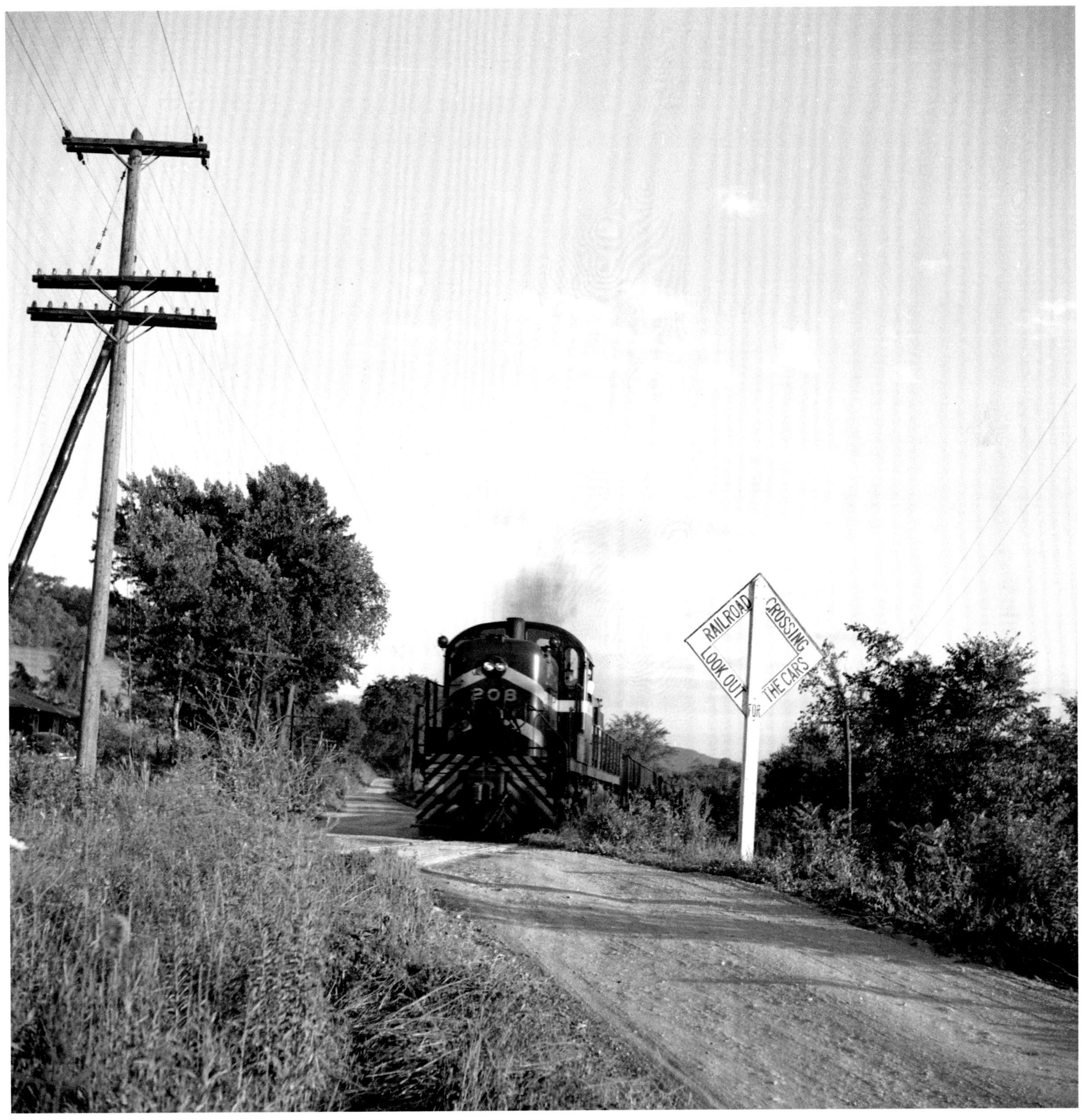
208
RAILROAD CROSSING
LOOK OUT FOR THE CARS

PORTFOLIO THREE

ACROSS NEW ENGLAND

Born a small-town New Englander, Phil Hastings grew up with a special eye for New England and the Canadian Maritimes. The first two portfolios in this book focus on specific railroads of New England—this portfolio reviews the remainder of Hastings's New England work.

Phil Hastings's views of the Grand Trunk Railway, a Canadian National subsidiary operating in New England, led to a book, *Grand Trunk Heritage*, published in 1978 by Hastings's friend John Krause.[1] Plates 31–34 depict this little-known carrier.

Plate 31 shows a Grand Trunk conductor signing the register book at the Grand Trunk station in North Stratford, New Hampshire, with the station's telegraph operator in the background. The image, taken in June 1949, depicts a classic railroad station interior. Plate 32 shows another iconic figure of the steam era on US railroads, a Grand Trunk fireman looking at Hastings from his side—the left—of the cab of Canadian National 6017. The Grand Trunk had a number of locomotives of its own, but engines from parent Canadian National also plied its rails. Plate 33 shows a Grand Trunk engineer climbing down from the cab of 2-8-2 3432 at Danville Junction, Maine. The final Grand Trunk image, plate 34, shows a Grand Trunk train on the trestle at Back Cove, Maine. Hastings took a number of excellent views at this location.

The Maine Central Railroad was closely aligned with Hastings's hometown railroad, the Boston & Maine. Plates 35–37 profile this iconic New England line. Plate 35 depicts a classic railroading scene, a railroader placing classification flags on Maine Central 369. Plates 36 and 37 show what may be the best-known survivor of the Maine Central, its former Mountain subdivision.[2] The most scenic parts of this line were revived by the Conway Scenic Railroad after its 1983 abandonment. Plate 36 shows a Maine Central freight at Willey House, New Hampshire, on the Mountain subdivision, and plate 37 shows a freight led by F-3 683 approaching the summit of famed Crawford Notch, New Hampshire.

The Bangor & Aroostook Railroad (BAR) served little-known and sparsely populated northern Maine. The Maine Central was one of its principal connecting railroads. The BAR was perhaps best known for carrying Maine potatoes to market. Plate 38, showing a Bangor & Aroostook plow at Brownville Junction, Maine, captures Maine's hard winters.

Plates 39 and 40 are views by Hastings of another Canadian National subsidiary operating in New England, the Central Vermont Railway.[3] Plate 39 shows an interesting pairing, Central Vermont steam switcher 501 with parent Canadian National C-liner diesel locomotives. Plate 40 is a creative view showing a Central Vermont engine profiled on a bridge. Hastings uses reflection here, as he often did, but the image does not include the reflected profile of the locomotive—an unusual touch.

Hastings loved short-line railroads, and his New England work is rich in views of such lines. Plates 41 and 42 focus on railroaders working for Vermont's Barre & Chelsea Railroad, which ran from Montpelier to Wells River, Vermont. Hastings had a special affinity for Vermont short line St. Johnsbury & Lake Champlain Railroad.[4] His first important publication, in the May 1947 issue of *Trains*, was a profile of this railroad. Plates 43–46 close this portfolio with views of the St. J.

Plate 43, one of Hastings's best-known images, is a panorama of the St. J at Walden, Vermont. There is not a train in sight—very innovative for a railroad-subject photo first published in 1947. Plate 44 shows a hard Vermont winter at the St. J station in Greensboro Bend. Plate 45 shows a more temperate station scene on the railroad at Cambridge Junction, Vermont. This New England portfolio closes with a St. J train crossing a trestle—a truly bucolic New England scene.[5]

***Facing,* Plate 31.** A conductor signs the register book at the Grand Trunk Railway station in North Stratford, New Hampshire, while the operator copies a train order. Hastings was to repeat this view in his photographic career, as did another frequent *Trains* contributor, O. Winston Link.

Courtesy of California State Railroad Museum. Philip Ross Hastings, MD, Collection, [Negative 9252].

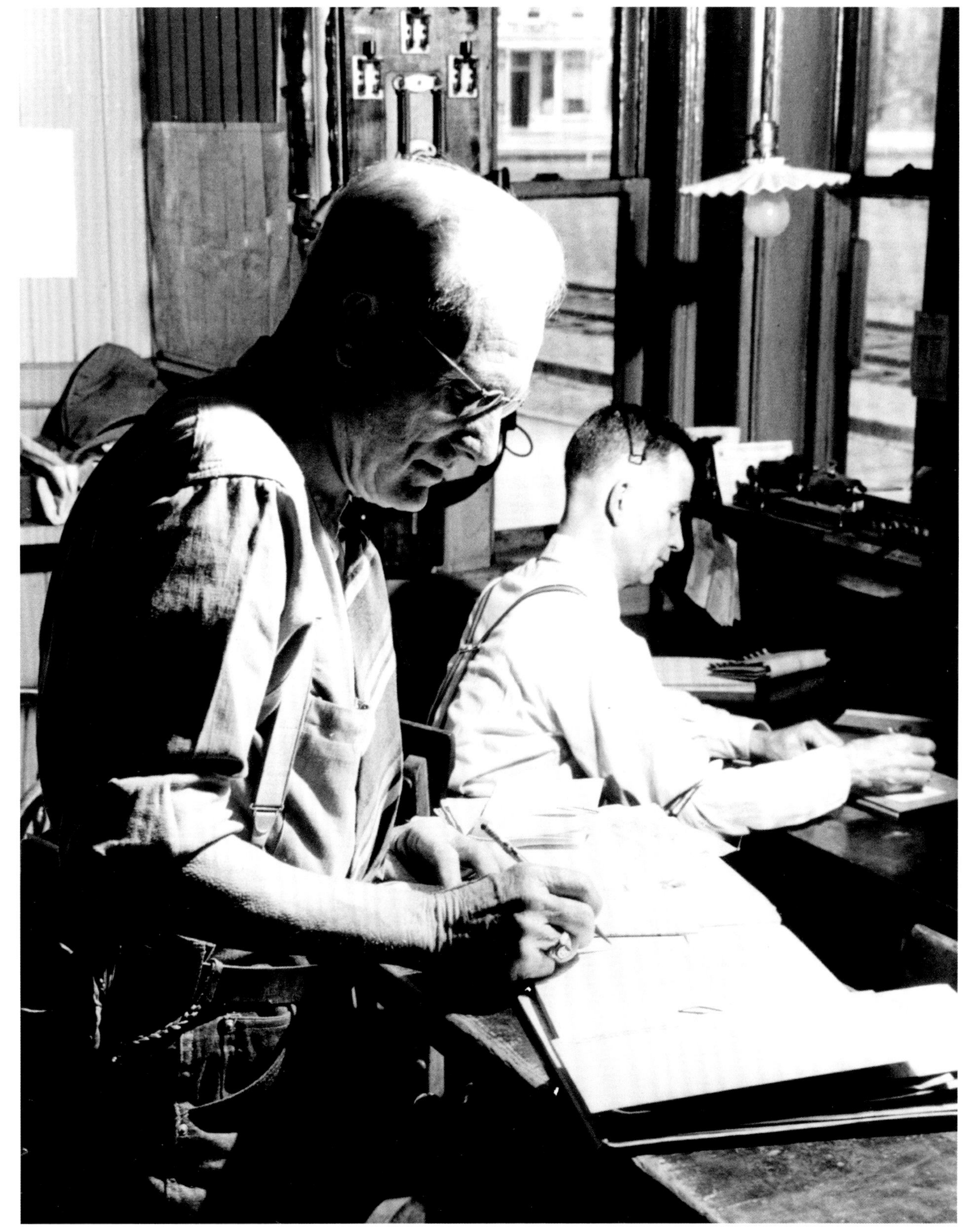

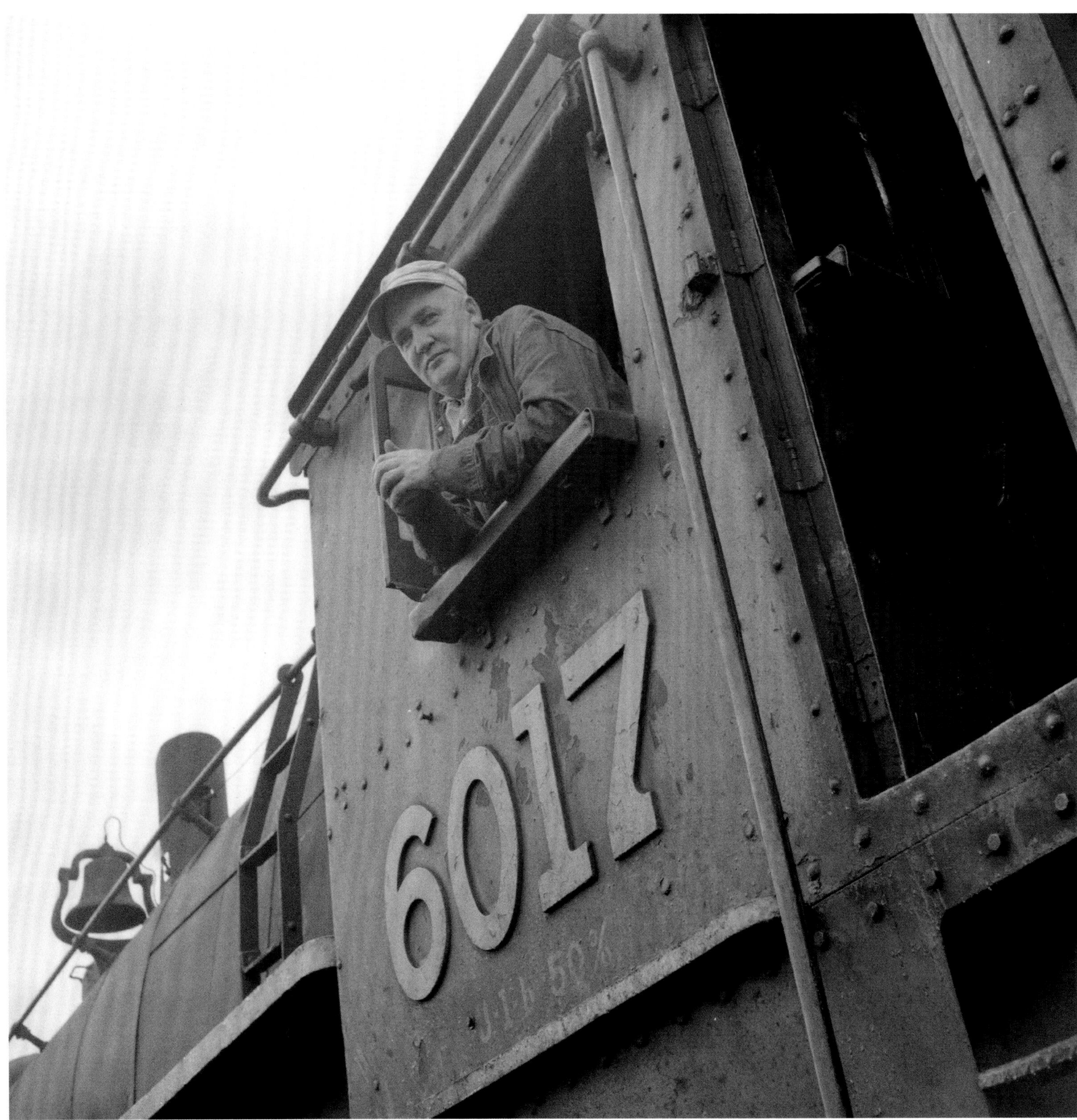
6017

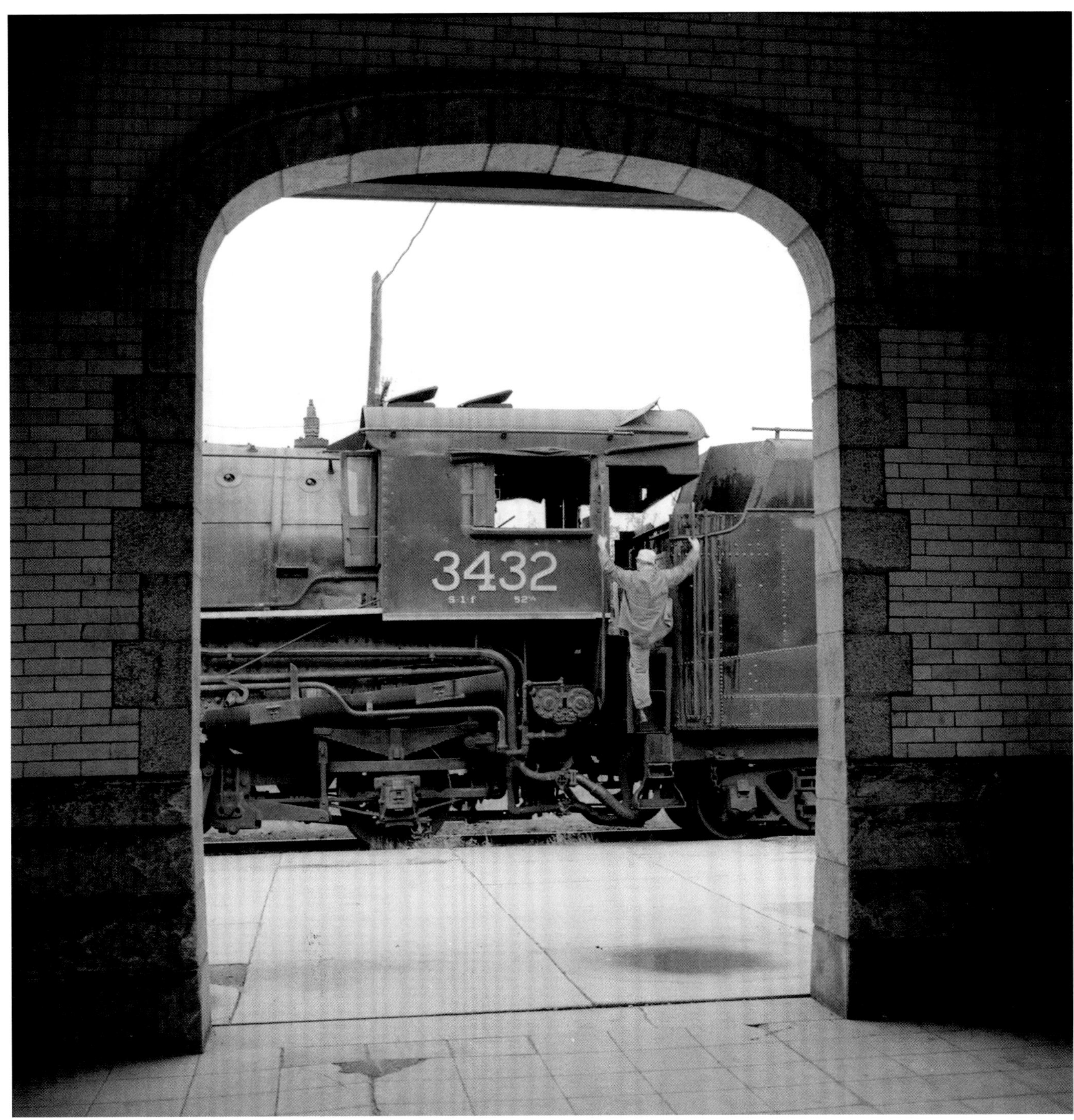

***Facing,* Plate 32.** A Grand Trunk fireman looks down from 6017 at Portland, Maine. Ahead of him is a 150-mile run to Island Pond, Vermont. The train is 17, bound for Montreal; the engine is a 4-8-2 "Mountain" type.

Courtesy of California State Railroad Museum. Philip Ross Hastings, MD, Collection, [Negative 8066].

Plate 33. A Grand Trunk engineer climbs down from the cab of 2-8-2 3432 at Danville Junction, Maine. His train is 188, running from Lewiston, Maine, to Danville Junction.

Courtesy of California State Railroad Museum. Philip Ross Hastings, MD, Collection, [Negative 8091].

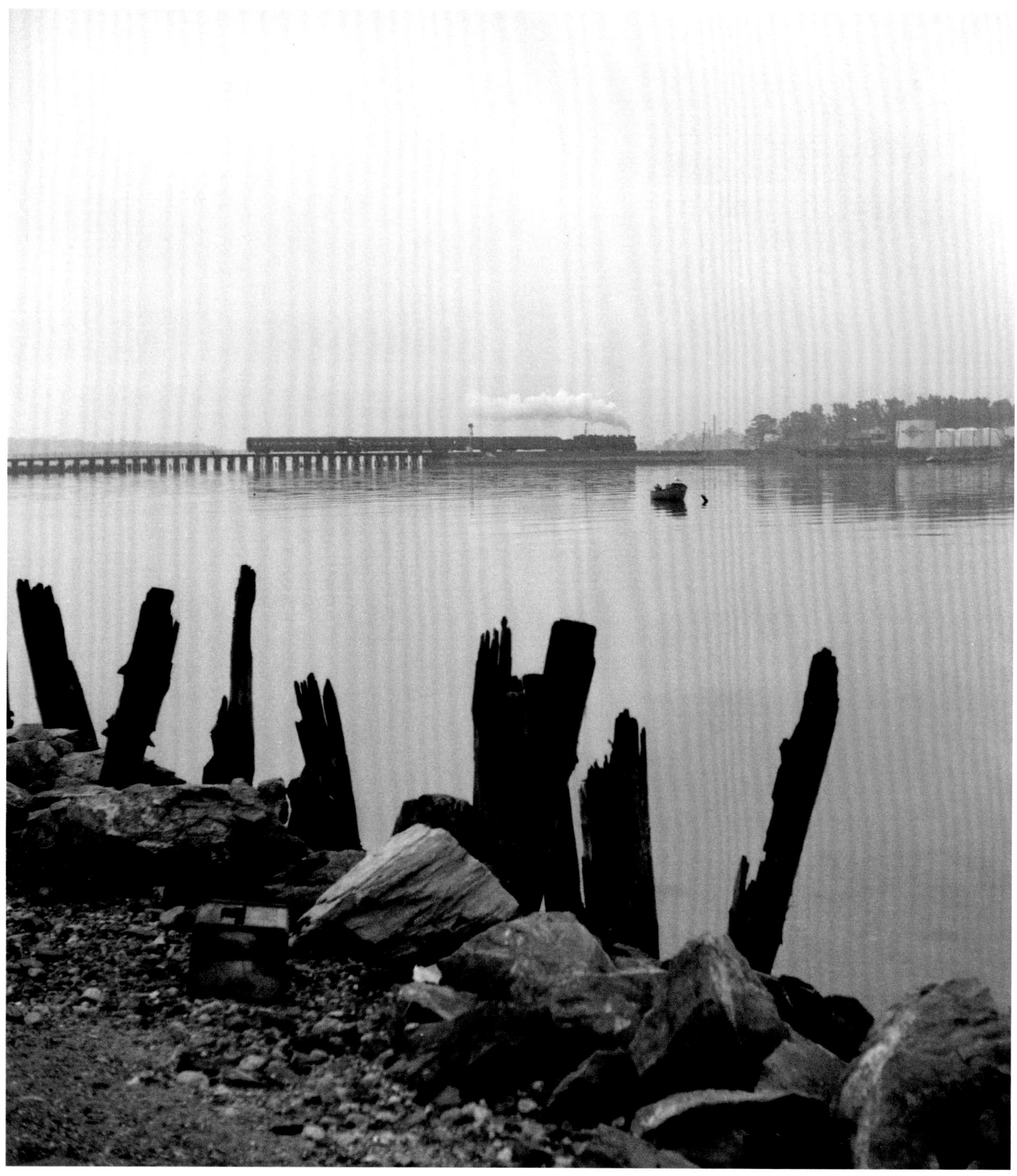

***Facing,* Plate 34.** A Grand Trunk train crosses the bridge at Back Cove, Maine, in the fog. This expert Hastings view is foregrounded by derelict pilings. It was taken on a trip with *Trains* editor David P. Morgan in the mid-1950s.

Courtesy of California State Railroad Museum. Philip Ross Hastings, MD, Collection, [Negative 10064].

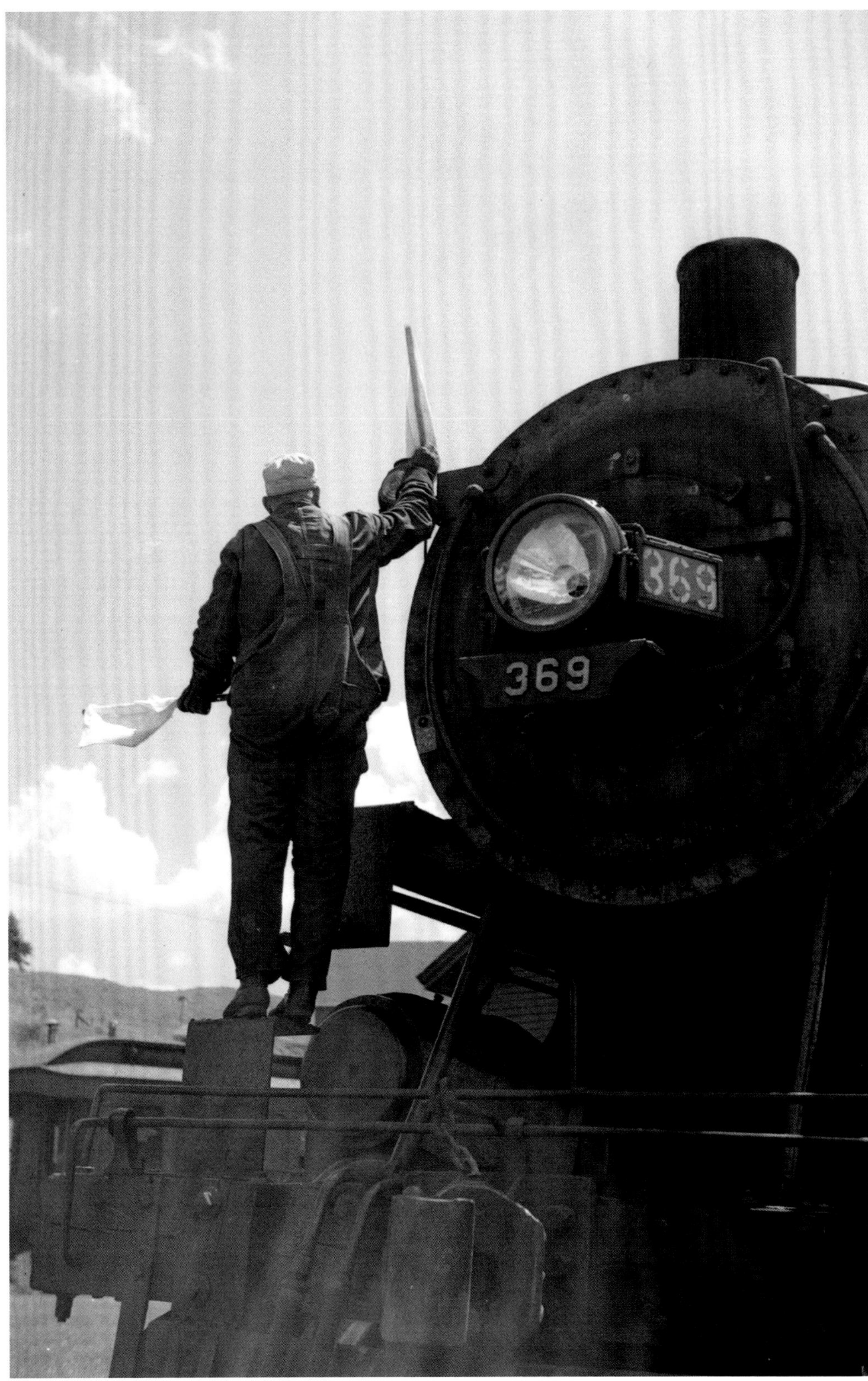

Plate 35. A Maine Central engineman puts up white classification flags in a classic steam-era pose. From the flags, the train is an extra; the engine is "Ten-Wheeler" 369. The photo was taken on the railroad's Beecher Falls (Vermont) branch.

Courtesy of California State Railroad Museum. Philip Ross Hastings, MD, Collection, [Negative 3611].

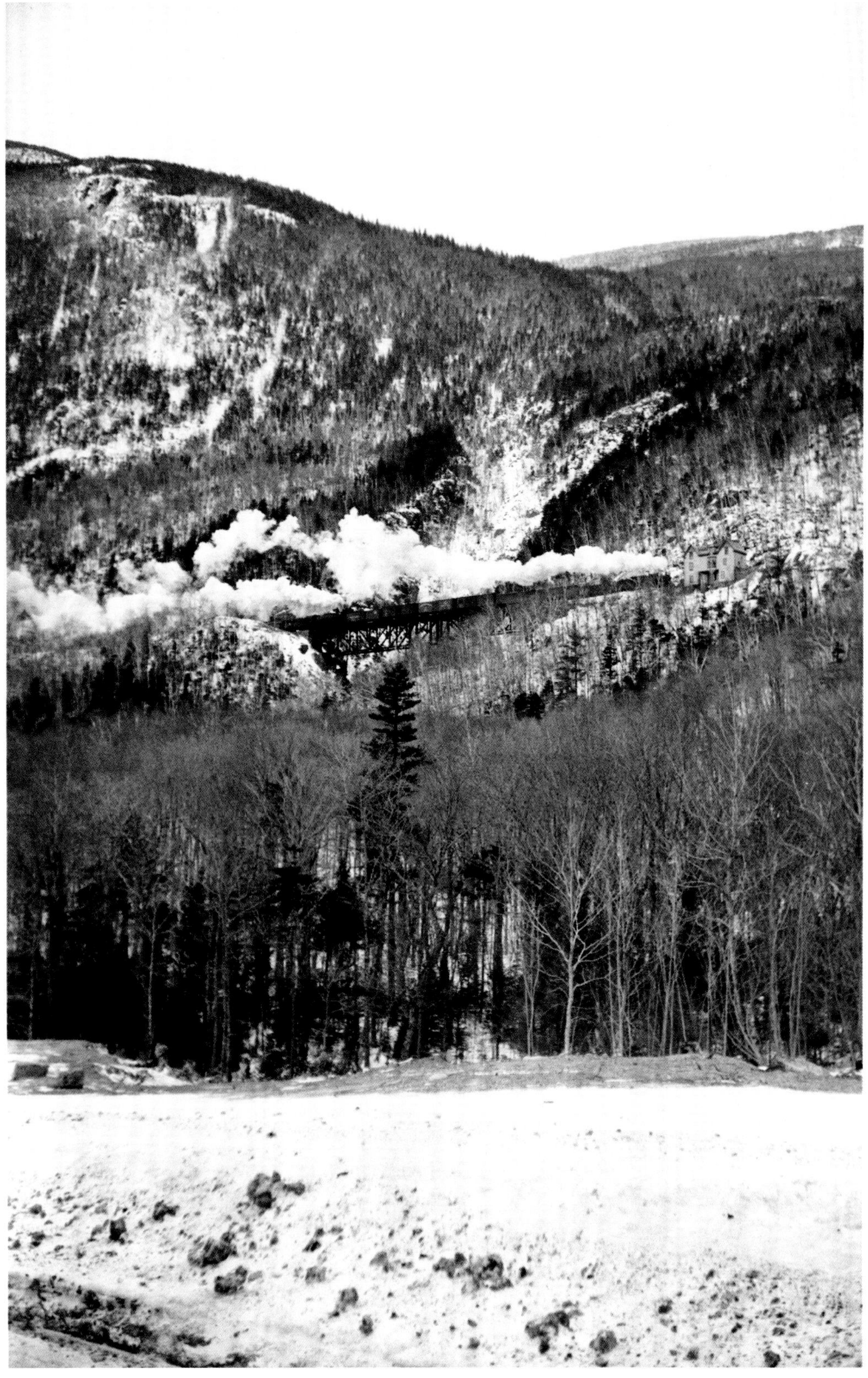

Plate 36. A Maine Central train passes Willey House on the railroad's Mountain subdivision in New Hampshire.

Courtesy of California State Railroad Museum. Philip Ross Hastings, MD, Collection, [Negative 3552].

Plate 37. This Maine Central train is a heavy freight led by F-3 683 approaching the summit of the grade at Crawford Notch, New Hampshire. The diesels are being helped by a pusher, 2-8-2 616. (See the smoke at the end of the train.) February 1950.

Courtesy of California State Railroad Museum. Philip Ross Hastings, MD, Collection, [Negative 3590].

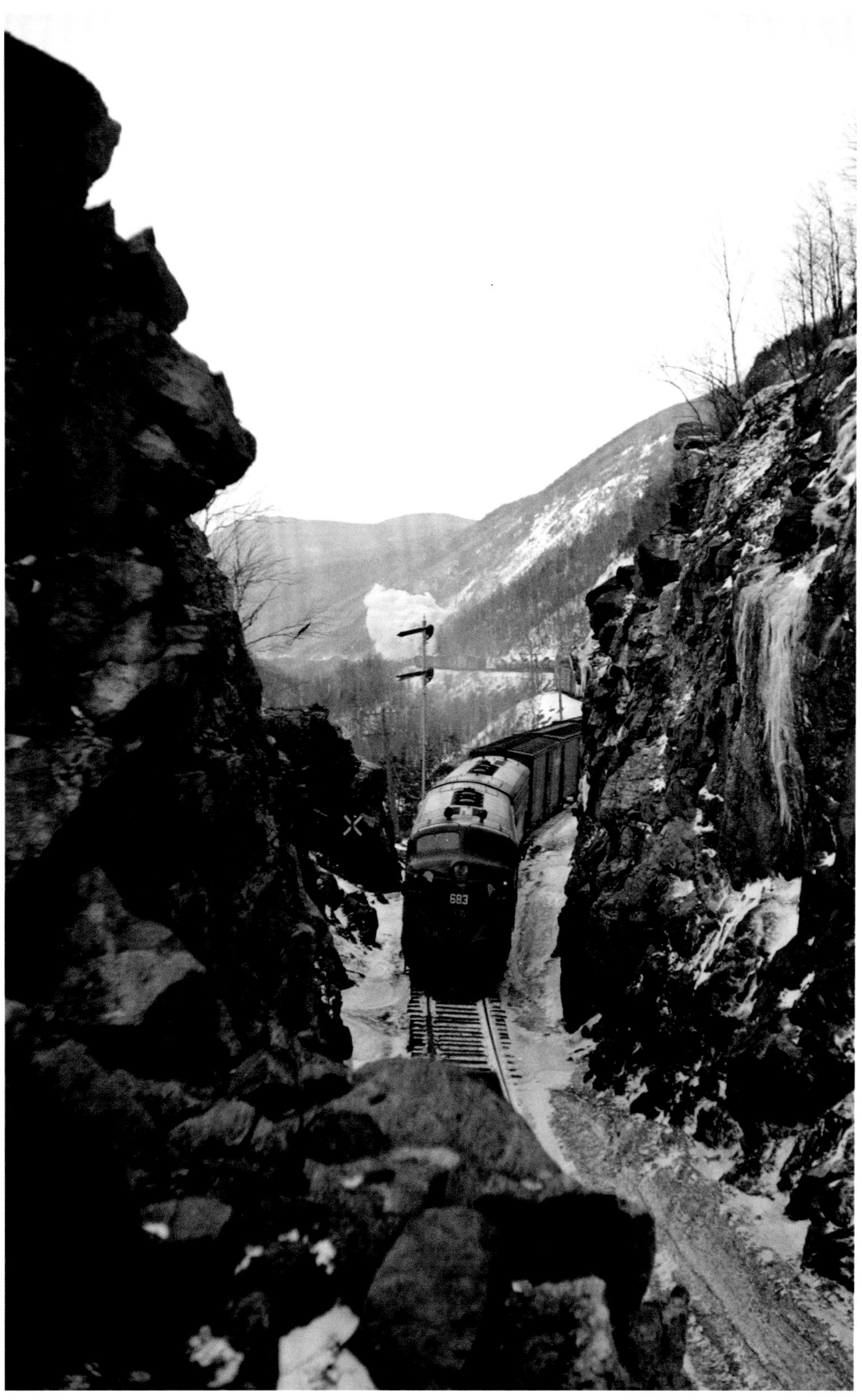

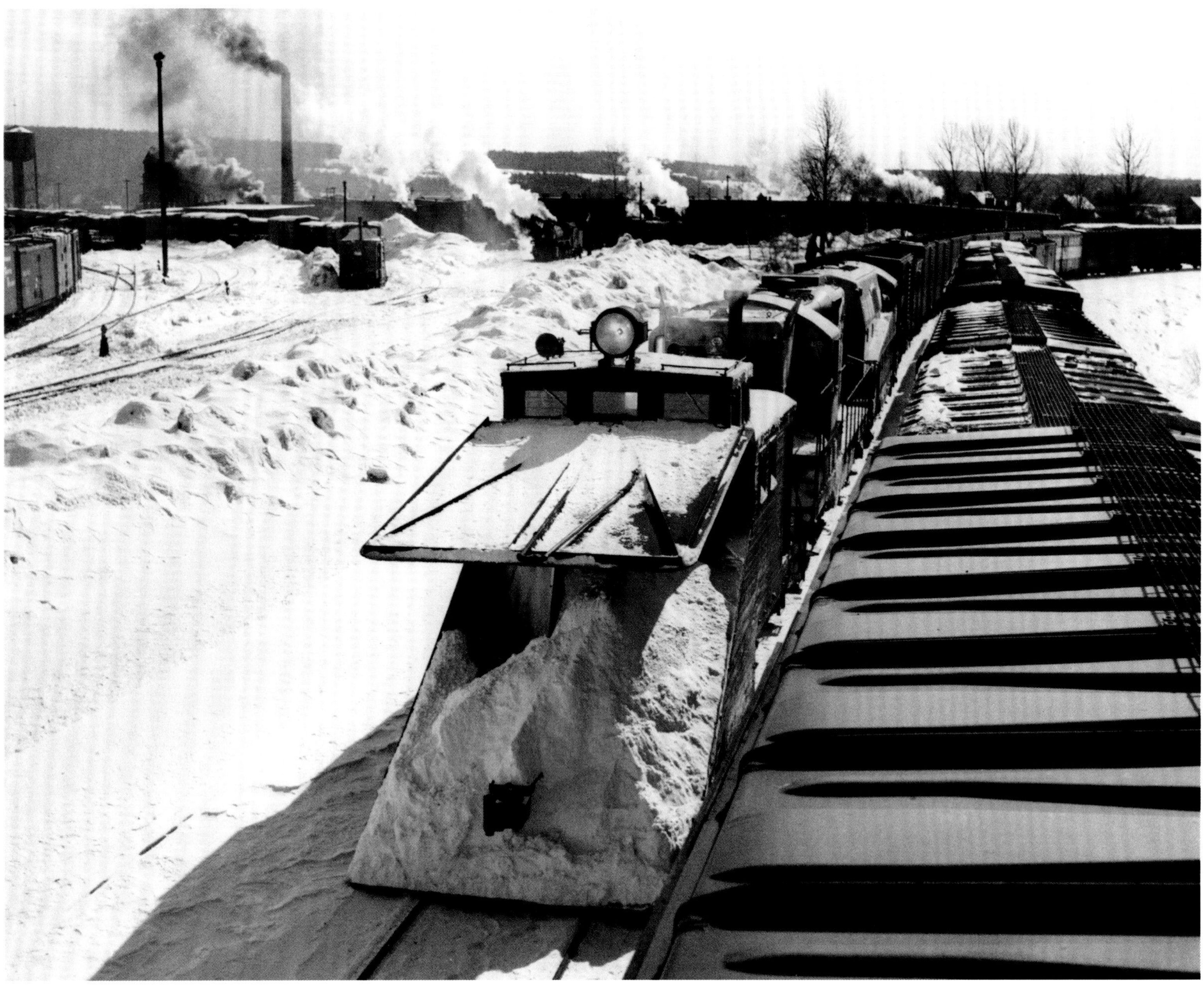

Plate 38. A Bangor & Aroostook plow precedes diesels at Brownville Junction, Maine. March 1955.

Courtesy of California State Railroad Museum. Philip Ross Hastings, MD, Collection, [Negative 10507].

***Facing,* Plate 39.** Central Vermont 501 with cars at Brattleboro, Vermont. An extra led by Canadian National "C-liners" is beside it.

Courtesy of California State Railroad Museum. Philip Ross Hastings, MD, Collection, [Negative 2678].

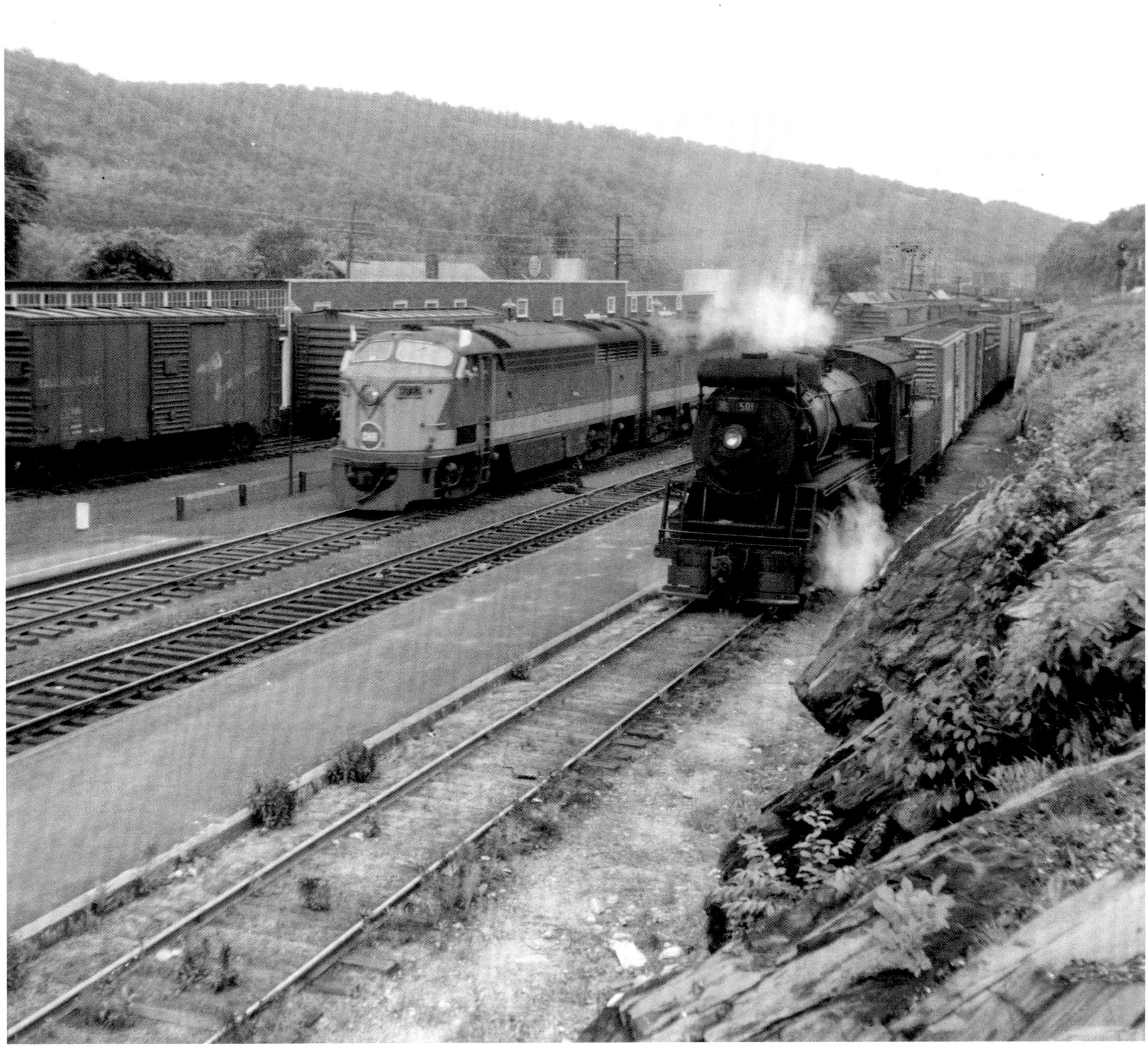

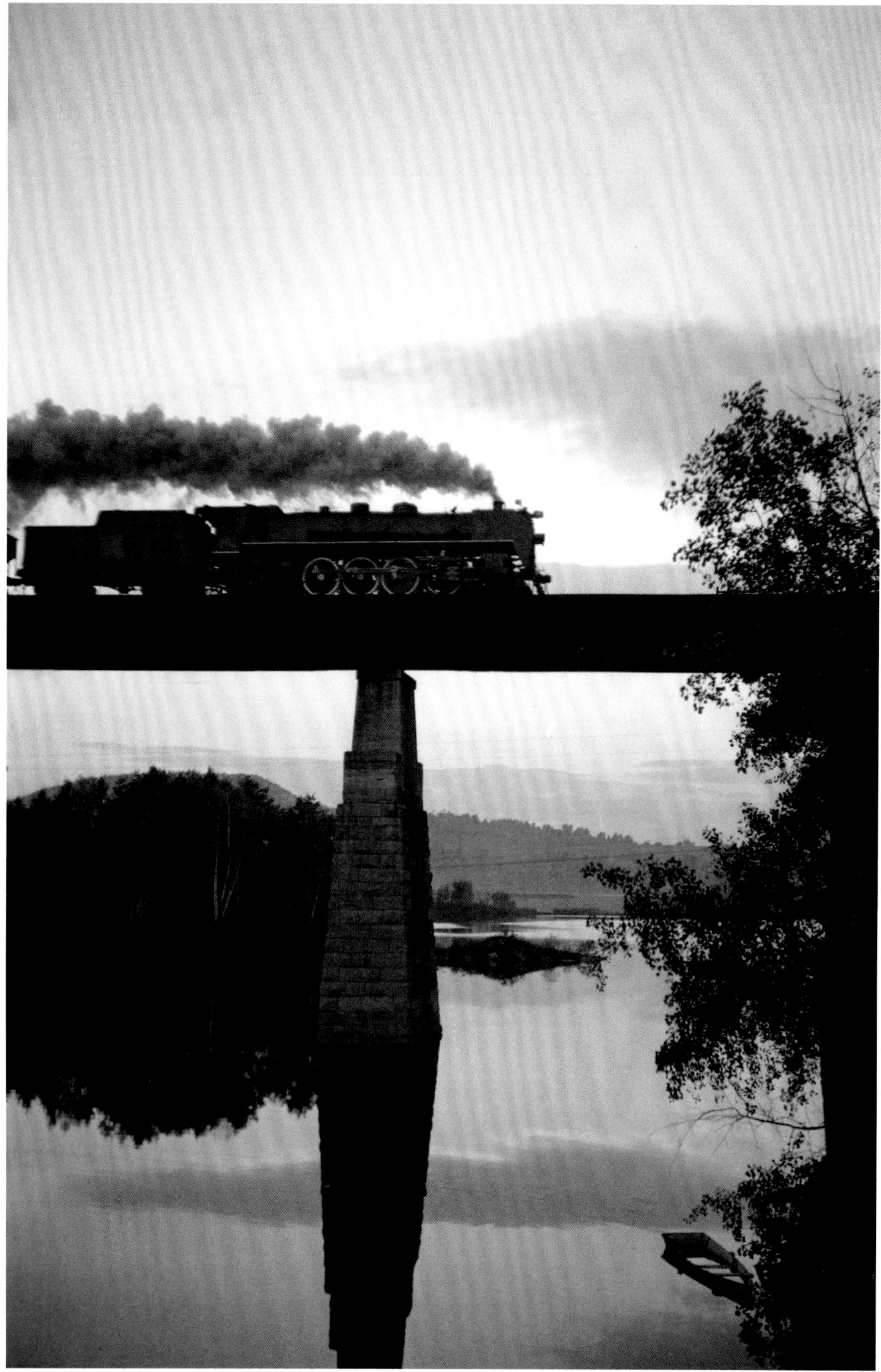

Plate 40. A Central Vermont engine is profiled crossing the White River with trees reflecting in the water below.

Courtesy of California State Railroad Museum. Philip Ross Hastings, MD, Collection, [Negative 2624].

***Facing,* Plate 41.** Hastings, like Archie Robertson, Lucius Beebe, and Charles Clegg, had a special love for American short lines. In this image, a female postal worker deals with the mail while a trainman, cigarette poised in his mouth, signals. According to Hastings's notes, the location is Fairmont, Vermont, on the Barre & Chelsea, September 15, 1947. Hastings's oeuvre includes a number of excellent shots of female post office and railroad employees.

Courtesy of California State Railroad Museum. Philip Ross Hastings, MD, Collection, [Negative 3984].

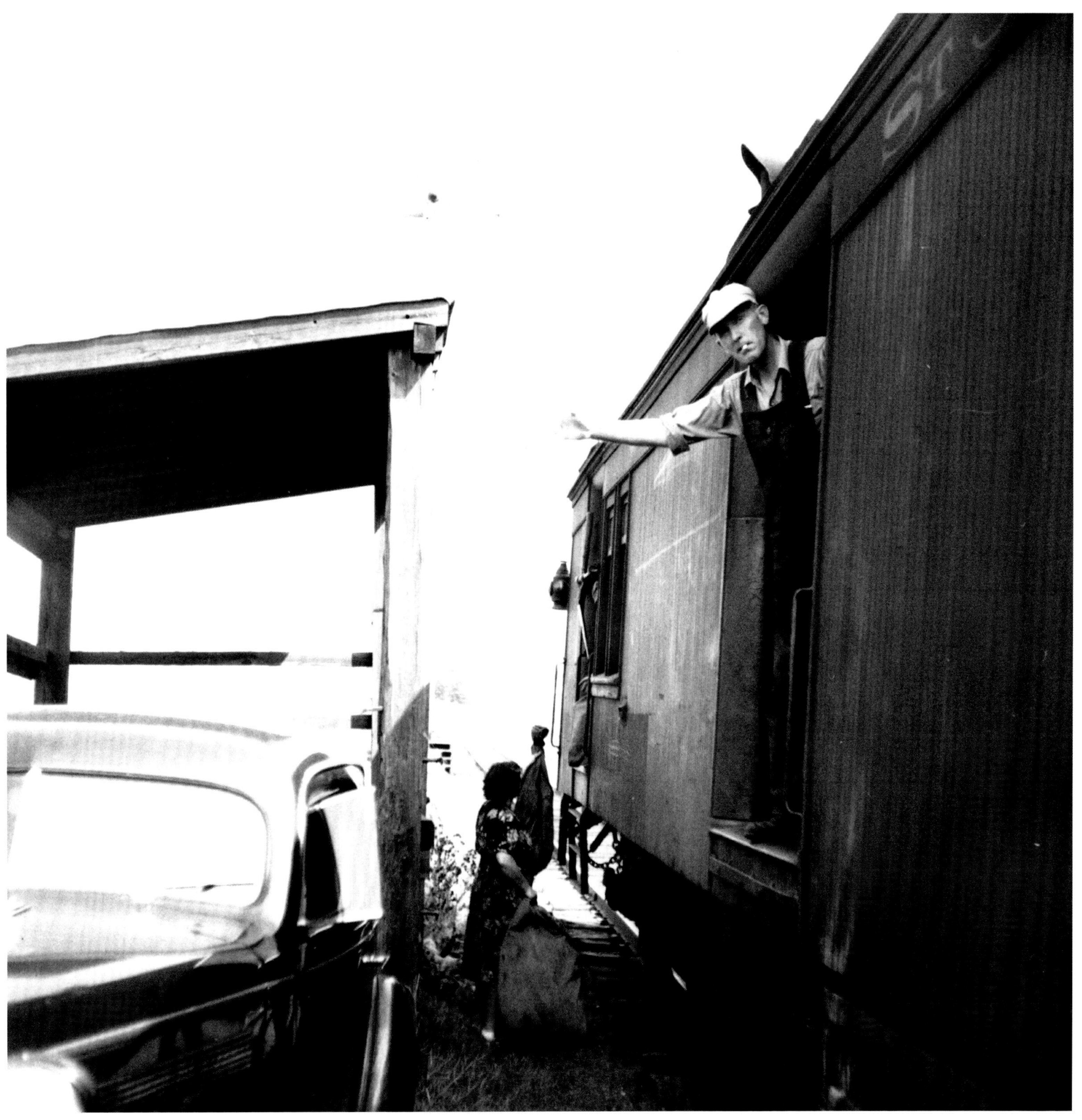

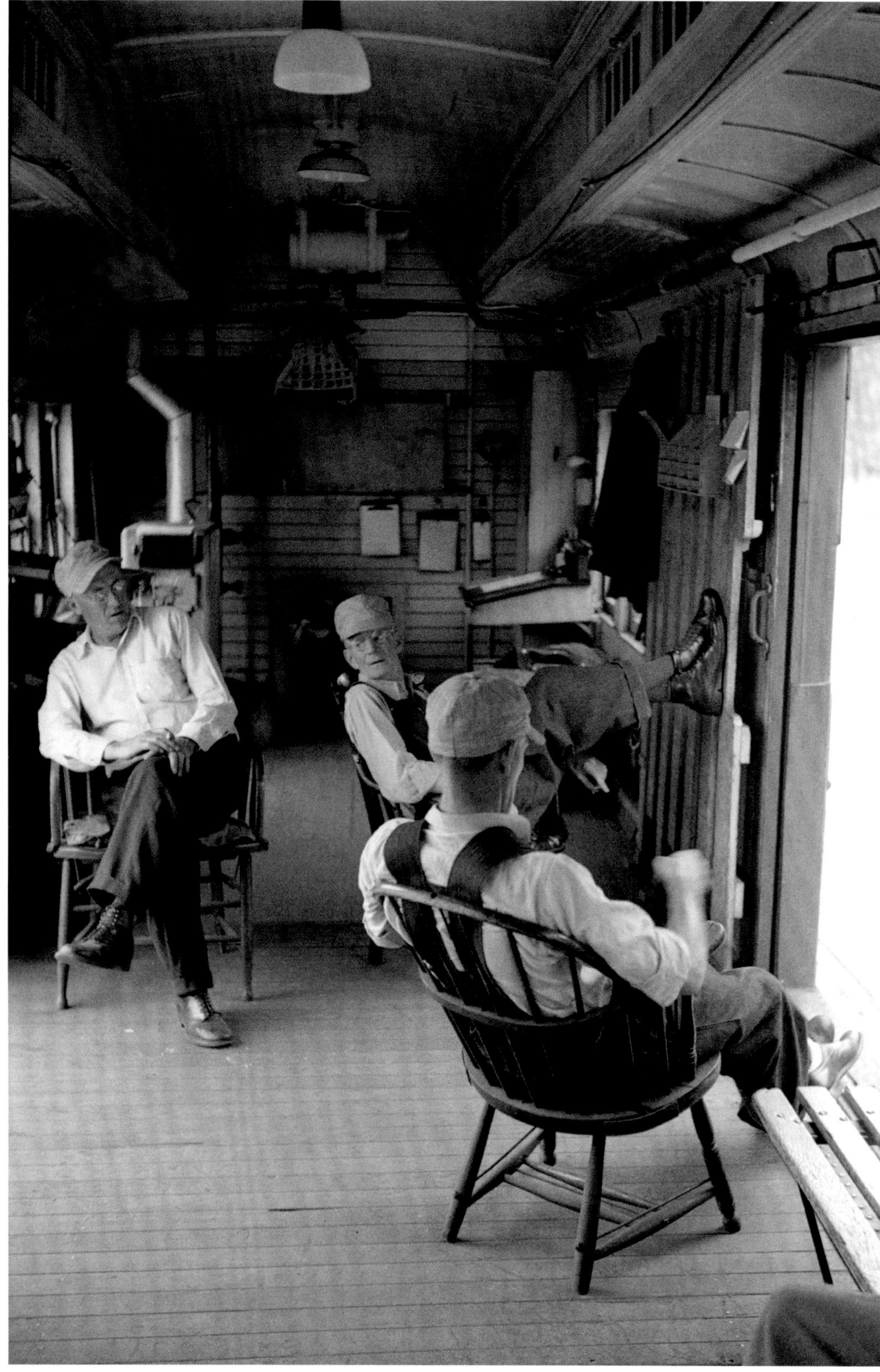

Plate 42. The crew of Barre & Chelsea train 4 relaxes in combine 14 after picking up a can of milk at Plainfield, Vermont. July 4, 1949.

Courtesy of California State Railroad Museum. Philip Ross Hastings, MD, Collection, [Negative 3985].

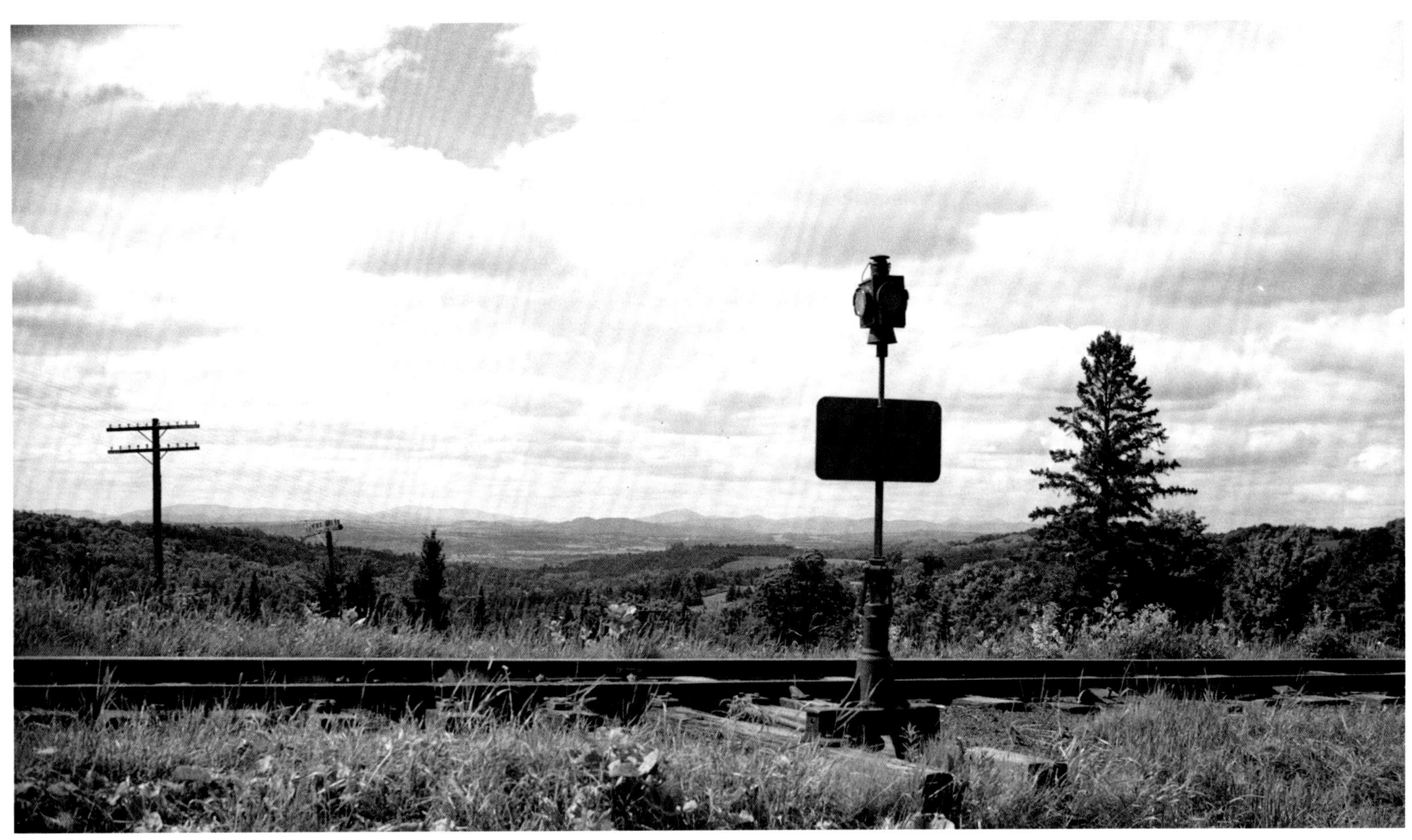

Plate 43. One of Phil Hastings's best-known images depicts a scene along the line of the St. Johnsbury and Lake Champlain Railroad, which became the St. Johnsbury & Lamoille County Railroad in 1948, so the name of the railroad depicted depends on the date of the image. This image is on the endpapers of Lucius Beebe and Charles Clegg's *When Beauty Rode the Rails* and also graces Hastings's first article in *Trains* magazine. The location is the railroad's summit (highest point at the top of a grade) at Walden, Vermont.

Courtesy of California State Railroad Museum. Philip Ross Hastings, MD, Collection, [Negative 10503].

Plate 44. On the St. Johnsbury and Lake Champlain, leased Barre & Chelsea 2-8-0 19 handles a westbound way freight. The location is Greensboro Bend, Vermont, 1942.

Courtesy of California State Railroad Museum. Philip Ross Hastings, MD, Collection, [Negative 10502].

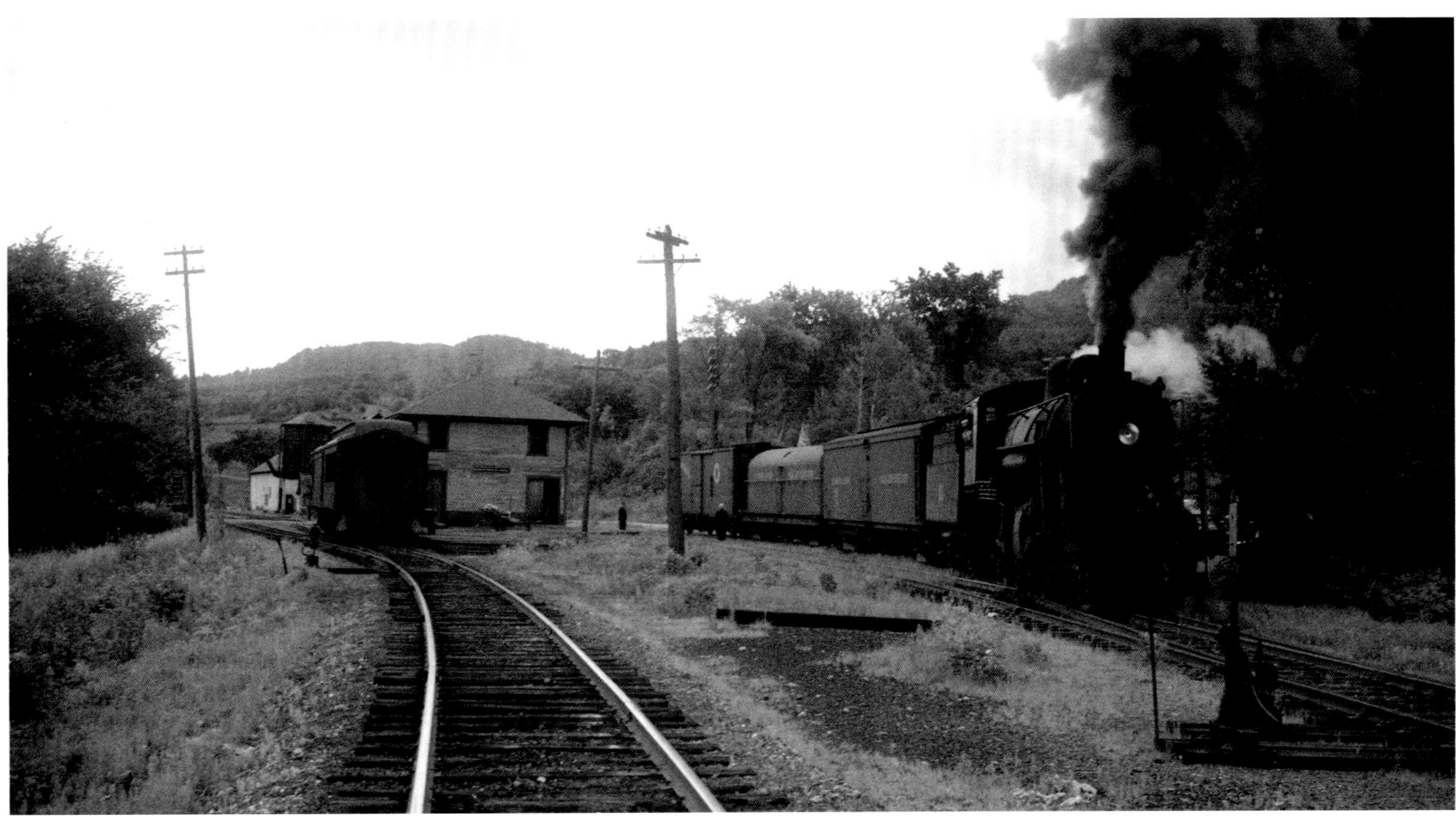

Plate 45. A St. Johnsbury & Lake Champlain Railroad train demonstrating the importance of milk traffic to this and other New England railroads. When milk and US mail traffic left the rails, many of these lines lost their reason for being. The location is Cambridge Junction, Vermont.

Courtesy of California State Railroad Museum. Philip Ross Hastings, MD, Collection, [Negative 8023].

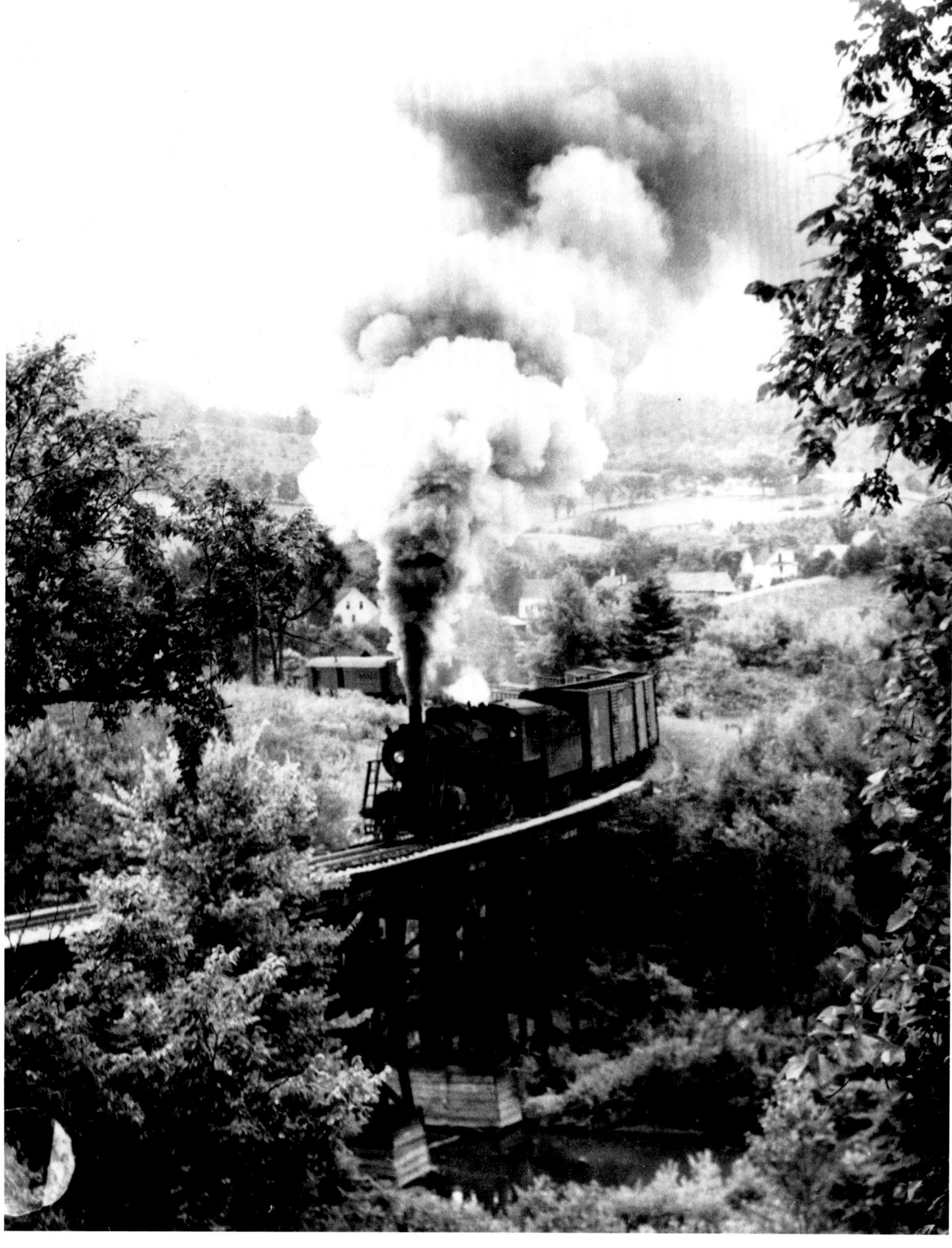

Plate 46. A St. Johnsbury & Lake Champlain train crosses a trestle—a bucolic New England setting. The location is the Sleepers River trestle on the stiff upgrade west from St. Johnsbury, Vermont.

Courtesy of California State Railroad Museum. Philip Ross Hastings, MD, Collection, [Negative 10505].

PORTFOLIO FOUR

O CANADA

Phil Hastings's New England railroad images show that he was inspired by his "home district" of the United States. The Canadian Maritimes, and much of Quebec, show similarities with New England, and Hastings's views of these parts of our great northern neighbor are also outstanding. Many of these were taken on "steam safaris" with David P. Morgan. Hastings also took a number of views in Ontario and a few of the provinces farther west. Of course, most of Hastings's Canadian views feature the two giant railroads of Canada, then and now the only true North American transcontinentals, the Canadian Pacific and the Canadian National.

Plates 47–56 feature the first North American transcontinental, "the impossible railway," the Canadian Pacific (CP). Plate 47 shows CP 2820, the first of the noted "Royal Hudson" steam locomotives, at CP's "home base," Windsor Station in Montreal, Quebec. Plate 48 shows another archetypal CP locomotive and location, engine 3004, a "Jubilee" type, at Gare du Palais Station in Quebec City, Quebec. Plate 49 shows the CP passenger depot at Sherbrooke, Quebec, as the overnight train from Halifax, Nova Scotia, pulls beside Quebec Central train 1.[1] Plate 50 shows Quebec Central train 1 crossing the St. Lawrence River.

Plate 51 returns this portfolio to Montreal, where milk is being loaded from a baggage car to a cart belonging to Montreal's famed Elmhurst Dairy. Plate 52 shows Hastings climbed a signal mast to frame a CP locomotive and crew switching freight cars. This type of image is creative but virtually impossible to emulate today.

Like Plate 52, plate 53 demonstrates the hardships of working outdoors in a Canadian winter. Here, a trainman clears a switch as another, in classic working garb, signals for a coupling. Plate 54 shows a CP engine crew checking the running gear of a "Royal Hudson" and oiling around. Plate 55, a later view, depicts a diesel-powered CP train in Paulson Gap, British Columbia. The CP series in this portfolio ends with plate 56, which shows a CP freight train leaving Brownville Yard in Brownville Junction, Maine.

The Canadian National was—and is—another transcontinental colossus. Plates 57–60 show this noted Canadian railroad. Plate 57 illustrates an unusual scene of great competitors combining efforts: it depicts a Canadian National / Canadian Pacific Toronto "pool train" at Montreal led by a Canadian National locomotive while a CP commuter train belches smoke at the right.

The Canadian National was government owned during Hastings's lifetime, and it served many small towns and branch lines. Plate 58 shows a crossing tender protecting a train at Palmerston, Ontario, a classic small "railroad town." Plate 59 takes us to the Canadian National's Waterloo Branch in Quebec. The last Canadian National view, plate 60, shows Hastings going to ground level to frame a Canadian National locomotive between two wheel blocks.

Finally, as plate 61 shows, US railroads had lines in Canada as well. The image shows New York Central "Ten-Wheeler" 1290 at Brigden, Ontario—an elderly steam engine framed by what was, at the time, already an archaic type of switch stand.

Plate 47. Canadian Pacific 2820, the first of the "Royal Hudsons," with a passenger train. The location is Windsor Station, Montreal, Quebec.

Courtesy of California State Railroad Museum. Philip Ross Hastings, MD, Collection, [Negative 2354].

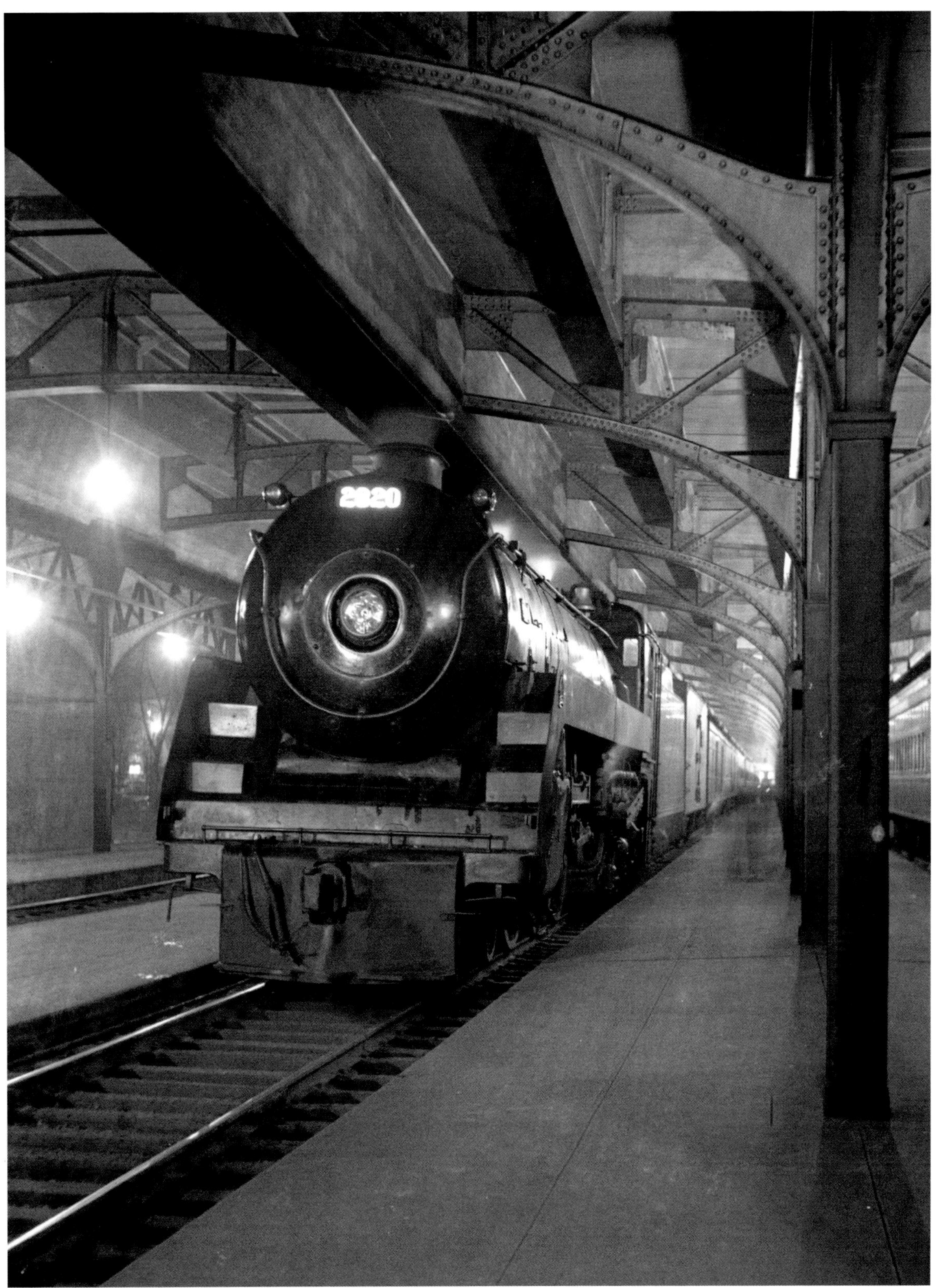

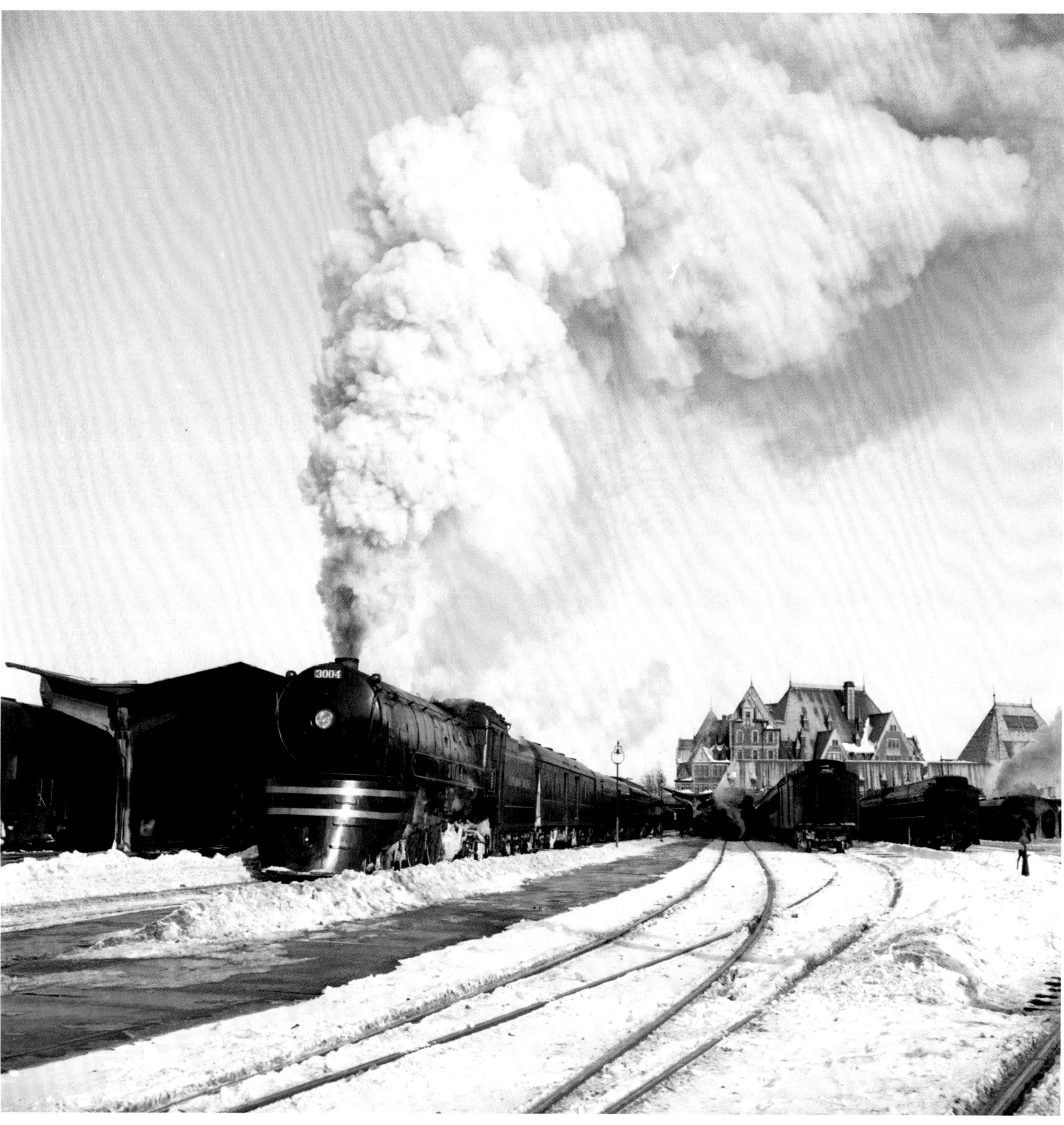
3004

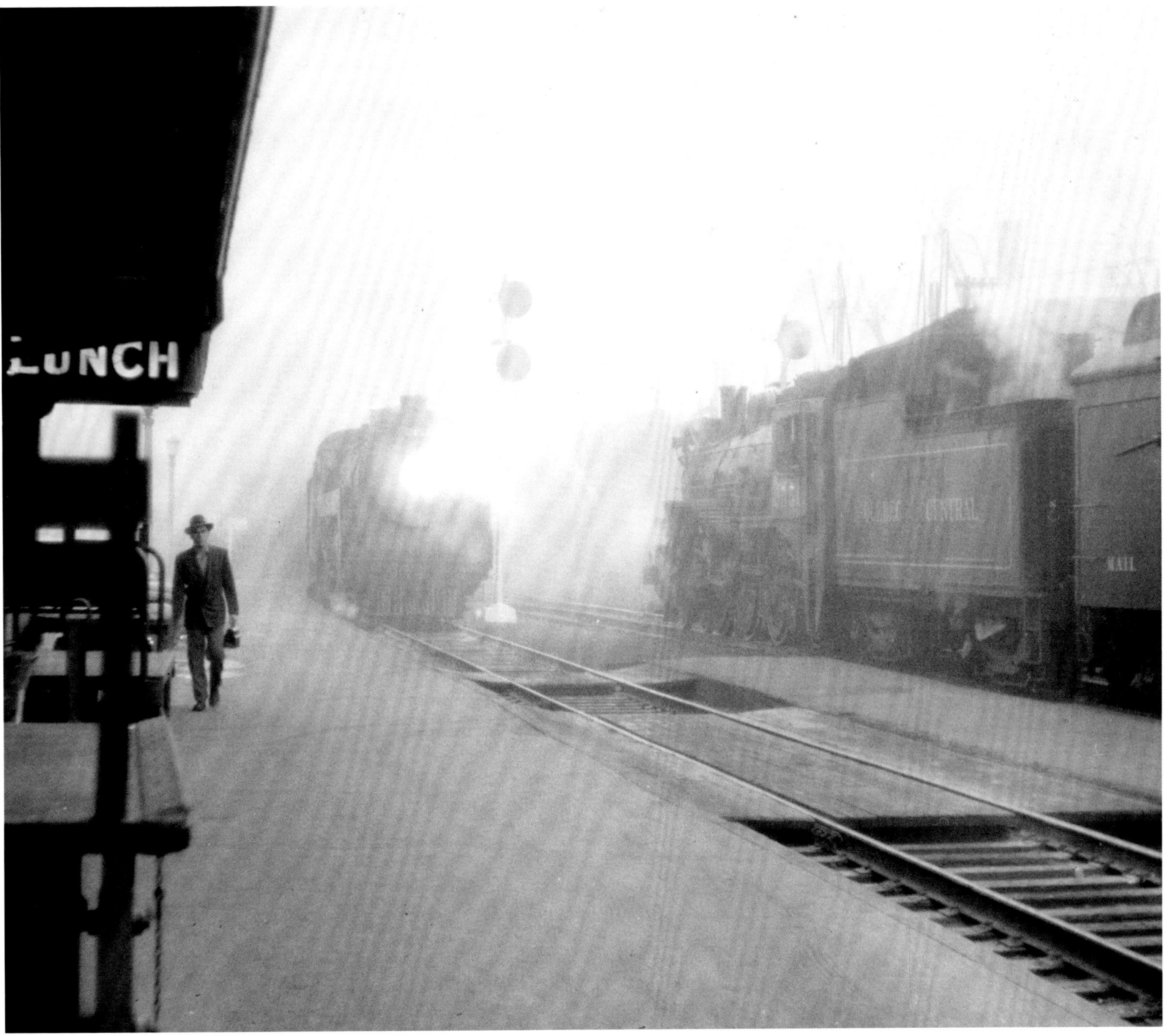

***Facing*, Plate 48.** Canadian Pacific 3004, a "Jubilee" type, with a passenger train. The location is Gare du Palais Station, Quebec City, Quebec.

Courtesy of California State Railroad Museum. Philip Ross Hastings, MD, Collection, [Negative 2577].

Plate 49. A foggy dawn envelopes the Canadian Pacific passenger station at Sherbrooke, Quebec. The overnight train from Halifax, Nova Scotia, is pulling in beside Quebec Central train 1, bound to Quebec City and led by light "Pacific" 2556.

Courtesy of California State Railroad Museum. Philip Ross Hastings, MD, Collection, [Negative 10510].

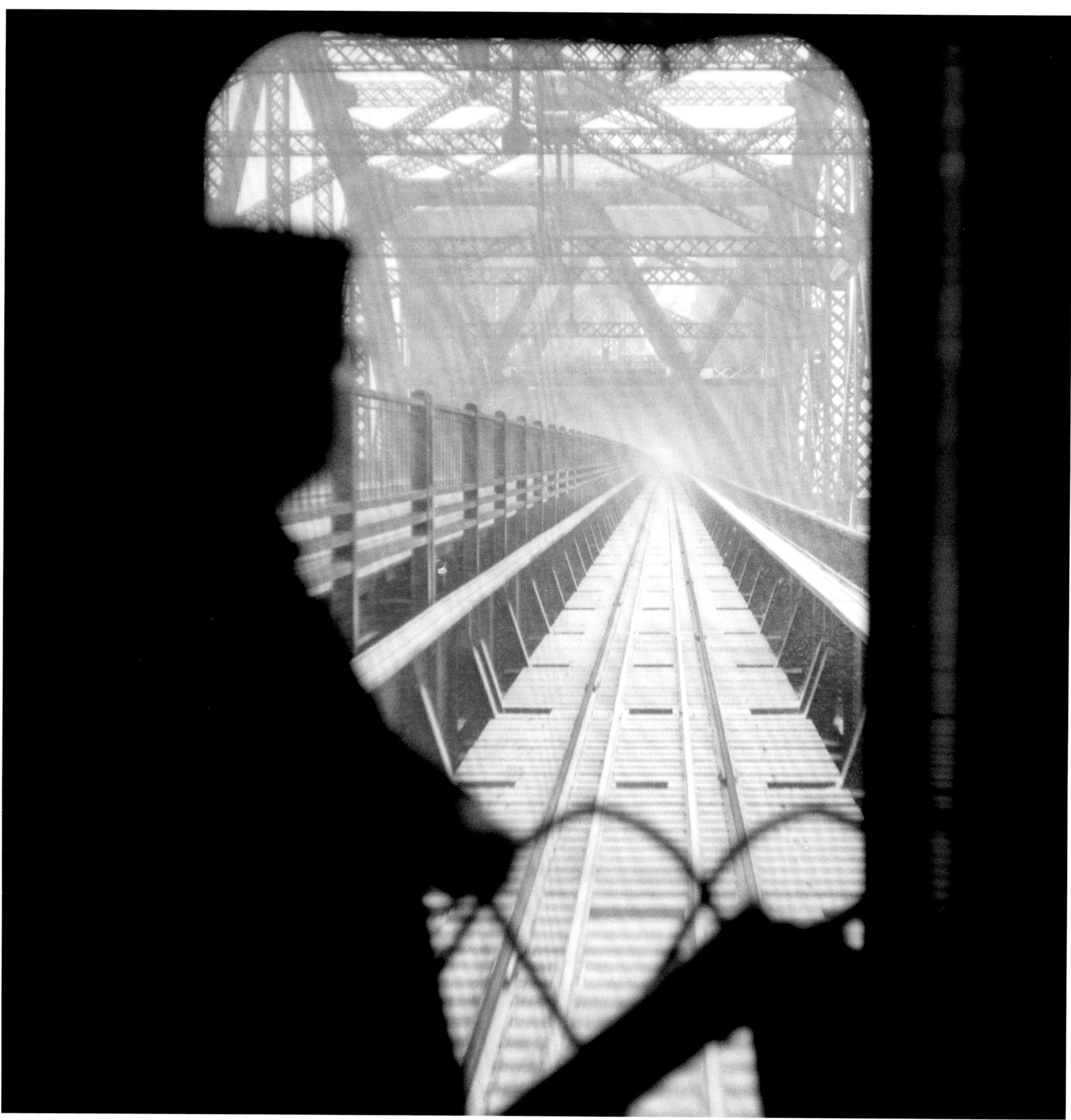

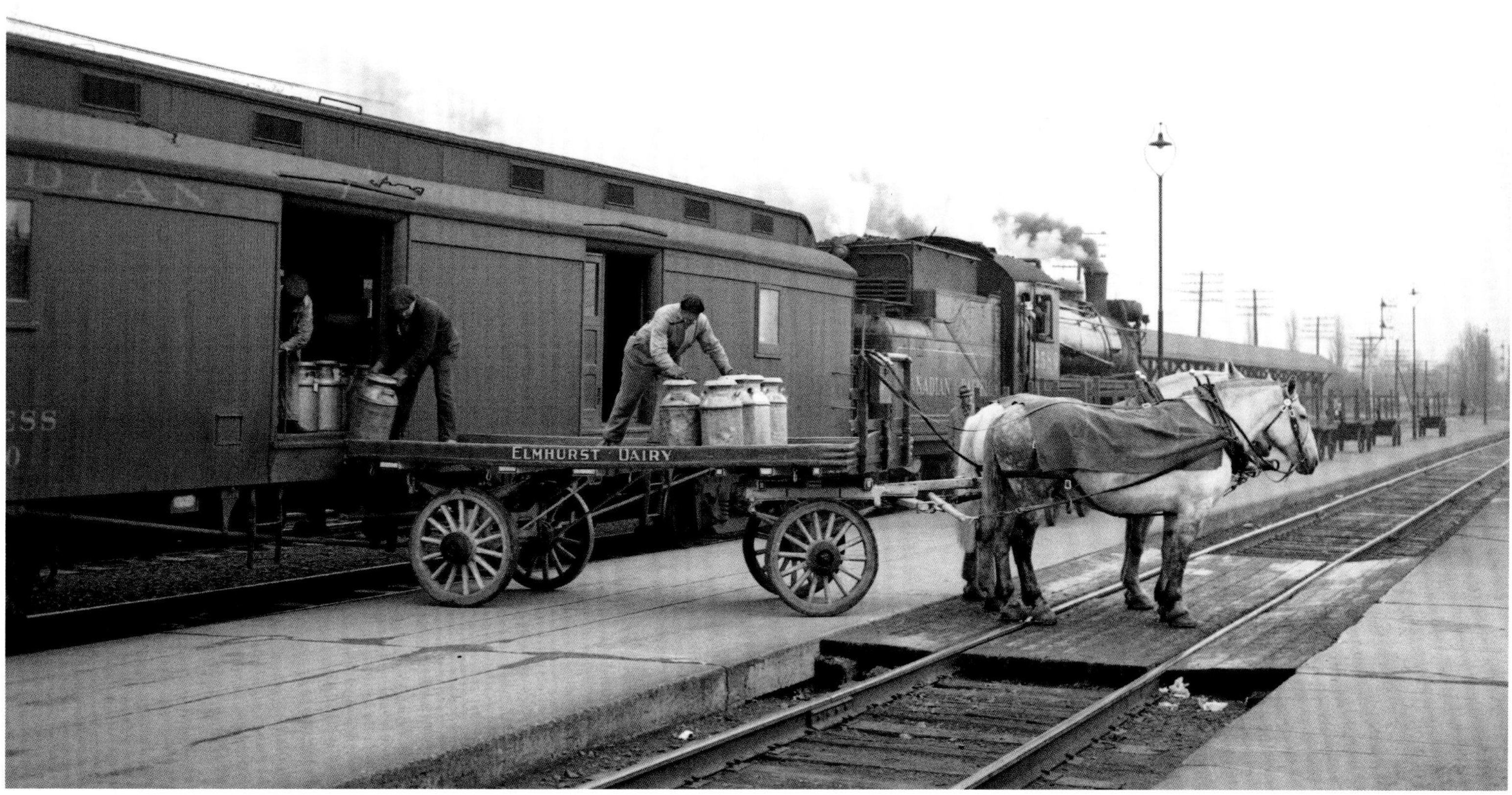

Plate 51. Milk was important traffic for Canadian railroads as well. In this scene, a horse-drawn Elmhurst Dairy cart loads milk from a Canadian Pacific baggage car at Montreal West, Quebec.

Courtesy of California State Railroad Museum. Philip Ross Hastings, MD, Collection, [Negative 2340].

***Facing,* Plate 50.** The flagman of Quebec Central train 1 looks out the rear door of his train as it crosses the dual rail and road bridge spanning the St. Lawrence River.

Courtesy of California State Railroad Museum. Philip Ross Hastings, MD, Collection, [Negative 8668].

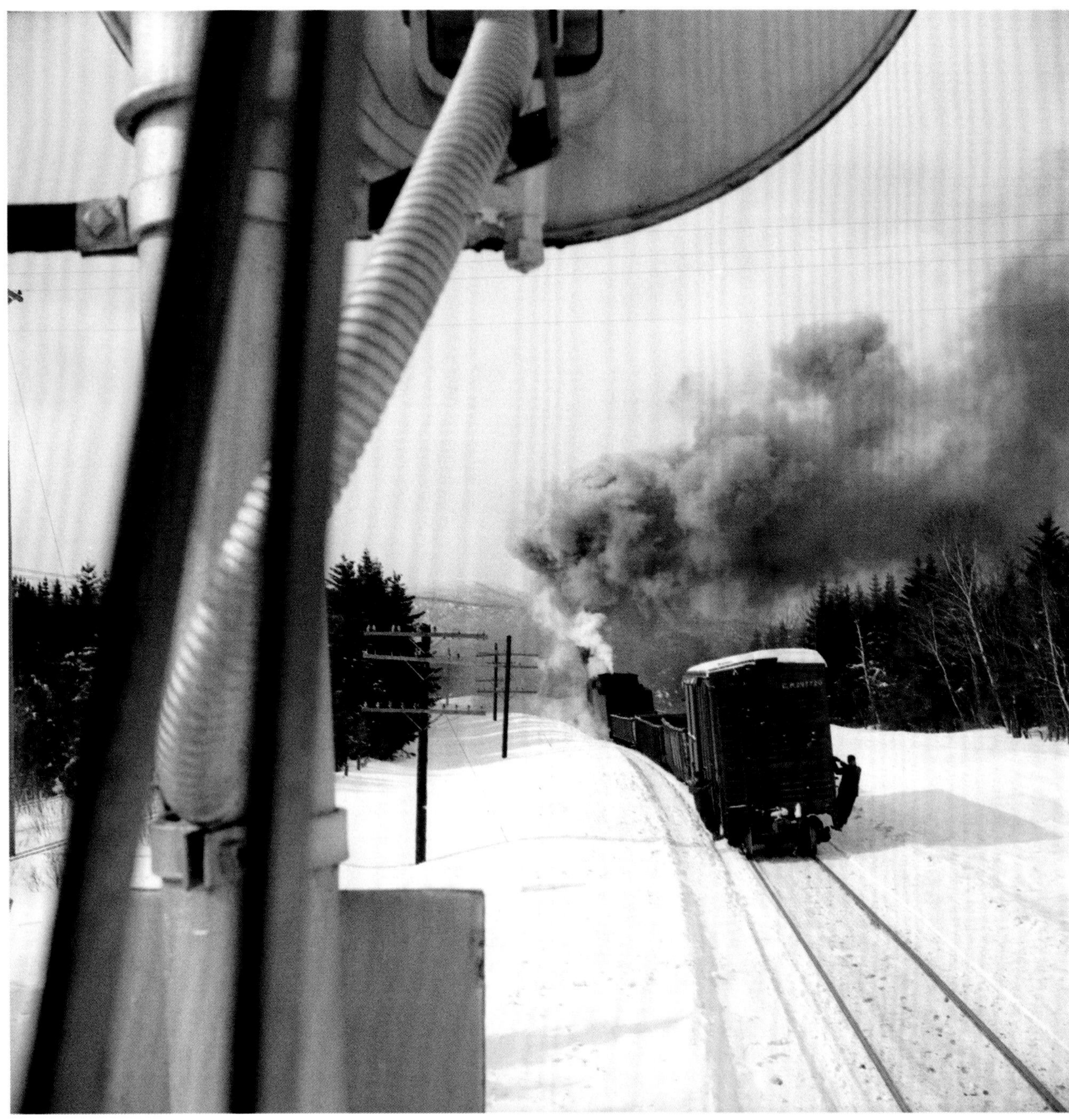

Plate 52. Hastings used a signal mast to access, and frame, this innovative overhead shot. In the view, a Canadian Pacific freight switches in the snow. Hastings, a Vermonter used to winter weather, captured a number of significant scenes of US and Canadian railroading during the winter months.

Courtesy of California State Railroad Museum. Philip Ross Hastings, MD, Collection, [Negative 2563].

***Facing,* Plate 53.** A Canadian Pacific trainman couples up two cars while a colleague clears snow out of a switch. A broom and another tool are stuck in the snow, ready for use. The workers are bundled against winter, and the trainman's hat, cigarette, jacket, and employee timetable are emblematic of railroaders during the steam era.

Courtesy of California State Railroad Museum. Philip Ross Hastings, MD, Collection, [Negative 2591].

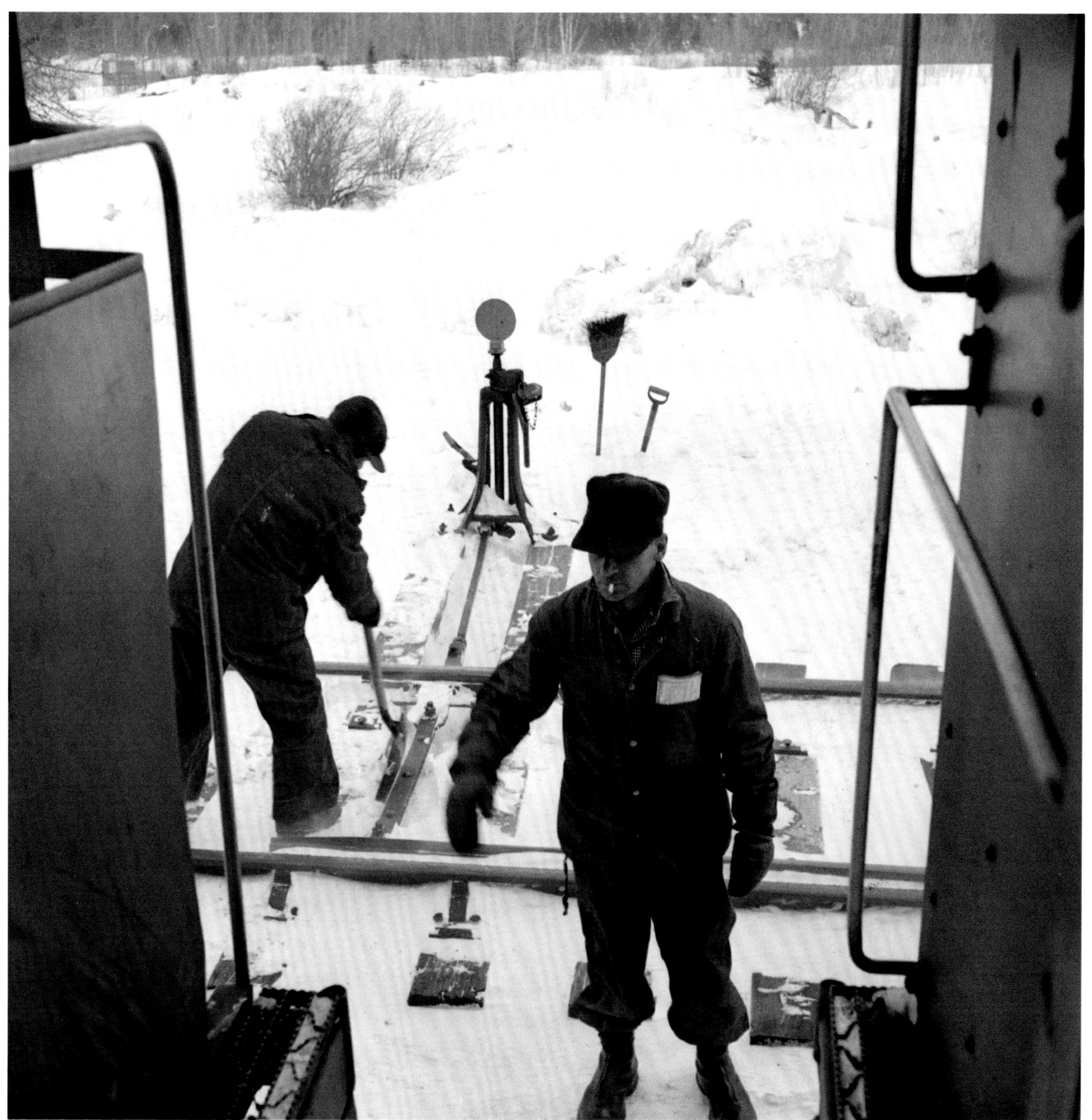

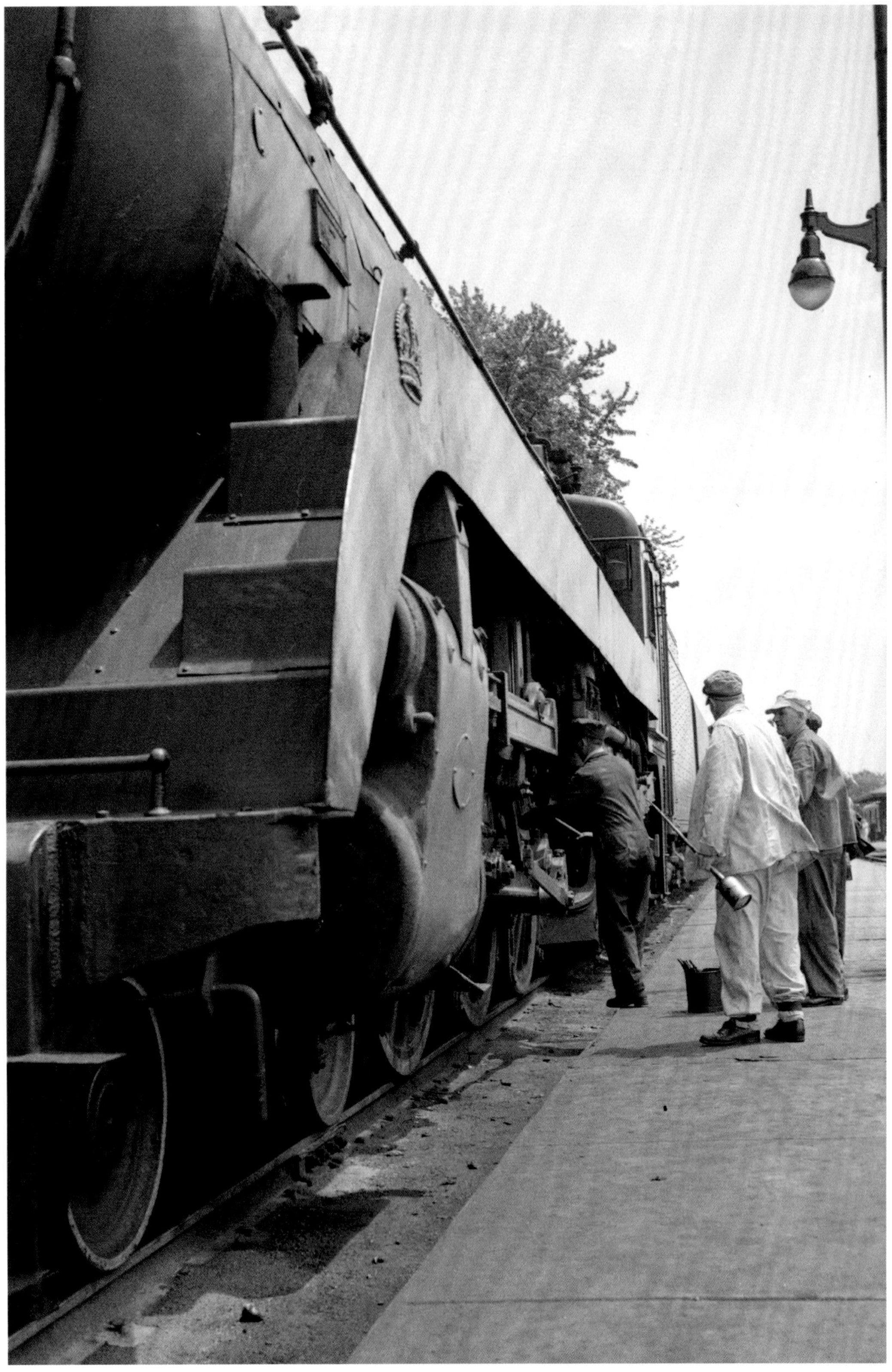

Plate 54. A Canadian Pacific engine crew checks the running gear of their locomotive and oils around. The crown on the engine's running board marks this as a "Royal Hudson."

Courtesy of California State Railroad Museum. Philip Ross Hastings, MD, Collection, [Negative 2551].

***Facing*, Plate 55.** In a later image, a diesel-powered Canadian Pacific train winds through the mountains. The location is Paulson Tunnel in Paulson Gap, west of Farron, British Columbia, on the CP's Kootenay division.

Courtesy of California State Railroad Museum. Philip Ross Hastings, MD, Collection, [Negative 2455].

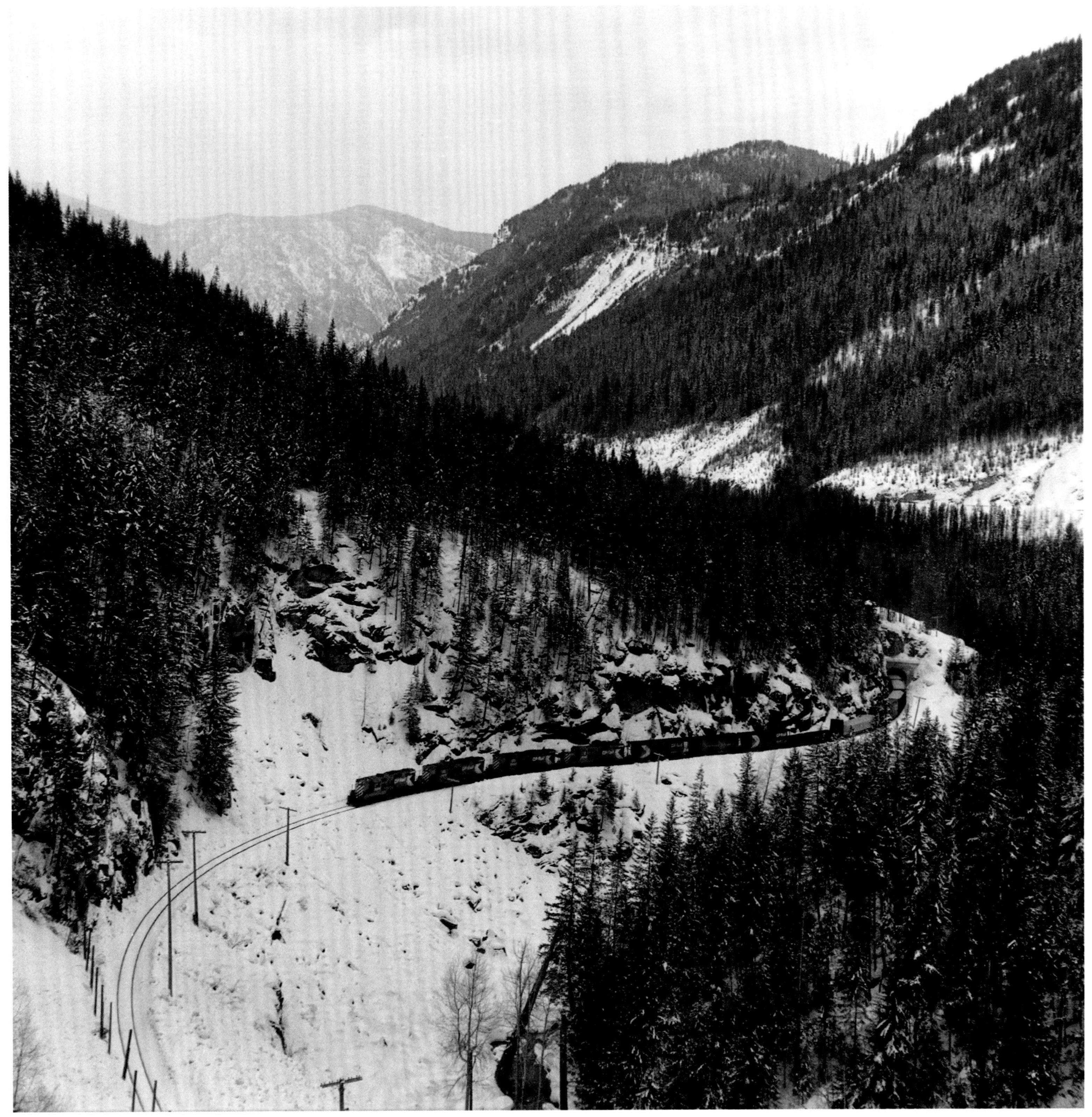

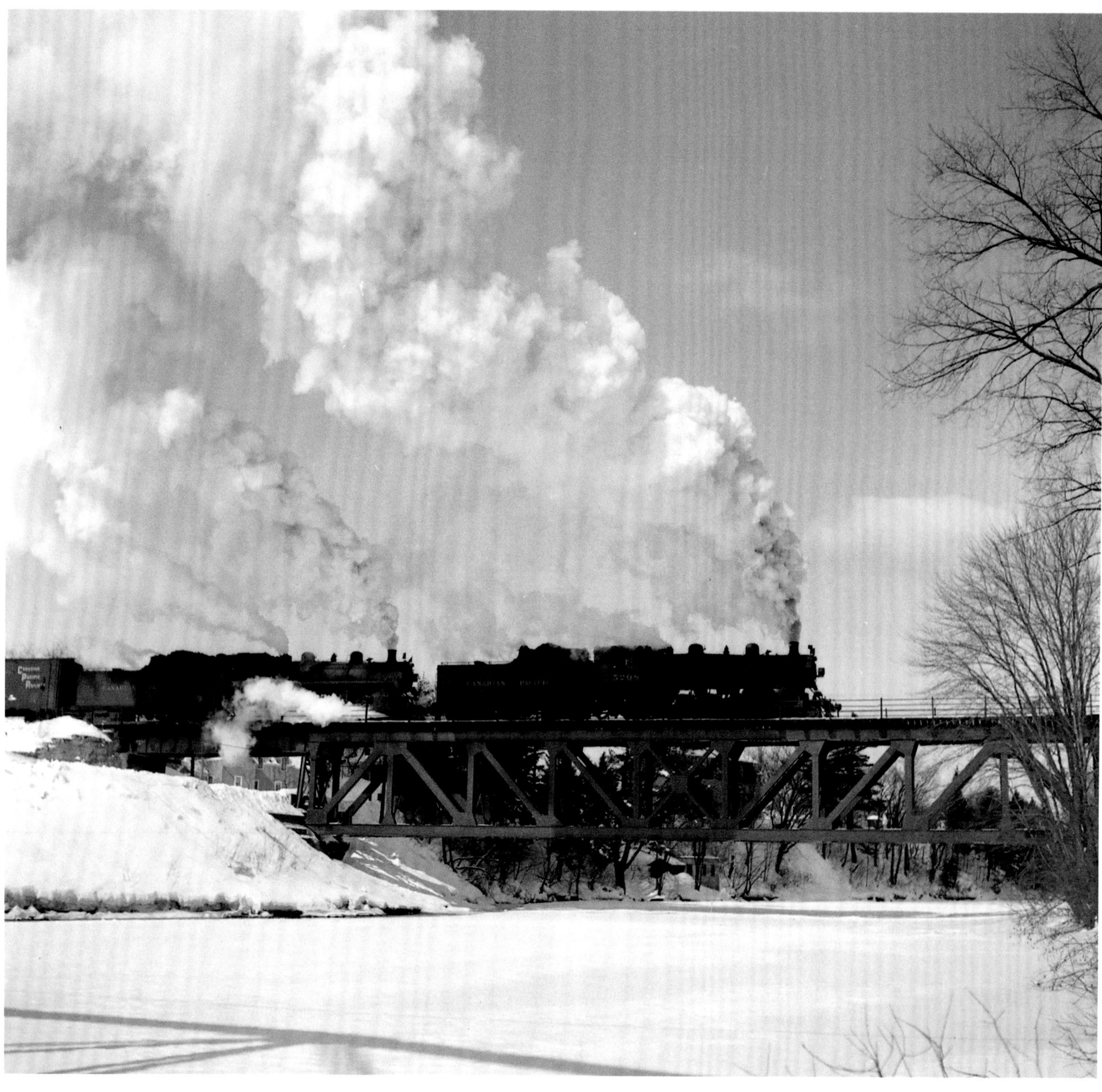
CANADIAN PACIFIC

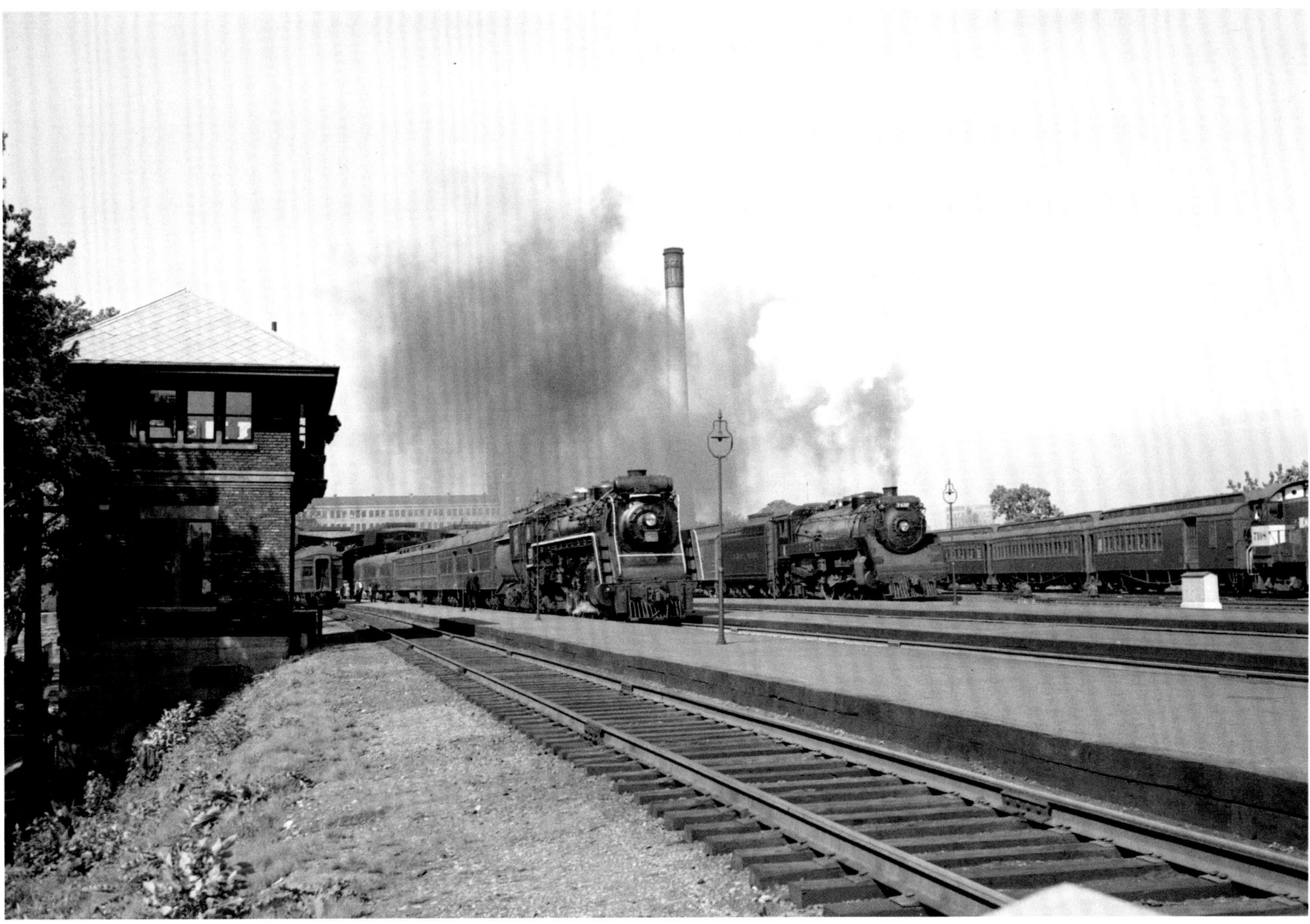

***Facing*, Plate 56.** Hastings titled this photo "Rails Move the River." In it, Canadian Pacific manifest freight 952 East attacks a 1 percent grade as it leaves the Brownville yard (Brownville Junction, Maine) with "Mikados" 5208 and 5217. The train is crossing the Pleasant River on March 8, 1955.

Courtesy of California State Railroad Museum. Philip Ross Hastings, MD, Collection, [Negative 2593].

Plate 57. Steam-powered passenger trains are lined up just behind a signal tower at Montreal's Windsor Station in this Hastings image. The train in the left foreground led by a Canadian National engine is a Canadian National / Canadian Pacific "pool train" to Toronto; the Canadian Pacific train on the right is a Montreal-area commuter train.

Courtesy of California State Railroad Museum. Philip Ross Hastings, MD, Collection, [Negative 2036].

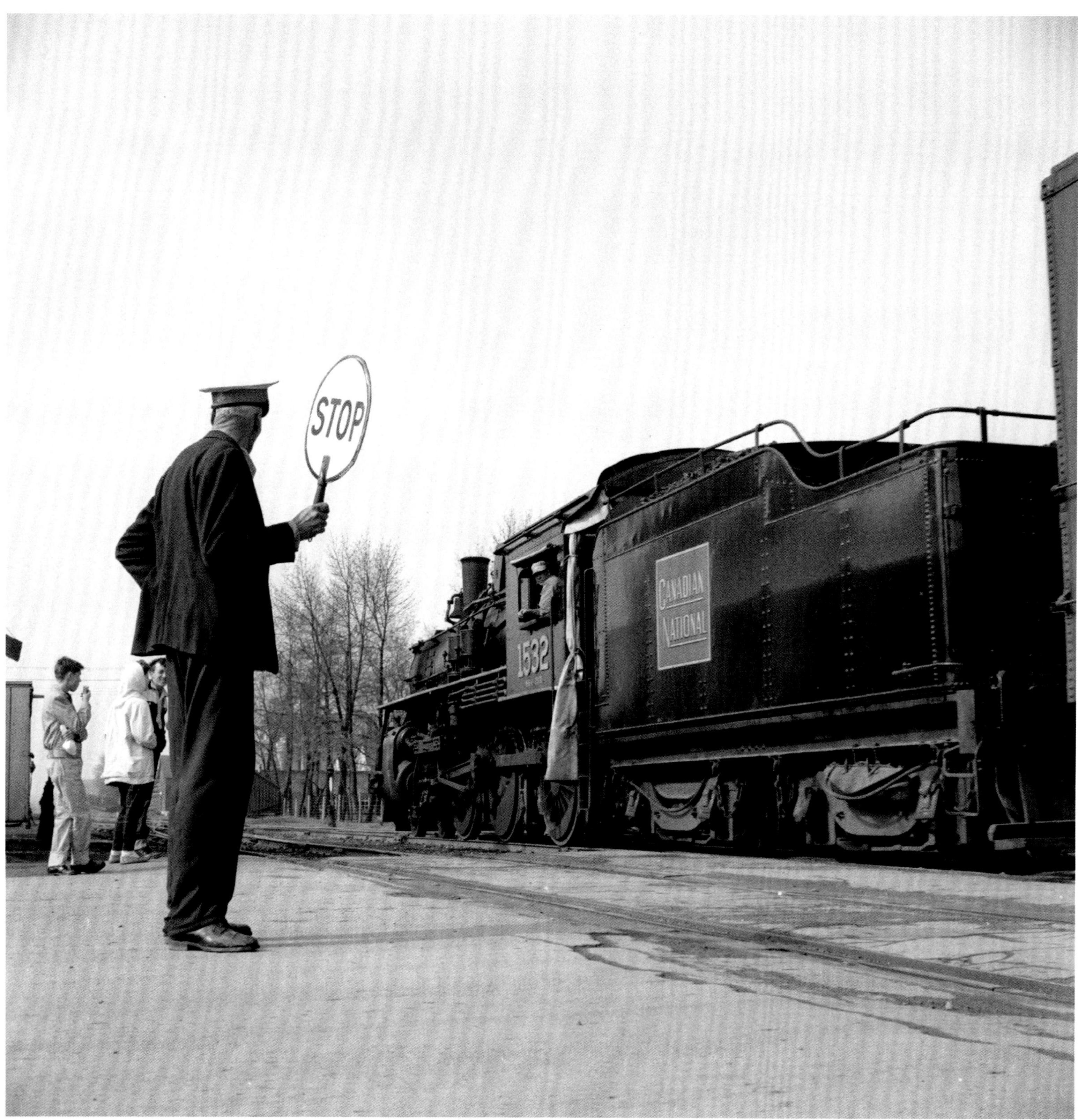
STOP
1532
CANADIAN NATIONAL

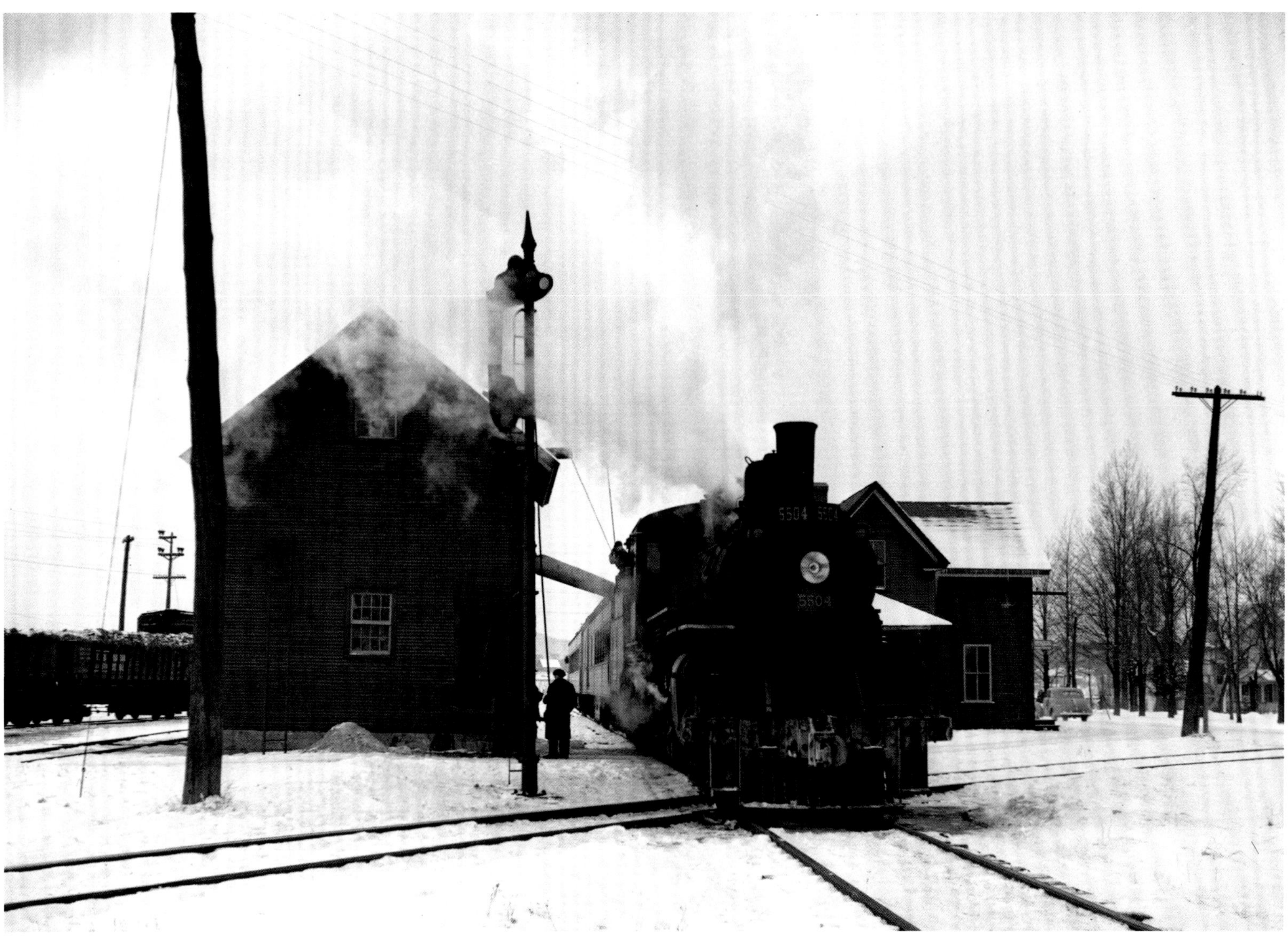

***Facing,* Plate 58.** In this 1957 image, Hastings focused on a crossing tender using his "stop" paddle to protect a group of teenagers from Canadian National Railways "Ten-Wheeler" 1532 and its train. The location is Palmerston, Ontario.

Courtesy of California State Railroad Museum. Philip Ross Hastings, MD, Collection, [Negative 2055].

Plate 59. In this winter image, Canadian National "Pacific" 5504 takes on water while sitting on a diamond on the railroad's Waterloo Branch at Waterloo, Quebec. It is crossing the Canadian Pacific's St. Guillaume subdivision.

Courtesy of California State Railroad Museum. Philip Ross Hastings, MD, Collection, [Negative 10034].

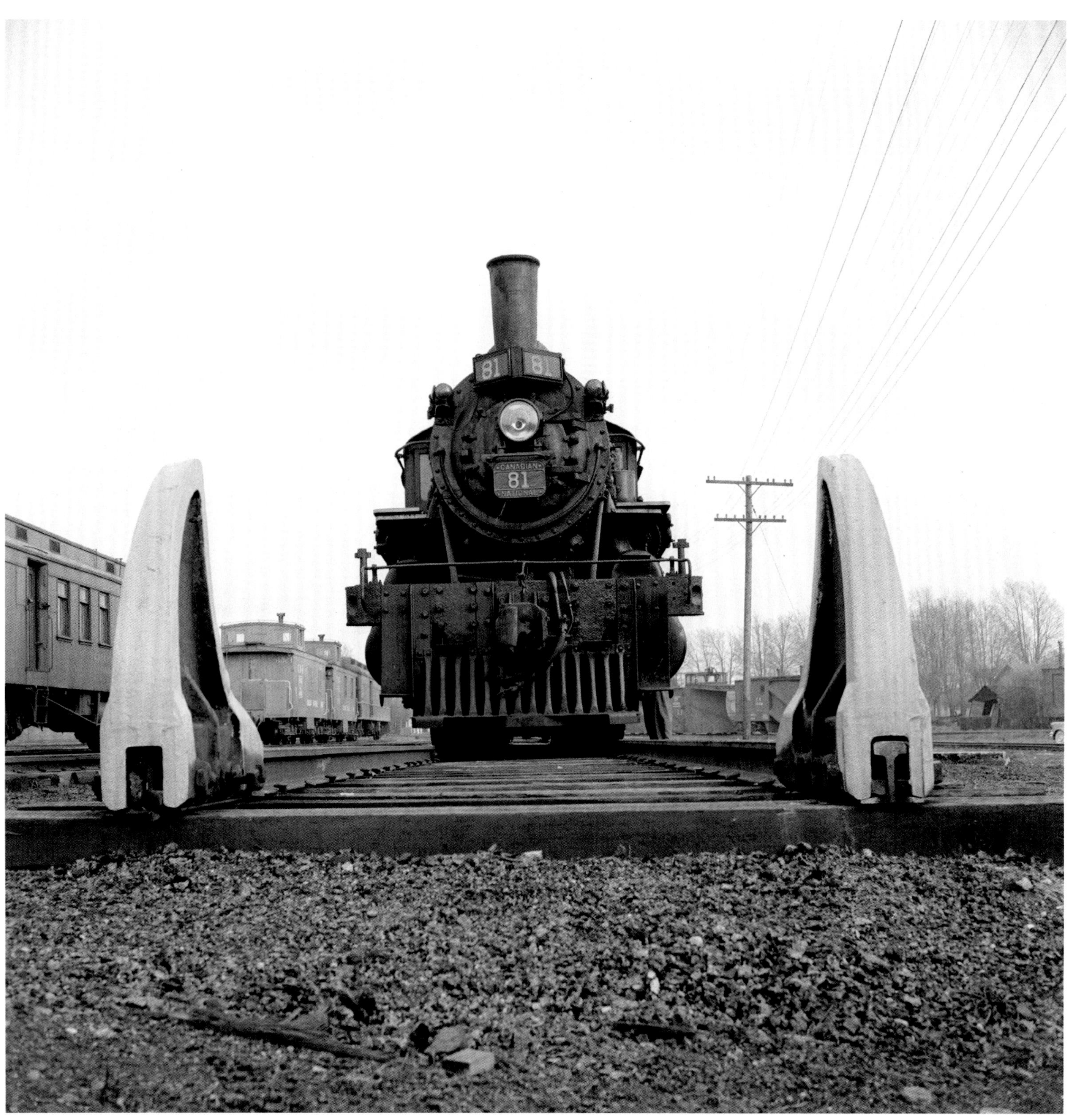
81
81
CANADIAN
81
NATIONAL

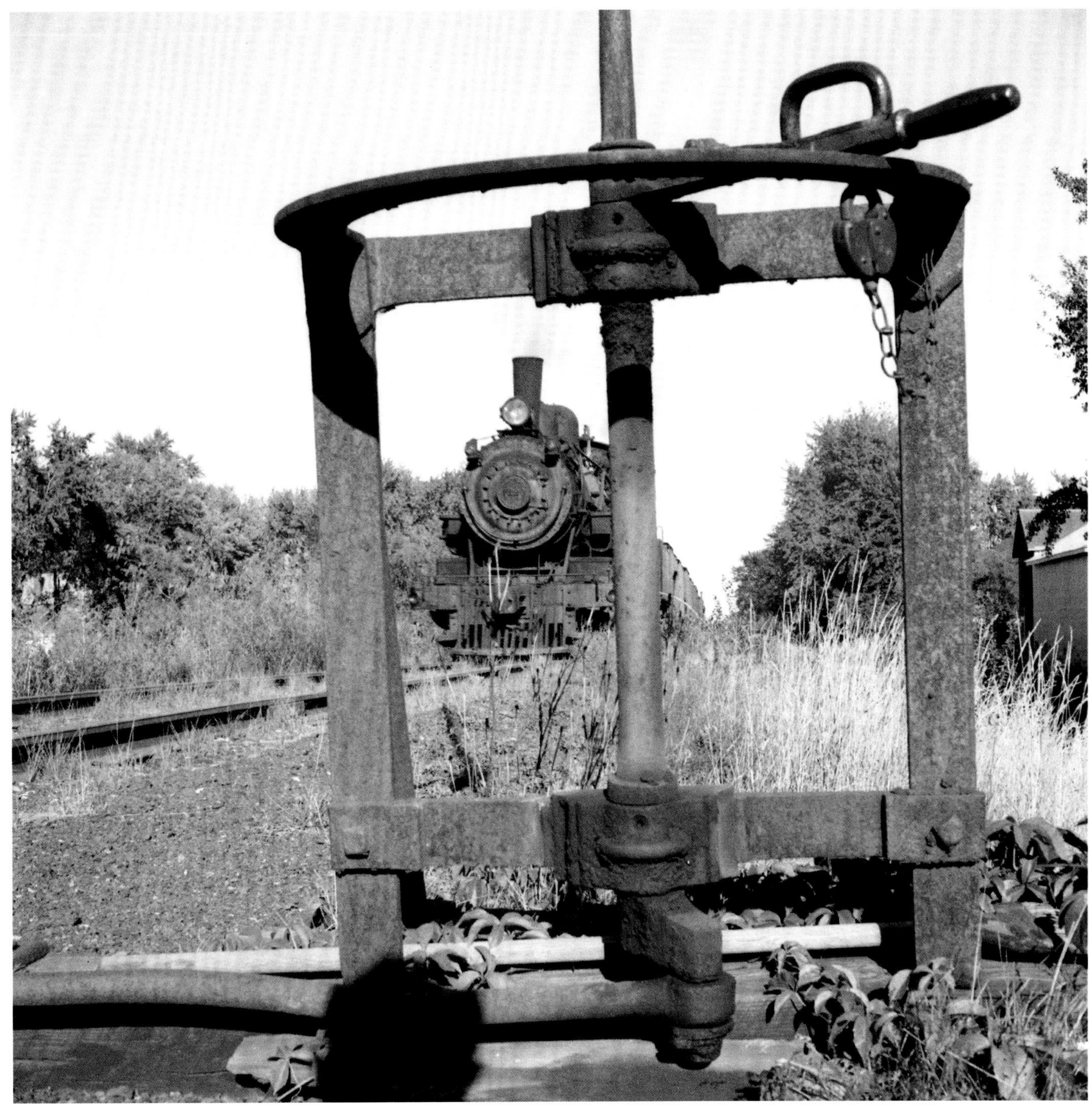

***Facing,* Plate 60.** In this image, Phil Hastings shot from ground level to frame a Canadian National steam locomotive between two end-of-track wheel blocks. The location is Palmerston, Ontario.

Courtesy of California State Railroad Museum. Philip Ross Hastings, MD, Collection, [Negative 3454].

Plate 61. American railroads also had lines in Canada. In this image, one of Hastings's better-known photos, he uses an archaic switch stand to frame New York Central "Ten Wheeler" 1290 at Brigden, Ontario.

Courtesy of California State Railroad Museum. Philip Ross Hastings, MD, Collection, [Negative 9745].

PORTFOLIO FIVE

NORTHEAST/MID-ATLANTIC

Phil Hastings's work includes good coverage of the northeastern and mid-Atlantic United States. Many of these images were taken on "steam safari" trips with *Trains* editor David P. Morgan. Hastings's coverage of the Pennsylvania Railroad in the Northeast is excellent and resulted in a posthumous book, *Philip R. Hastings: Portrait of the Pennsylvania Railroad*.[1]

Plates 62–64 depict America's first important railroad, the Baltimore & Ohio (B&O). Plate 62 shows a Black railroader, probably a Pullman porter, on a B&O Korean War–era troop train. Plate 63 depicts a B&O commuter train formed of Budd RDC (Rail Diesel Car) cars at the classic Point of Rocks, Maryland, station. Finally, plate 64 shows B&O 7602 in a wedge shot framed vertically to catch a plume of black smoke.[2]

Plates 65 and 66 depict George Gould's also-ran and competitor to the B&O, the Western Maryland Railway. Plate 65 shows a contrast between Western Maryland passenger engine 202 and a child. Plate 66, which also includes a child for contrast with the massiveness of railroad equipment, shows a Western Maryland freight passing the station in Frostburg, Maryland. The diesels shown here, in a 1953 photo, are vanquishing steam on the Western Maryland and soon will win this battle in the US and then Canada.

Plates 67, 68, 69, and 70 depict the "Standard Railroad of the World," the Pennsylvania Railroad (PRR). Plate 67 shows a classic Pennsylvania K4s–type leading a local at Huntingdon, Pennsylvania. Hastings's eye led him to frame the locomotive between the "Clasters" truck to the left and the crossing tower to the right.

Plates 68 depicts one of the best-known features of the Pennsylvania Railroad, Rockville Bridge across the Susquehanna River. Plate 69, a notable pan shot, shows PRR Baldwin "Centipede" 5829 serving as a pusher and helping a freight train cross the Alleghenies. Plate 70—in the view of this observer one of Hastings's most notable images—shows a Pennsylvania freight crossing Rock Stream in New York.

The next four images in this portfolio depict New Jersey locations. Plates 71 and 72 were taken on the Pennsylvania-Reading Seashore Lines (PRSL), a very unusual railroad—a joint venture between the Pennsylvania and a close competitor, the Reading Company. There was sometimes humor in the chalked graffiti left on railroad equipment by railroaders and others; in fact, a chalked message is how the Union Pacific "Big Boys" got their name. In plate 71, graffiti on a tiny 0–4–0 switcher, a Pennsylvania Railroad A5s, says, "DONT LAUGH IM TRYING." Plate

72 shows a PRSL engineman, probably an engineer, checking his watch as he waits by his engine, a Pennsylvania Railroad "Atlantic."[3]

Plates 73 and 74 also show New Jersey scenes but on the Jersey Central.[4] Both depict a "Camelback" locomotive.[5] The first of these, a view reminiscent of a noted Lucius Beebe image, shows CNJ fireman Frank Ballinger at his post in the rear of a "Camelback." The second shows the engineer of CNJ "Camelback" 754 waiting at a grade crossing.

This portfolio closes with a southern flavor, in West Virginia. Plates 75 and 76 depict the Chesapeake & Ohio Railway (C&O), largely a coal hauler carrying black diamonds from the mines of West Virginia to Tidewater Virginia. Plate 75 shows a member of one of the C&O's most famous classes of locomotives, 2-6-6-6 "Allegheny" 1624, in the New River Gorge town of Thurmond, West Virginia.

This portfolio closes with plate 76, showing a Black section worker going out to inspect a section of the C&O's track on a velocipede.[6]

***Facing*, Plate 62.** Photographs of Black railroaders during the steam era are relatively rare. Here, Hastings captures a Black railroader, probably a Pullman porter, looking out a vestibule door on a Baltimore & Ohio (B&O) troop train, May 20, 1953.

Courtesy of California State Railroad Museum. Philip Ross Hastings, MD, Collection, [Negative 102].

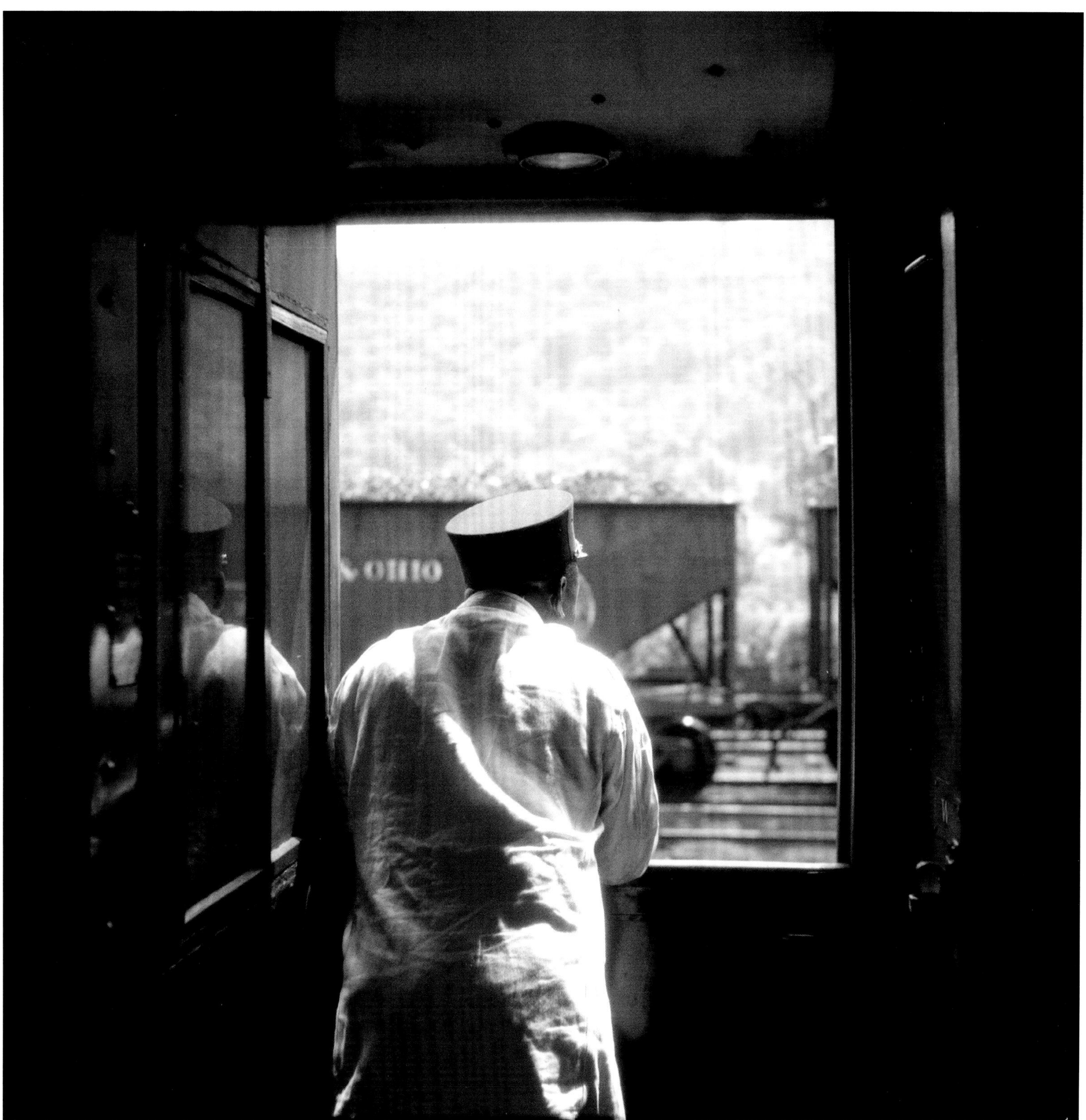
& OHIO

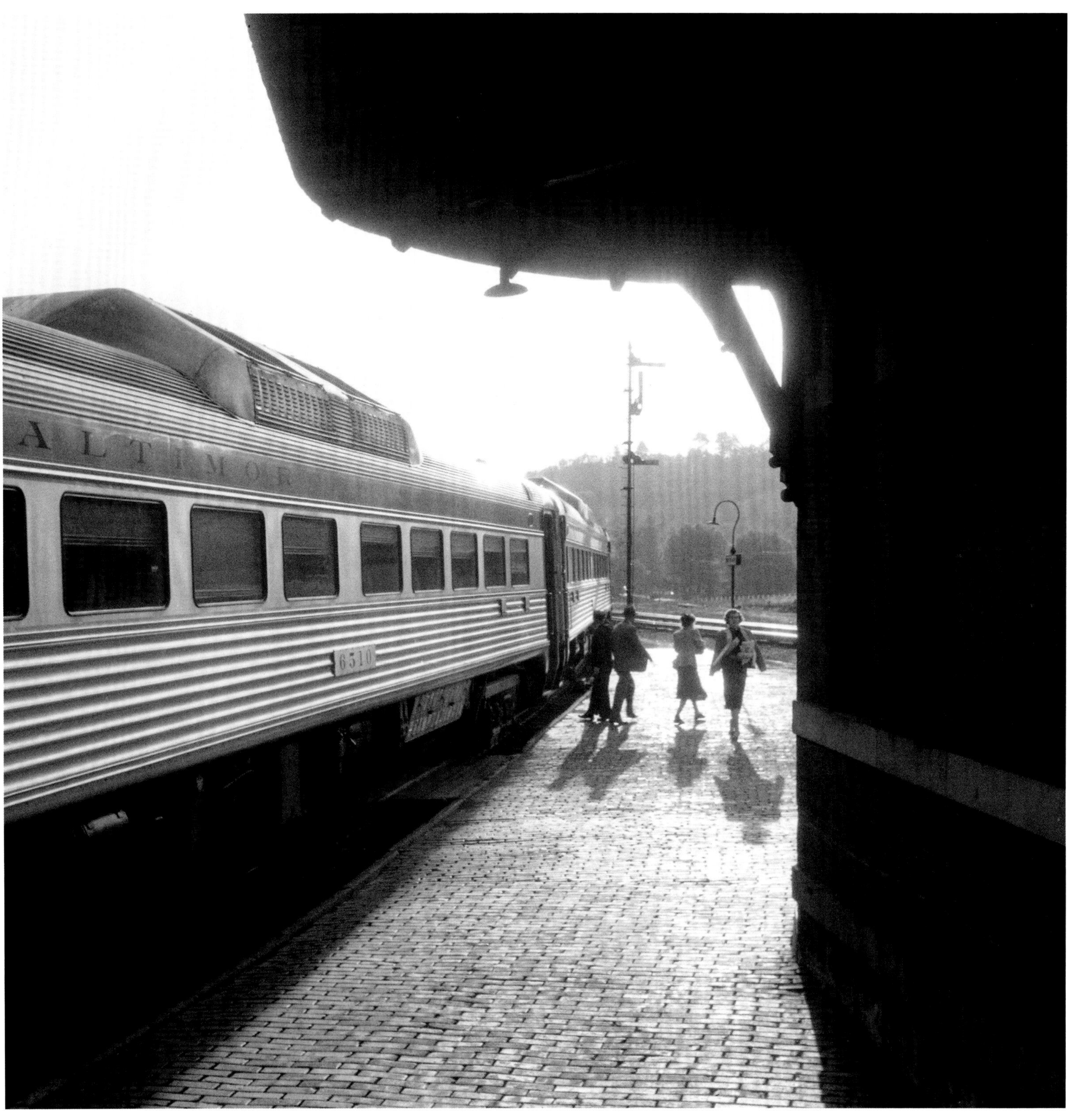
6510

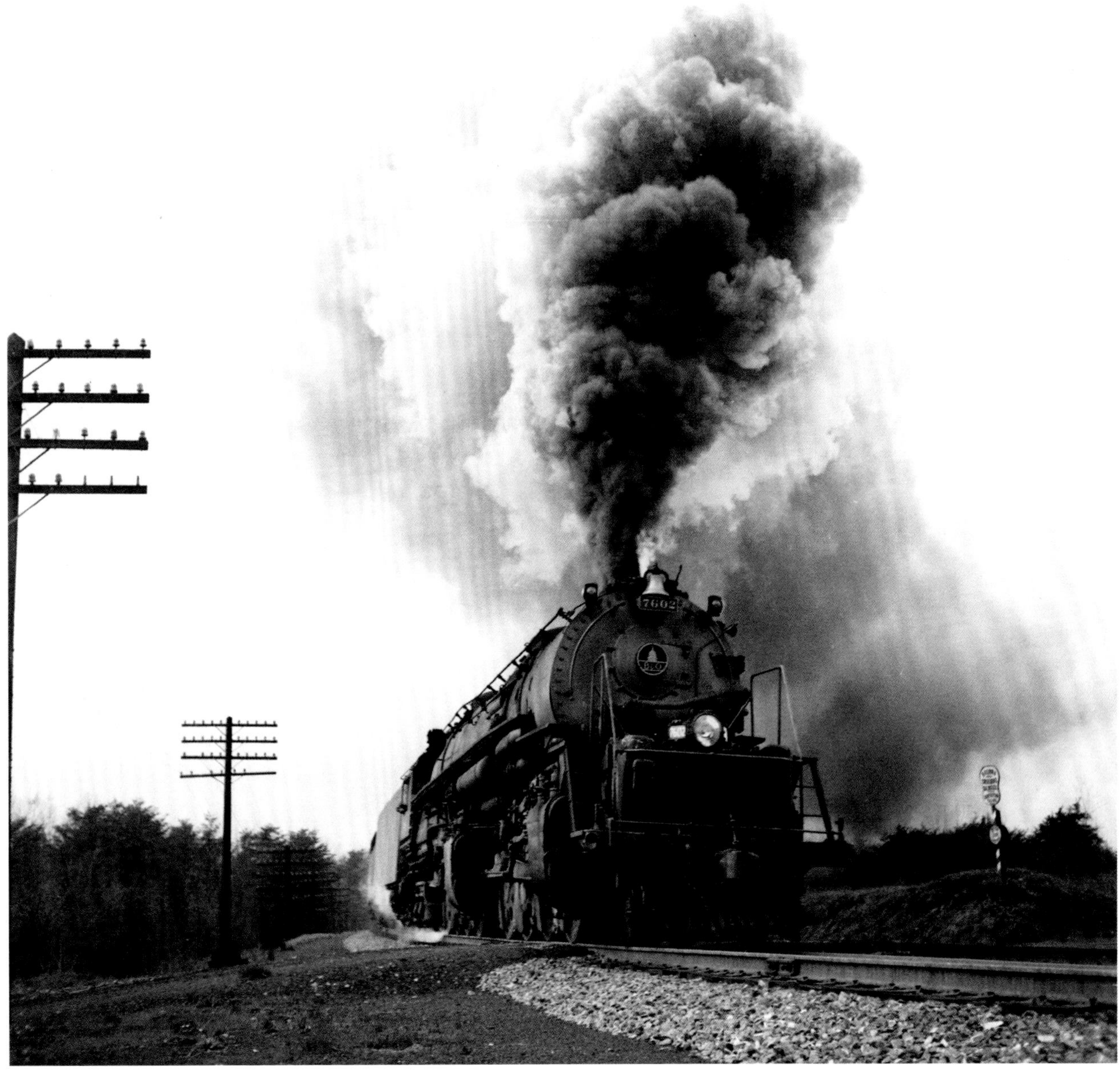

***Facing,* Plate 63.** Hastings often used reflections, usually in trackside waterbodies, in his images. In this photo, passengers detrain from RDC cars (Budd Rail Diesel Cars) at the B&O station at Point of Rocks, Maryland. The detraining passengers and a B&O trainman are shadowed by the sun on the brick station walkways. The finely detailed shadows resemble reflections.

Courtesy of California State Railroad Museum. Philip Ross Hastings, MD, Collection, [Negative 79].

Plate 64. Massive B&O 2-8-8-4 articulated steam locomotive 7602 belches black smoke in this Hastings image showing the power of steam.

Courtesy of California State Railroad Museum. Philip Ross Hastings, MD, Collection, [Negative 108].

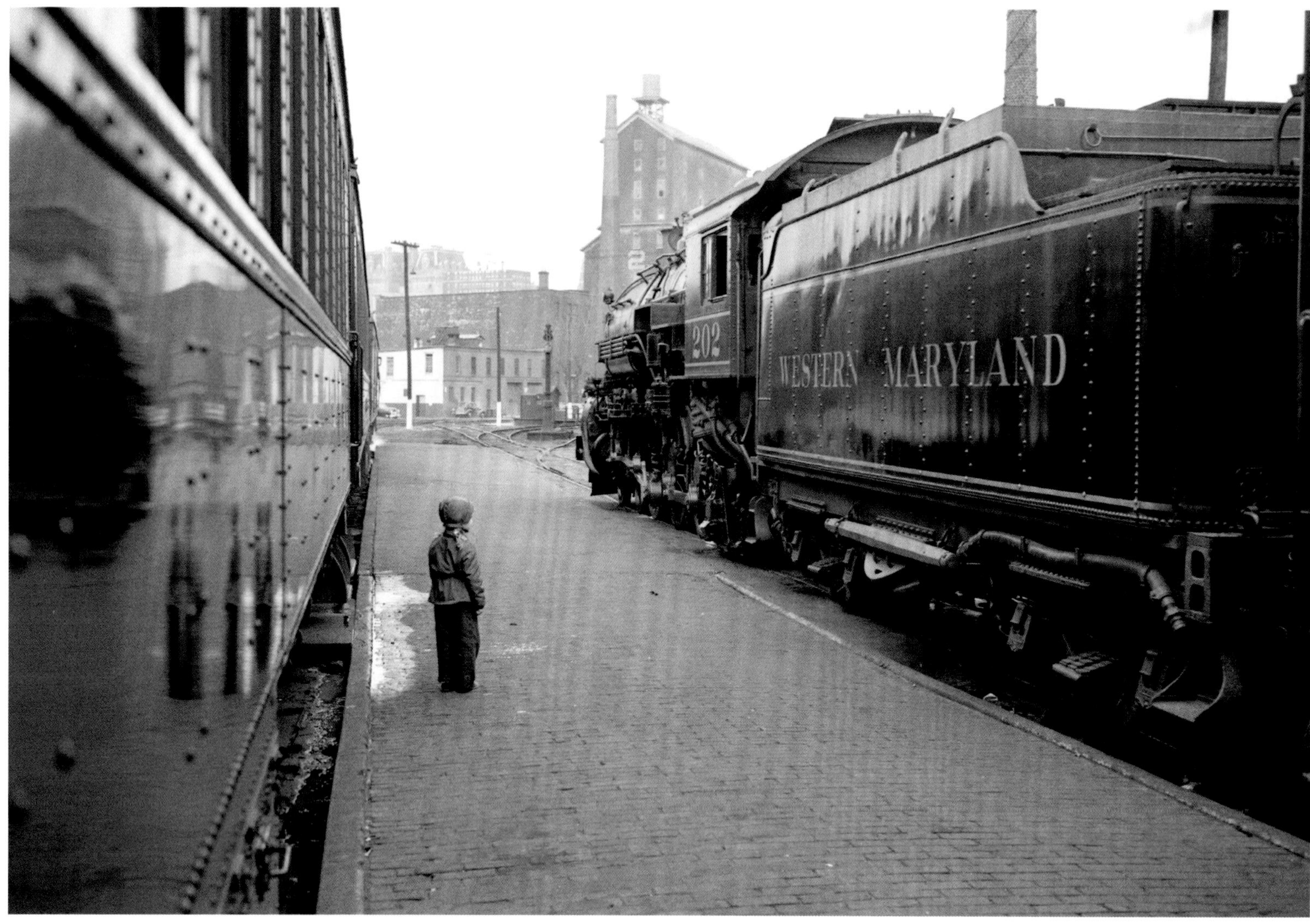

Plate 65. During his early years as a photographer, Hastings often used his children as subjects in his images, although his captions often did not identify them as such. The little girl, who appears to be Hastings's daughter, Pamela, his oldest child and his only daughter, presents an interesting contrast to Western Maryland locomotive "Pacific" 202. The 202 survives, in City Park, Hagerstown, Maryland.

Courtesy of California State Railroad Museum. Philip Ross Hastings, MD, Collection, [Negative 3642].

***Facing,* Plate 66.** A Western Maryland freight, with F-7A diesels 65 and 59 pushing behind the caboose, climbs Frostburg Hill, at Frostburg, Maryland. Eighty-six cars ahead, two more F-7As lead the train. June 6, 1953.

Courtesy of California State Railroad Museum. Philip Ross Hastings, MD, Collection, [Negative 3699].

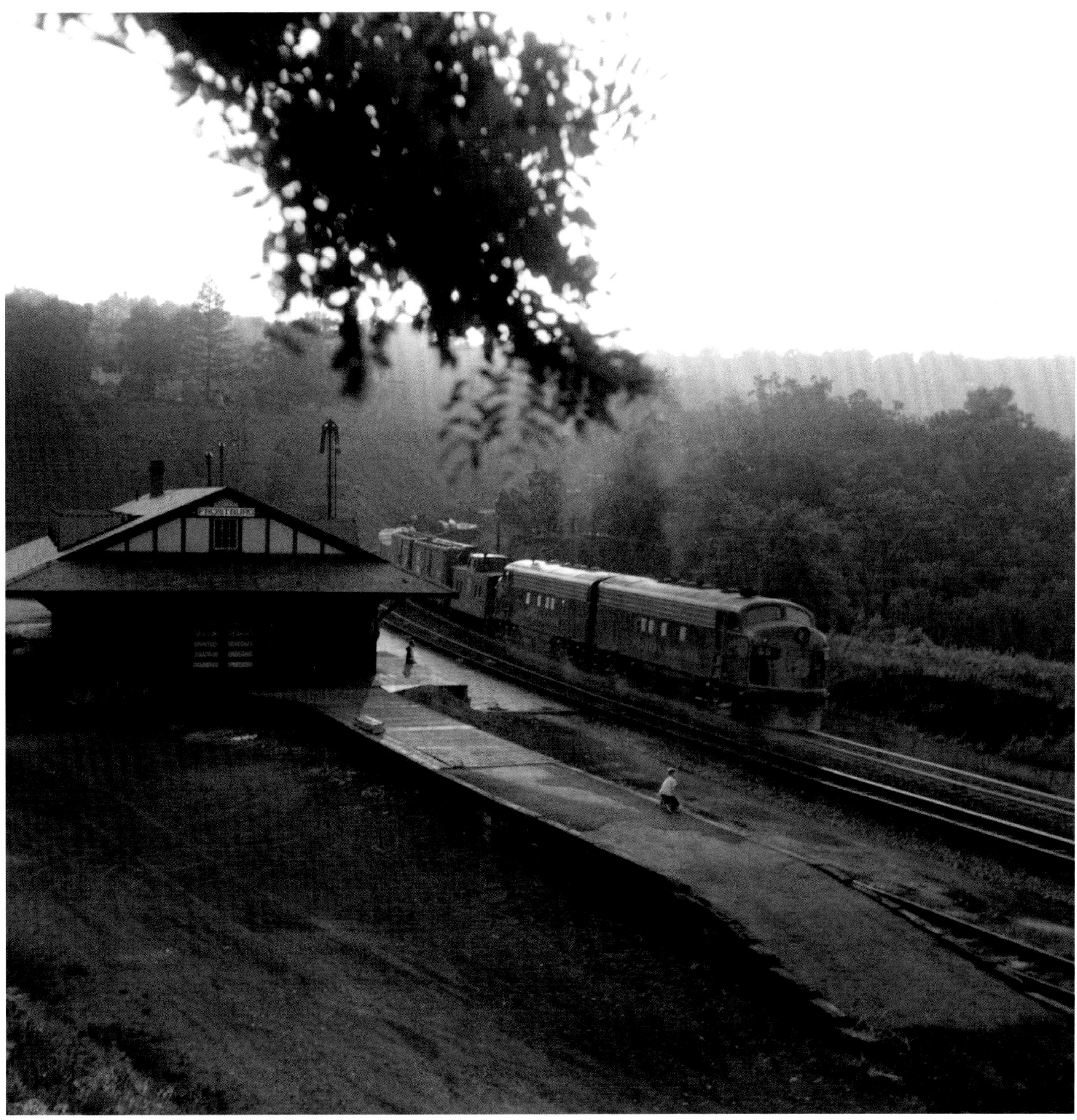

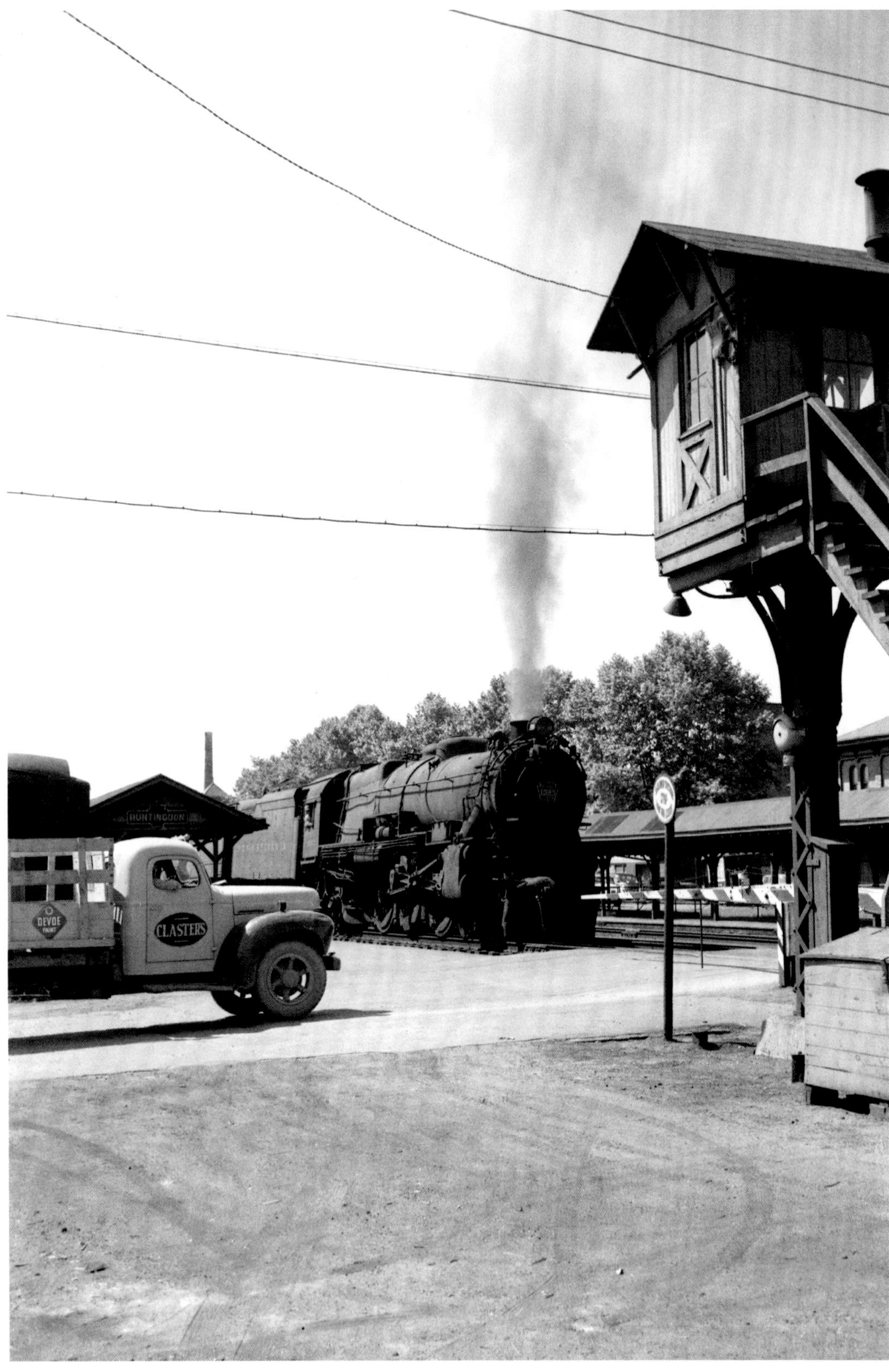

Plate 67. A "Clasters" truck waits at the crossing gates, below a crossing tower, for a Pennsylvania Railroad Harrisburg, Pennsylvania–bound local led by K4s type 1983. The Huntingdon, Pennsylvania, station is in the background. June 1952.

Courtesy of California State Railroad Museum. Philip Ross Hastings, MD, Collection, [Negative 3856].

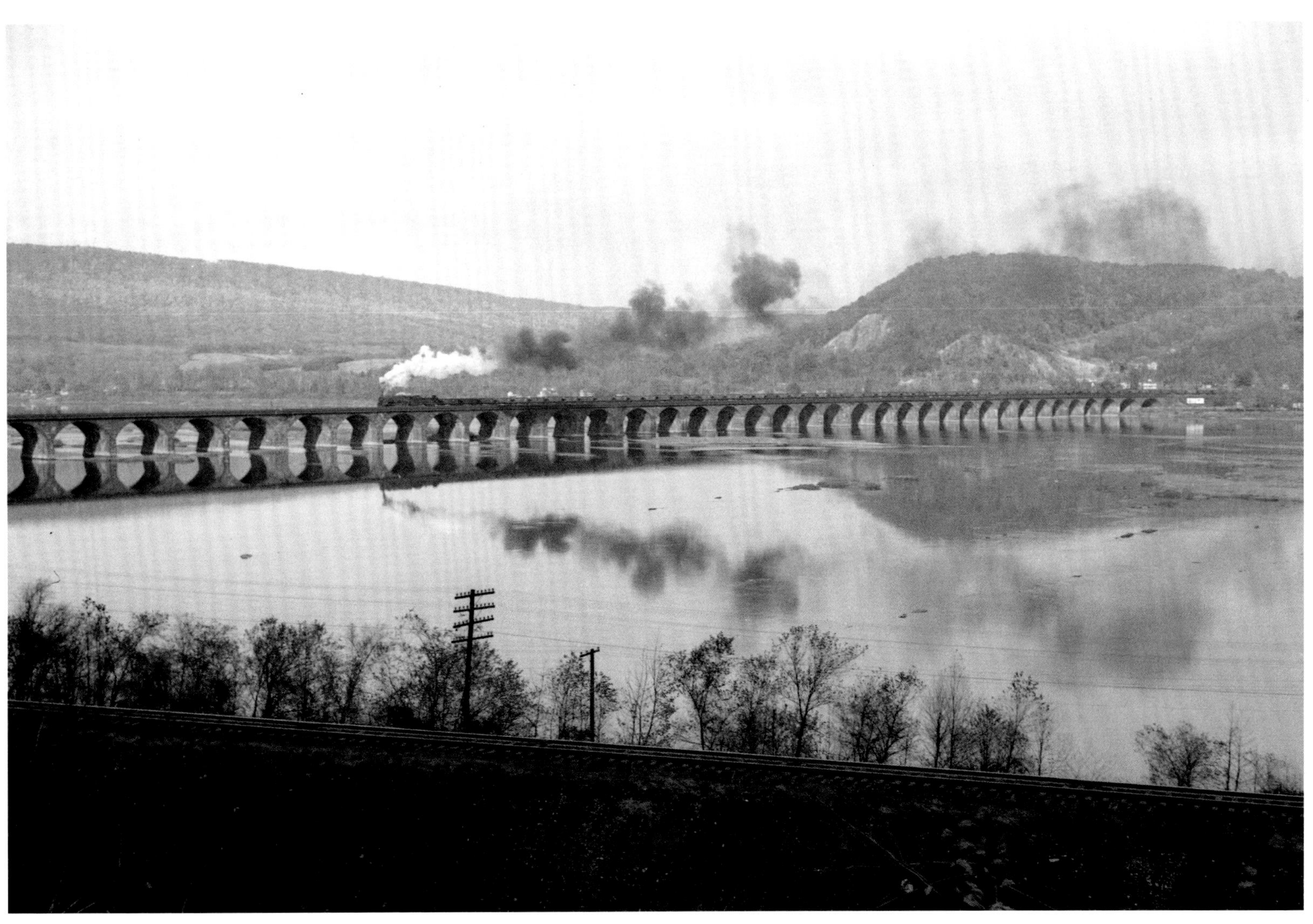

Plate 68. A westbound train of empty hoppers crosses the Pennsylvania Railroad's noted Rockville Bridge on its way back to the coal mines. Rockville Bridge crosses the Susquehanna River near Harrisburg, Pennsylvania.

Courtesy of California State Railroad Museum. Philip Ross Hastings, MD, Collection, [Negative 6510].

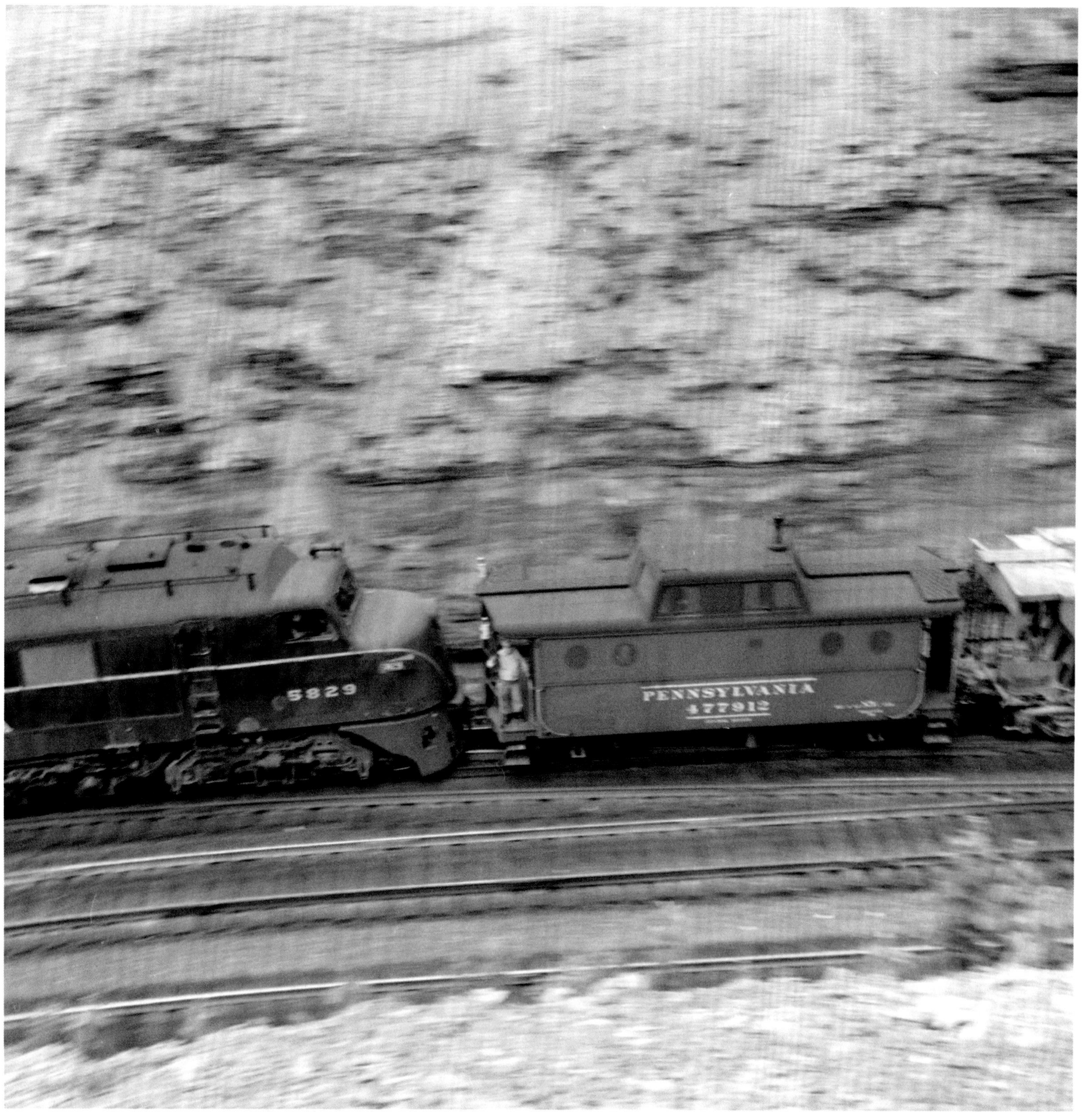
5829
PENNSYLVANIA
477912

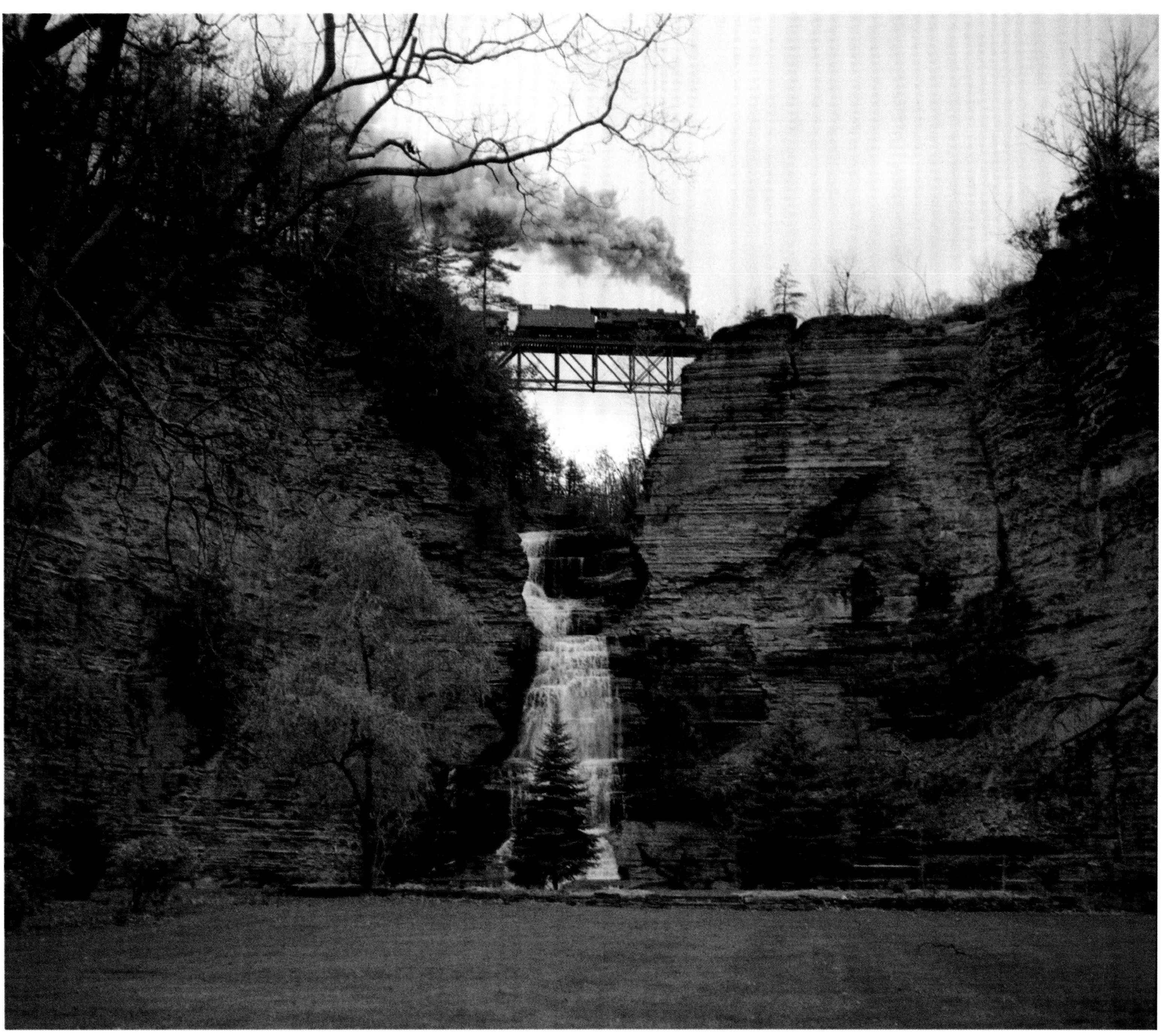

***Facing,* Plate 69.** Hastings was a master of the pan shot. In this image, he captures Pennsylvania Railroad Baldwin "Centipede" 5829 pushing on the end of a freight. Just ahead of the Baldwin is Pennsylvania Railroad World War II–era cabin car (caboose) 477912.

Courtesy of California State Railroad Museum. Philip Ross Hastings, MD, Collection, [Negative 4023].

Plate 70. In one of his most notable and creative photos, Hastings caught a Pennsylvania "Decapod" crossing Rock Stream, in New York. The engine leads a northbound coal train heading for Sodus Point, New York.

Courtesy of California State Railroad Museum. Philip Ross Hastings, MD, Collection, [Negative 3865].

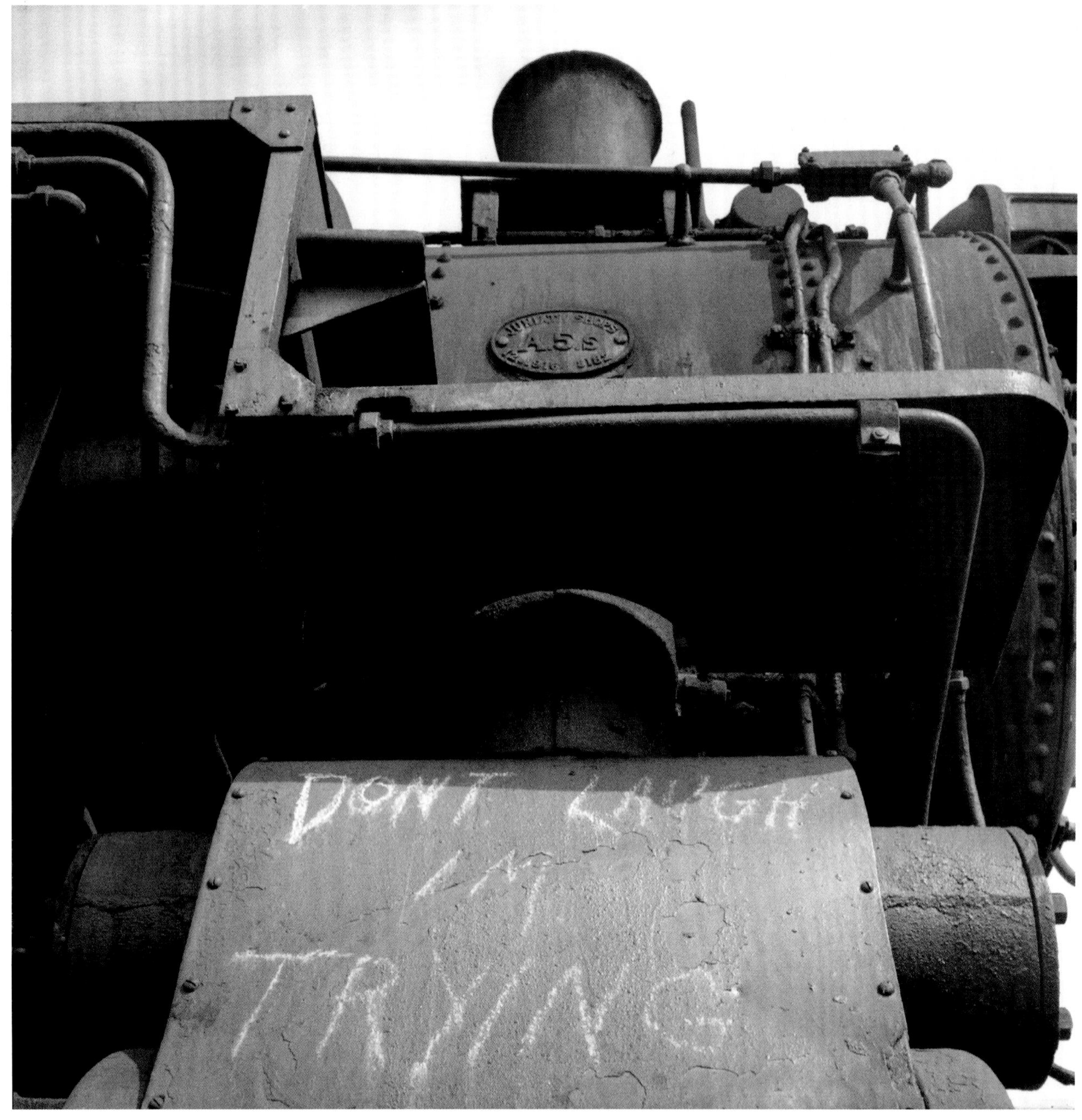

Plate 71. "DONT LAUGH IM TRYING." Chalked graffiti on a Pennsylvania Railroad A5s type 0-4-0 switcher built by the railroad at its Juniata Shops. Here, it is operating on the Pennsylvania-Reading Seashore Lines. One A5s is preserved at the Railroad Museum of Pennsylvania.

Courtesy of California State Railroad Museum. Philip Ross Hastings, MD, Collection, [Negative 9848].

***Facing,* Plate 72.** A Pennsylvania-Reading Seashore Lines trainman, probably an engineer, chomps on his cigar and checks the time as he waits by his engine. The location is Tuckahoe, New Jersey; the locomotive in the background is the "Lindbergh Special" engine, E6 "Atlantic" 460, which survives at the Railroad Museum of Pennsylvania. Hastings's portraits excel in their depiction of railroaders at the end of the age of steam.

Courtesy of California State Railroad Museum. Philip Ross Hastings, MD, Collection, [Negative 9831].

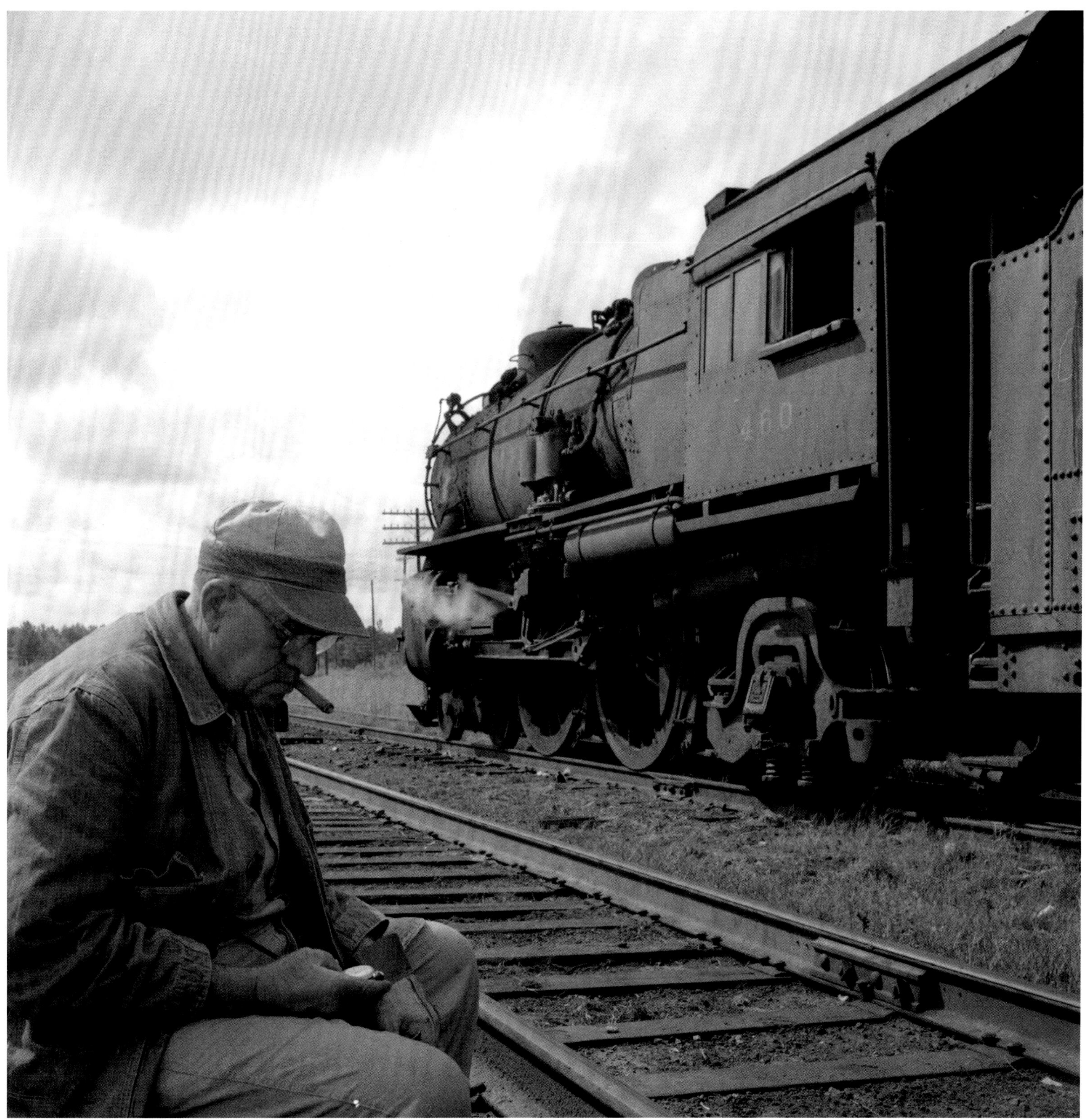
460

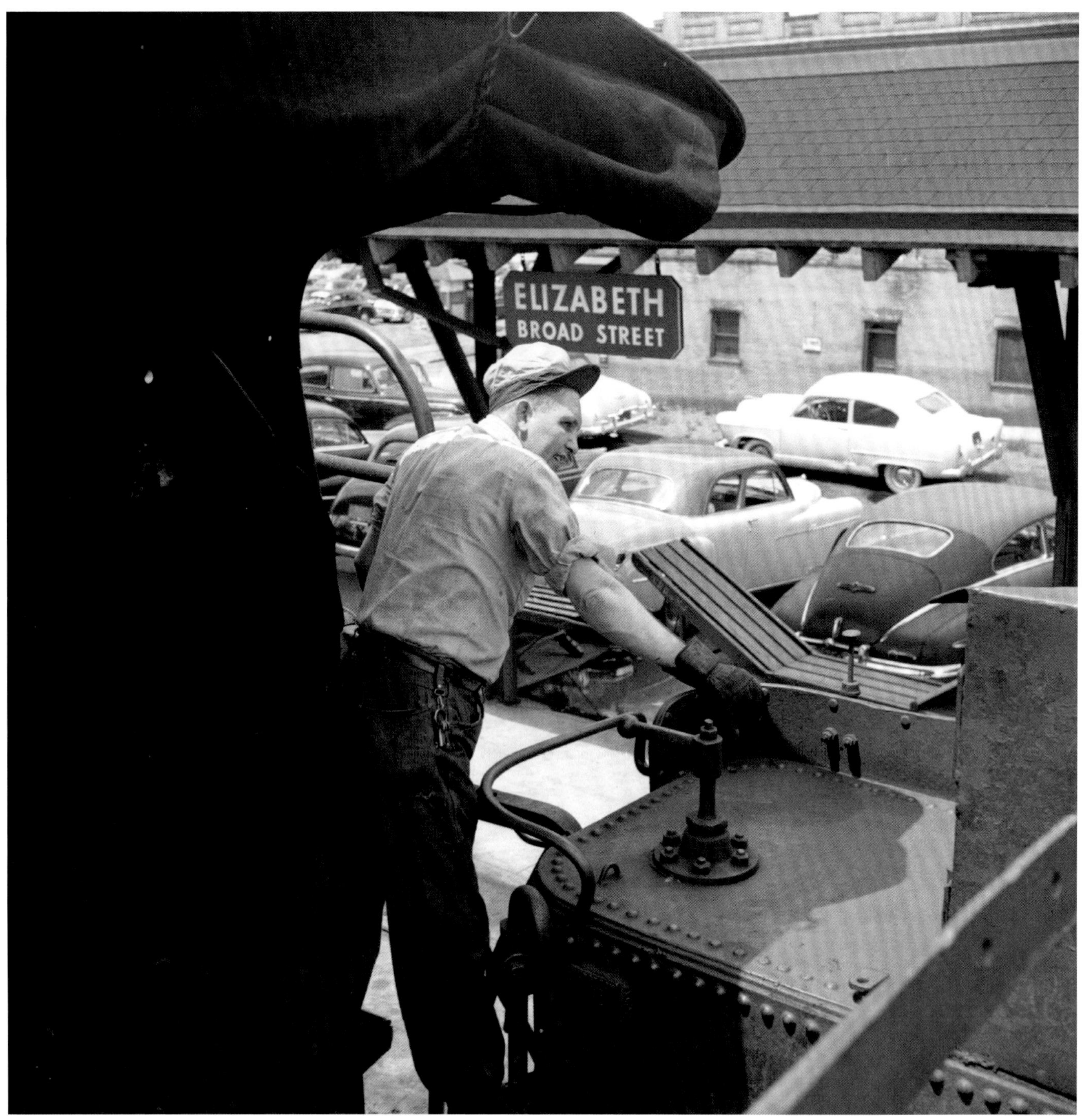

Plate 73. Jersey Central (Central Railroad of New Jersey) fireman Frank Ballinger, in the rear cab of a "Camelback" (center-cab) locomotive, waiting for the highball. The location is Elizabeth, New Jersey.

Courtesy of California State Railroad Museum. Philip Ross Hastings, MD, Collection, [Negative 10494].

***Facing,* Plate 74.** Here, Hastings gives us a view of the engineer's cab, and the engineer, of Jersey Central "Camelback" 754 at Dunellen, New Jersey. A period truck crosses the tracks through a crossing gate in the background.

Courtesy of California State Railroad Museum. Philip Ross Hastings, MD, Collection, [Negative 2735].

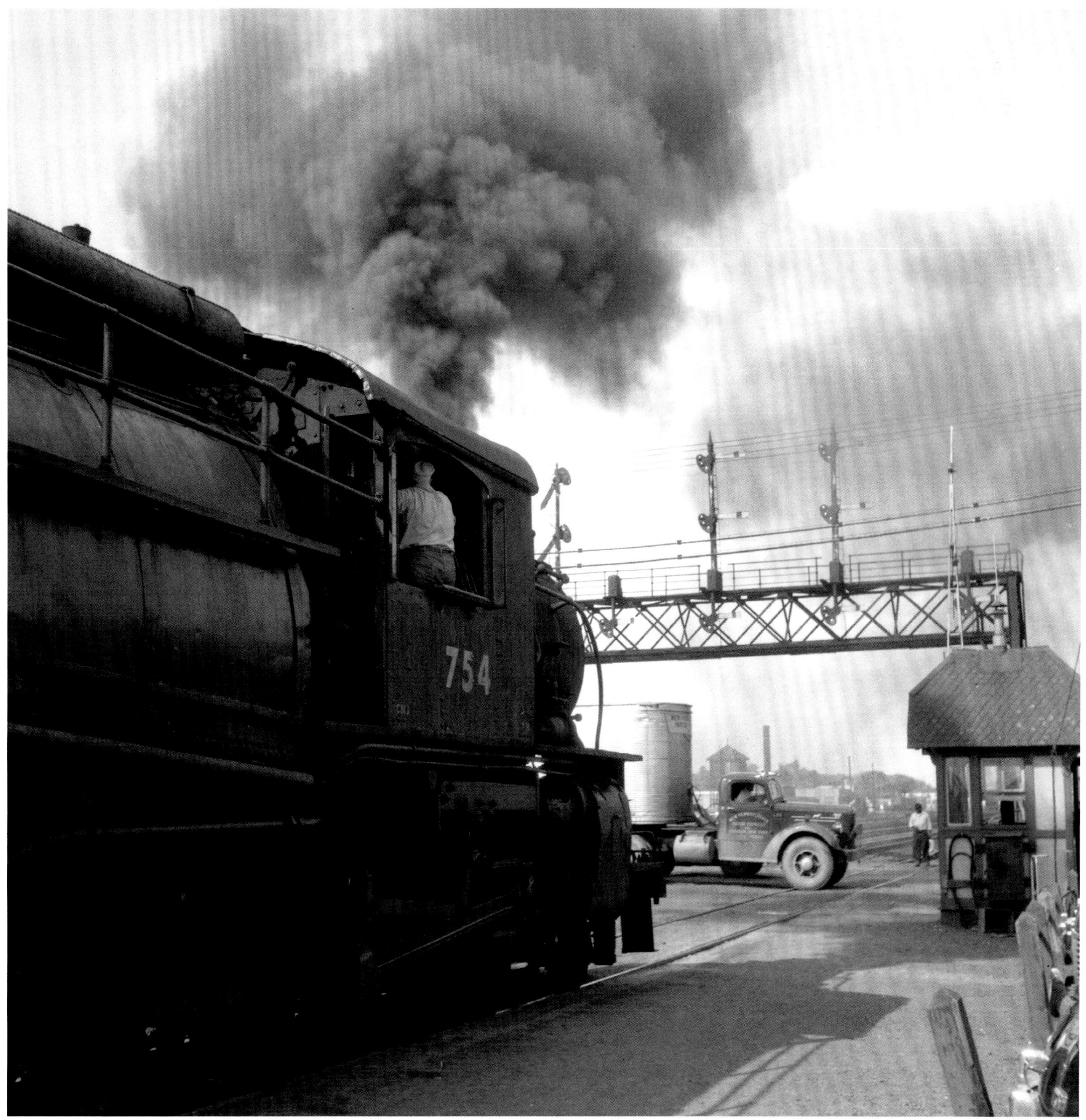
754

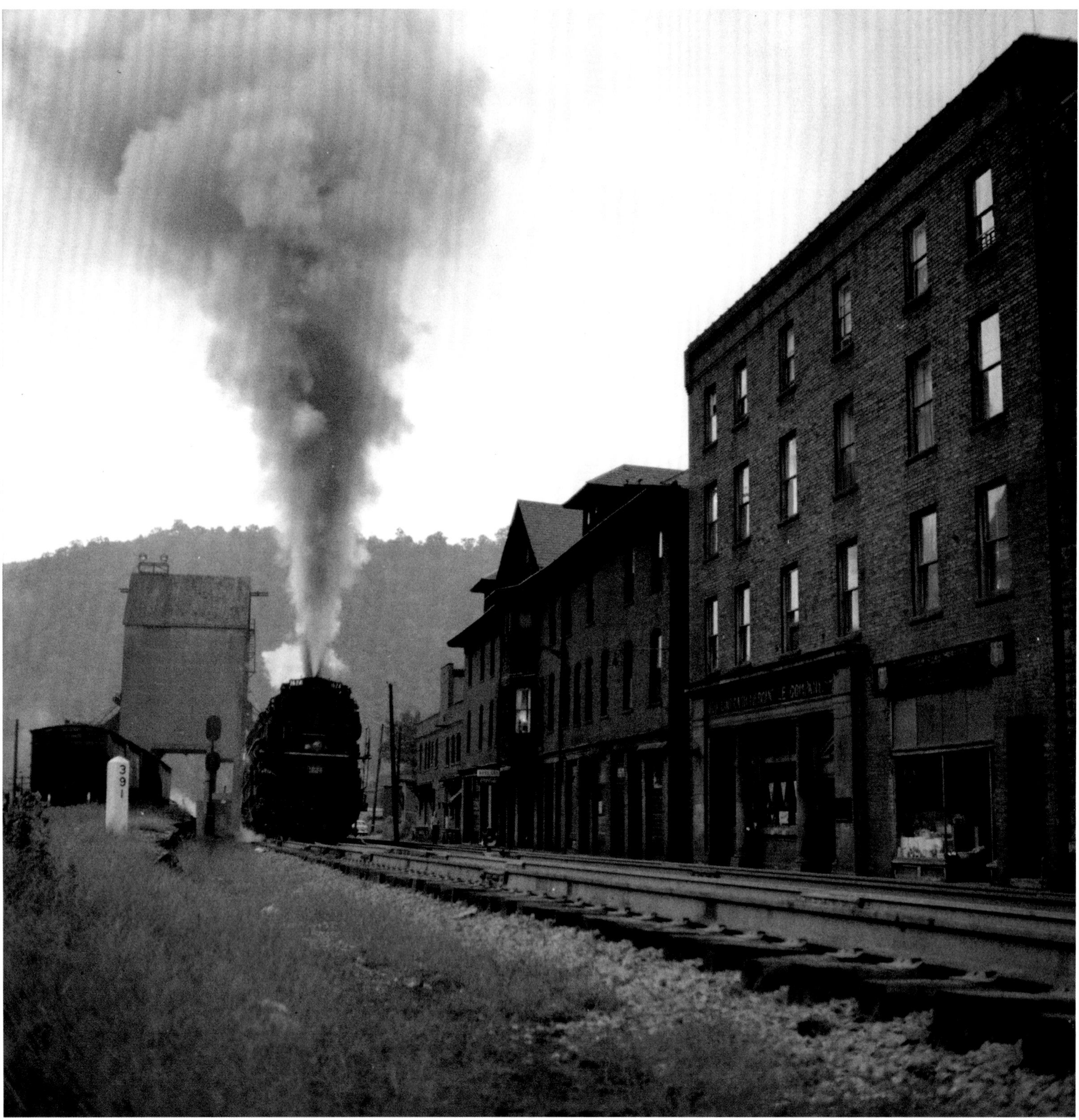
391

***Facing,* Plate 75.**
Chesapeake & Ohio 2-6-6-6 1624 passes one of America's most notable railroad photo locations, the storefronts along the C&O in Thurmond, West Virginia. The 1624 is pulling train Extra 1624 East. Hastings took this shot on a "Steam in Indian Summer" steam safari with David P. Morgan.

Courtesy of California State Railroad Museum. Philip Ross Hastings, MD, Collection, [Negative 2748].

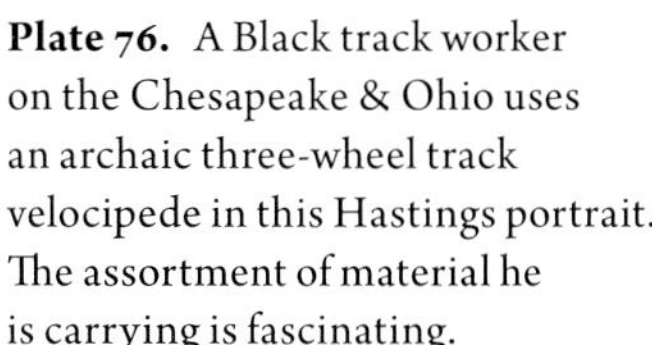

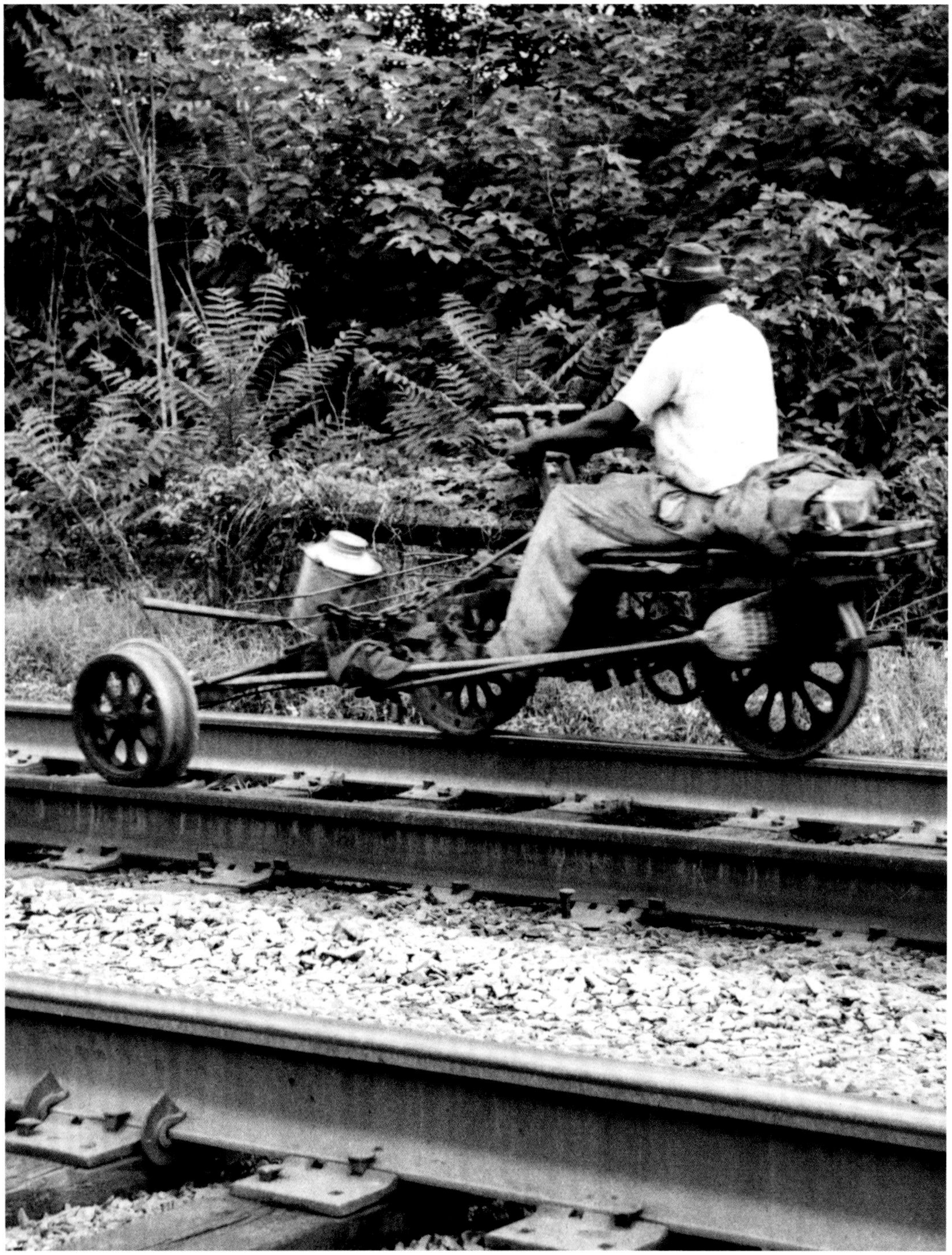

Plate 76. A Black track worker on the Chesapeake & Ohio uses an archaic three-wheel track velocipede in this Hastings portrait. The assortment of material he is carrying is fascinating.

Courtesy of California State Railroad Museum. Philip Ross Hastings, MD, Collection, [Negative 4063].

PORTFOLIO SIX

MIDWEST

In 1959, Phil Hastings's career took him to Waterloo, Iowa. He was to spend the rest of his life in this midwestern town, and he was soon busy with a family of five and his psychiatric practice. He also spent a great deal of his railroad-related time at the Mid-Continent Railway Historical Society in North Freedom, Wisconsin. His photographic work was relatively sparse for a number of years but, in the late 1960s, he began to document the vanishing secondary passenger trains of the Midwest—work that appeared as a series of articles in *Passenger Train Journal* in the 1970s.[1] For all of these reasons, the bulk of Hastings's later work focuses on the railroads of the Midwest, as does some of his 1950s photography. The Chicago Great Western Railway (CGW) and the Chicago, Rock Island and Pacific Railway (Rock Island or Rock Island Line) were among Hastings's favorite subjects during the later years of his life. This reflects his long residency in Waterloo, Iowa, which was served by the CGW, the Rock Island, the Illinois Central Railroad, and a short line, the Waterloo, Cedar Falls and Northern Railway.

This portfolio of Hastings's midwestern work begins with a steam-era photo, plate 77, showing an interesting rail-level view on the Nickel Plate in central Illinois.[2] Plate 78 follows and depicts the "Main Line of Mid-America," the Illinois Central (IC). In the photo, the IC's 2520 blackens the sky past a classic grain elevator.

Plates 79–81 are a condensed photo essay depicting "the Mohawk that refused to abdicate"—the locomotive that provided the title for Hastings's (and David P. Morgan's) best-known book. In the first plate, New York Central Railroad engineer John Hitchko impatiently awaits the highball in Galion, Ohio. He is pulling a "junk train," and his engine looks tired and worn, but it is a famed New York Central "Mohawk." Hitchko's train pulled a drawbar (broke in two) soon after leaving Galion and tied up one of the two tracks of this New York Central main line. Plate 80, taken thirteen miles away on the same New York Central main line in Shelby, Ohio, shows a diesel-powered New York Central train passing the signal tower in Shelby.

But where was Hitchko, "Mohawk" 3005, and their train? Hitchko told Morgan he'd make at least sixty miles an hour through Ohio that day. As Hastings, Morgan, and the operator in the tower waited, smoke appeared in the distance and the wail of a fast-moving train was heard. All present assumed it was a fast passenger train. Then, in plate 81, perhaps Hastings's best-known image, Hitchko drives 3005 by the tower, leading a train of empties, gondolas full of scrap, and bad-order (damaged) cars through Shelby in a banging, crashing cacophony. The image—see the dust trailing the train—captures it all.

Plates 82–84 form another midwestern portfolio, this one focusing on the then surviving Wabash Railroad "Moguls." An extended portfolio of these Hastings images has been published twice before, as "The quaint and the quiet" in *The Mohawk That Refused to Abdicate, and Other Tales* and "Mogul Suite" in Lucius Beebe and Charles Clegg's *The Age of Steam*. Plate 82 shows an elderly engineer, bearing the badges of his trade, oiling an equally elderly Wabash "Mogul" in Bluffs, Illinois. The light "Moguls" were used on this Wabash branch from Bluffs, Illinois, to Keokuk, Iowa, due to loading limits on the line's bridge across the Illinois River at Meredosia, Illinois. Plate 83 shows a "Mogul" doubleheader, with Wabash engines 573 and 576, crossing a trestle on this branch. Plate 84 shows "Mogul" 576 at the water tank in Meredosia. Hastings took this shot from the bridge there, allowing him to frame the locomotive within the first truss.

The Soo Line—the Minneapolis, St. Paul and Sault Ste. Marie Railroad, a Canadian Pacific subsidiary—has not received the photographic coverage accorded to its midwestern peers. In this view, plate 85, Hastings shows track workers working on a switch in front of Soo Line 2702 and the railroad's station in Duluth, Minnesota.[3]

Waterloo, Iowa, Hastings's adopted home beginning in 1959, was a major railroad center at the time. One of the railroads serving Waterloo was the CGW. Hastings took a number of significant images of the line, resulting in the book *Chicago Great Western Railway: Iowa in the Merger Decade*. These images are diesel-era photos taken about a decade after Hastings's work with David P. Morgan. Plates 86–88 depict the CGW, including a train at Cedar Falls Junction, Iowa; RS-2 56 at Tripoli, Iowa; and a well-bundled trainman with his train at Waterloo's Highland Yard. The CGW was merged into the Chicago and North Western in 1968.

The Rock Island—the Chicago, Rock Island & Pacific—also served Waterloo. Hastings's diesel-era photos of the Rock Island also resulted in a book, *Remember the Rock*. Plates 89–91 represent Hastings's views of the Rock Island Line. They include a section gang with their speeder at Malcolm, Iowa; the depot at Walker, Iowa; and a portrait of agent-operator Earl C. Berry adjusting train-order hoops at Marengo, Iowa. The run-down Rock Island depot and right-of-way in plate 90 show the condition of the railroad, which was liquidated from bankruptcy in 1980.

Finally, in this midwestern survey, plates 92 and 93 represent the Chicago and North Western Railway (C&NW). Plate 92 is a close-up of workers laboring over the trailing truck journal of C&NW 395. Plate 93, a fitting farewell to the Midwest before the era of great railroad mergers, shows the "Way Bills" box at the C&NW depot in Mercer, Wisconsin—a late Hastings view taken in 1981. The Union Pacific, one of today's "big six" Canada and US railroads, acquired the C&NW in 1995.

***Facing,* Plate 77.** As in plate 60, Hastings went to rail level to capture a Nickel Plate (New York, Chicago & St. Louis Railroad) locomotive framed by a rail on the lower left. Two railroaders wait in the background. The location is Illinois.

Courtesy of California State Railroad Museum. Philip Ross Hastings, MD, Collection, [Negative 9806].

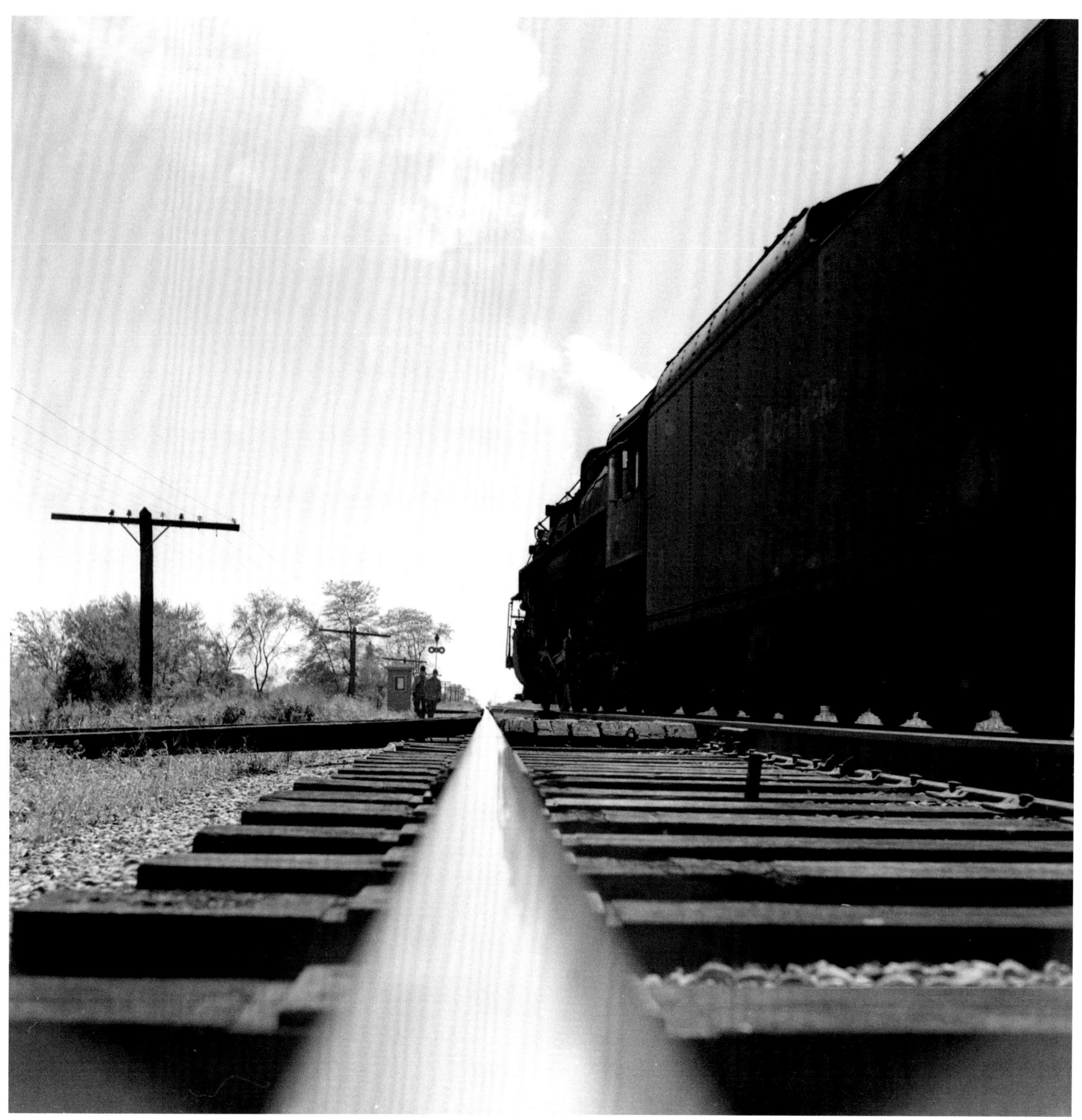

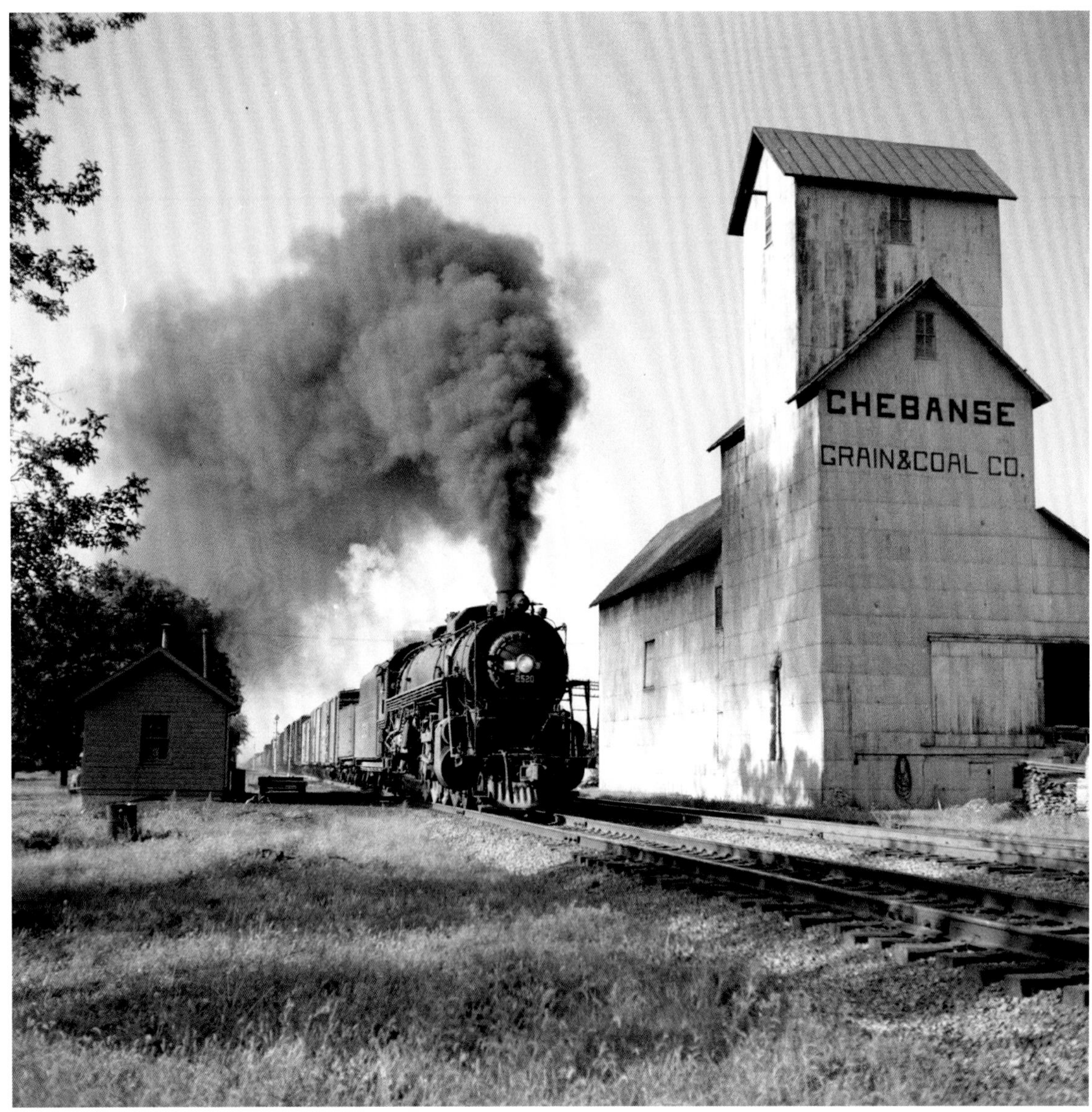

Plate 78. Illinois Central "Mountain" 2520 passes the Chebanse Grain & Coal Co. in Chebanse, Illinois. Hastings often used unusual trackside buildings—many with engaging names—as framing points in his images.

Courtesy of California State Railroad Museum. Philip Ross Hastings, MD, Collection, [Negative 10498].

***Facing,* Plate 79.** A photo essay called *The Mohawk That Refused to Abdicate, and Other Tales,* from which the title of the Morgan and Hastings book is drawn, contains what is arguably Hastings's best-known image. Plates 79–81 are an abbreviated version of this photo essay. Here, New York Central engineer John Hitchko waits, impatience showing in his features, in the cab of his engine, powerful "Mohawk" 3005. The location is Galion, Ohio; the date is September 1955. The "Mohawk" has been downgraded from passenger service to pulling what Morgan called "dead freight." Morgan asked Hitchko what he'd be able to do with this train and he replied, "Sixty" [miles per hour]. Hastings and Morgan were incredulous. Soon after leaving Galion, this train, Extra 3005 East, was delayed by a pulled drawbar.

Courtesy of California State Railroad Museum. Philip Ross Hastings, MD, Collection, [Negative 10500].

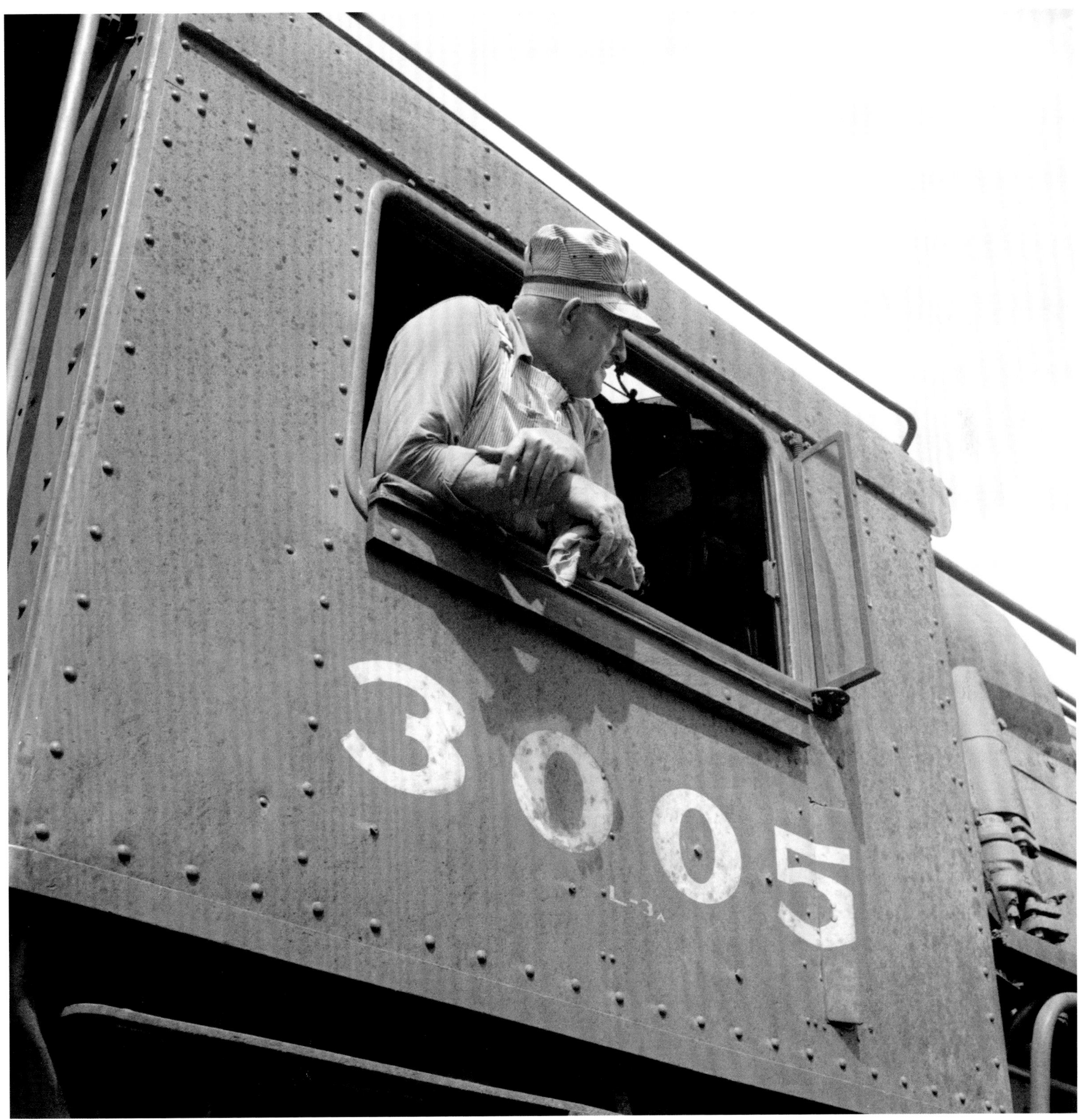
3005
L-3A

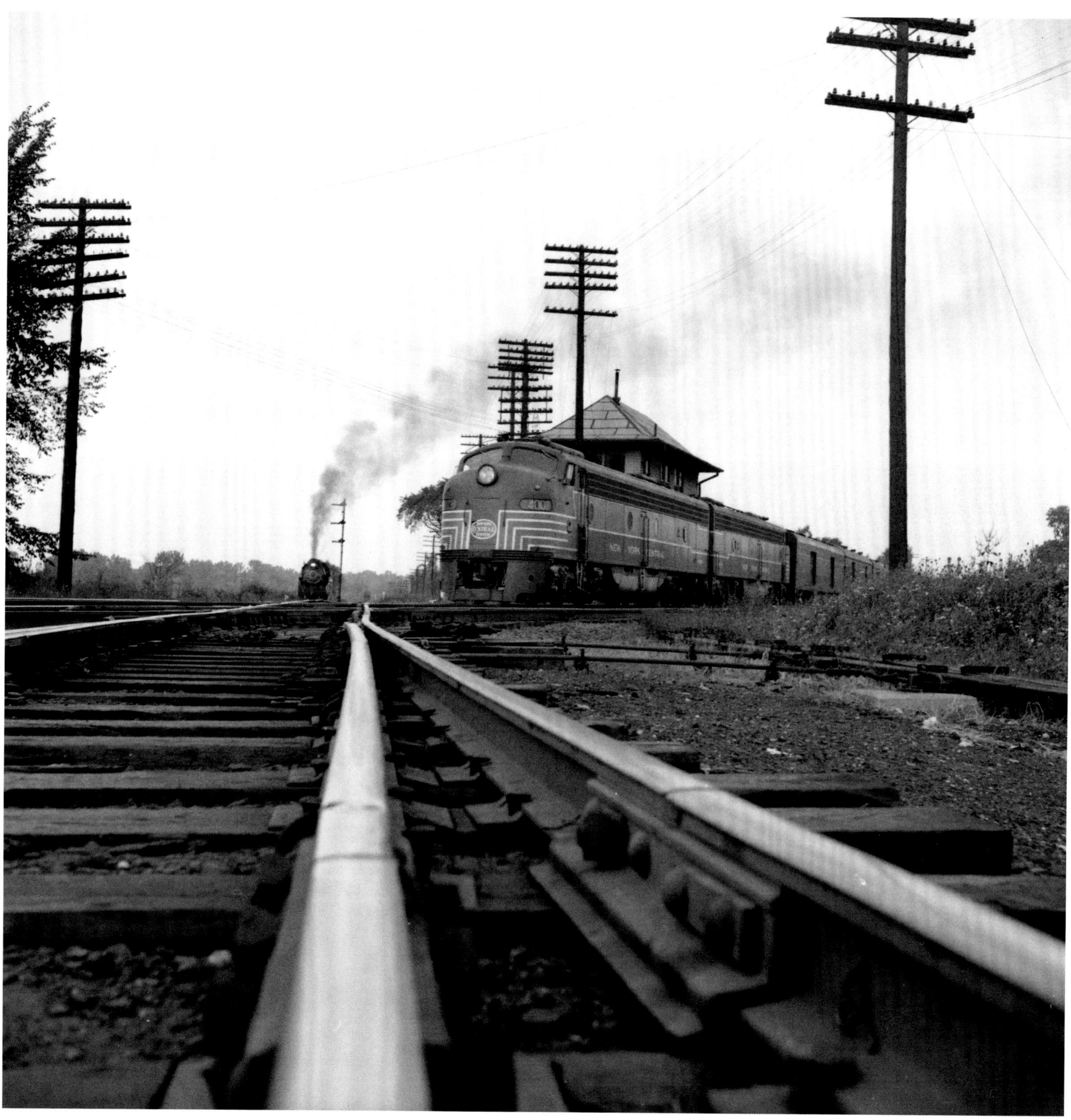

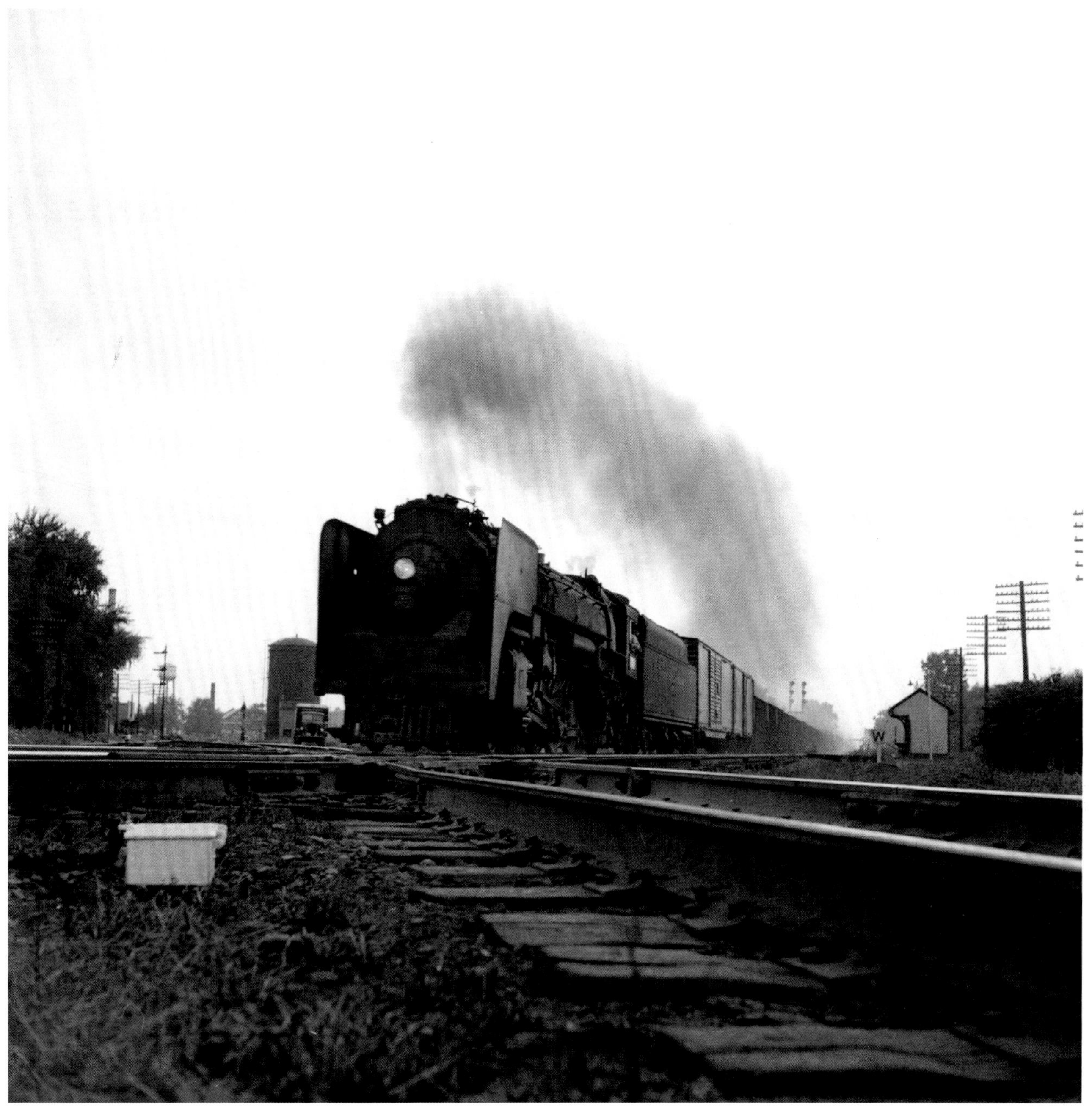

***Facing,* Plate 80.** Hastings and Morgan drove from Galion to Shelby, Ohio, where the New York Central main crossed a Baltimore & Ohio branch line. In this image, a passenger train led by a New York Central pair of E-8s slams across the diamond at Shelby Tower. Meanwhile, the New York Central dispatcher—this was before train crews commonly used radios—didn't know the exact location of Extra 3005 East.

Courtesy of California State Railroad Museum. Philip Ross Hastings, MD, Collection, [Negative 4095].

Plate 81. A smudge of smoke and the blast of a whistle allowed Hastings to set up for one of his outstanding images. Under a plume of black smoke, and trailing dust that testifies to its speed, engineer Hitchko takes 3005 and his train across the Shelby diamond at sixty miles an hour. The ninety-eight cars behind him, many of them destined for the scrapper, rattled and rocked as they passed Hastings and Morgan.

Courtesy of California State Railroad Museum. Philip Ross Hastings, MD, Collection, [Negative 1761].

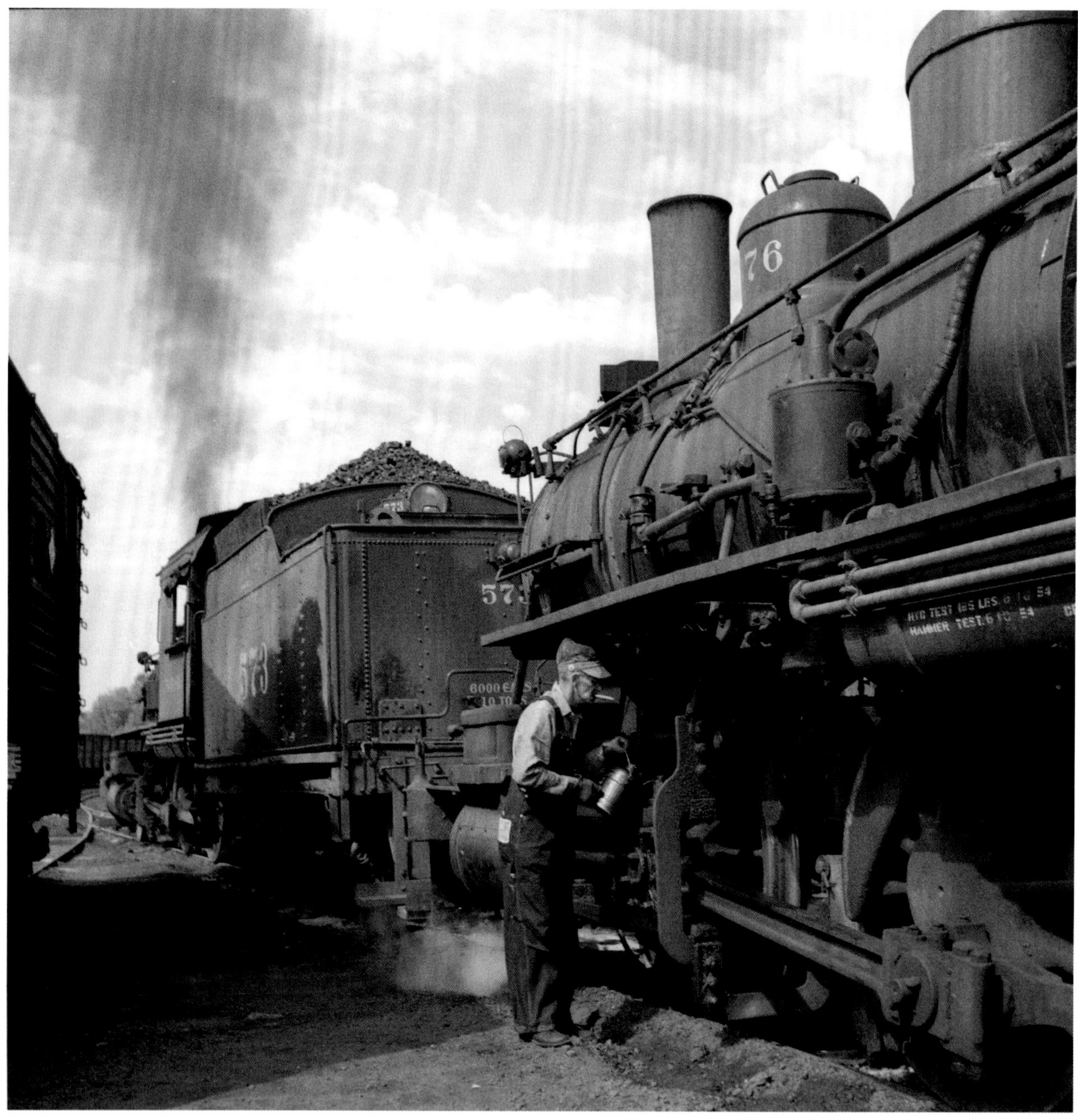

Plate 82. Plates 82–84 are also an abbreviated photo essay, this one focusing on the ancient Wabash "Moguls," which served the railroad's branch from Bluffs, Illinois, to Keokuk, Iowa. A bridge with a light load limit across the Illinois River at Meredosia, Illinois, extended the working life of these small engines. In this photo, an elderly engineer—with the ever-present billed cap—oils up "Mogul" 576, which is double-headed with "Mogul" 573. The location is Bluffs, Illinois; the year is 1954.

Courtesy of California State Railroad Museum. Philip Ross Hastings, MD, Collection, [Negative 3741].

***Facing,* Plate 83.** In this image, the "Mogul" double-header is silhouetted on a trestle.

Courtesy of California State Railroad Museum. Philip Ross Hastings, MD, Collection, [Negative 3721].

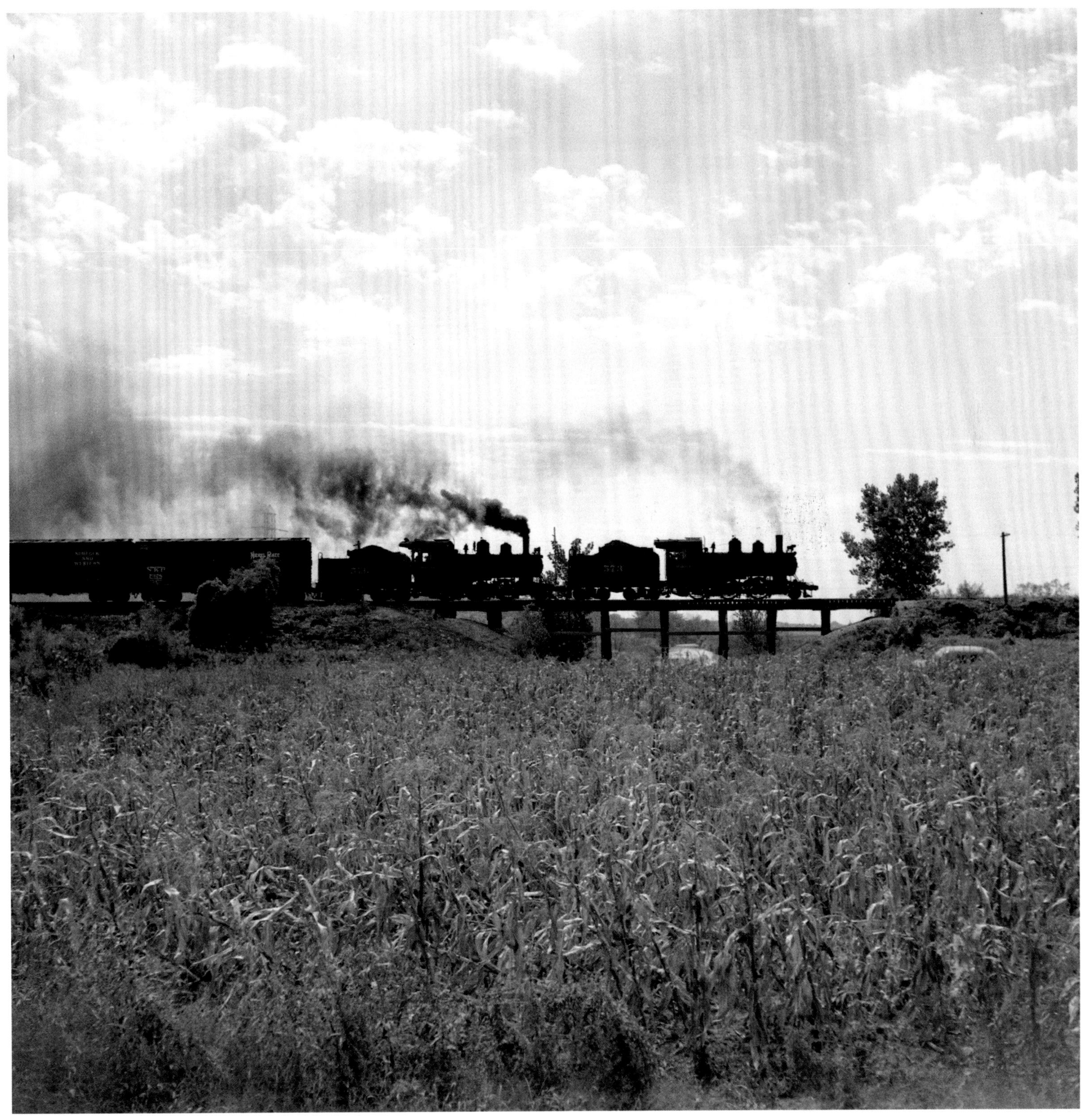

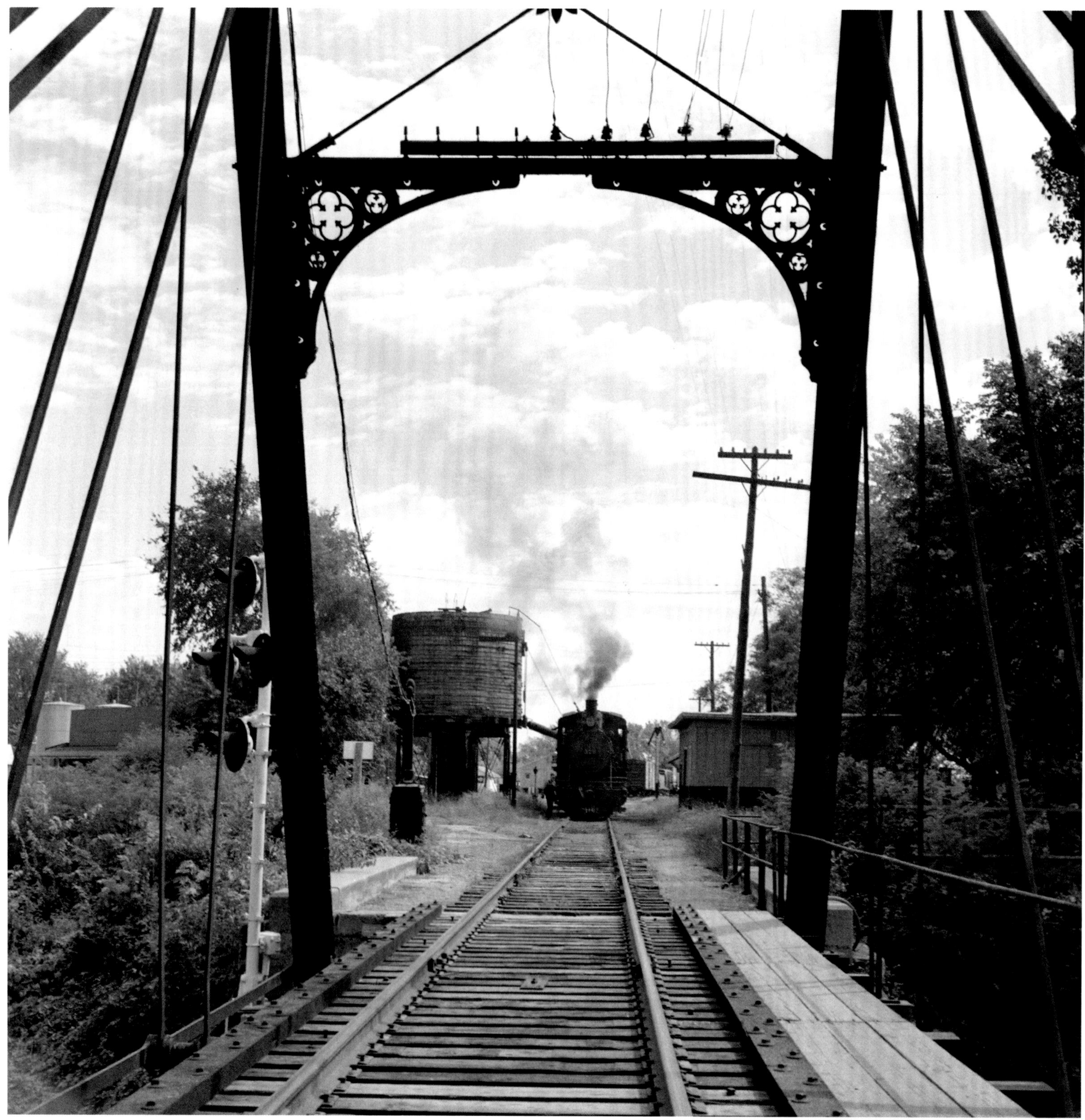

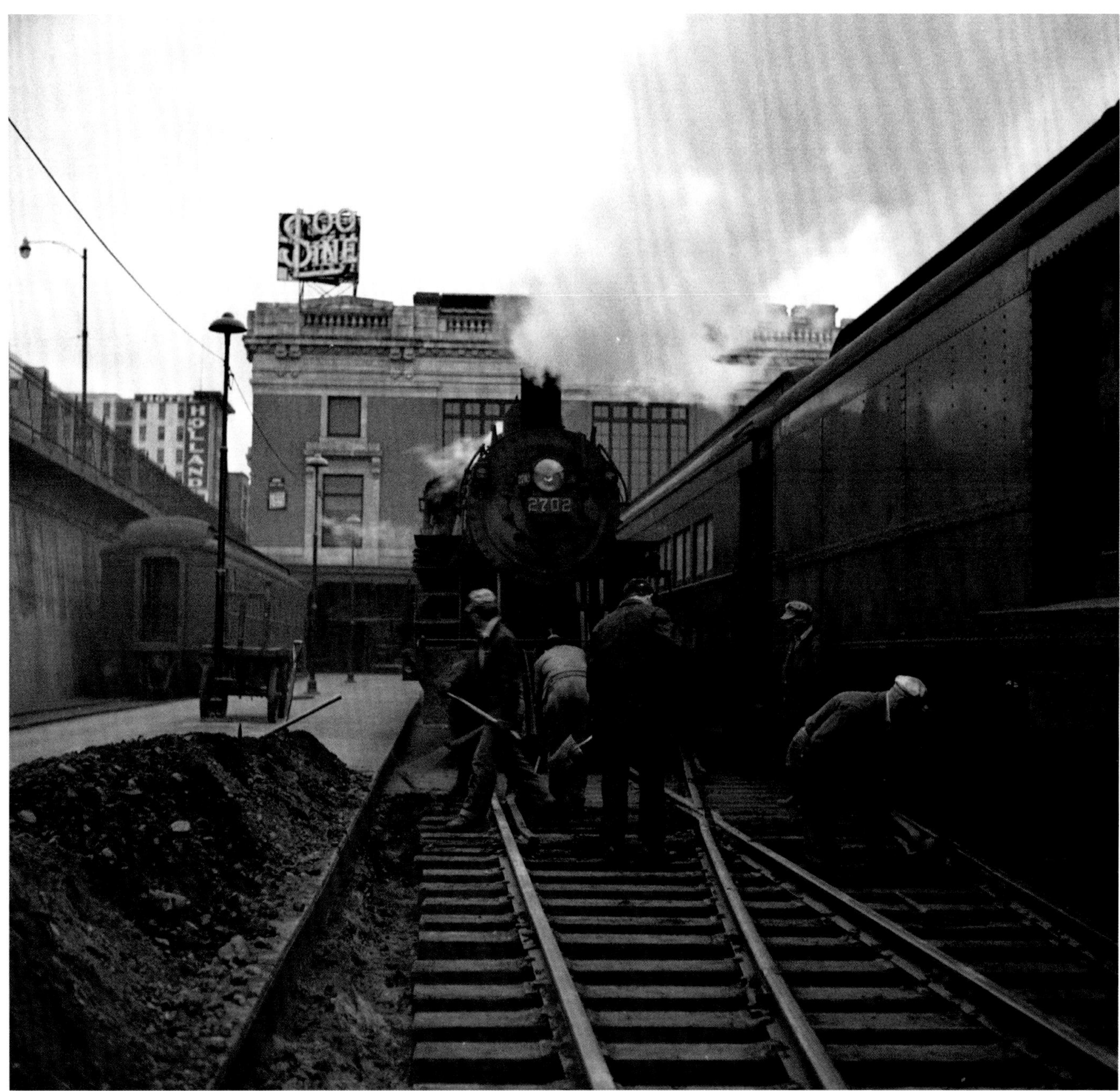

***Facing,* Plate 84.** Here, one of the "Moguls" takes on water, framed by the bridge at Meredosia, Illinois, in 1954. Versions of the Wabash "Mogul" photo essay may be found in Lucius Beebe and Charles Clegg's *The Age of Steam* and in *The Mohawk That Refused to Abdicate, and Other Tales.*

Courtesy of California State Railroad Museum. Philip Ross Hastings, MD, Collection, [Negative 3725].

Plate 85. Images of track workers from the age of steam in America are relatively scarce. In this Soo Line (Minneapolis, St. Paul and Sault Ste. Marie Railroad) image, Hastings shows track workers laboring in front of Soo Line "Pacific" 2702. The image was taken on September 14, 1954. Hastings did not note this location, but it appears to be the station in Duluth, Minnesota.

Courtesy of California State Railroad Museum. Philip Ross Hastings, MD, Collection, [Negative 4058].

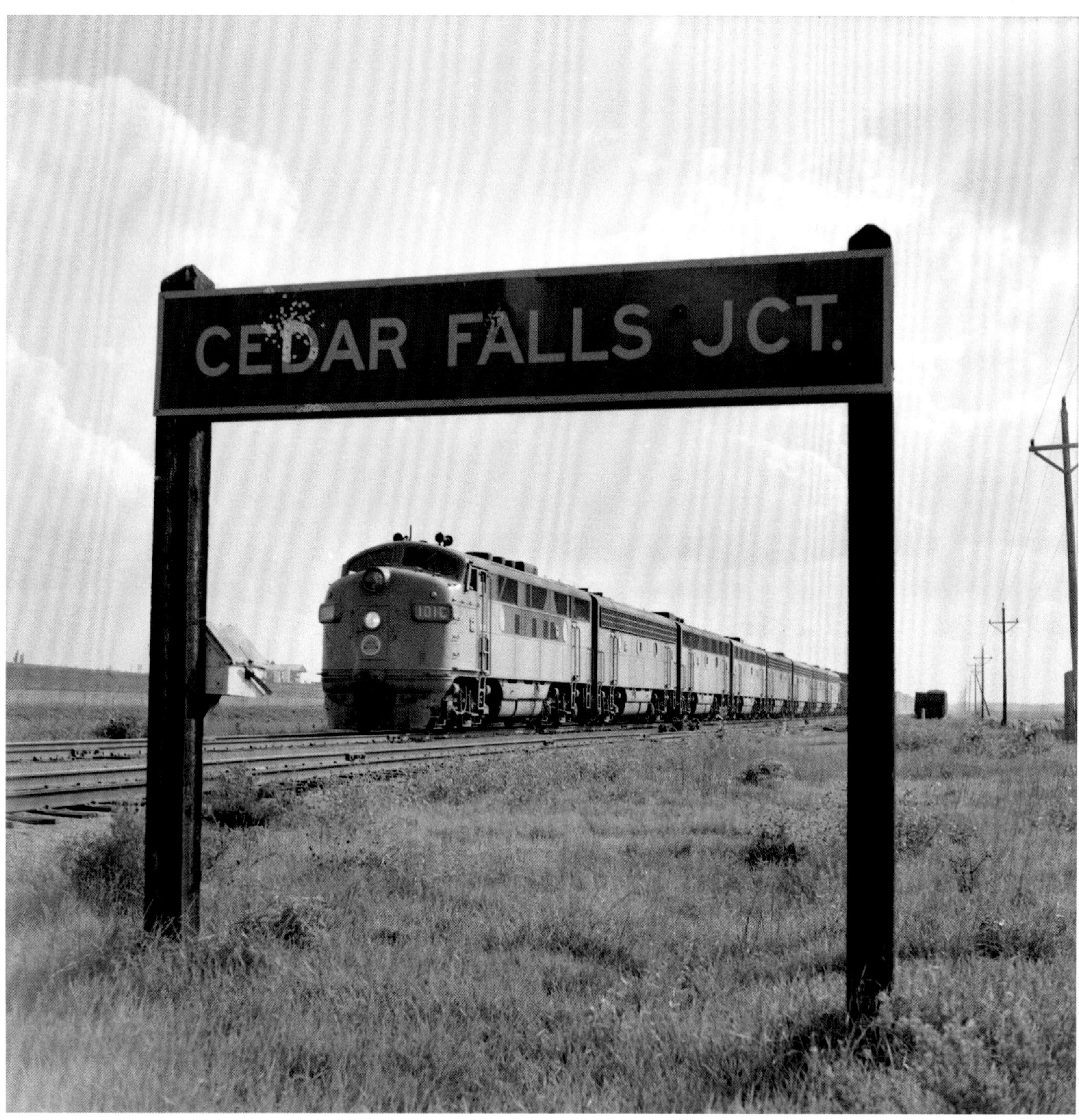

Plate 86. Chicago Great Western F-3A 101C and a string of diesel units is framed under a railroad station sign for Cedar Falls Junction, Iowa. Hastings, like O. Winston Link, sometimes used station signs of this type to frame locomotives and trains.

Courtesy of California State Railroad Museum. Philip Ross Hastings, MD, Collection, [Negative 3093].

***Facing*, Plate 87.** Chicago Great Western RS-2 56 with a train. The decrepit Tripoli, Iowa, depot provides an apt background. May 28, 1967.

Courtesy of California State Railroad Museum. Philip Ross Hastings, MD, Collection, [Negative 3061].

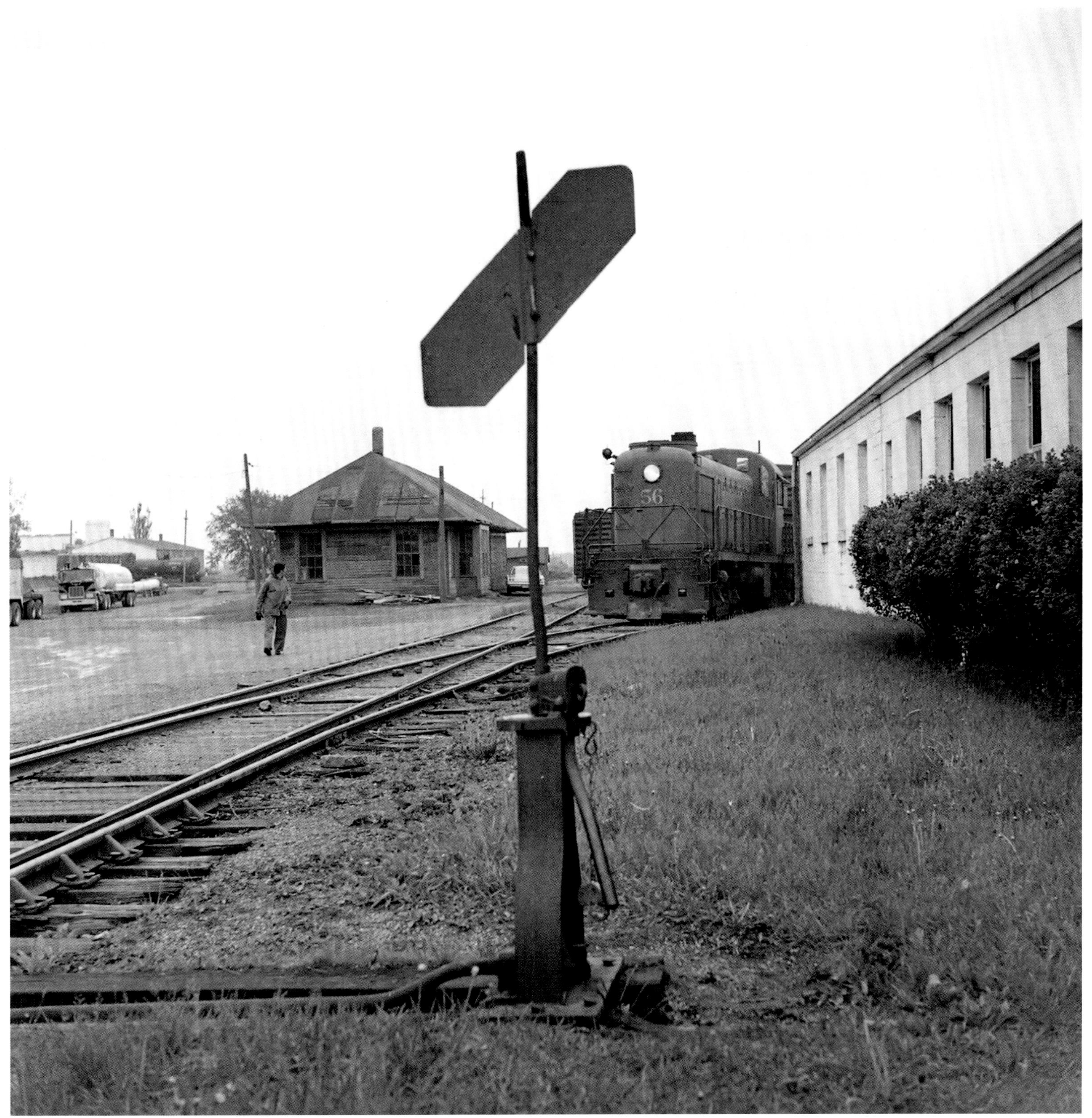
56

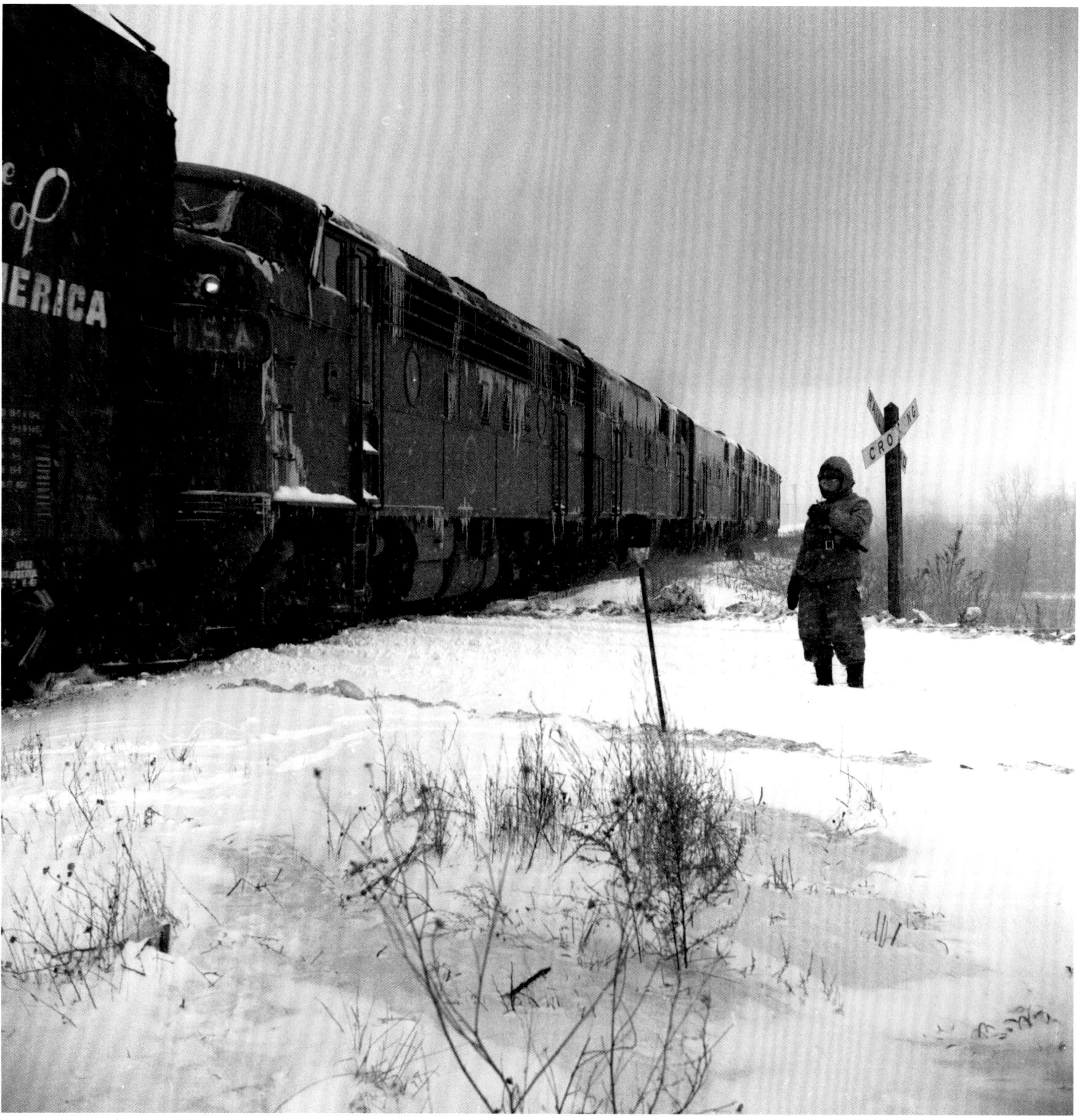
of
ERICA
CRO

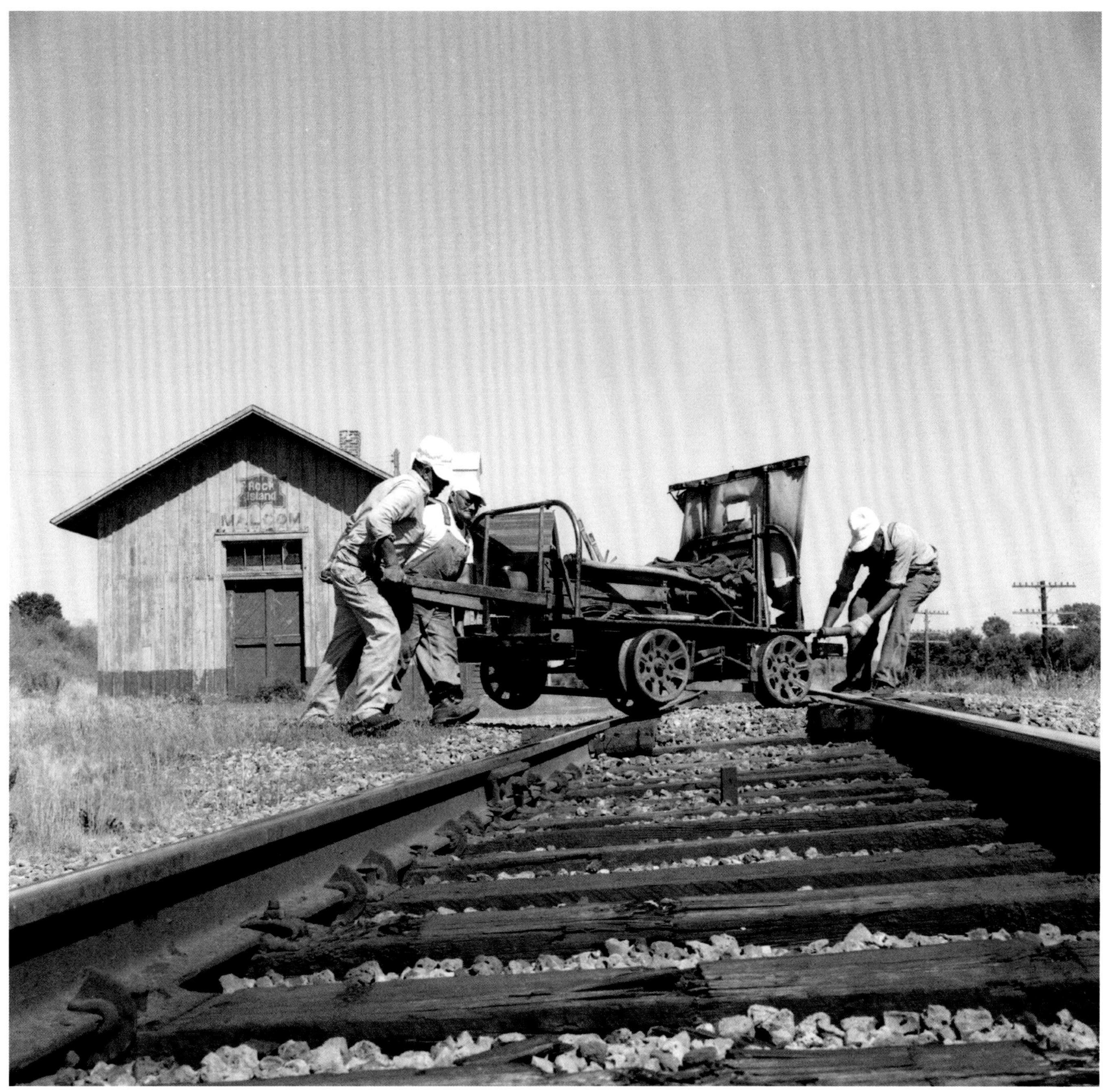

***Facing,* Plate 88.** In an image that suggests frigid cold, a bundled-up Chicago Great Western trainman talks the engineer of his train, Extra 161, back into Highland Yard, Waterloo, Iowa, to set out cars there. As we see in this view, radio greatly simplified railroad work.

Courtesy of California State Railroad Museum. Philip Ross Hastings, MD, Collection, [Negative 7888].

Plate 89. This image was the cover photo of the *Railroad History* issue featuring this author's article, "Artist of the Rail: Phil Hastings." In the image, which captures Black railroad workers, a section gang lifts their "speeder" onto the Rock Island (Chicago, Rock Island & Pacific Railroad) tracks at Malcom, Iowa.

Courtesy of California State Railroad Museum. Philip Ross Hastings, MD, Collection, [Negative 3011].

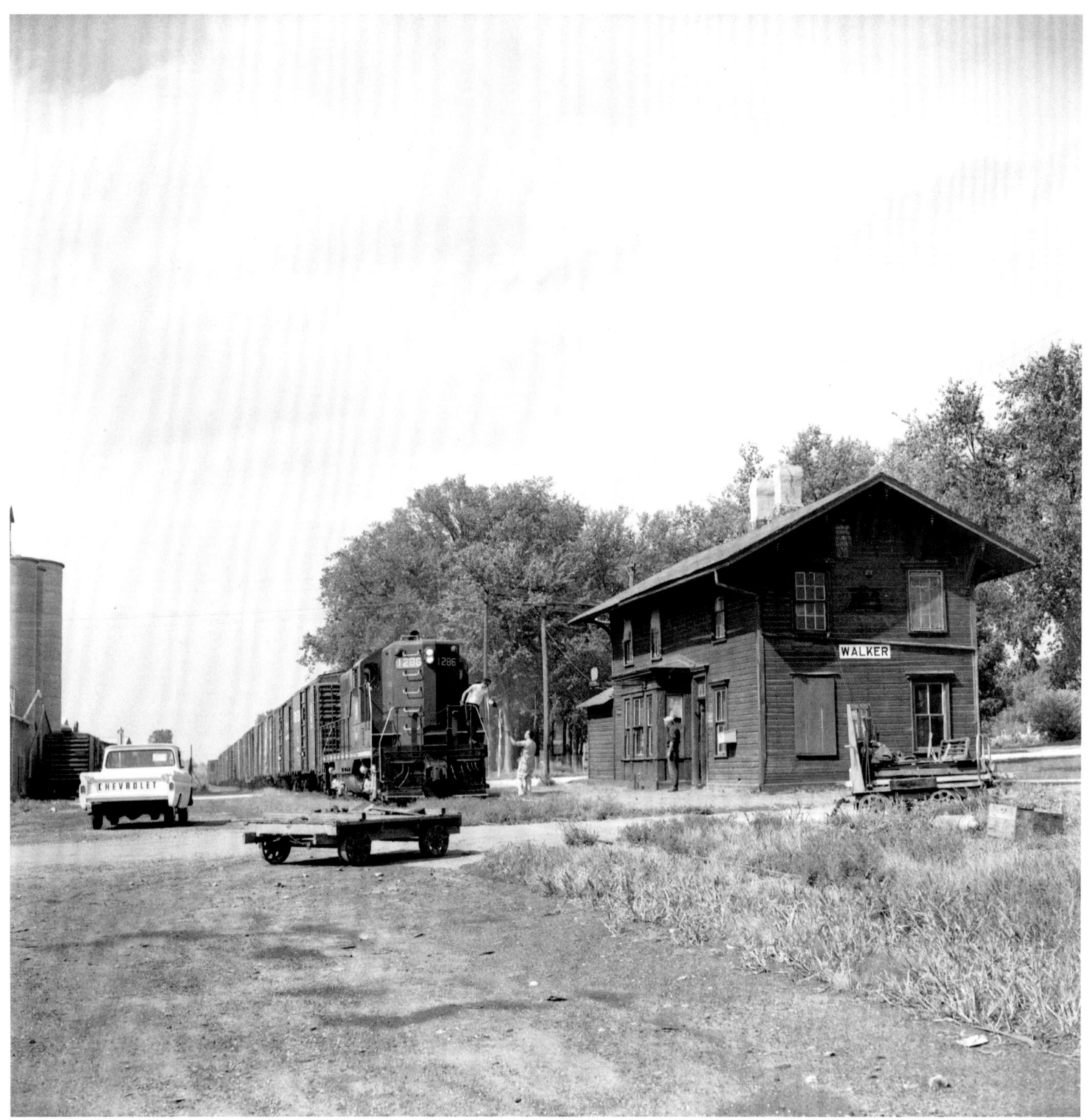

Plate 90. The agent at Walker, Iowa, hands waybills up to the head brakeman on a freight train led by Rock Island GP-7 1286. The two-story wooden station is spectacularly decrepit in this 1964 view.

Courtesy of California State Railroad Museum. Philip Ross Hastings, MD, Collection, [Negative 3257].

Facing, Plate 91. In this interesting view, Hastings captures Rock Island agent-operator Earl C. Berry as he adjusts train-order hoops for the crew of westbound train 7, the *Cornhusker*. Marengo, Iowa, November 19, 1966.

Courtesy of California State Railroad Museum. Philip Ross Hastings, MD, Collection, [Negative 3209].

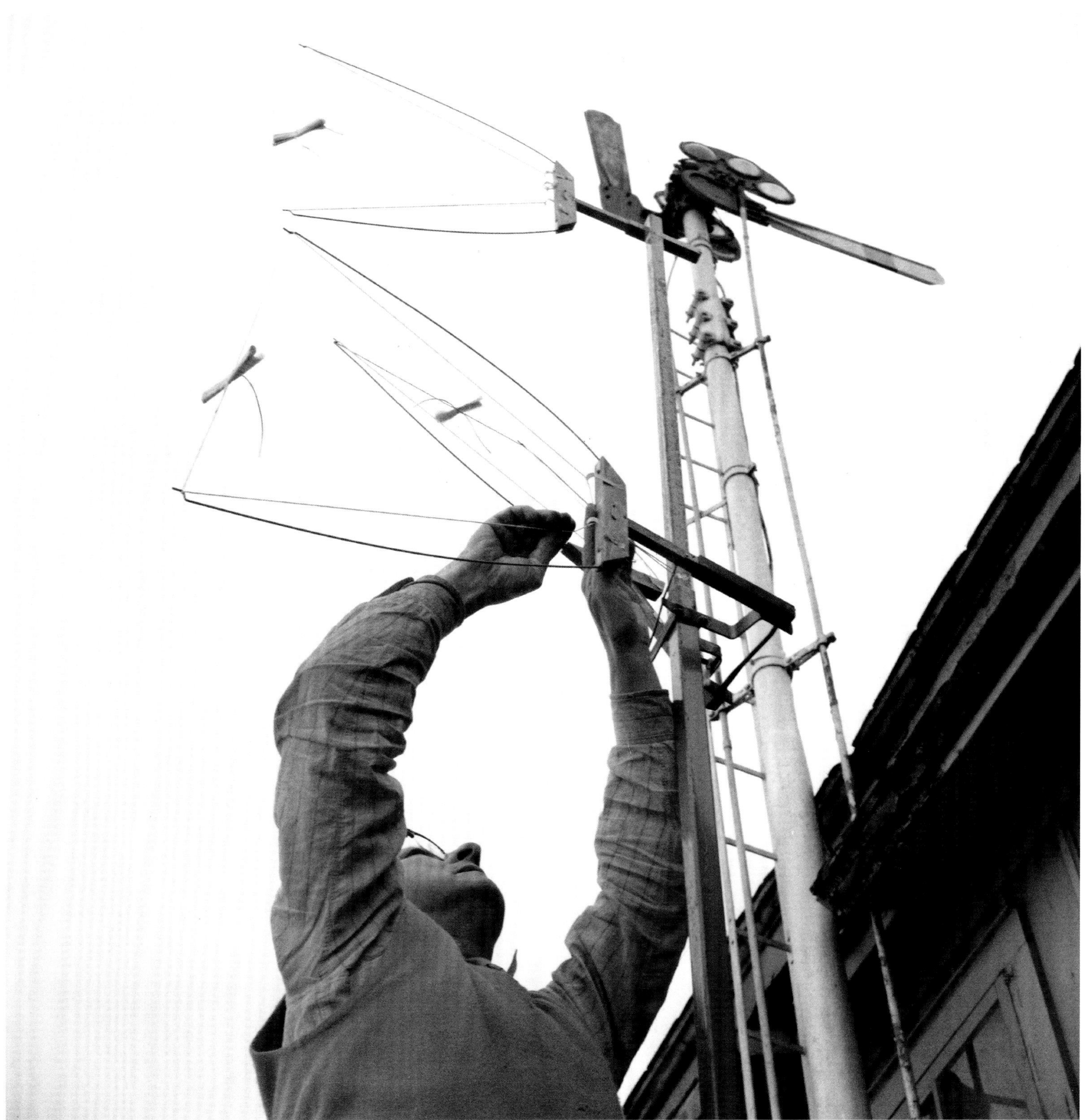

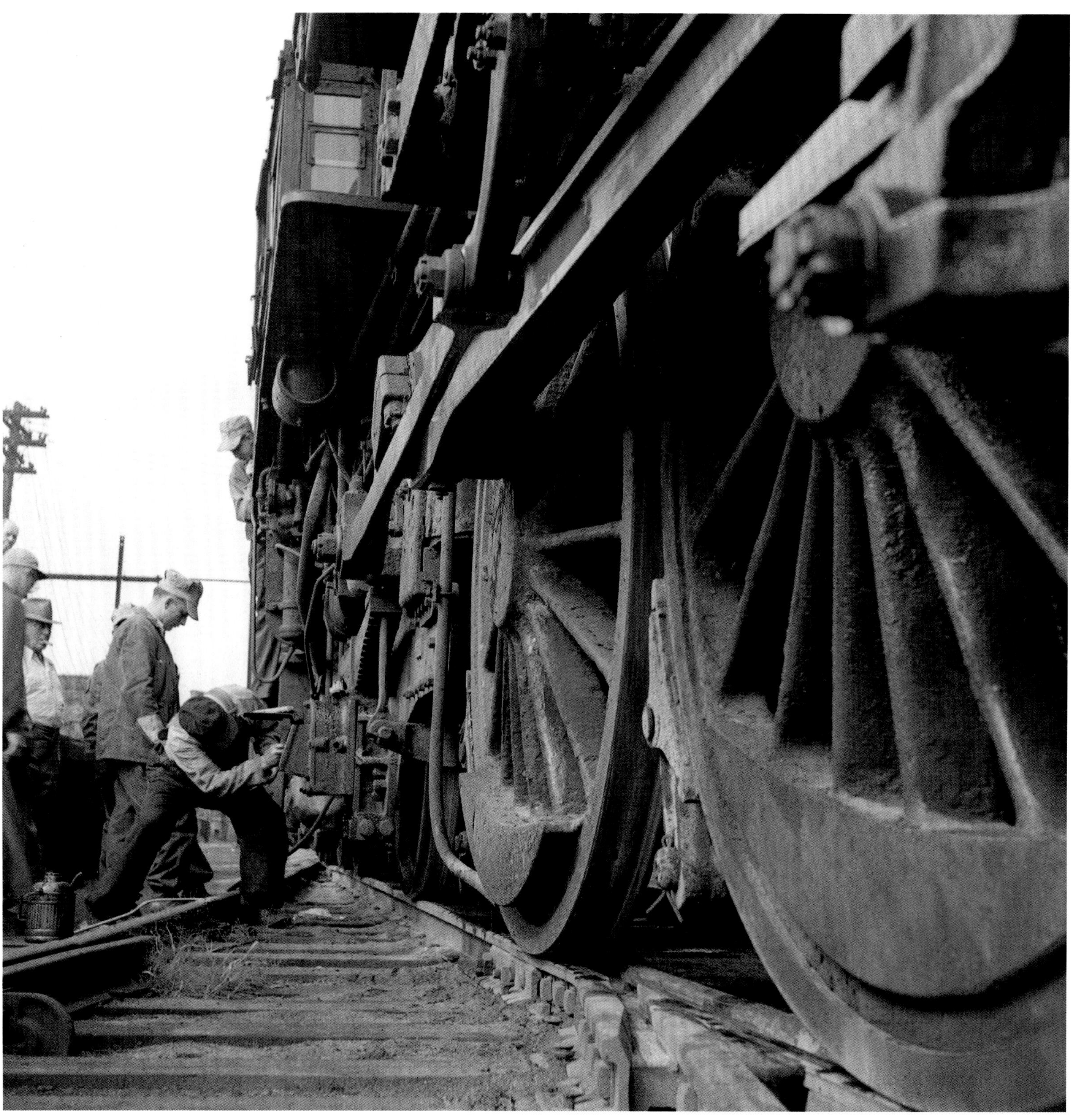

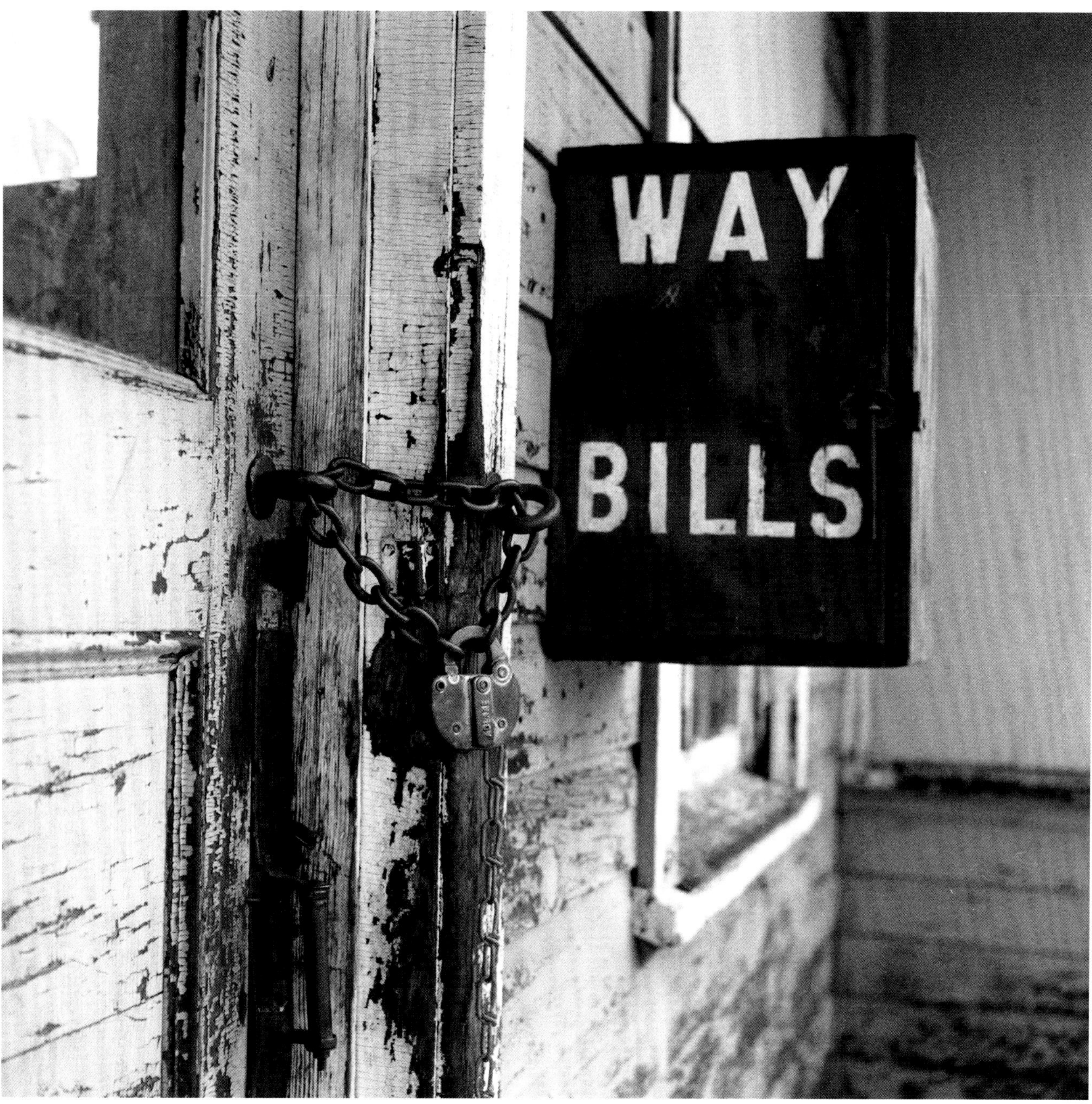

***Facing,* Plate 92.** In this close view, Hastings compares the massive drivers of Chicago & North Western Railway "Atlantic" 395 to railroaders laboring to fix a hotbox on one of the engine's trailing truck journals. The location is Madison, Wisconsin, and the photo was taken during a Railroad Club of Chicago excursion recognizing the retirement of this locomotive, built in 1908.

Courtesy of California State Railroad Museum. Philip Ross Hastings, MD, Collection, [Negative 2889].

Plate 93. Hastings's view of a waybill box outside the Chicago & North Western depot in Mercer, Wisconsin, taken in 1981. The image tells us a lot, without any words, about the decline of midwestern "Granger" railroads, such as the Milwaukee Road, the Rock Island, the Chicago Great Western, and even the North Western.

Courtesy of California State Railroad Museum. Philip Ross Hastings, MD, Collection, [Negative 2965].

PORTFOLIO SEVEN

WEST

Phil Hastings joined in the US Army in 1943 and then attended Tufts College, Fordham University, and New York University. He received an MD from the University of Vermont in 1950. After graduating, he rejoined the army and was posted to a number of different locations. Hastings took advantage of living in these areas to take railroad-subject images as much as he could, given that he was an army doctor with a growing family. During his photographic career, he took many notable photos of the American West—so many that one or more photo books could easily be drawn from this part of his oeuvre alone.

Portfolio Seven looks at his images of the West.[1] Although a New Englander, Hastings's photographs show that he was able to incorporate the vastness, and even the eeriness, of the West into his railroad-subject photography.

In many ways, Texas is a gateway—at least a gateway in American folklore—to the West. It is a divided state, with its eastern counties reflecting the landscape, population, and mores of the South. Houston is the megapolis of this part of Texas. As you go west in this vast state, however, especially as you pass Dallas–Fort Worth, the landscape becomes more and more barren, until you reach the plains around Lubbock and Amarillo, or the archetypal border city of El Paso, adjacent to Ciudad Juárez, Mexico.

This review of Hastings's West starts with plate 94, taken in the Upper Gulf Coast region of Texas at T&NO Junction on the south edge of Houston. This location was highlighted in Hastings's article in the February 1952 issue of *Railroad* magazine. The framing of the train under the station sign in this image is notable. The railroads crossing here are the Texas & New Orleans (a Southern Pacific subsidiary) and the Gulf, Colorado & Santa Fe (a Santa Fe subsidiary).

Plate 95, also taken on the Texas & New Orleans, is included here as it depicts a rare view of the interior of a sand house. The location is the major south Texas city of San Antonio. Plate 96, taken in Houston, is a Hastings view of the Santa Fe (Atchison, Topeka & Santa Fe Railway) and one of its DL-109 Alco locomotives. The dusty road and scrubby weeds suggest the humid heat of this part of the Lone Star State.

Like Lucius Beebe and Charles Clegg before him, Hastings was drawn to the narrow-gauge railroads of Colorado—at least to the ones that survived by the time he was able to visit. Plates 97, 98, and 99 depict the narrow-gauge lines of the Denver & Rio Grande Western Railroad (D&RGW) in Colorado. The trackside café is an icon of American railroading. Plate 97 is an enormously successful view of a train from such a café—an image underrepresented in American railroad-subject photographs. Plate 98 depicts a switchback (a track configuration for climbing very steep gradients); one of the switchbacks on the D&RGW's Monarch Branch. These were the only switchbacks on the D&RGW system at the time. Finally, plate 99 is a winter scene at Cumbres Pass, high above Chama, New Mexico. This location may still be reached by train and is served by the Cumbres & Toltec Scenic Railroad.

Plate 100 shows another iconic railroad pass of the West, but a very different one on a very different, standard-gauge line. This is the Union Pacific Railroad's "Big Boy" 4019 at Dale, Wyoming. Plate 101, taken in northern Idaho, shows a Northern Pacific Railway (NP) "doodlebug" (self-propelled passenger railcar) on the NP/Union Pacific–owned Camas Prairie Railroad.

Hastings took a number of photographs of the Milwaukee Road (Chicago, Milwaukee, St. Paul and Pacific Railroad). The Milwaukee Road's network was an odd duality: the railroad was primarily a midwestern carrier, but in a fit of overreach, it constructed the last transcontinental railroad in the United States—its "Pacific Extension," completed in 1909. Six hundred and forty-five miles of the extension were later electrified, an innovative move for the early twentieth century, but a step that only added to the tremendous costs of this line. The Milwaukee Road remained financially unstable after this overbuilding and declared bankruptcy for the third time in 1977. Plate 102 shows Milwaukee steam engines with an electric "Boxcab," and plate 103 is Hastings's view of the railroad's beautiful Spokane River viaduct in the snow.

In a view emblematic of a closing era, plate 104 shows a Great Northern "op" (telegraph operator) with his "bug" (high-speed telegraph) key watching a train. Plates 105–107 depict the NP. Plate 105 shows 2-8-8-2 4021, with characteristic front-mounted air pumps and low headlight, under a plume of smoke.[2] Plate 106 depicts a prototypical small-town depot, and plate 107 shows the soon-to-be motive power victor, represented here by NP F-7A 6512 followed by two of its kin. Plate 108 remains in the Great Northern / NP domain: it shows a Spokane, Portland and Seattle (SP&S) Railway train led by massive 4-6-6-4 911. The SP&S was co-owned by Great Northern and NP.

This portfolio of Hasting images of the US West closes with the silhouette of a Southern Pacific trainman in his caboose as his train goes over Donner Pass.

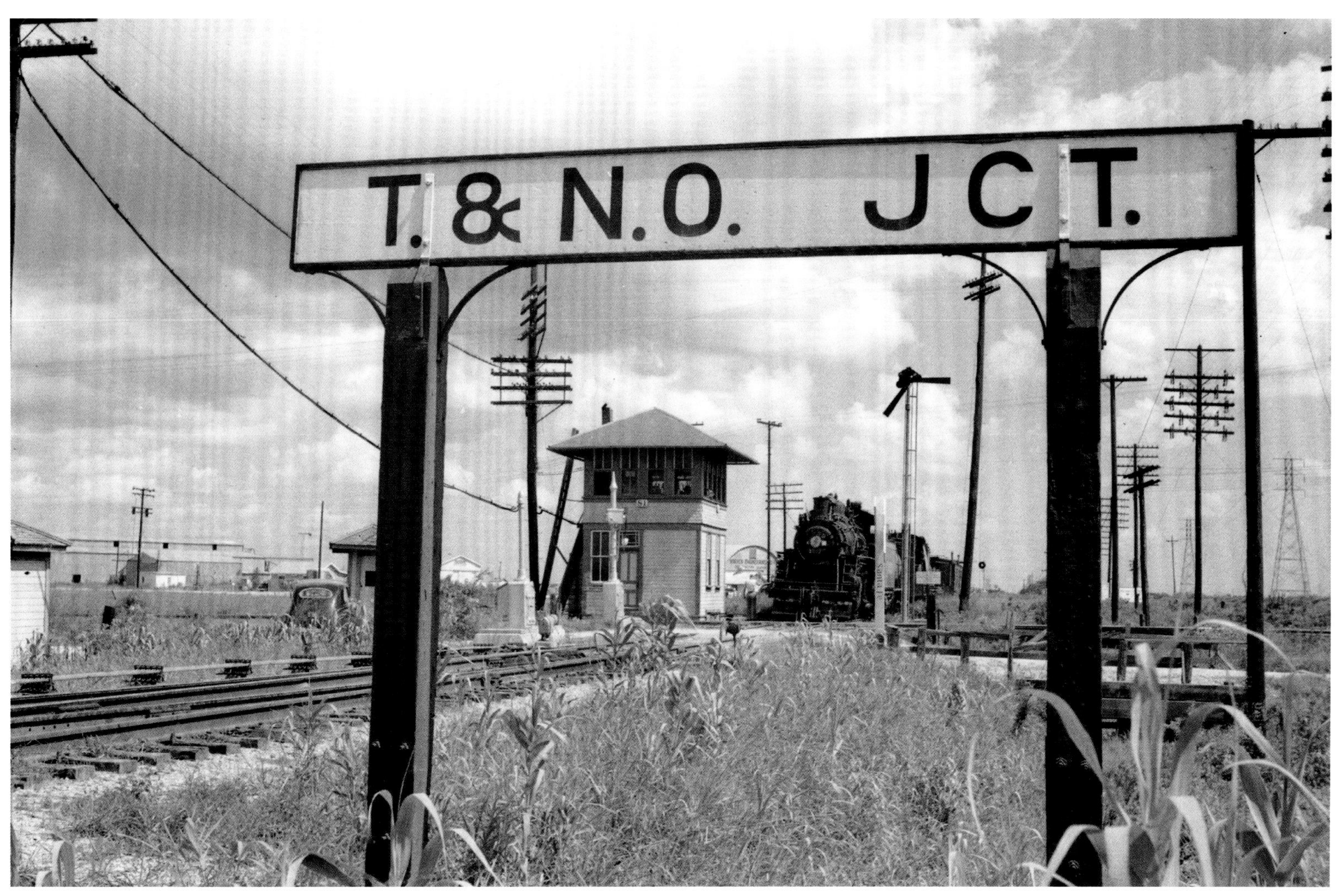

Plate 94. A Missouri Pacific freight passing Tower 81 at T&NO (Texas & New Orleans) Junction is framed under the T&NO Junction station sign. See plate 86 for a similar image.

Courtesy of California State Railroad Museum. Philip Ross Hastings, MD, Collection, [Negative 8146].

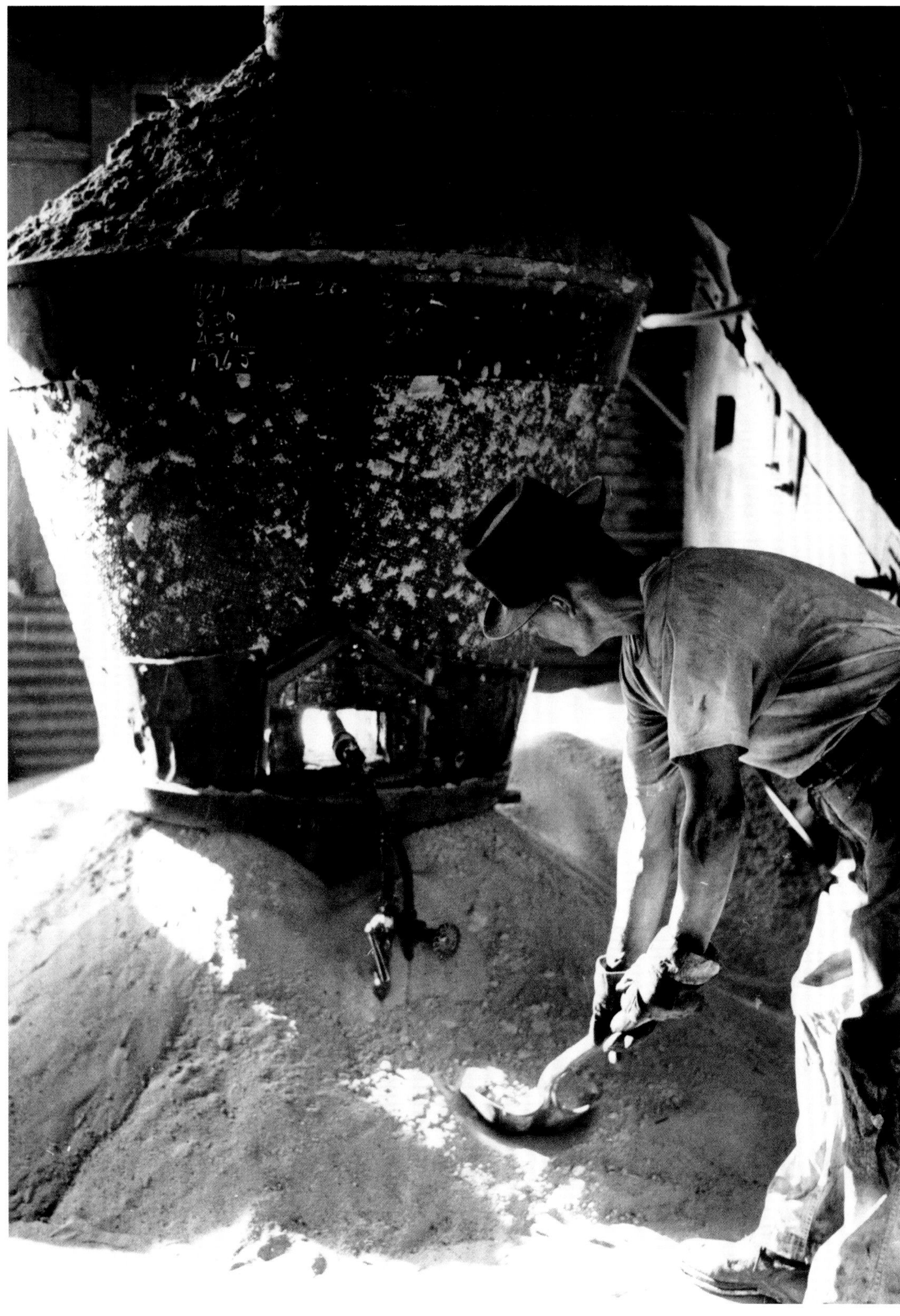

Plate 95. Here, Hastings captures a rarely recorded image of railroading—a railroader drying sand in a sand house on the Texas & New Orleans Railroad, San Antonio, Texas, July 11, 1948. The T&NO was a subsidiary of the Southern Pacific Company.

Courtesy of California State Railroad Museum. Philip Ross Hastings, MD, Collection, [Negative 10511].

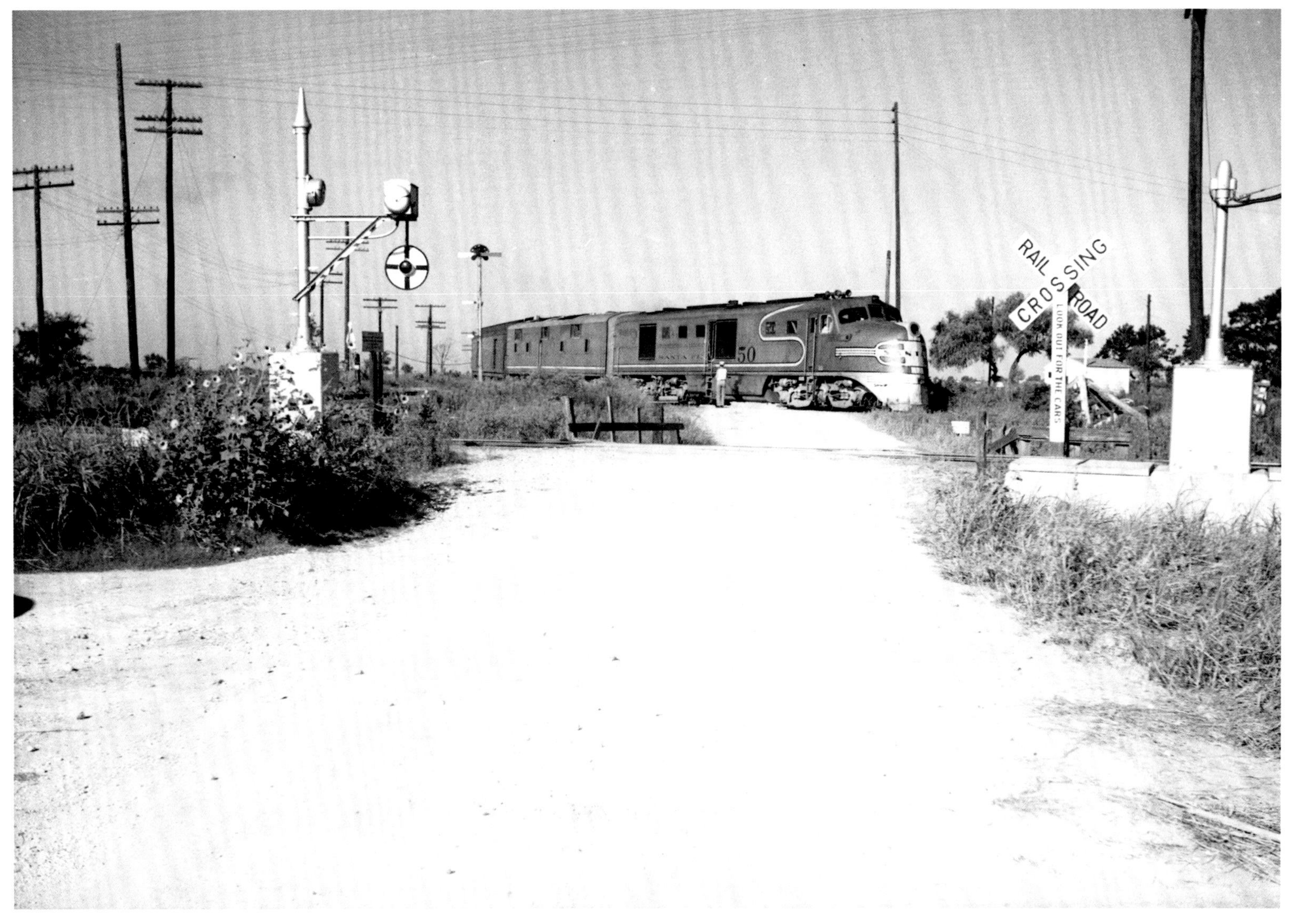

Plate 96. Atchison, Topeka and Santa Fe Railway DL-109 50 with a train, in Houston, Texas. Hastings framed the uncommon diesel unit between a "wig-wag" signal and a railroad crossing sign. A train order signal in the background adds to the effect.

Courtesy of California State Railroad Museum. Philip Ross Hastings, MD, Collection, [Negative 24].

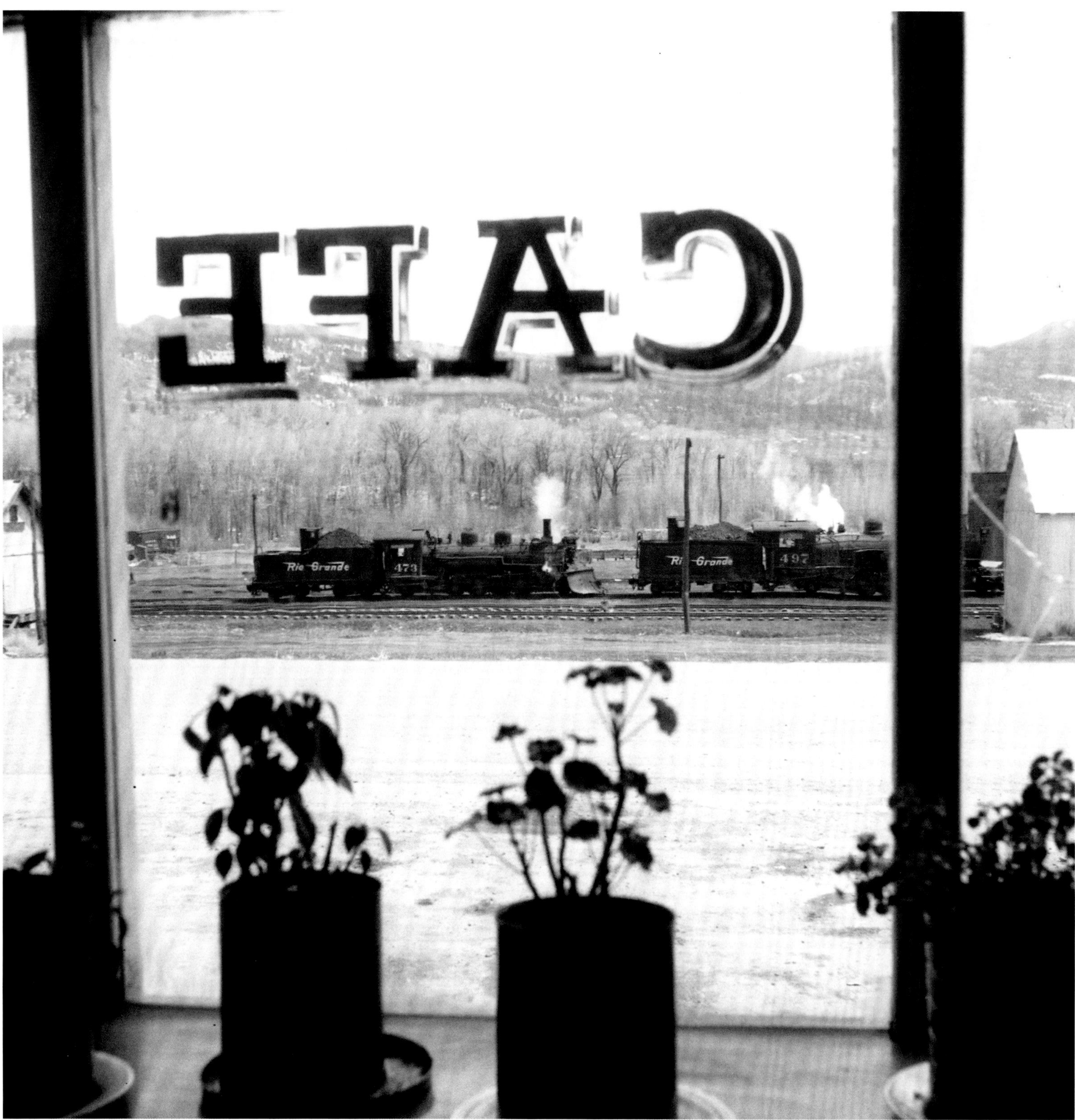
CAFE
Rio Grande
473
Rio Grande
497

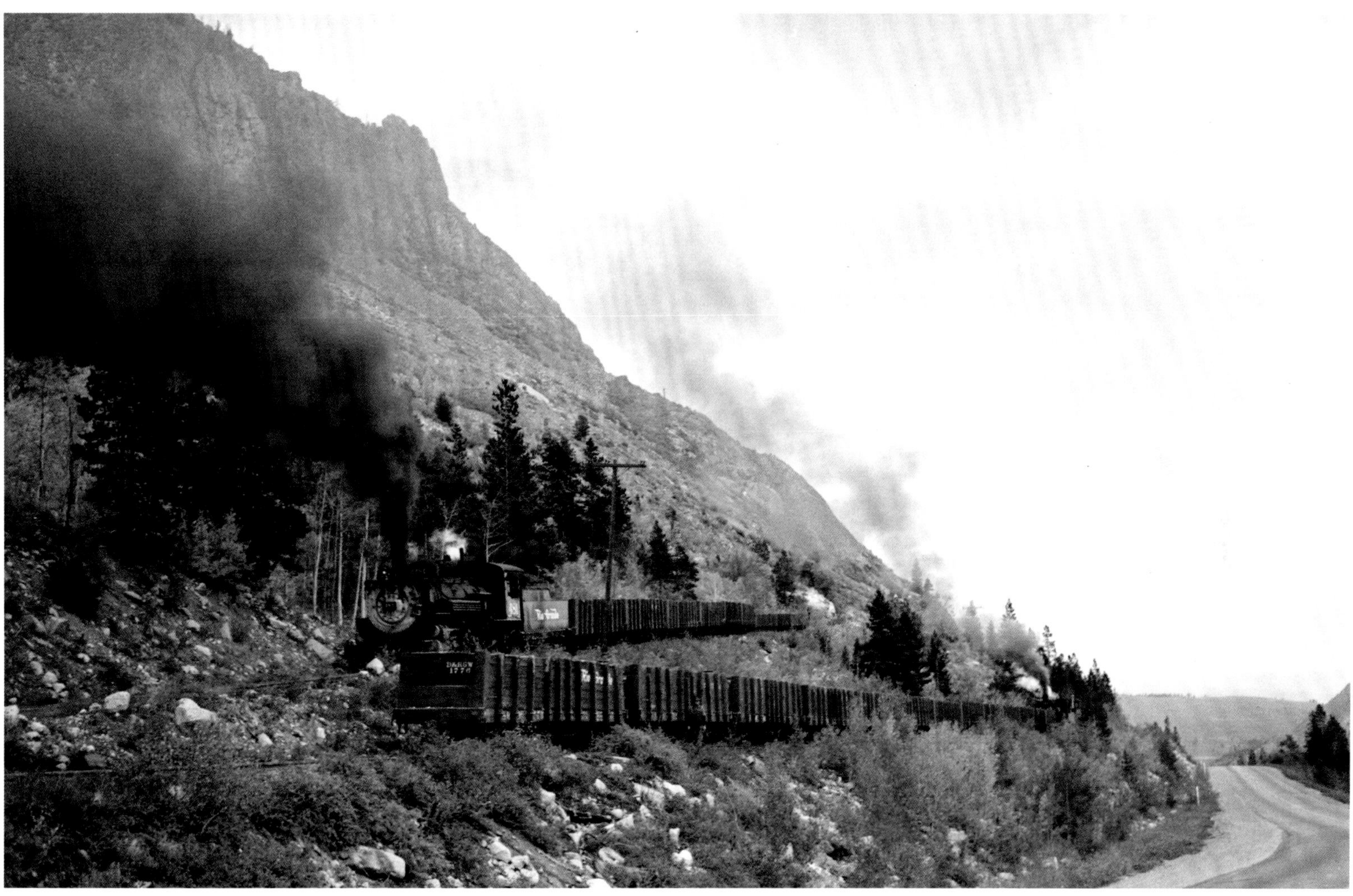

***Facing,* Plate 97.** Narrow-gauge Denver & Rio Grande Western locomotives 473 and 497 from a café window. The locomotives had both come in on a freight from Durango, Colorado, and had been turned and serviced for their return trip. Note how Hastings framed the locomotives between the backward "CAFE" and the plants on the windowsill. K-28 473 survives on the Durango & Silverton Narrow Gauge Railroad in Colorado, and K-37 497 survives on the Cumbres & Toltec Scenic Railroad, which runs in both New Mexico and Colorado. The location is Annie's Café in Chama, New Mexico.

Courtesy of California State Railroad Museum. Philip Ross Hastings, MD, Collection, [Negative 232].

Plate 98. Denver & Rio Grande Western K-36 481 on a switchback. The location is the Monarch branch, which ran from Poncha Junction, Colorado, to a quarry. The locomotive survives at the Durango & Silverton Narrow Gauge Railroad.

Courtesy of California State Railroad Museum. Philip Ross Hastings, MD, Collection, [Negative 8320].

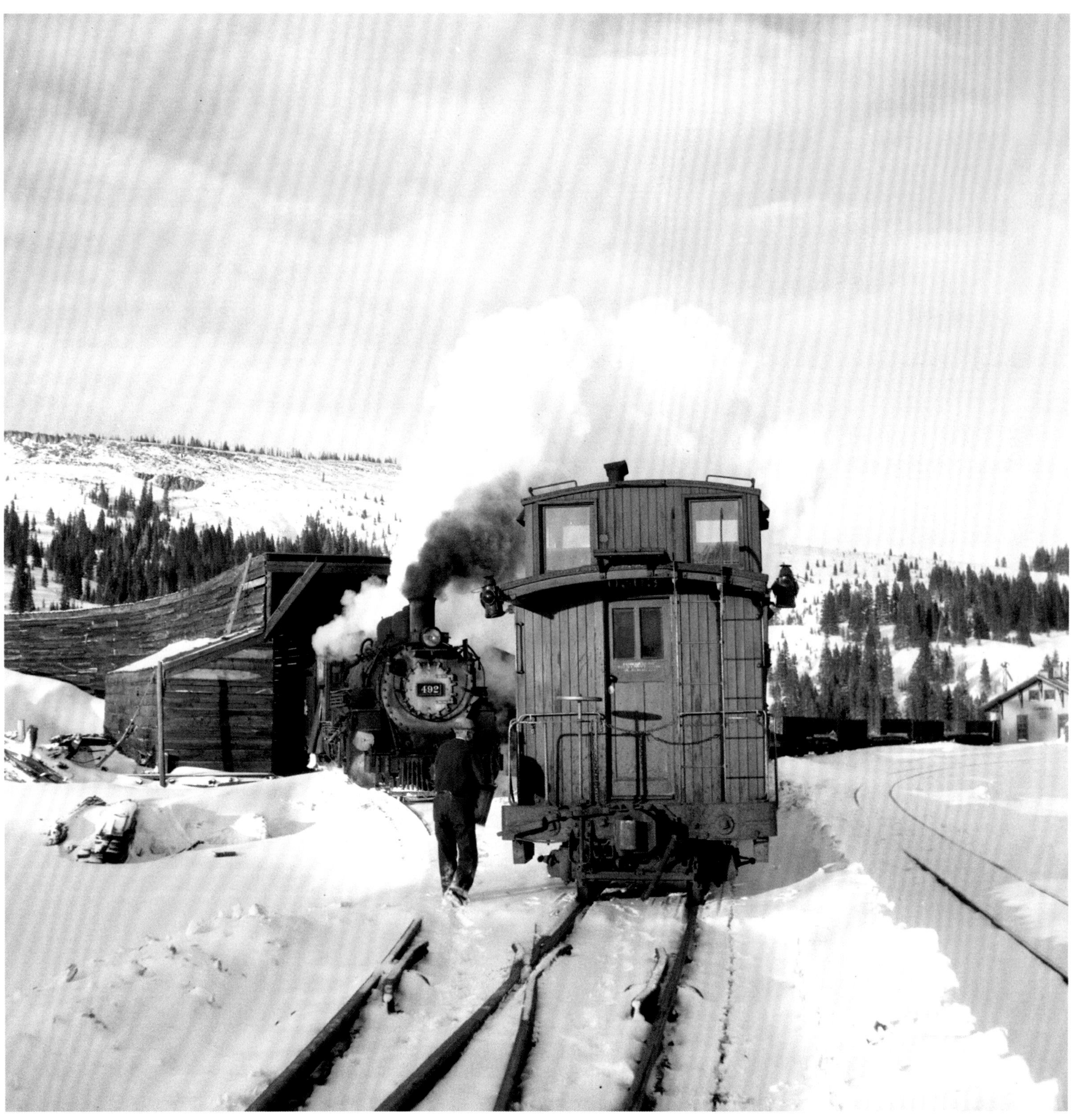
492

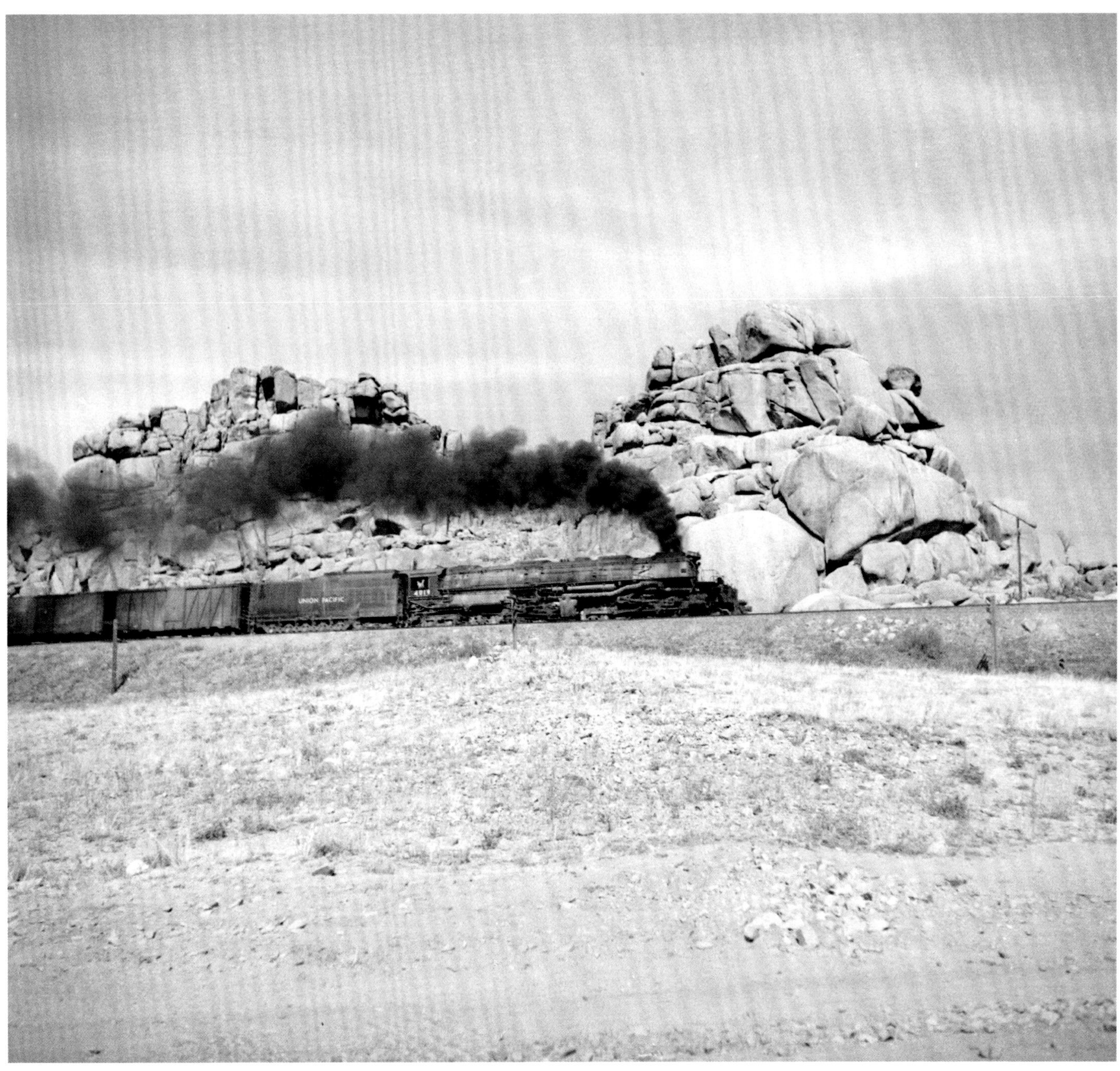

***Facing*, Plate 99.** A brilliant Hastings tableau of a narrow-gauge caboose in the snow with a snow shed, station, and K-37 492 in the background. The locomotive survives at the Cumbres & Toltec Scenic Railroad. This is Cumbres Pass, still served by the trains of the Cumbres & Toltec, when the station and wye snow shed still survived—a small section of the snow shed remains.

Courtesy of California State Railroad Museum. Philip Ross Hastings, MD, Collection, [Negative 3108].

Plate 100. Every railroad-subject photographer who could travel West in the 1940s and 1950s tried to capture the Union Pacific 4-8-8-4 "Big Boys," by many measures the largest steam locomotives ever built. Here, Hastings captures "Big Boy" 4019 at Dale, Wyoming.

Courtesy of California State Railroad Museum. Philip Ross Hastings, MD, Collection, [Negative 3769].

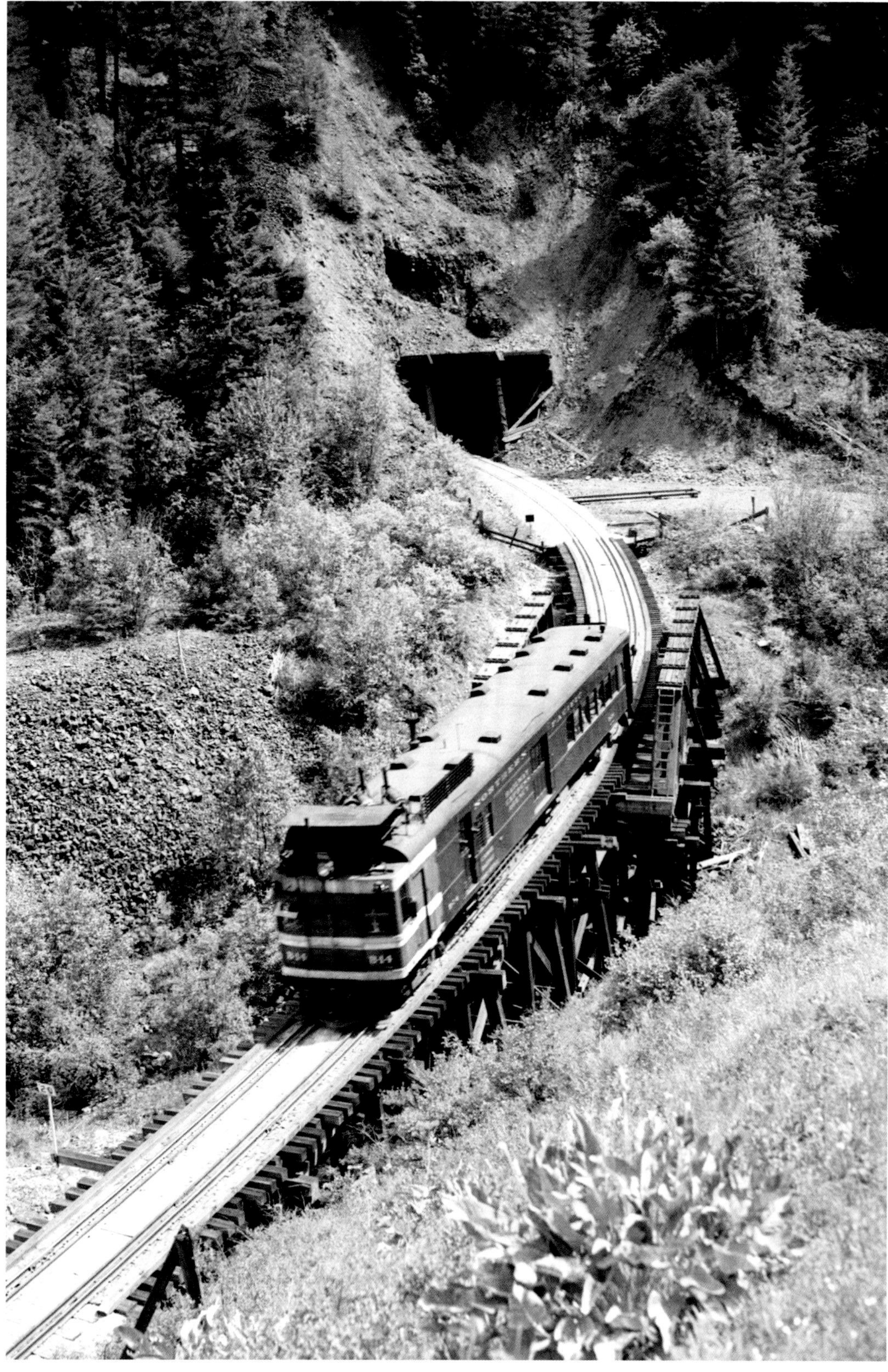

Plate 101. Northern Pacific "doodlebug" B-14 exits the horseshoe tunnel at the apex of Lapwai Canyon on the Camas Prairie Railroad and crosses a trestle. The doodlebug is running as train 343, bound from Graingeville to Lewiston, Idaho. The Camas Prairie, known as "the railroad on stilts" because of the many trestles on its line, was owned by the Northern Pacific and the Union Pacific. May 28, 1951.

Courtesy of California State Railroad Museum. Philip Ross Hastings, MD, Collection, [Negative 1889].

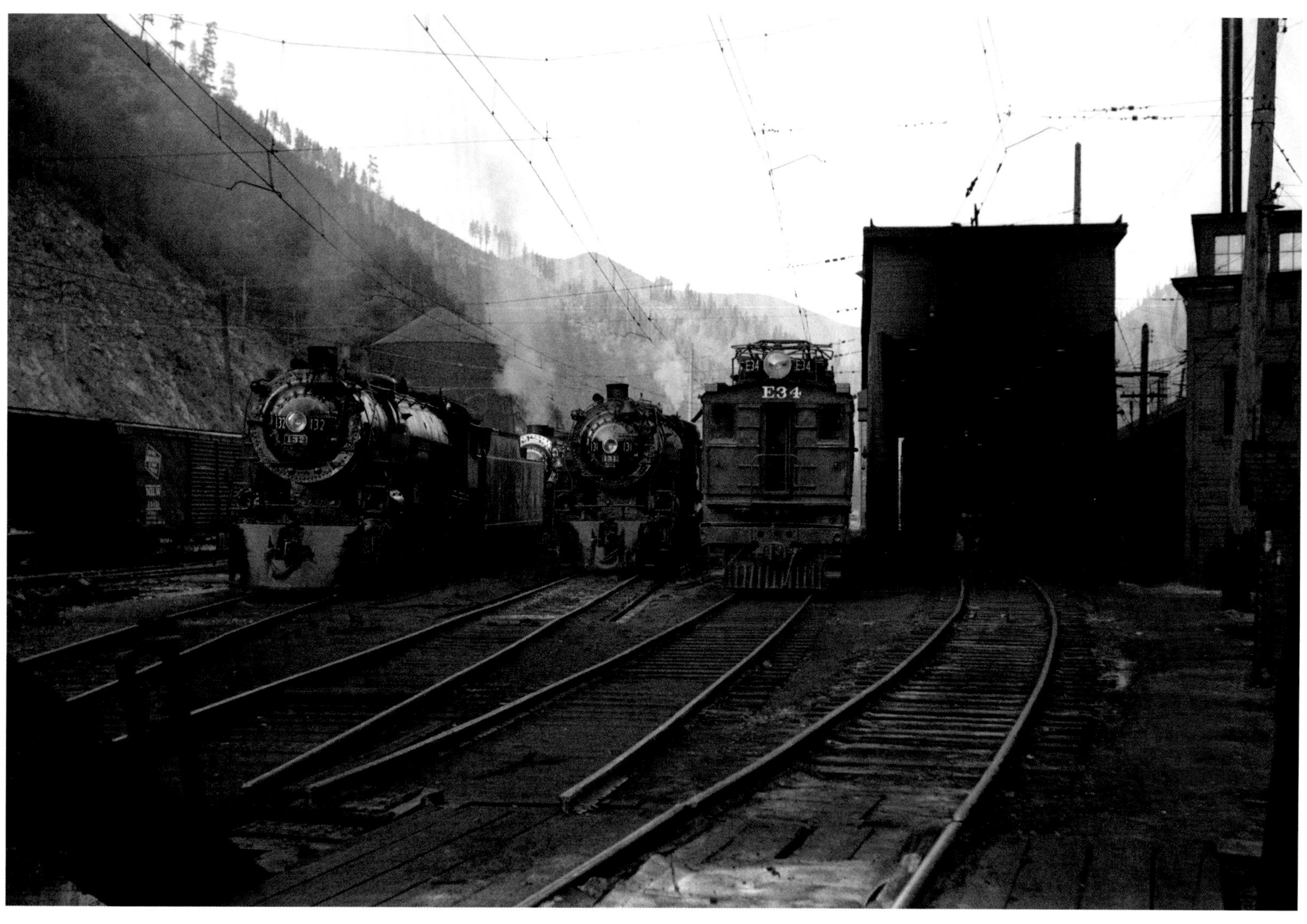

Plate 102. In this photo, Phil Hastings caught three Milwaukee Road (Chicago, Milwaukee, St. Paul and Pacific Railway) steam engines on the "Pacific Extension" with an electric locomotive, "Boxcab" E34. The identifiable steam locomotives are sister "Baltics" (4-6-4s), 131 and 132. The location is probably Avery, Idaho.

Courtesy of California State Railroad Museum. Philip Ross Hastings, MD, Collection, [Negative 3127].

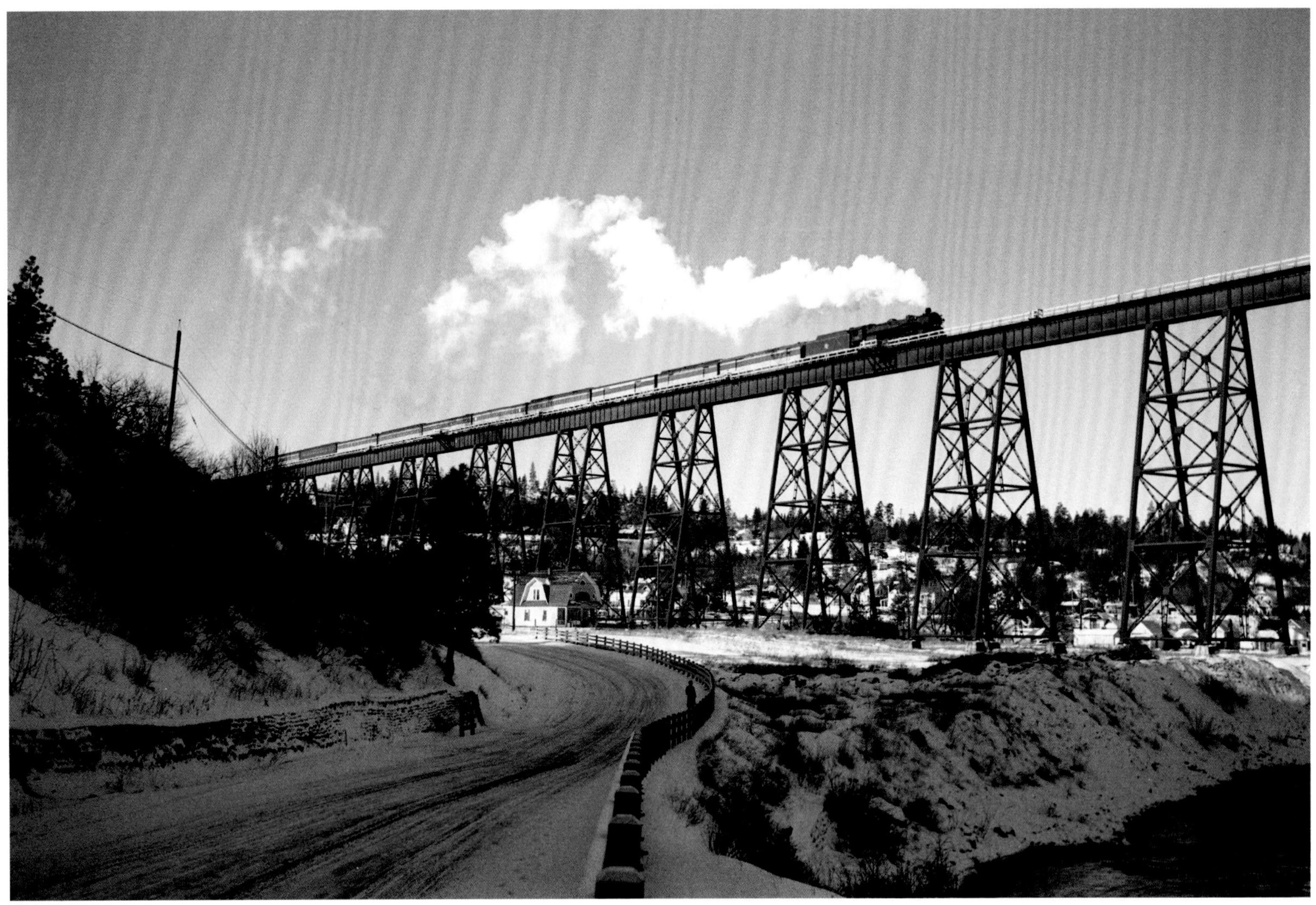

Plate 103. In this beautiful winter view, Phil Hastings catches Milwaukee Road train 18, the eastbound *Columbian*, crossing the Spokane River viaduct in Spokane, Washington, 1951. The train is led by engine 251, a 4-8-4.

Courtesy of California State Railroad Museum. Philip Ross Hastings, MD, Collection, [Negative 3172].

***Facing*, Plate 104.** This Hastings scene, which reflects many paintings done for the classic pulp *Railroad* magazine, captures an agent-operator with his "bug" high-speed telegraph key at the Great Northern station in Priest River, Idaho. The train order signal handles are hand-labeled "west bound" and "east [bound]."

Courtesy of California State Railroad Museum. Philip Ross Hastings, MD, Collection, [Negative 1978].

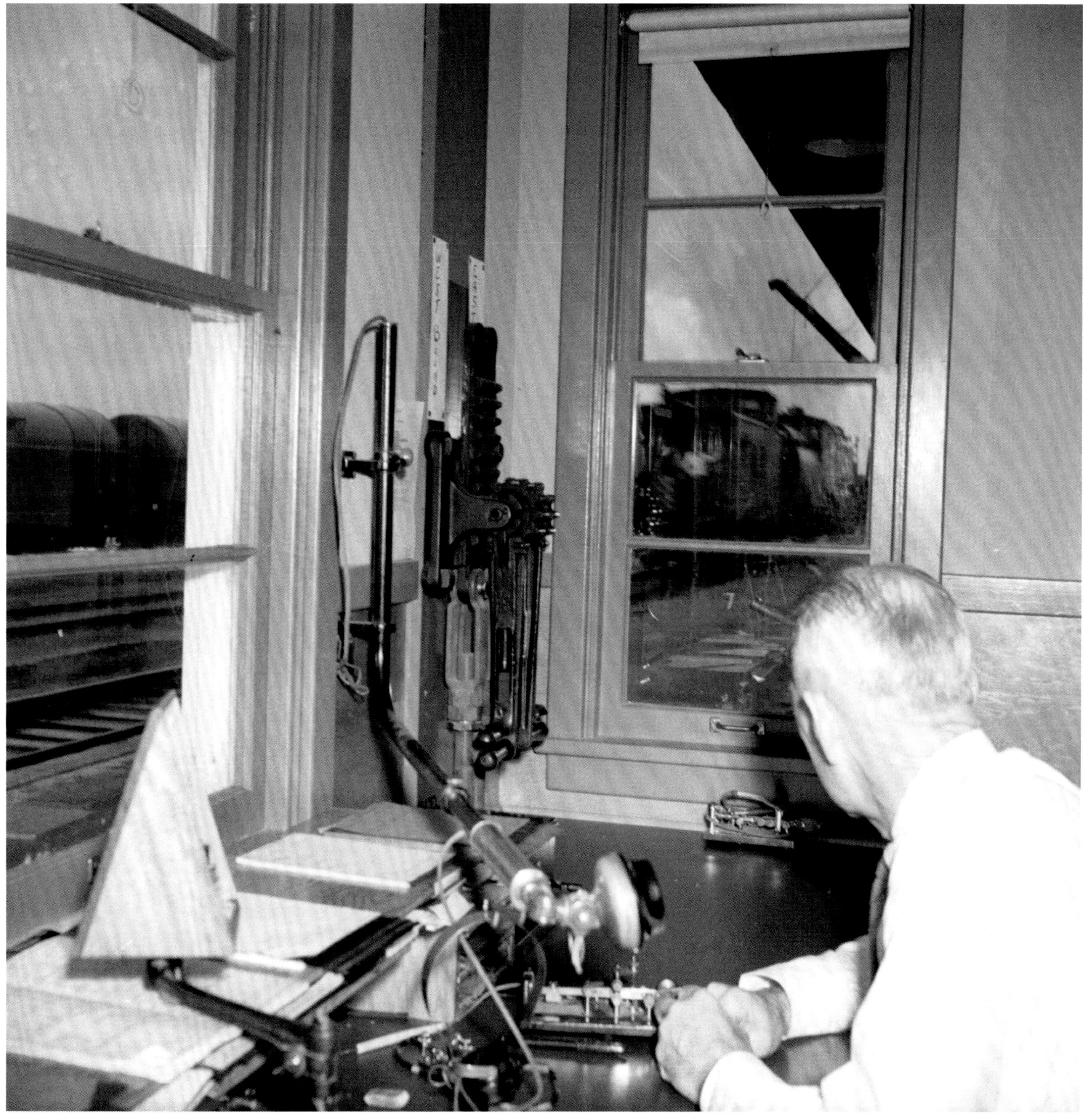

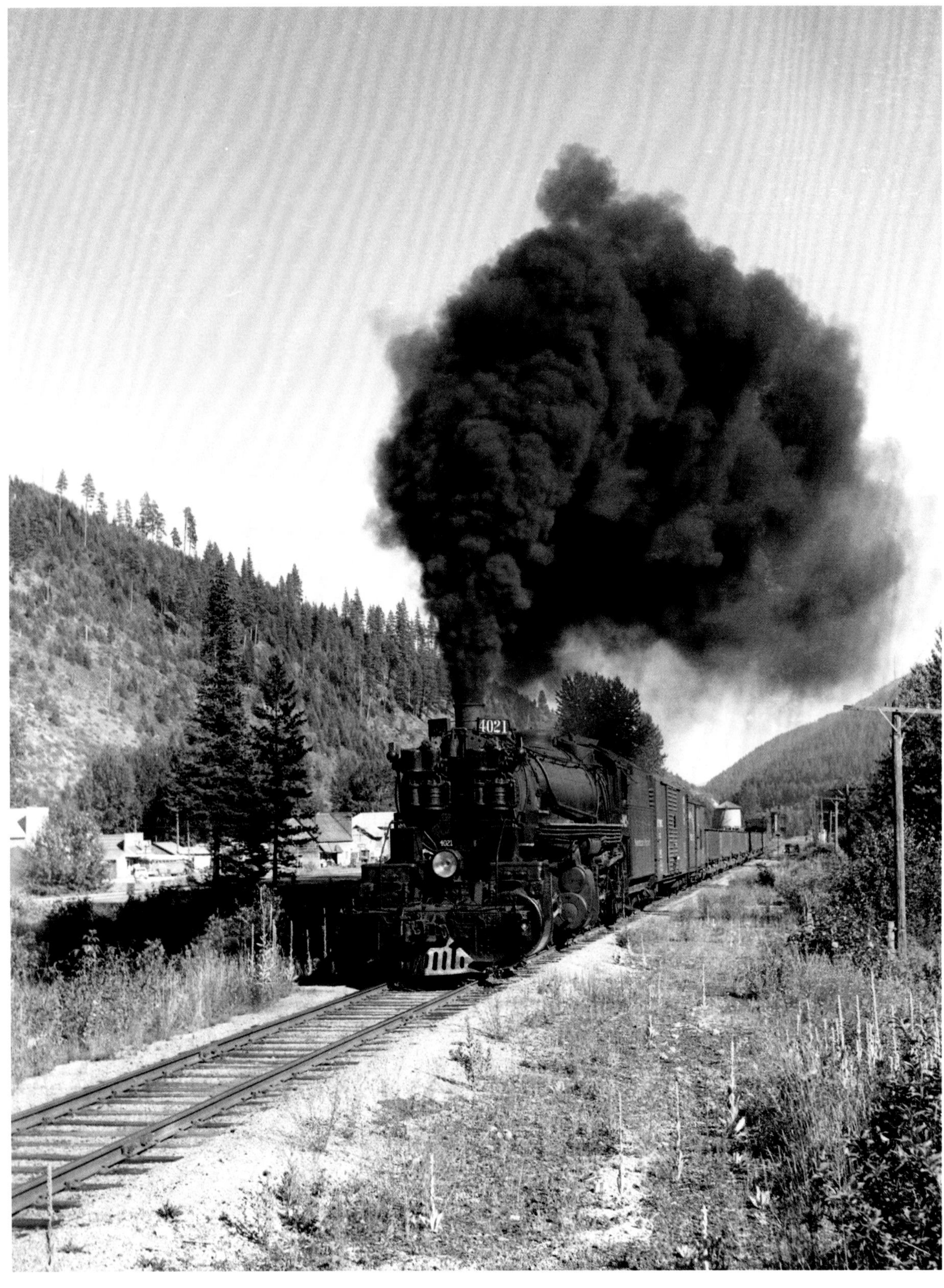

Plate 105. The influence of Lucius Beebe and Charles Clegg is reflected in this vertically framed three-quarters shot of Northern Pacific Railroad engine 4021, a 2-8-8-2, under a plume of black smoke.

Courtesy of California State Railroad Museum. Philip Ross Hastings, MD, Collection, [Negative 8537].

Plate 106. In this Northern Pacific image, Hasting expertly frames an engine, 1787 (a 2-8-2), under an archaic train order signal and between a station with its Western Union sign and a trackside building reading "Grain & Pea Co." Like Walker Evans, Hastings used America's large inventory of unusual buildings and building names to great effect in his images.

Courtesy of California State Railroad Museum. Philip Ross Hastings, MD, Collection, [Negative 450].

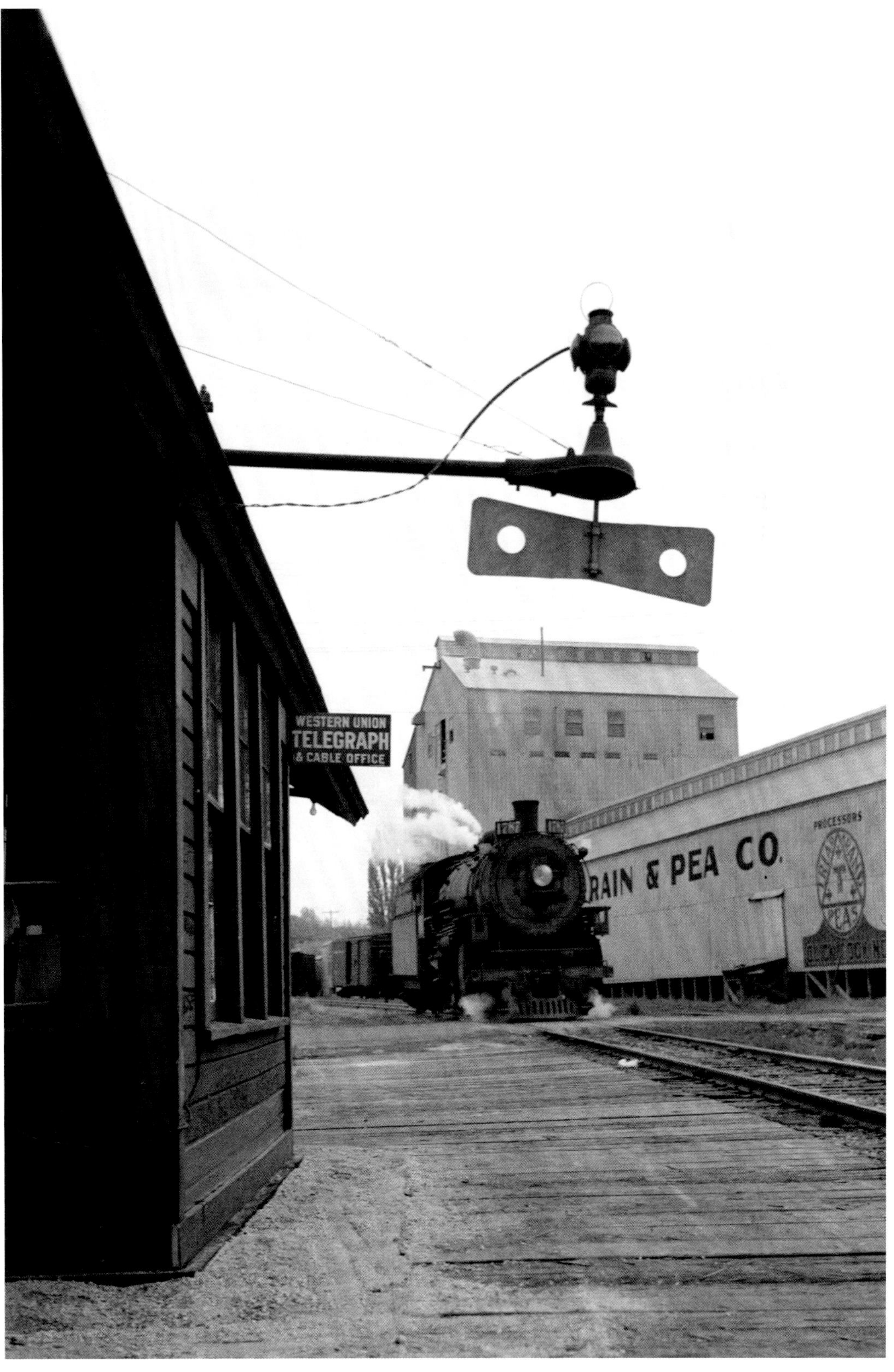

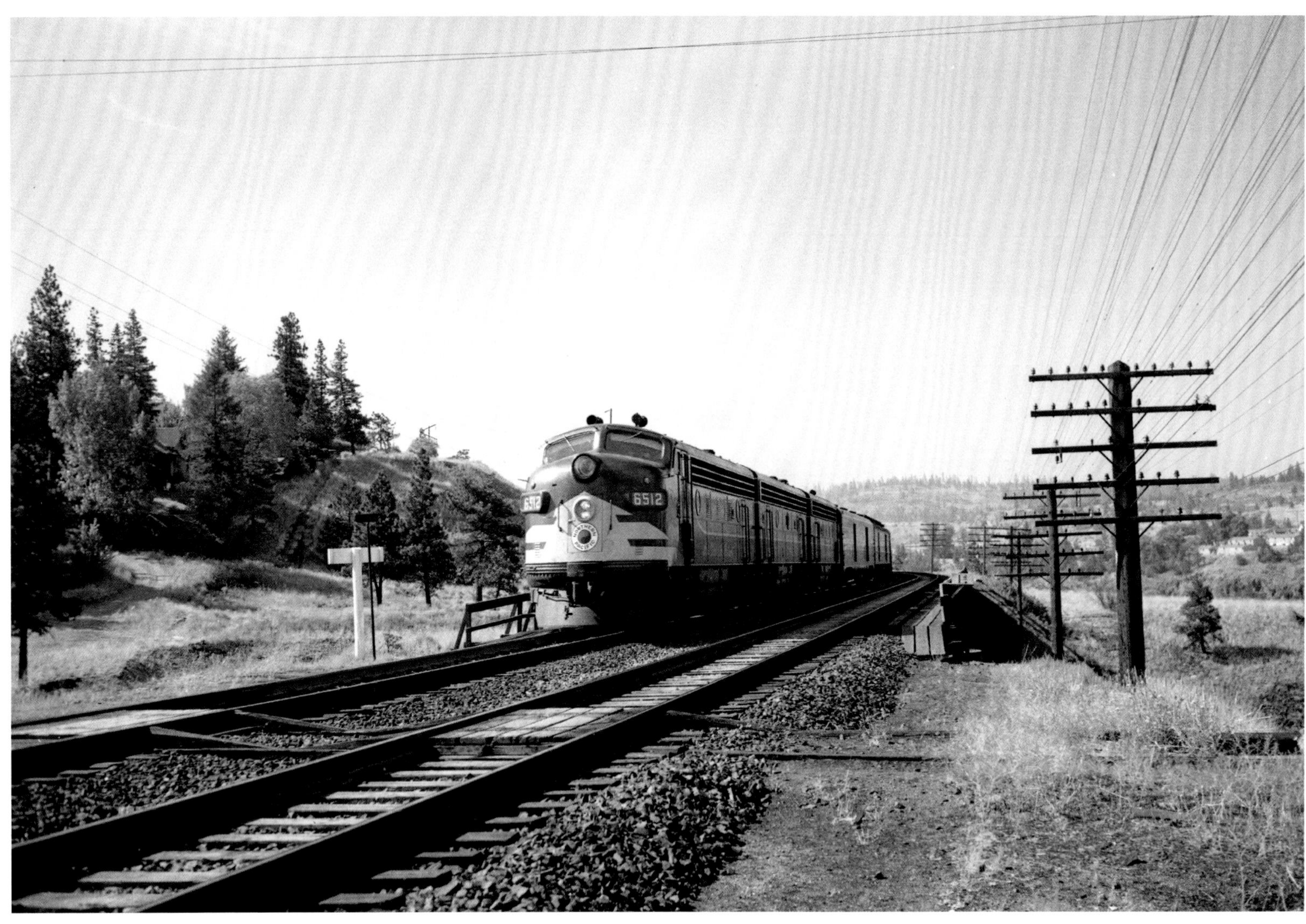

Plate 107. Northern Pacific 6512 leads two other units pulling a passenger train in this view of the early diesel age of American railroading.

Courtesy of California State Railroad Museum. Philip Ross Hastings, MD, Collection, [Negative 8542].

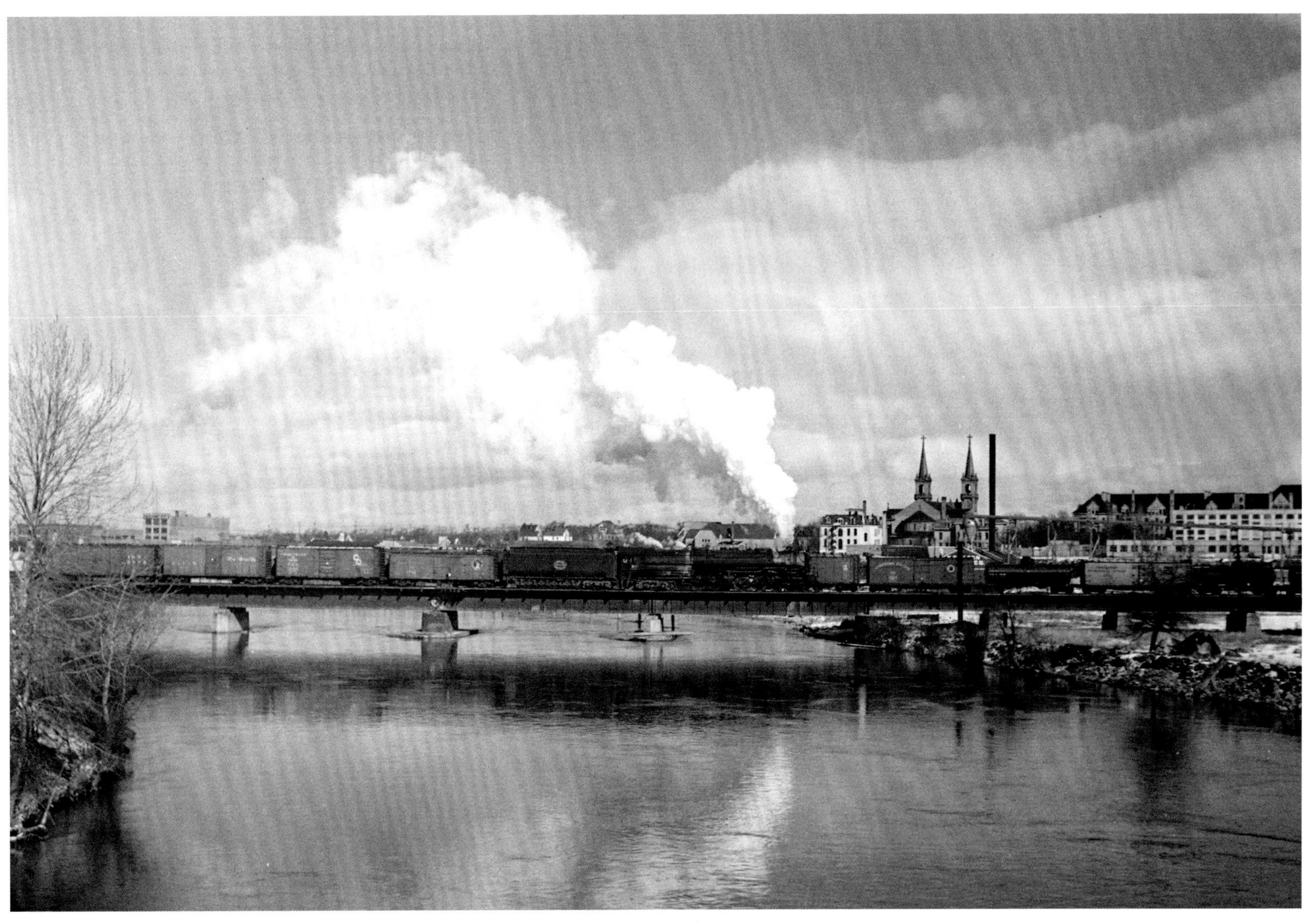

Plate 108. The Spokane, Portland and Seattle Railway (SP&S) was a regional railroad owned by the Great Northern and Northern Pacific. In this image, Hastings captures SP&S 911 4-6-6-4 broadside, leading a freight train over a photogenic bridge.

Courtesy of California State Railroad Museum. Philip Ross Hastings, MD, Collection, [Negative 3813].

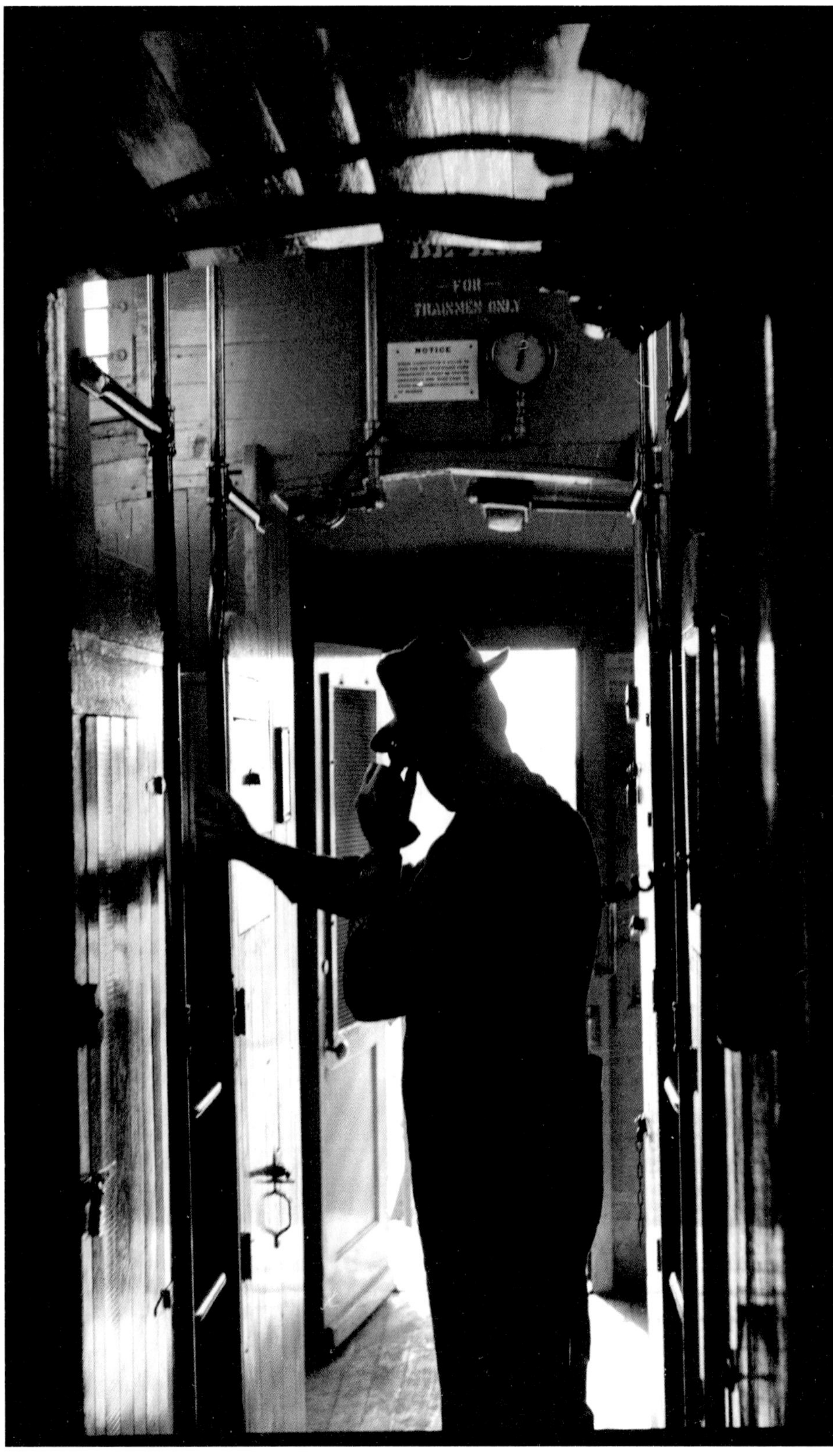

Plate 109. In this iconic silhouette, taken on a Southern Pacific freight crossing Donner Pass, Hastings captures a SP trainman in his caboose. The image was taken on a ride with *Trains* editor David P. Morgan.

Courtesy of California State Railroad Museum. Philip Ross Hastings, MD, Collection, [Negative 10279].

PORTFOLIO EIGHT

NOT AS LONG, BUT JUST AS WIDE

Trains editor David P. Morgan and Phil Hastings traveled throughout the United States during the mid-1950s and documented the end of steam on the railroads of the United States and Canada. Many of these images were featured in *Trains* and then in the book *The Mohawk That Refused to Abdicate, and Other Tales.*

Fortunately for today's readers and observers, most of whom were born after the end of the age of steam, Morgan and Hastings had complementary interests. As Morgan said in the epilogue to *The Mohawk That Refused to Abdicate, and Other Tales,* "We did not agree on politics or religion, to say nothing of locomotives. He preferred little engines, squat Ten-Wheelers, sawed-off saddletankers, fast-breathing Shays, and the like. The bigger the power, the better I liked it."[1]

From the evidence in the *Philip Ross Hastings, MD Collection* at the California State Railroad Museum, Morgan and Hastings worked together on their joint itineraries—and at least some of the time, Hastings got the first draft. If, like this observer, you follow the path of Hastings in preferring the unusual, the short line, and the regional railway, this was fortunate. Like Beebe and Clegg before them, Hastings and Morgan spent a good deal of their time documenting American and Canadian short lines and little-known, neglected branch lines that were part of major carriers, such as the Canadian National, the New York Central, and the Wabash. From the evidence of his images, Hastings was inspired by short lines in the same way he was by New England regionals, such as the Boston & Maine, the Central Vermont, and the Grand Trunk. This portfolio explores his views of short line railroading across the United States. The photos are sequenced geographically.

The dispatcher was the king of the railroad in terms of control of traffic, but he—this was really not a position open to women in the US during this time period—held an inside job rarely depicted by photographers. In plate 110, the first in this series, we see a dispatcher with his train sheet and a train order, controlling New York's tiny Grasse River Railroad. The Grasse River was a lumber railroad that also carried passengers in a service largely patronized by guests of the Conifer Inn in Conifer, New York. Plate 111 shows the Grasse River Railroad tracks at Conifer blanketed by winter snow.

Hastings, according to David P. Morgan, a "taciturn Vermonter," clearly loved his home region.[2] His depictions of New England were generally masterful. In plate 112, the famed Suncook Valley "Blueberry Express," an engine and an RPO/

combine, gets ready to depart the train shed of the majestic, long-vanished Concord, New Hampshire, station. Plate 113 takes this portfolio back to New York and a signature view of the Dansville & Mount Morris Railroad, shot in 1955 on the "Steam in Indian Summer" railroad safari with Morgan. The image is featured in *The Mohawk That Refused to Abdicate, and Other Tales* as a thumbnail—it shines out as a full-page view.[3]

Archie Robertson and Lucius Beebe led the way in exploring the short lines of the US South.[4] Phil Hastings was also an avid explorer of our southern US short line heritage. Plate 114, taken in the Appalachian fringes of the region, shows a Meadow River Lumber Company engineer with his charge. Plate 115 is one of Hastings's best-known images, but it deserves a place here given the example it sets with its unusual, blurred silhouette view. It depicts a crew walking toward a scrap train during the dismantling of Tennessee's Oneida & Western Railroad. Plates 116 and 117 take us to the next state east of Tennessee, North Carolina, for views of caboose cookery on the Winston-Salem Southbound Railway and an abandoned day coach on the Atlantic & Western Railway. Our tour of the South and its short lines concludes in the Deep South, with two views, plates 118 and 119, taken on an iconic Georgia short line, the Gainesville Midland Railroad.

Hastings's home region from 1959 until his death in 1987, the Midwest, is represented by a regional railroad, the Toledo, Peoria & Western Railway (plate 120), which operated—and operates, as it survives today—in Indiana and Illinois. The locomotive is an Alco RS-2, one of the finest examples of Art Deco–influenced diesel locomotive design.

The remainder of the short lines in this portfolio are in the US West. Plates 121 and 122 depict the West Side Lumber Company's operations, which were centered on Tuolumne, California. The locomotive is a Heisler, one of the three major types of geared American locomotives.

Many short lines replaced engine-hauled passenger trains with railcars in an effort to save money. This happened across the United States, from the Atlantic & Western in North Carolina to the California Western Railroad. Plate 123 depicts an unusual railcar, the Washington, Idaho & Montana Railway's *The Potlatcher*, constructed by Fairmont Railway Motors. Hastings took an extensive series of photos of the Washington, Idaho & Montana (WI&M). Plate 124, the final image in this portfolio, depicts a WI&M freight train—a steam engine and three cars—seemingly about to disappear into the vastness of "big sky country."

Plate 110. In another classic, but rarely captured, image, Hastings looks over the shoulder of a Grasse River Railroad dispatcher with his train sheet and a train order. The Grasse River Railroad, a lumber railroad, ran from Childwold to Cranberry Lake, New York. Photo taken December 24, 1949.

Courtesy of California State Railroad Museum. Philip Ross Hastings, MD, Collection, [Negative 9638].

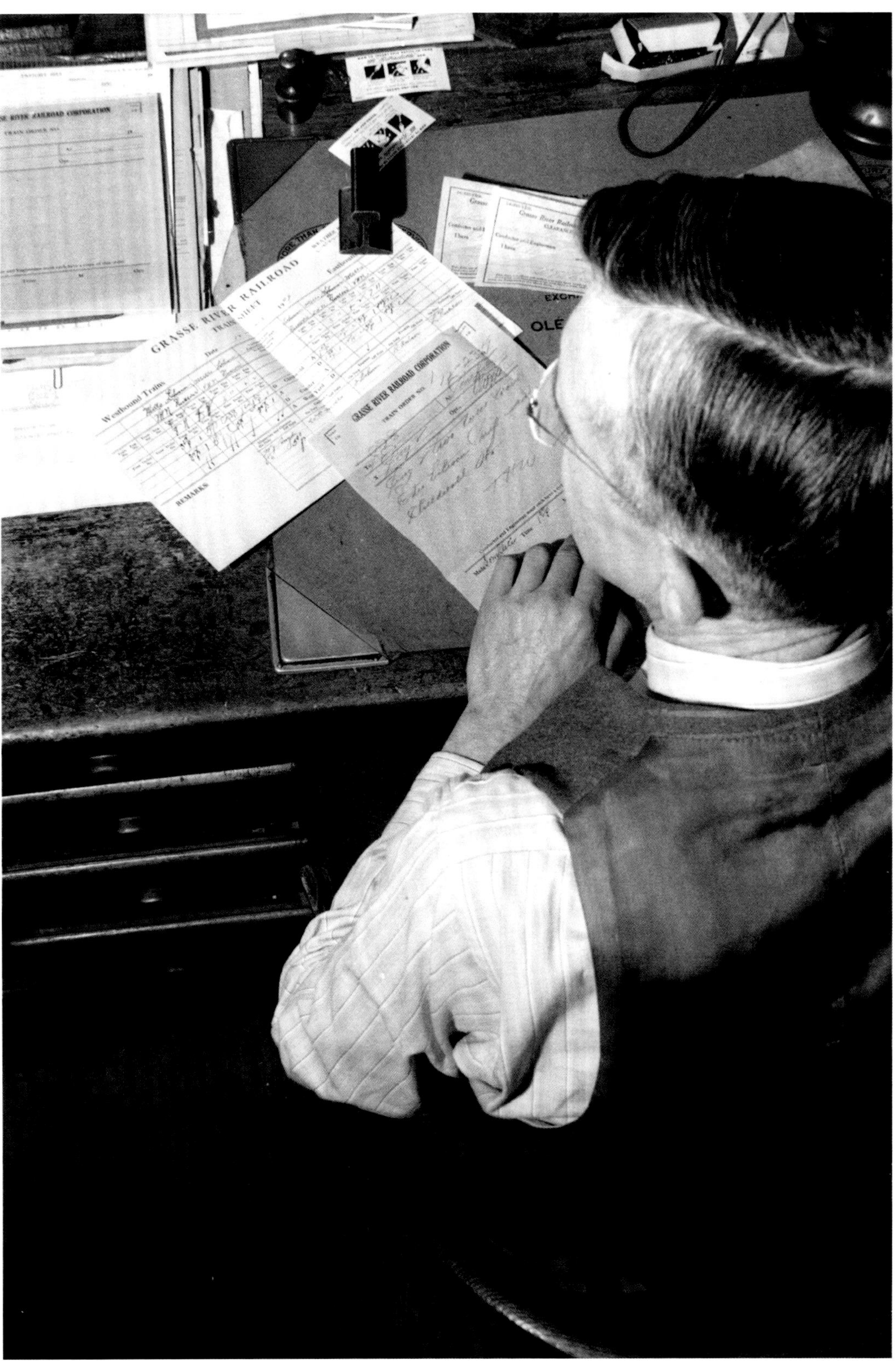

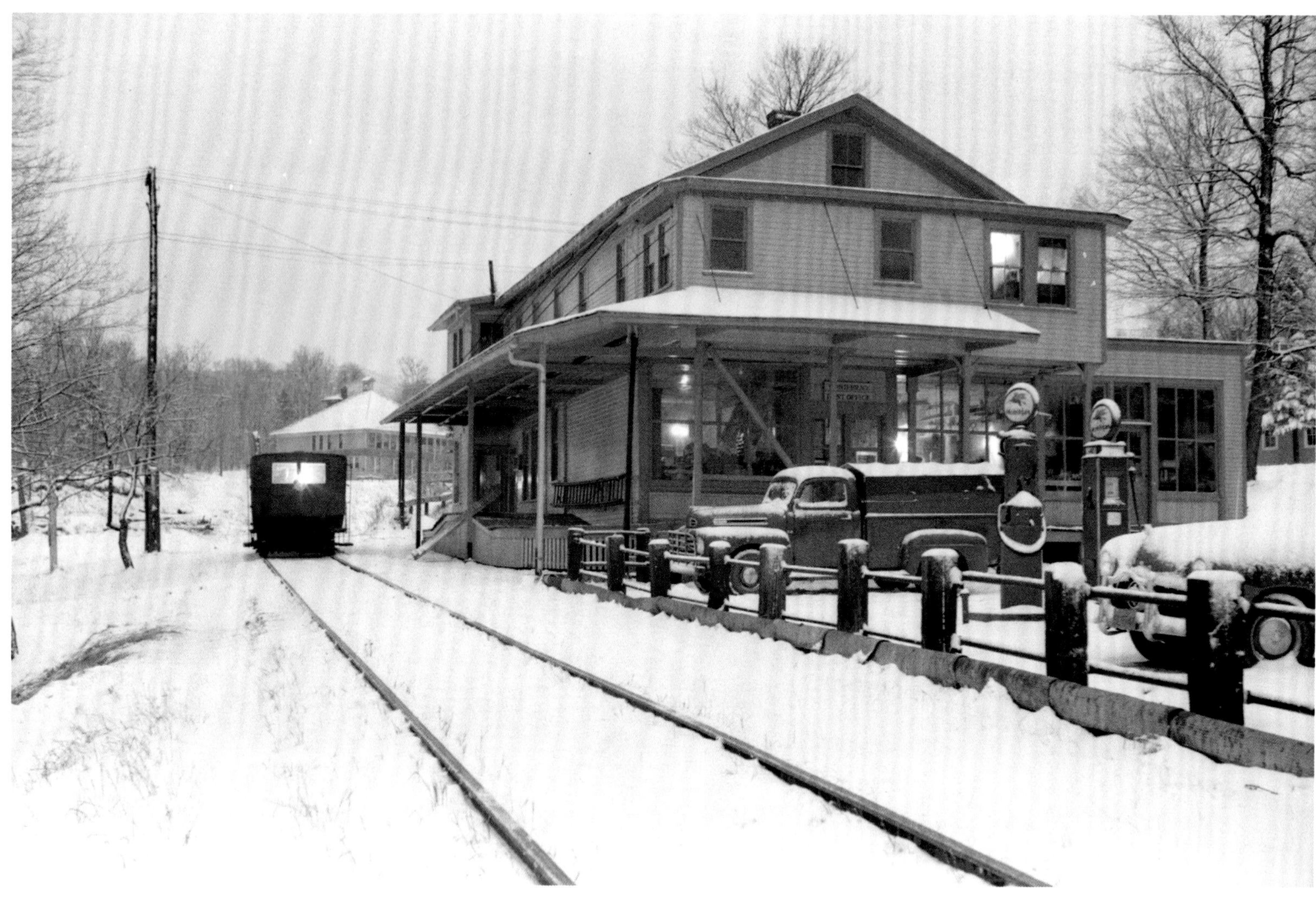

Plate 111. The Grasse River Railroad at Conifer, New York, an impressive Hastings view in the snow that includes "Mobilgas" gas pumps and a speeder. The Grasse River's passenger service served the Conifer Inn in Conifer.

Courtesy of California State Railroad Museum. Philip Ross Hastings, MD, Collection, [Negative 9643].

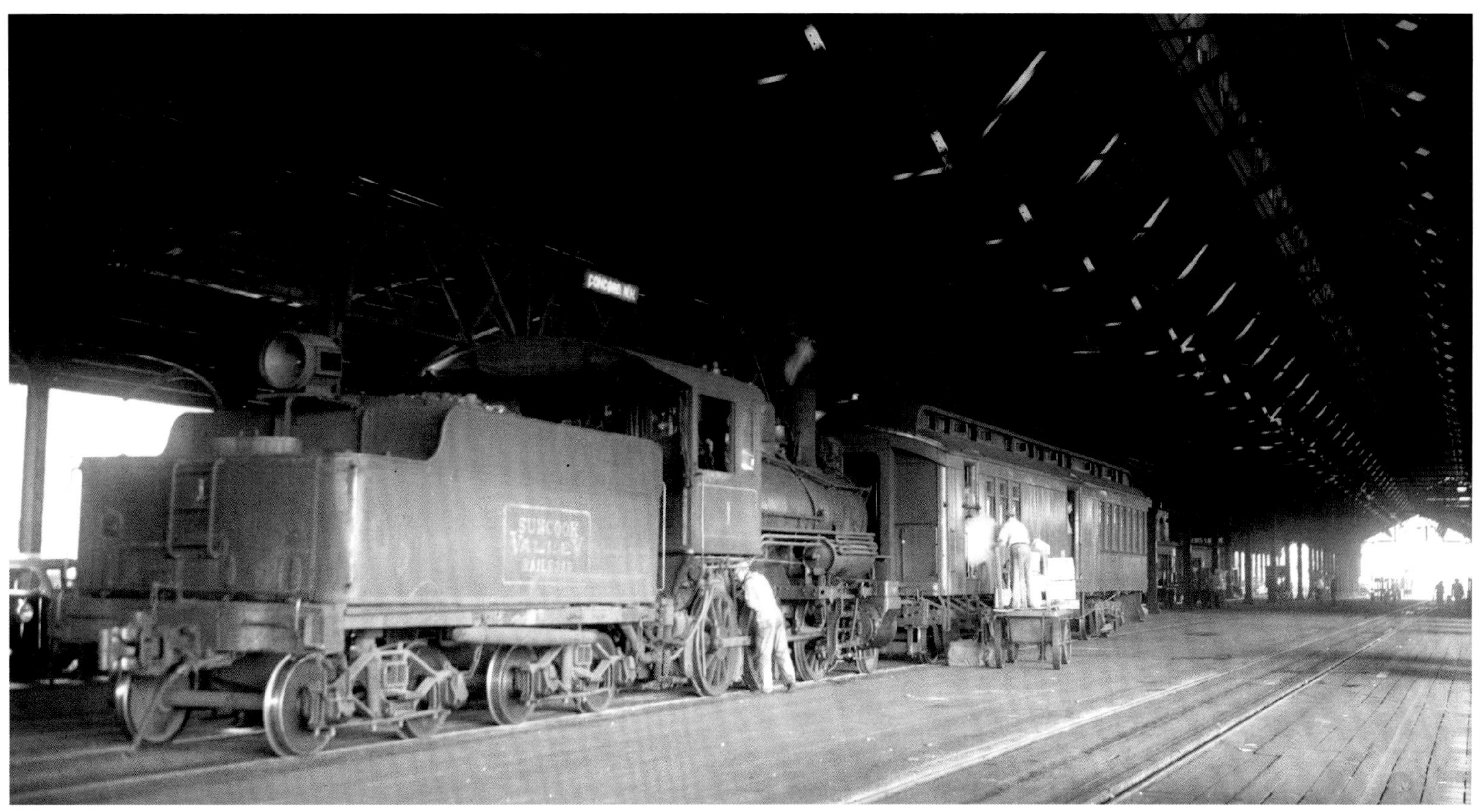

Plate 112. The Suncook Valley, route of the "Blueberry Express," was a traditional New England short line. Here, Suncook Valley locomotive 1, backward, sits with a train consisting of a railway post office (RPO) combine. The mail and express being loaded suggests how this tiny railroad was able to survive as long as it did; the railroad was abandoned in 1952. The location is the train shed of the grand railroad station in Concord, New Hampshire, demolished in 1959. For a great profile of this train, see Archie Robertson's classic *Slow Train to Yesterday*.

Courtesy of California State Railroad Museum. Philip Ross Hastings, MD, Collection, [Negative 9458].

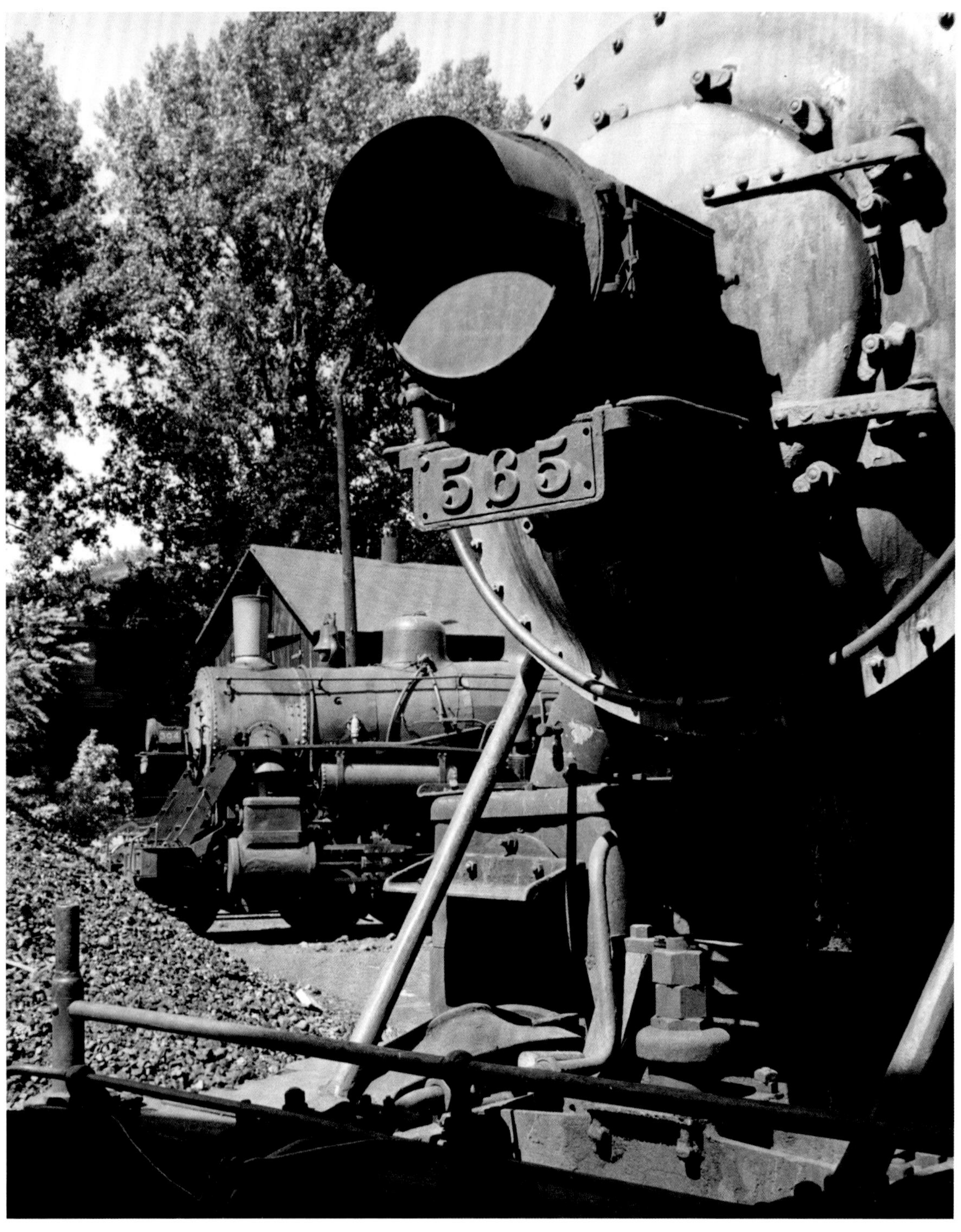

Plate 113. Hastings's close-up of Dansville & Mt. Morris Railroad engines 565 (a 2-6-0 built in 1908) and 304 (a 4-6-0 built in 1905). The Dansville & Mount Morris, now part of the Rochester and Southern Railroad, ran from Dansville to Mount Morris, New York.

Courtesy of California State Railroad Museum. Philip Ross Hastings, MD, Collection, [Negative 10508].

***Facing,* Plate 114.** A Meadow River Lumber Company engineer looks ahead from his Shay as he works in the woods near Rainelle, West Virginia, 1955.

Courtesy of California State Railroad Museum. Philip Ross Hastings, MD, Collection, [Negative 10499].

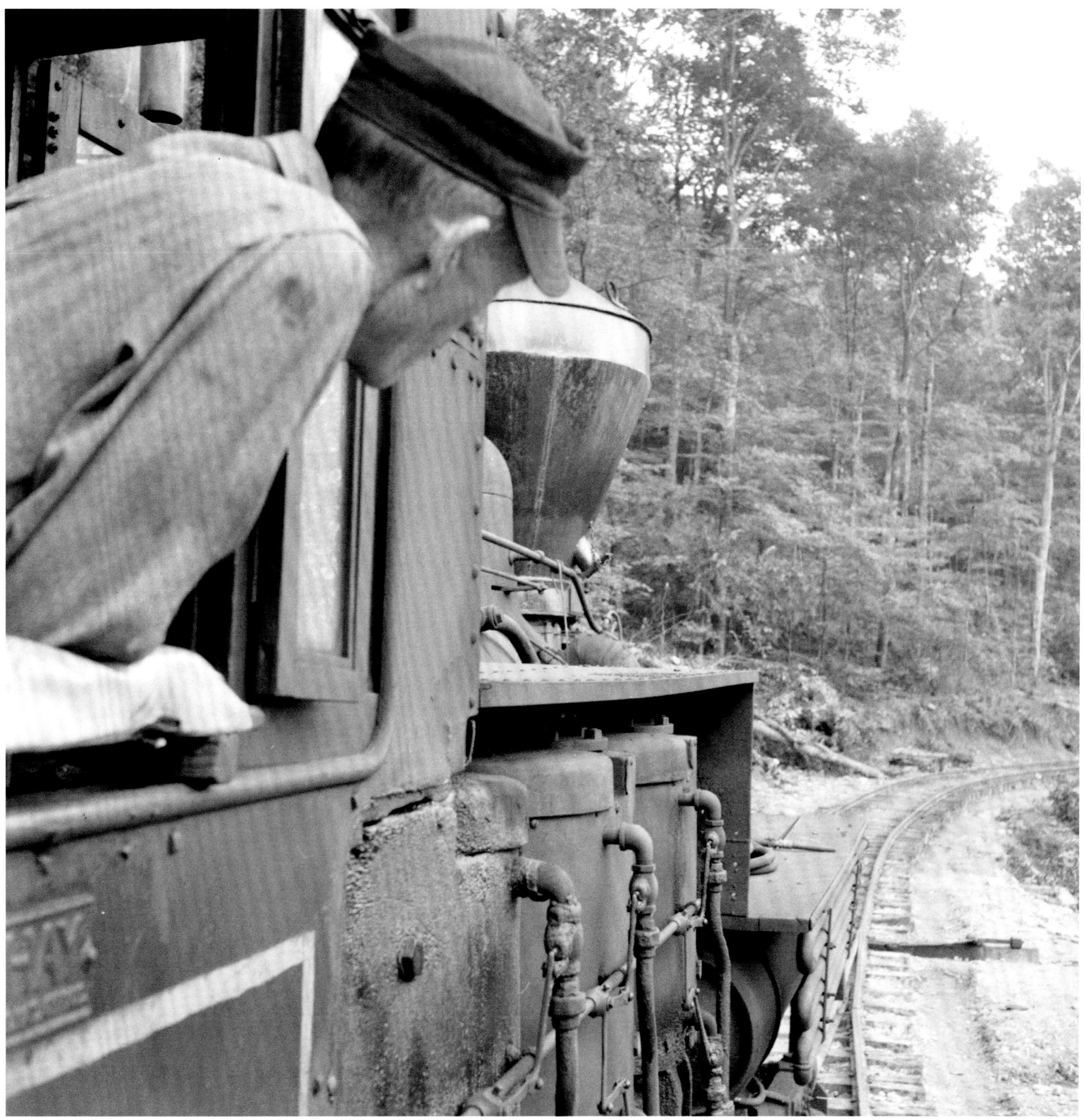

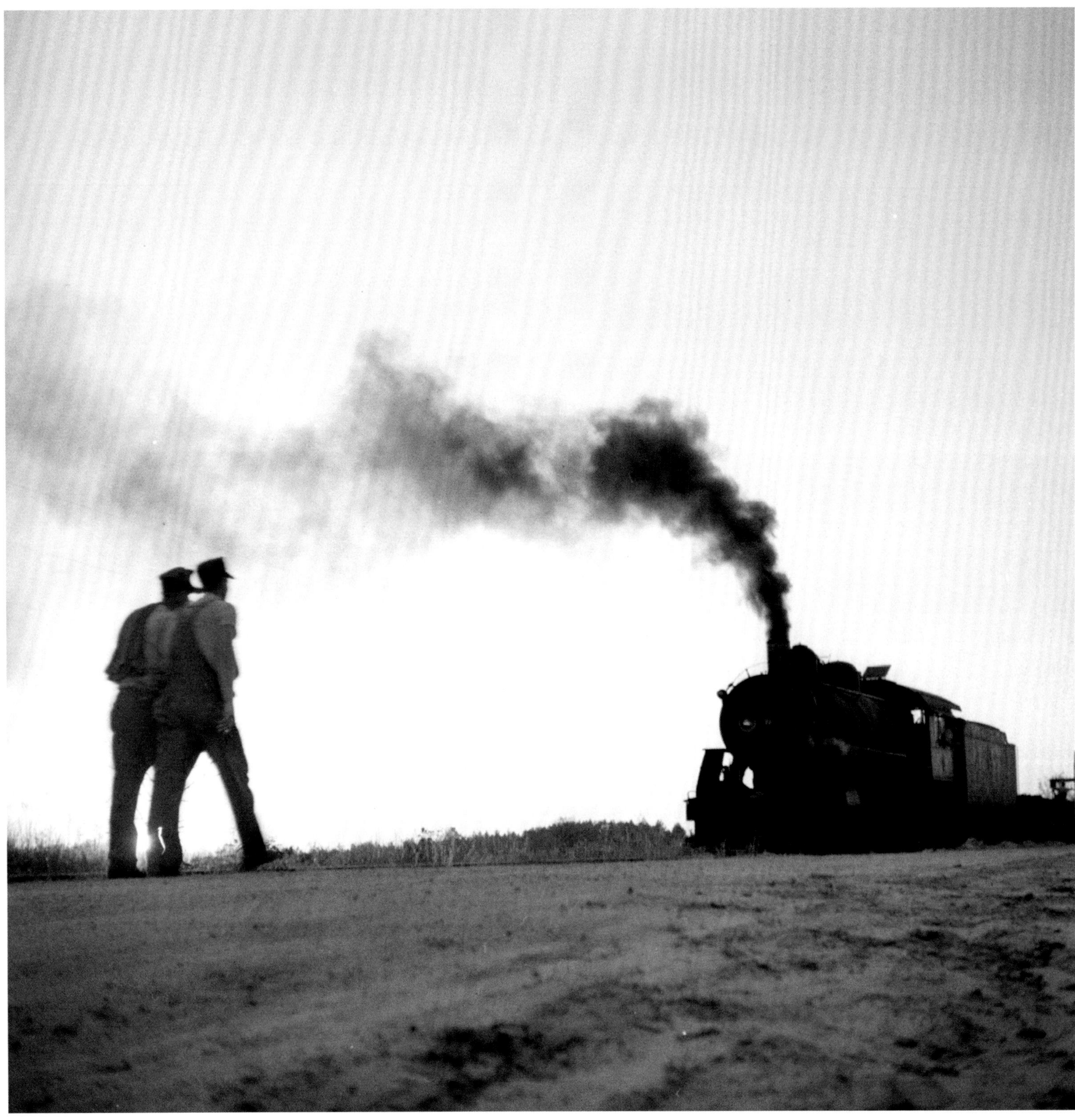

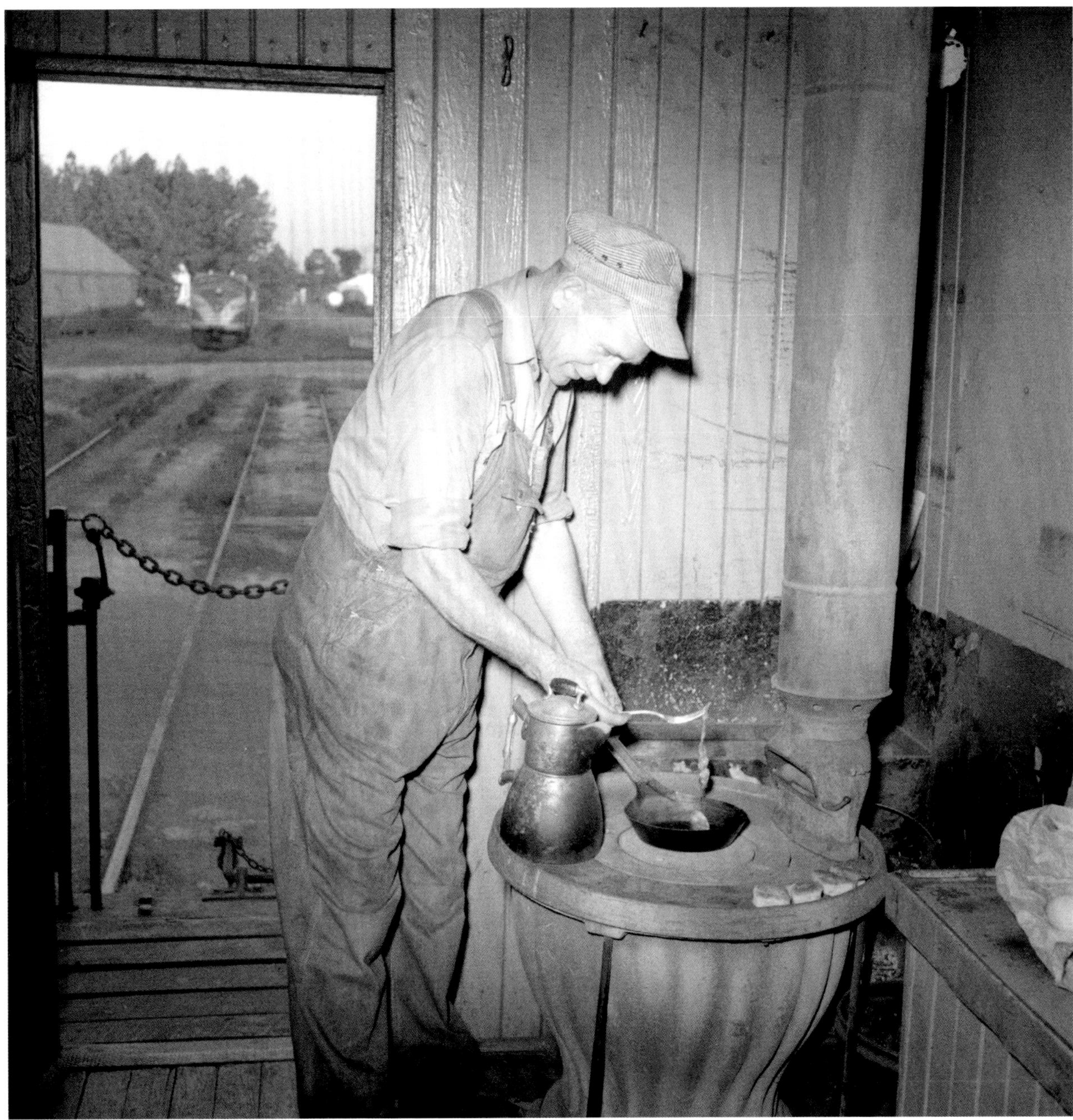

***Facing,* Plate 115.** In one of his best-known photos, Phil Hastings combines two of his signatures—a silhouette of railroad workers or patrons and darkness or near darkness. This image is of what David P. Morgan called, "The saddest train of all," a train scrapping the Oneida & Western Railroad. The Oneida & Western ran from Oneida to Jamestown, Tennessee.

Courtesy of California State Railroad Museum. Philip Ross Hastings, MD, Collection, [Negative 10501].

Plate 116. Here, Hastings captures another once common but rarely photographed image of steam-era railroading: caboose cookery. The scene is a caboose on North Carolina's Winston-Salem Southbound, then jointly owned by the Norfolk & Western Railway and the Atlantic Coast Line Railroad. The railroad still exists and is owned by N&W and ACL successors Norfolk Southern and CSX; it runs from Winston-Salem to Wadesboro, North Carolina.

Courtesy of California State Railroad Museum. Philip Ross Hastings, MD, Collection, [Negative 5672].

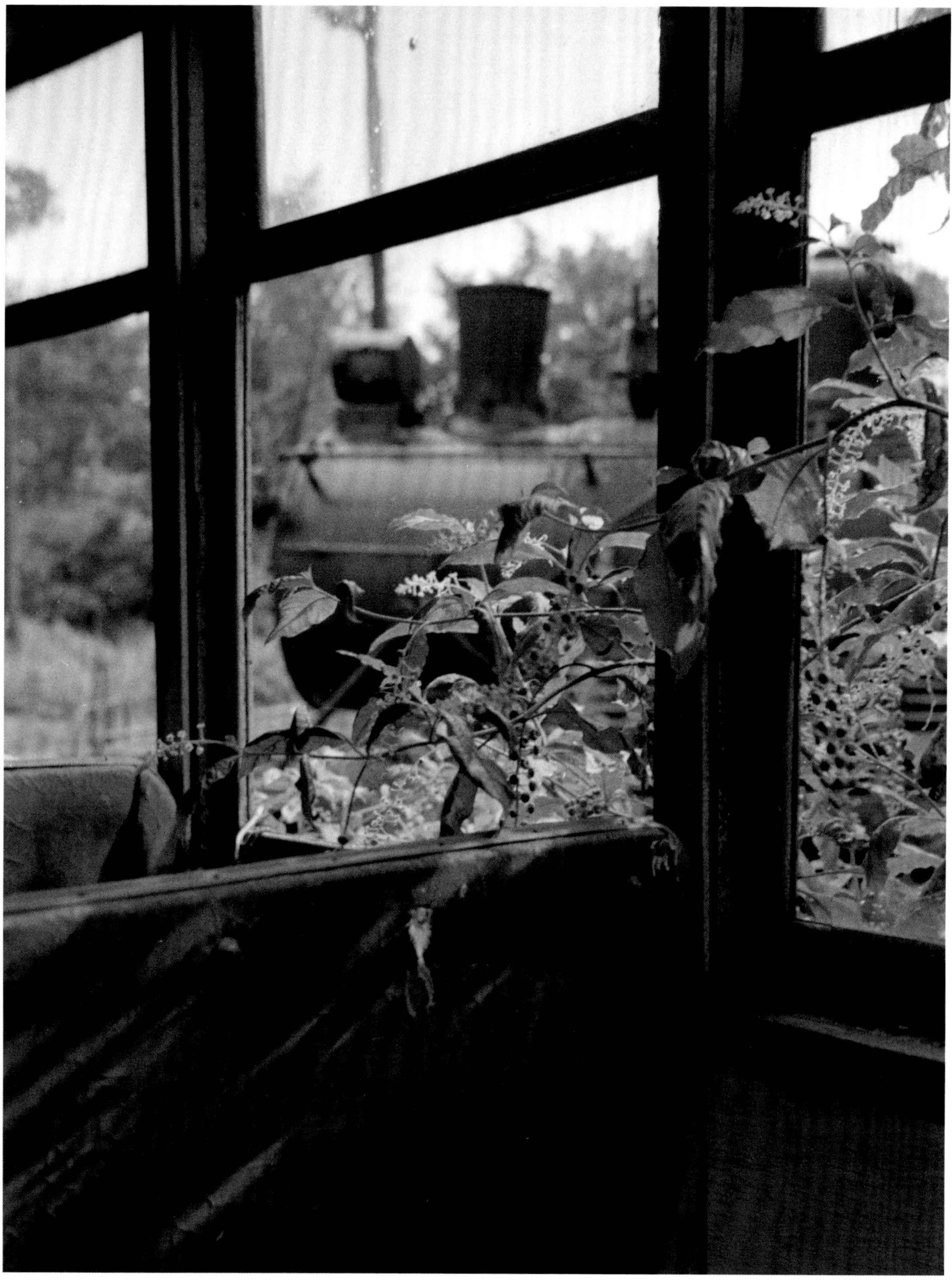

Plate 117. The town of Sanford, North Carolina, is not too far from Winston-Salem. In this image, taken in Sanford, Hastings captured an Atlantic & Western Railroad locomotive through the window of an abandoned A&W coach. By including pokeweed in the image, Hastings tells us, without words, that we are in the US South. The Atlantic & Western survives today, although much of its line was abandoned in the early 1960s.

Courtesy of California State Railroad Museum. Philip Ross Hastings, MD, Collection, [Negative 6015].

***Facing,* Plate 118.** Hastings followed in the footsteps of Lucius Beebe and Charles Clegg as he captured Gainesville Midland Railroad "Decapod" 207 at an interchange with the Seaboard Air Line Railway in Athens, Georgia.

Courtesy of California State Railroad Museum. Philip Ross Hastings, MD, Collection, [Negative 5529].

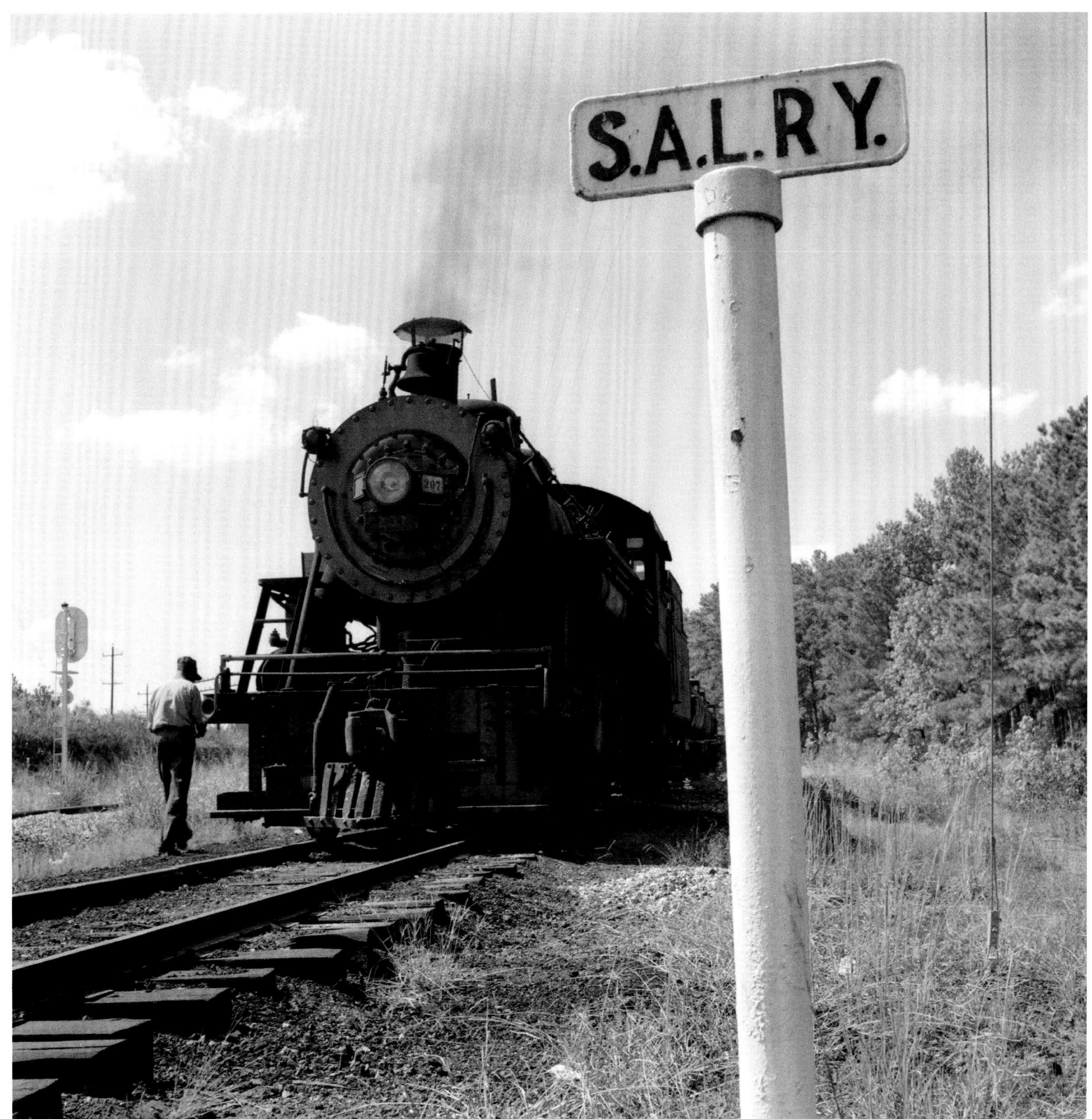
S.A.L.RY.

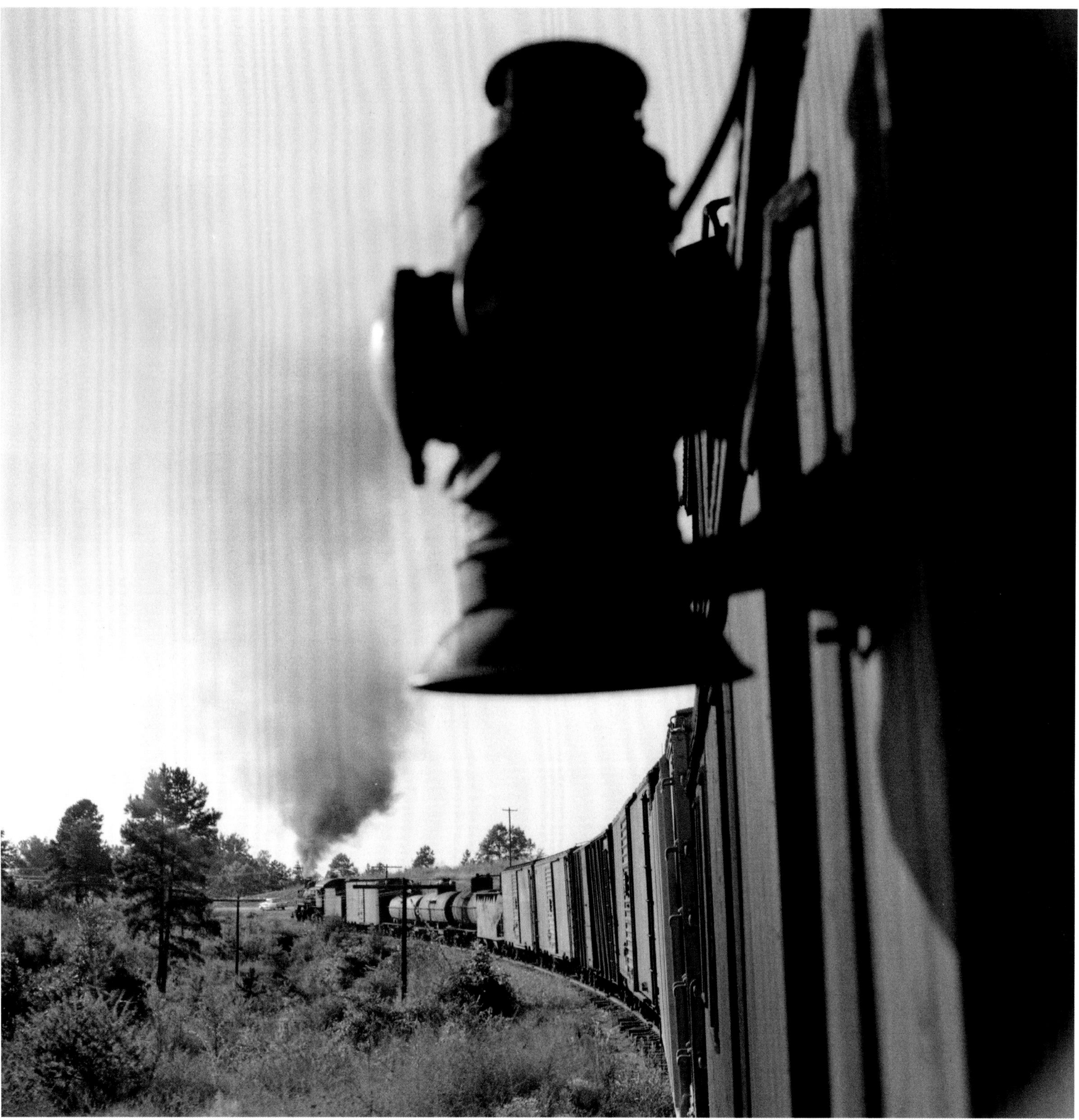

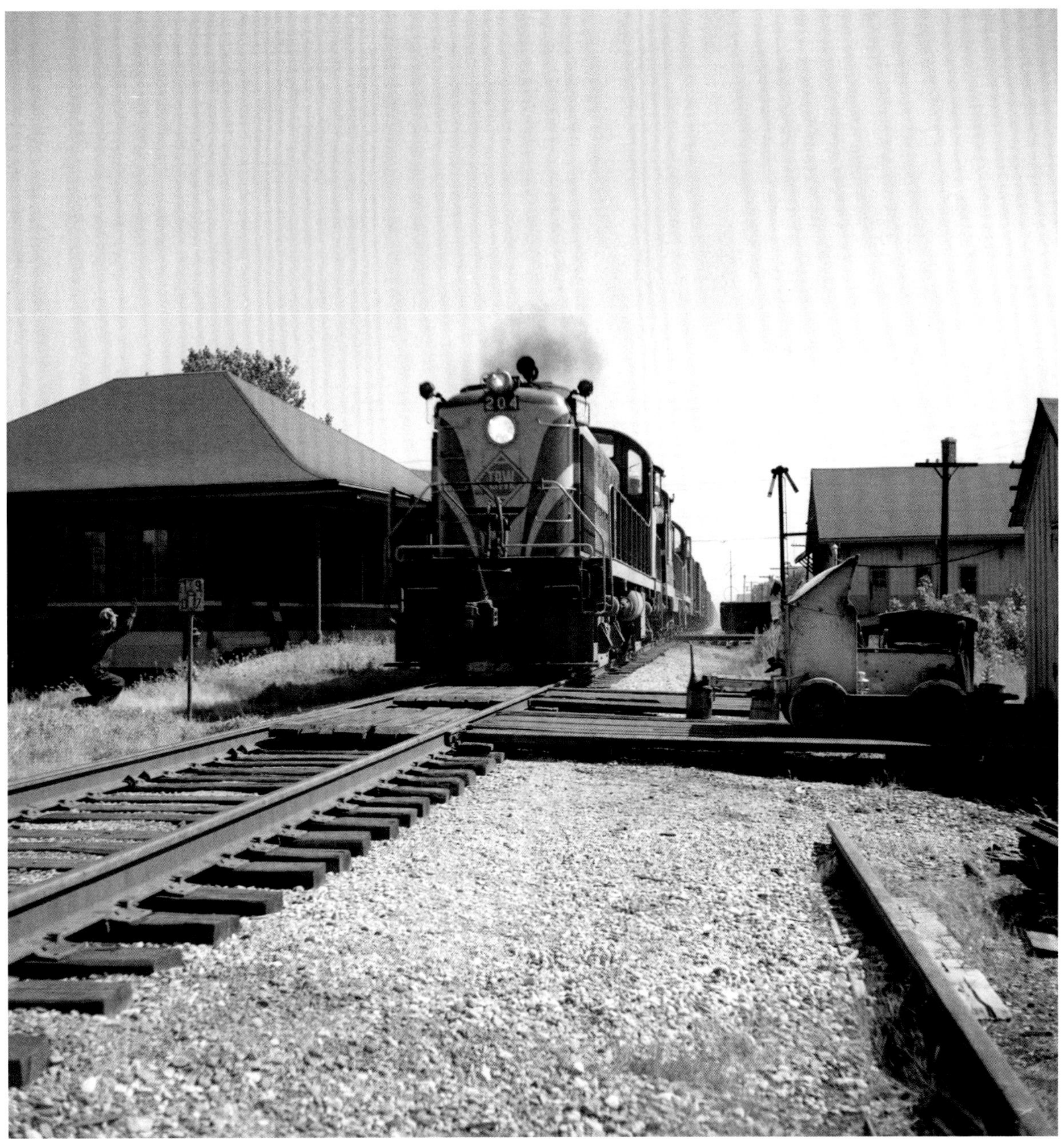

***Facing,* Plate 119.** An image Hastings tried to capture a number of times is a train taken from the rear with a marker light foregrounded in the upper right third of the view. Marker lights were required in order to designate a train. They were turned red when the train was on the operating line and green or yellow (depending on the railroad's rules) to show it was safely in a siding. This image was taken on the Gainesville Midland. The Gainesville Midland was purchased by the connecting Seaboard Air Line in 1959.

Courtesy of California State Railroad Museum. Philip Ross Hastings, MD, Collection, [Negative 5511].

Plate 120. In this view, taken September 18, 1954, at Gilman, Illinois, a Toledo, Peoria & Western Railway westbound manifest freight led by Alco RS-2 204 passes the Illinois Central (left) and TP&W (right) stations. Hastings sometimes included section gang speeders in his views, usually to great effect, and this image is foregrounded by one—no workers are present in the image, but a can is set out for their use. The TP&W, an Illinois/Indiana regional, survives today.

Courtesy of California State Railroad Museum. Philip Ross Hastings, MD, Collection, [Negative 3756].

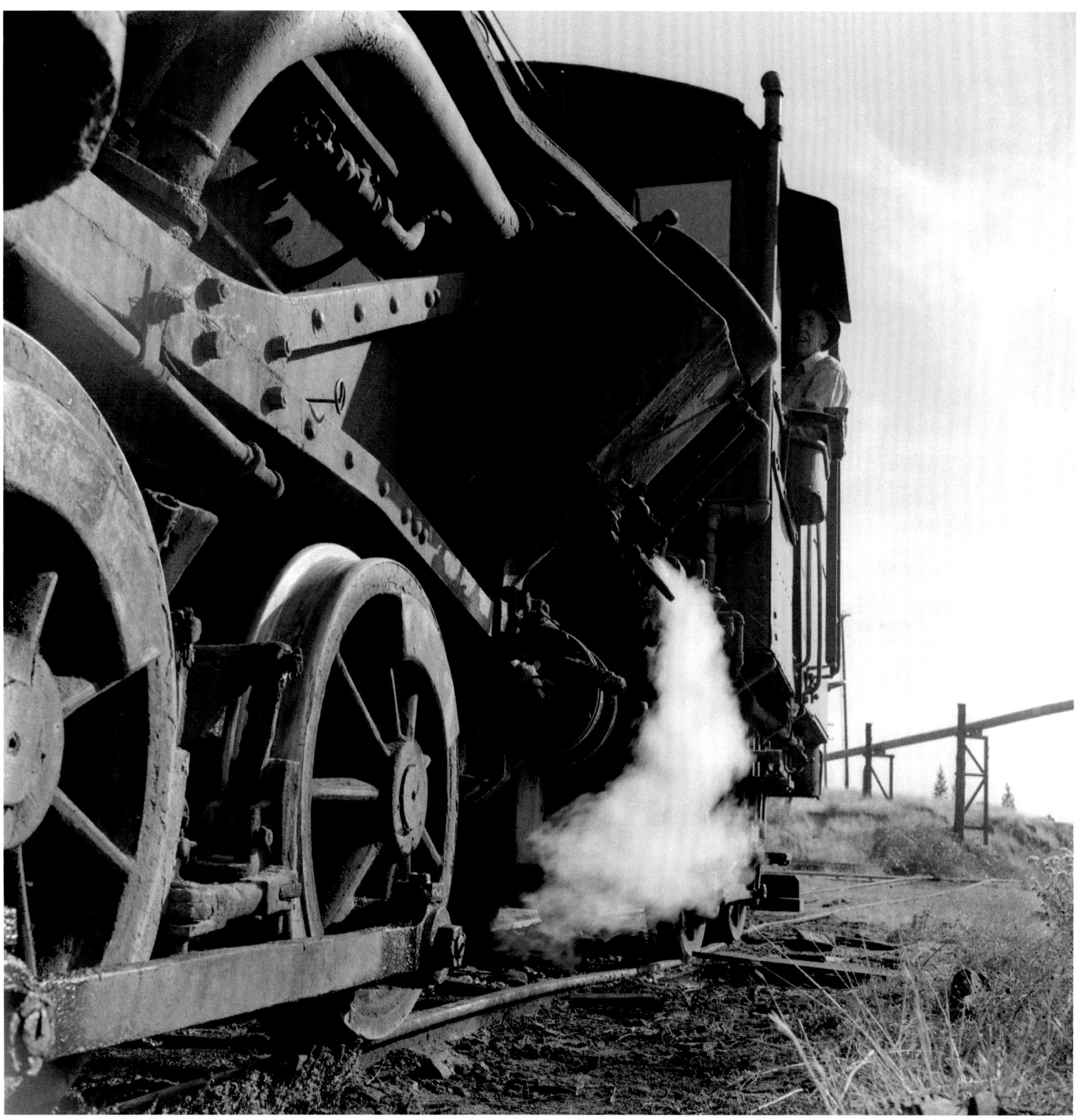

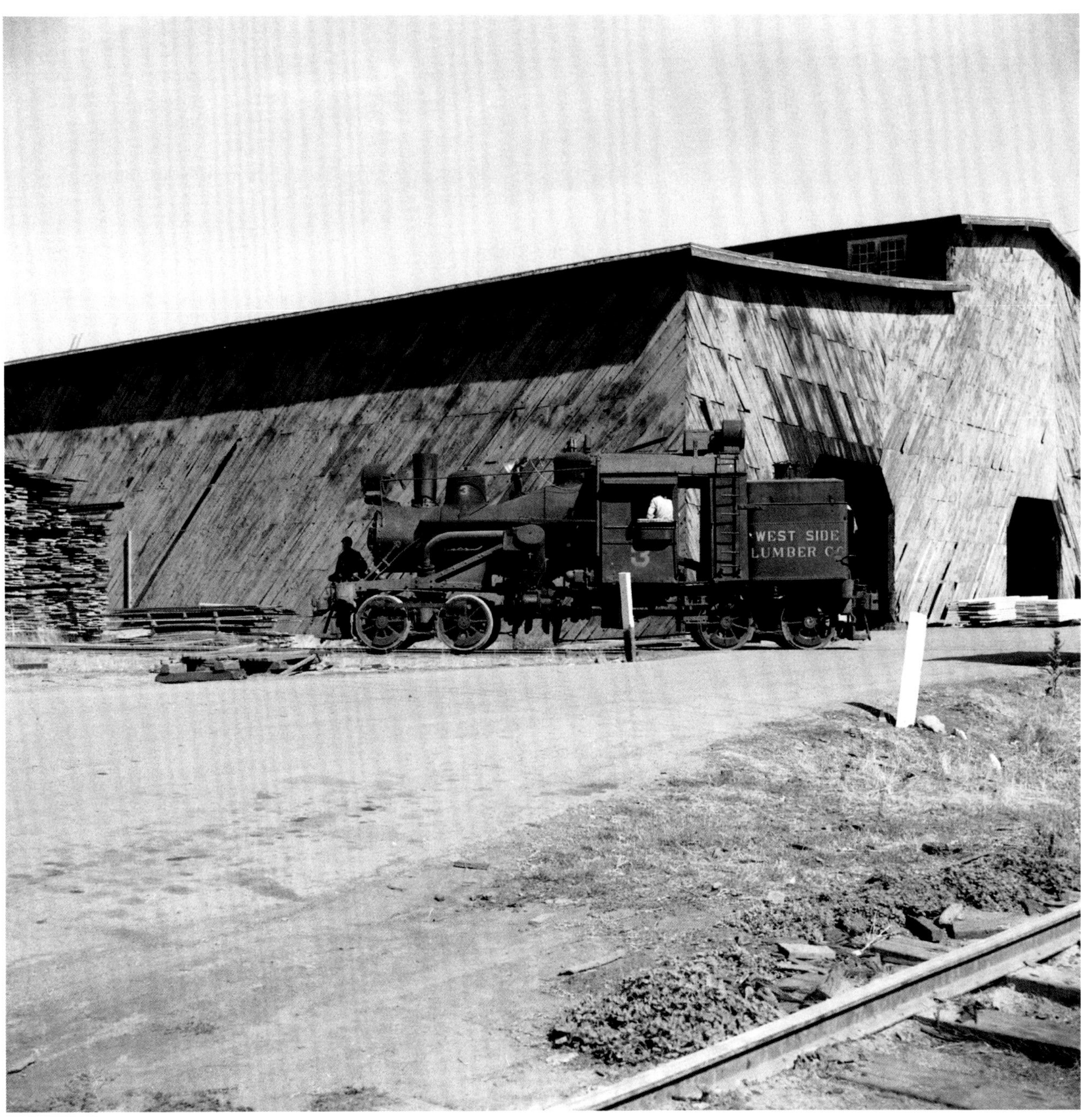

***Facing,* Plate 121.** In this view of West Side Lumber Company Heisler 3, Hastings shoots upward from track level, placing an engineman on the upper right third point of the image. The image was taken in Tuolumne, California, in 1957. The West Side Lumber Company's railway was the last three-foot-gauge lumber railroad operating in the US West.

Courtesy of California State Railroad Museum. Philip Ross Hastings, MD, Collection, [Negative 10184].

Plate 122. In this view of the same locomotive, West Side Lumber Company Heisler 3, Hastings captures the engine in front of a building with distinctive, and visually interesting, slanted wood siding. The image tells us, without words, that lumber was plentiful in Tuolumne. The tracks in the foreground form an interesting, broken visual *V* with the track hosting locomotive 3. 1957.

Courtesy of California State Railroad Museum. Philip Ross Hastings, MD, Collection, [Negative 10176].

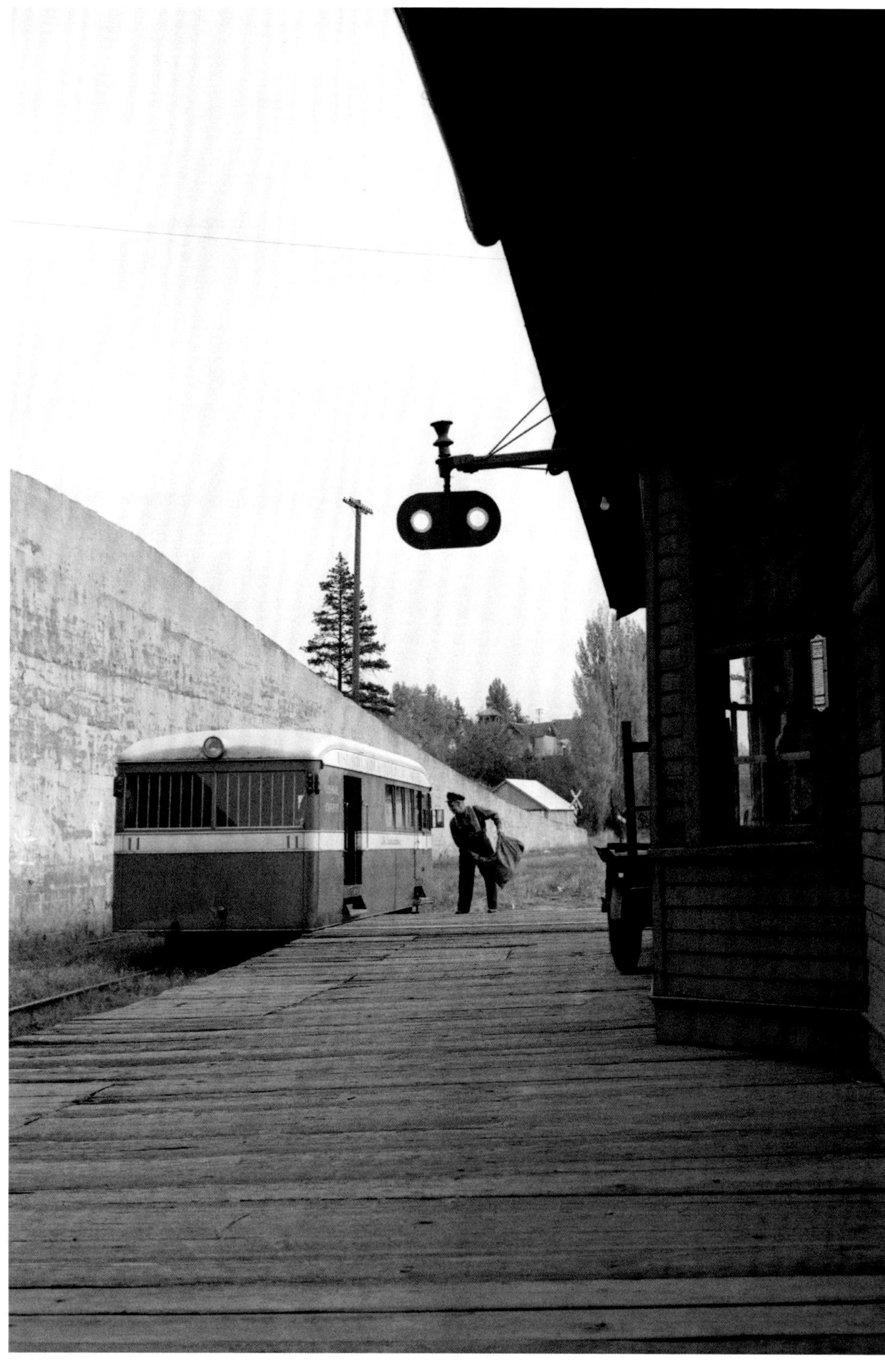

Plate 123. Hastings had an affinity for the archaic "turn" type of train order signal. In this view, a signal of this type crowns an image of a trainman loading mail into a tiny Washington, Idaho & Montana Railway railcar at a classic steam-era station. The railcar is the *Potlatcher* (named for the railroad's owner, Potlatch Lumber Company), built by Fairmont Railway Motors—better known for its speeders. The *Potlatcher* provided the railroad's passenger service from 1938 to 1955, when passenger service ended.

Courtesy of California State Railroad Museum. Philip Ross Hastings, MD, Collection, [Negative 3310].

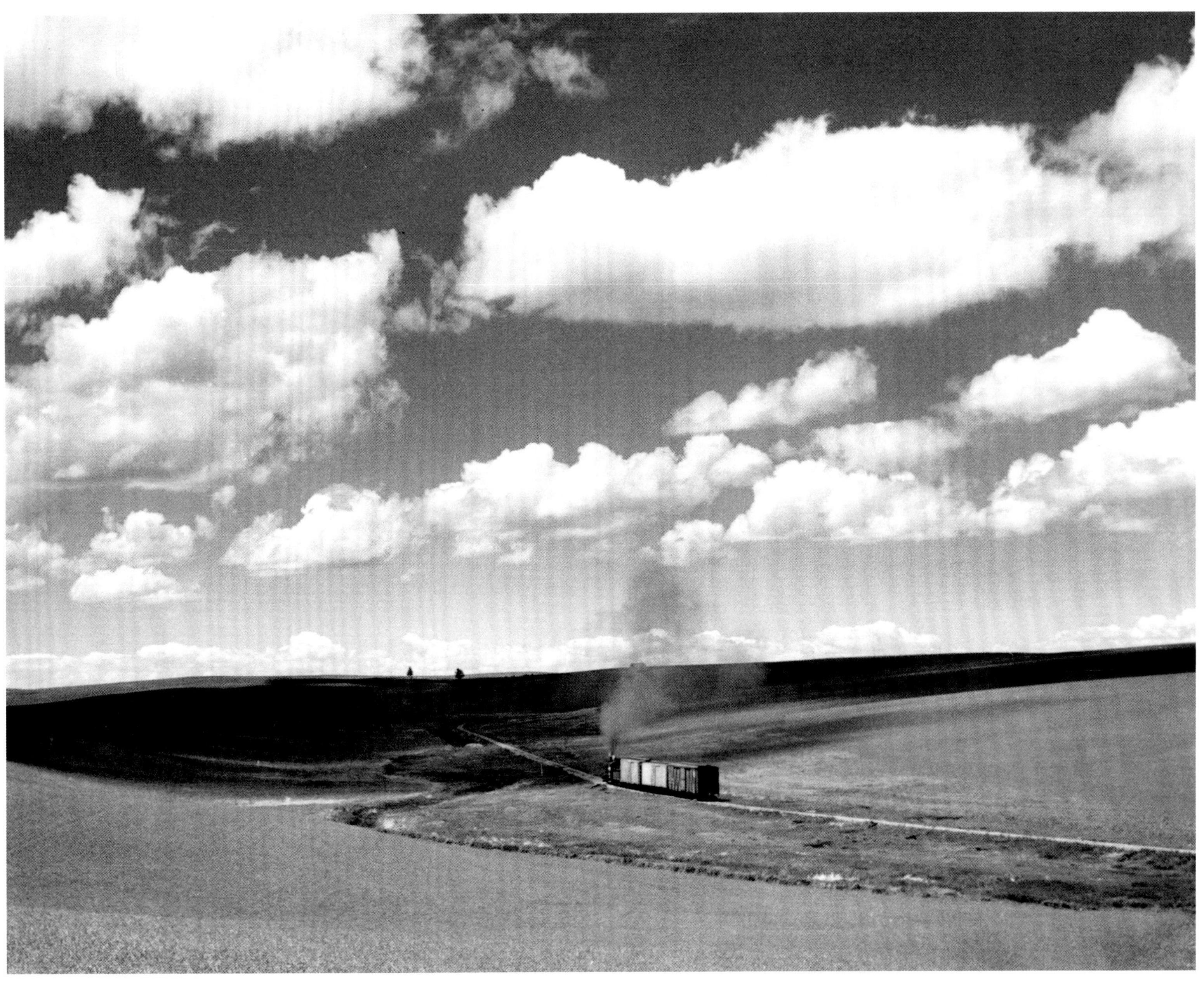

Plate 124. In the final Hastings short line view in this portfolio, a Washington, Idaho & Montana freight train, just three cars sans caboose, is about to be swallowed up by "big sky country."

Courtesy of California State Railroad Museum. Philip Ross Hastings, MD, Collection, [Negative 10512].

PORTFOLIO NINE

IN THE NIGHTTIME

Phil Hastings was a great innovator in night and low-light railroad-subject photography. As his friend Jim Shaughnessy, said, "I truly feel that Phil Hastings originated the night railroad photo, at least originated the art for the average railfan."[1] In advancing this technique, Hastings was joined by his contemporaries, both fellow *Trains* magazine contributors, O. Winston Link and Jim Shaughnessy. Shaughnessy, who followed Link and Hastings in the chronology of their images, acknowledged the influence of the two older photographers. Link famously, and categorically, denied that he was influenced by other railroad-subject photographers or contemporary art photographers, such as Walker Evans, and claimed to be unaware of their work.

Unlike Hastings, Link's reputation has crossed solidly over into the realm of art photography and so he has had an influence on art photographers following him who are interested in photography in darkness or, like Gregory Crewdson, in posed tableaux images. In recent years, due largely to two books, *Essential Witness* and *The Call of Trains*, Shaughnessy's work has also gained some—admittedly limited—recognition in this world.[2]

To this observer's eye, Phil Hastings's pioneering night photography, much of which precedes the beginning of O. Winston Link's Norfolk & Western work in 1955, is clearly an influence on those who followed. A full range of his work has not been gathered together in one book, irrespective of subject, before. Hopefully, a reappraisal of the uniqueness of his night images may follow.

Hastings's 1950s work, and that of Link and Shaughnessy, not only precedes the invention of sensitive digital cameras but also the advent of strobe flashguns. These men worked with flashbulbs, light bulbs that could only be used once. In this environment, there was only one technique, open shutter, that didn't require additional equipment beyond a camera, tripod, and a shutter-release cable. In this technique, the photographer holds the shutter open to collect ambient light. Exposure times are critical and often uncertain. Hastings did use this technique.

In terms of techniques requiring additional equipment, flash fill was the next step up. In this technique, the open shutter is used, but fill light is applied with a battery-powered piece of equipment that uses flashbulbs—today, strobe flash guns are used. Hastings used this technique as well. Finally—and, due to the cost of the equipment involved, a technique usually only available to well-funded professional photographers—synchronized flash lighting can be used. This requires a camera with a shutter that is synchronized with a linked set of flashbulb guns, the entire setup normally being battery powered. O. Winston Link was a master of this technique. Hastings sometimes used this technique as well but with a limited number of flashbulb guns.[3]

Contemporary railroad-subject photographer Dick Steinheimer said this of Hastings's nighttime work: "Hastings' equipment was simple: a twin lens reflex, light tripod, and one or two flash guns. Relying mostly on available light from station platforms or quickly vanishing daylight (he was a superb master of low-light, mixed source photography), his techniques were straightforward."[4]

This portfolio is organized geographically, but the time line is also of interest. The earliest image featured here, which seems to be taken with ambient light, was shot in 1948. Hastings also took a number of interesting self-portraits in darkness (see fig. 3 in the introduction), many of them dating from the early 1950s. The majority of the images featured here were taken in the mid-1950s. Soon after this period, Hastings moved to Iowa and began his professional career as a psychiatrist.[5] Probably because of his career and his family, we largely see a hiatus in images of this type until another group emerges in the mid-1960s.

This portfolio begins with one of Hastings's best-known night images, plate 125, showcasing a "meet" of trains on the Canadian National at Green River, New Brunswick. A technique that Hastings used from time to time with great effect is showcased here—his flash illuminates falling snow in the foreground and, combined with ambient light, the railroad-subject scene.

Plate 126, not dated but probably taken in the 1950s, shows Hastings using ambient light from the Toronto, Canada, skyline to create a background for a night image of a Canadian National locomotive taken from overhead.

Moving south and east from Canada, plate 127, one of Hastings's early photos, depicts a Boston & Maine local at Hastings's hometown, Bradford, Vermont. Light reflecting on the RPO car and the combine provides interest, as does the railroader and the sack of mail in the foreground.

Plate 128, also undated but taken after World War II and before 1955, shows a meet between the New York, New Haven and Hartford Railroad and the Boston & Maine. This very posed tableau, including four railroaders, one of them holding a lantern, seems to reflect O. Winston Link's influence—but it actually predates the first publications of Link's Norfolk & Western night photographs. Plate 129 is another posed, if less complex, image taken of a Central Vermont switch engine at Brattleboro, Vermont, in 1956.

In addition to the Boston & Maine, Hastings had a special affinity for another classic New England railroad, the Rutland.[6] In the next night image, plate 130, taken before Rutland passenger service ended in the summer of 1953, we see another conductor with a brightly lighted lantern—an effect that would become a trademark technique for Link later in the decade.

In plate 131, a resplendent New York Central "Niagara" sits beside a Baltimore & Ohio locomotive at an engine terminal. The "Niagaras" were scrapped in 1955 and 1956. The 6000 was the first "Niagara" built. In plate 132, a stunning image taken in 1956 that seems years ahead of its time in terms of framing, Hastings looks back from a helper as a train led by E-7A 5867 leaves Altoona, Pennsylvania, to climb the westbound grade to Horseshoe Curve and the Gallitzin tunnels. The distorted face of the engineer, seen through the wet cab window, adds a surreal, uncanny vibe to the image—something that is unusual for Hastings. In a final eastern view before we move to the Midwest, plate 133 shows the East Broad Top Railroad and Coal Company (EBT) roundhouse and turntable at Orbisonia, Pennsylvania. The image was taken in 1952, before EBT service ended in 1956. (Figure 2 in the introduction was taken during a visit to the EBT by Hastings and his family.)[7]

Hastings's move to Waterloo, Iowa, in 1959 put railroads such as the Burlington Route, the Rock Island, and the Chicago Great Western squarely in his viewfinder. Hastings's 1960s nighttime portrait of a Railway Express agency clerk, taken on the Burlington at Omaha, Nebraska, plate 134, is one of his most noted images. As might be expected, Hastings took a number of images in his new hometown, Waterloo, Iowa, and many of them were night images. Plate 135, whose lighting shows the gaudy cigarette ads—perhaps a silent comment from a psychiatrist/physician—and the train, is an example.

Turning to the western US, any railroad-image photographer of the mid-twentieth century worth his or her salt made the pilgrimage—popularized by Lucius Beebe and Charles Clegg—to the narrow gauge lines of the Rio Grande Southern Railroad and the Denver & Rio Grande Western. In this noted night image, plate 136, Hastings used lighting ahead of the locomotive profiled—in this case, D&RGW 499—to suggest its headlight penetrating the dark unknown before it. Plate 137 is a night image of another favorite photographers' quarry of the 1940s and 1950s, a Union Pacific "Big Boy." Both are mid-1950s images.

Hastings took many great railroad-subject images with Pacific Northwest settings—a book featuring them would be a worthwhile endeavor. Plate 138 is an early Hastings image, taken in 1951, but it depicts a relative newcomer, Great Northern F-3A diesel 359 at Spokane, Washington. As with the Toronto skyline image in plate 126, the lighted Great Northern Clocktower adds to the image. Plate 139, another "flash and snowflake" image, is a photo taken in the darkness of the famed Norden Summit Southern Pacific snow shed. The Norden complex was an amazing, now largely vanished, piece of railroad infrastructure.

This view of Phil Hastings's "In the Night Time" and this book-length survey of his work ends with an iconic 1955 image of a conductor and an operator on the night shift, plate 140. Conductor S. M. Surratt's train will leave just after midnight, and the standard Western Union clock in the photo leaves us in no doubt as to the time.

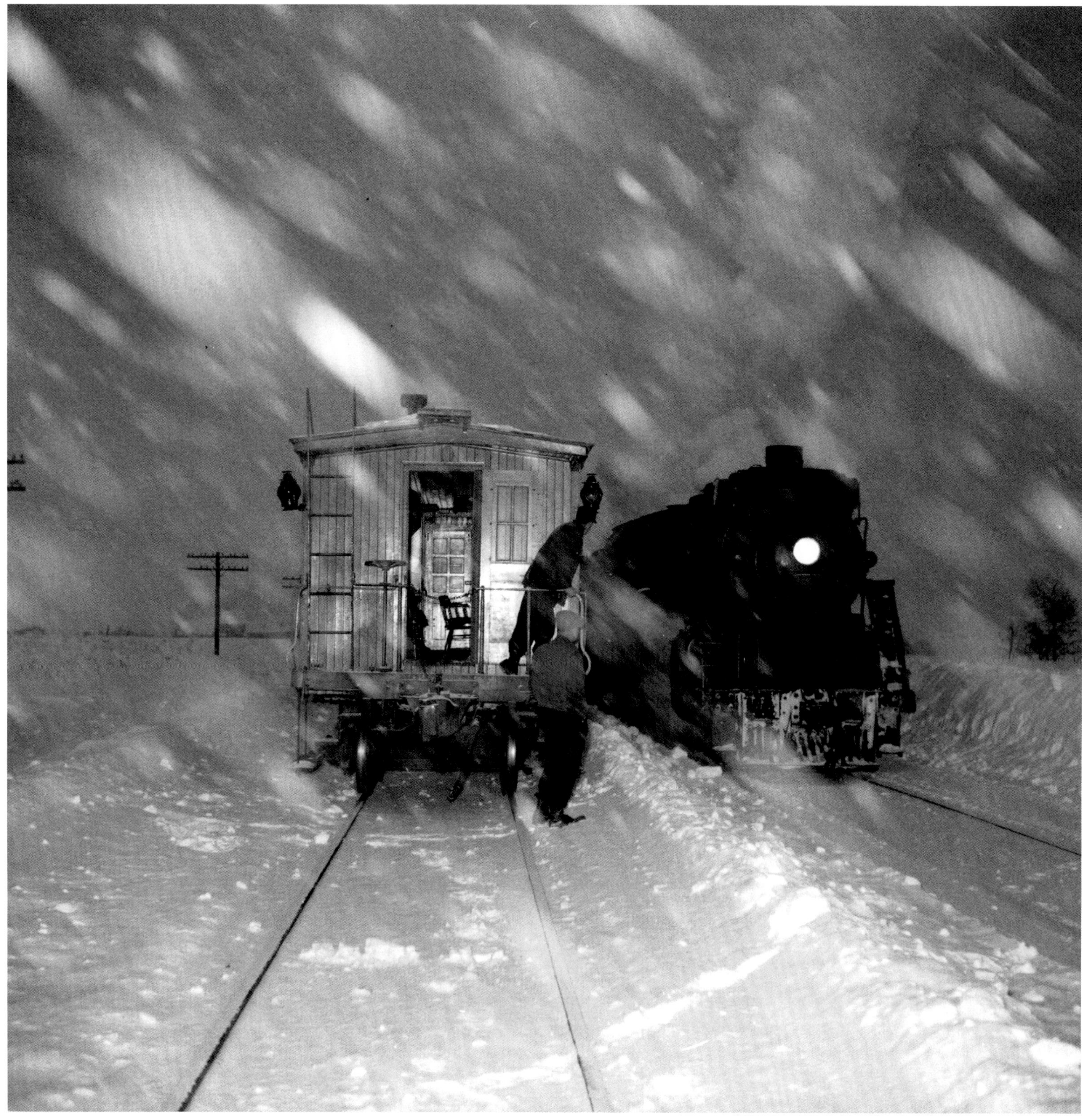

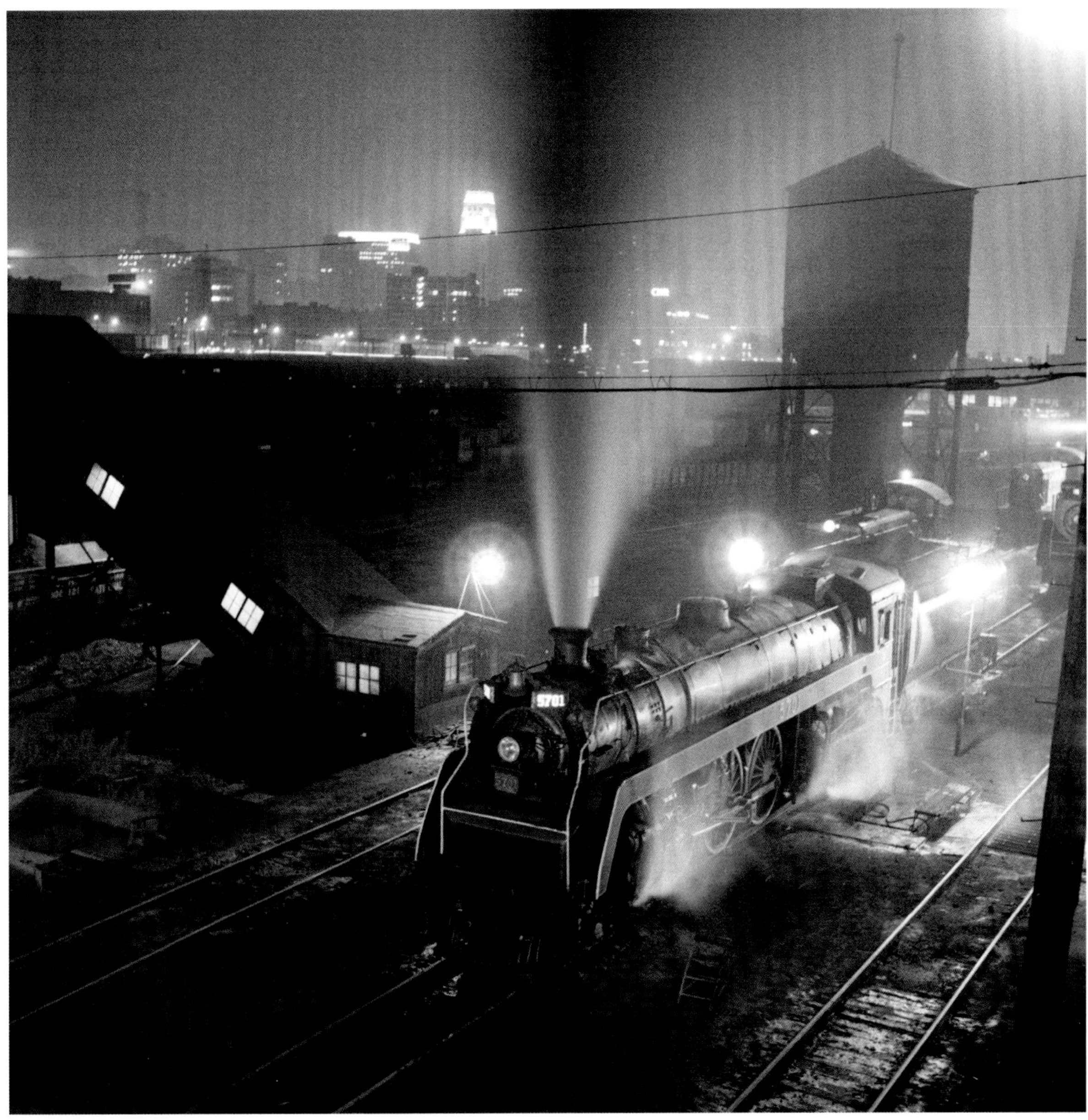

***Facing,* Plate 125.** In a well-known image, Phil Hastings captured a meet in near darkness during a blinding snowstorm. The blurred flakes—an effect Hastings tried for a number of times but achieved most successfully here—suggest the storm, while the attire of the trainmen on the caboose suggests both the cold of night and the warmth of their mobile home away from home. Hastings used flash, much of it reflecting from the stark, white snow, to capture this view. It was taken in Green River, New Brunswick, in 1955. The train that the conductor and rear brakeman are looking over is a westbound extra headed by Canadian National 4-6-2 5258.

Courtesy of California State Railroad Museum. Philip Ross Hastings, MD, Collection, [Negative 2016].

Plate 126. In another Canadian National night view, taken at a very different place, Hastings captures Canadian National 5701 from overhead, posed in front of the lights of the Toronto skyline. An open shutter technique with stationary subjects allowed Hastings to capture these lights. The 5701 was a Class K-5-a 4-6-4.

Courtesy of California State Railroad Museum. Philip Ross Hastings, MD, Collection, [Negative 1995].

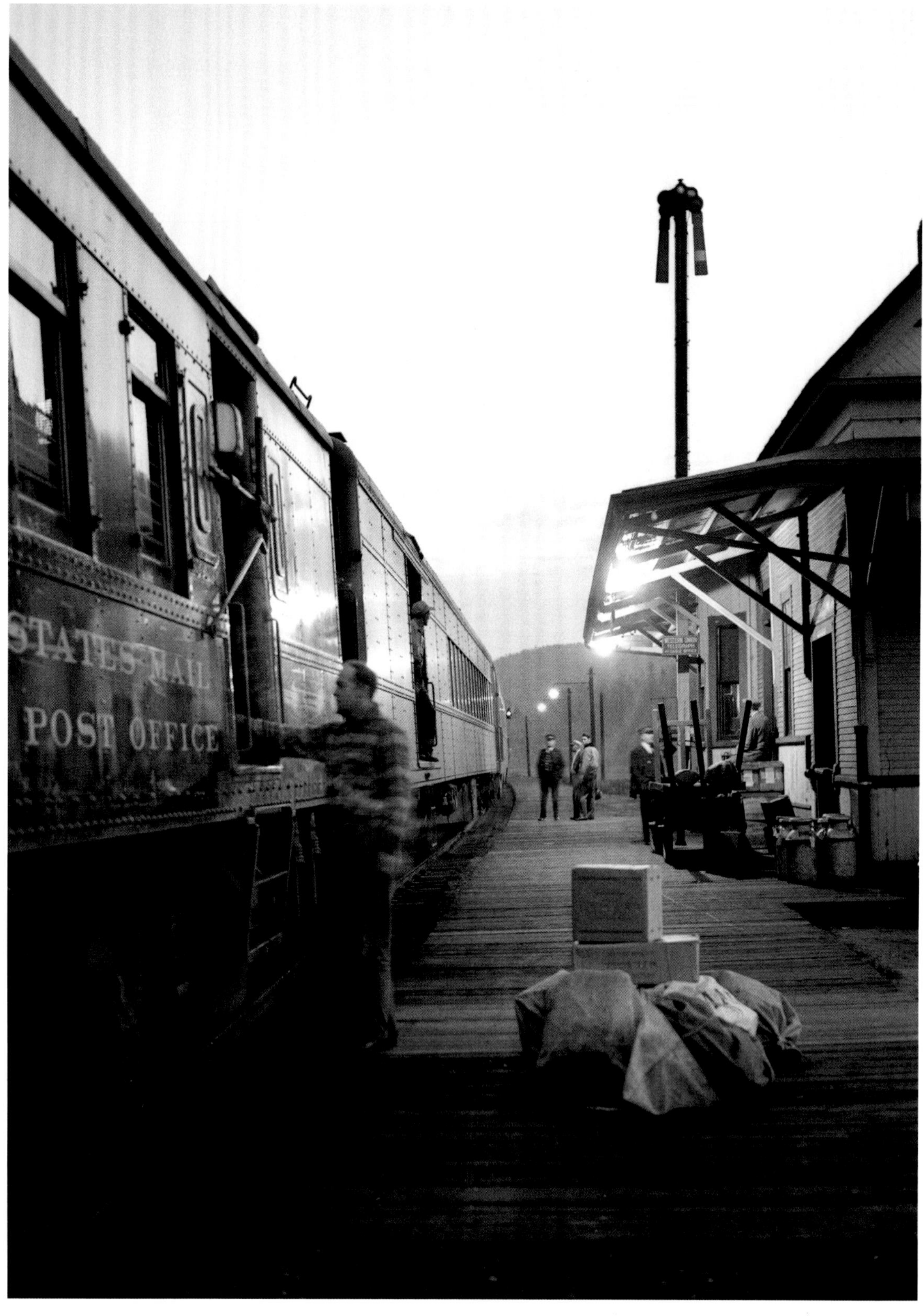

Plate 127. In this view, taken at dusk in October 1948, a Boston & Maine train stops at Phil Hastings's hometown, Bradford, Vermont. A railroader, in the foreground, helps unload mail from the train's Railway Post Office (RPO) car.

Courtesy of California State Railroad Museum. Philip Ross Hastings, MD, Collection, [Negative 388].

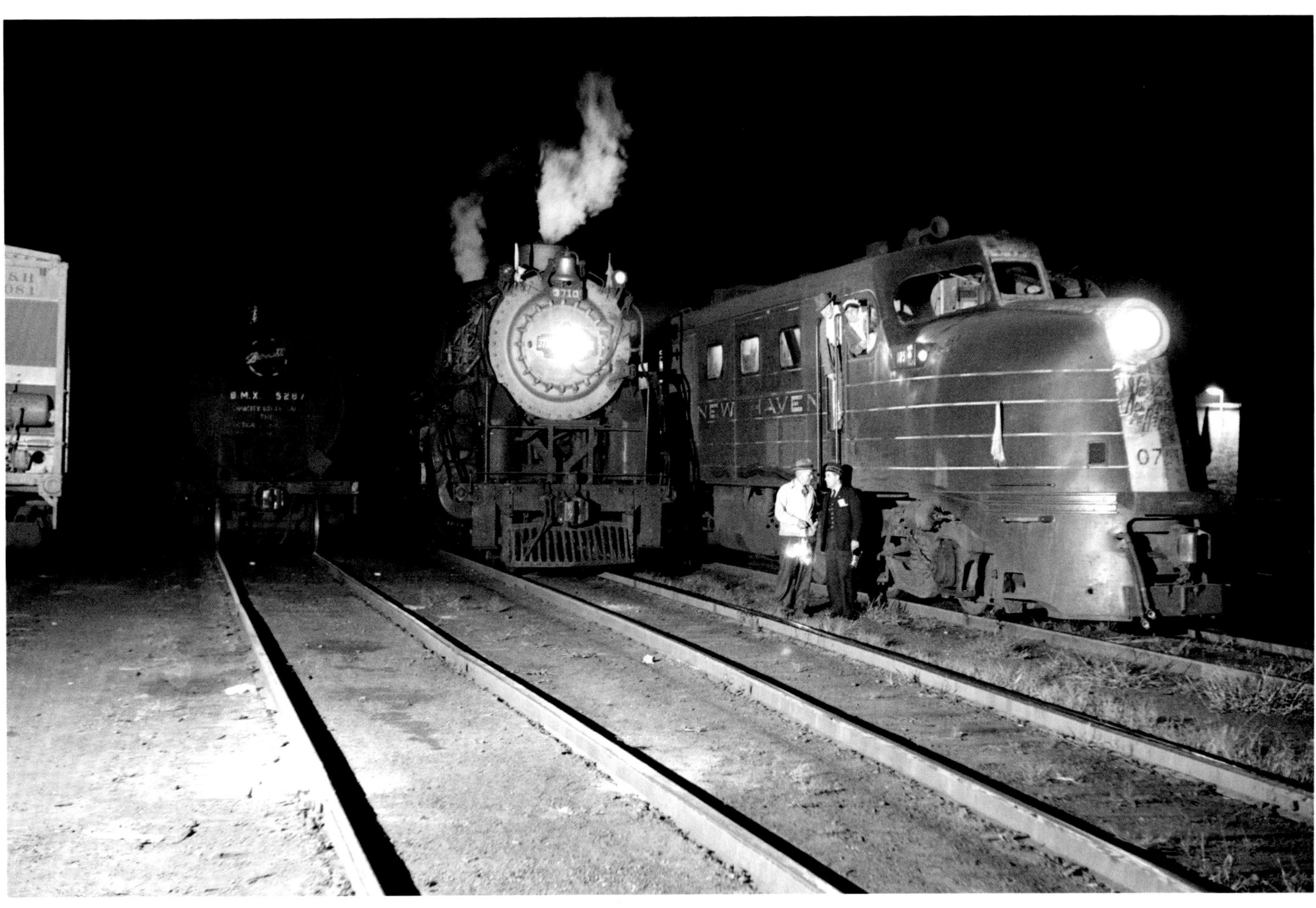

Plate 128. In this posed Hastings nighttime view, the engineer, and what seems to be a "brass hat" such as a road foreman of engines, look from the cab window and door of New York, New Haven and Hartford Railroad DL-109 0751 while a passenger trainman with an unlighted electric lantern and another railroader with a lighted lantern confer. The lighted lantern effect resembles the effect in O. Winston Link's noted photo, "Birmingham Special, Rural Retreat, Virginia." The steam locomotive next to the DL-109 is Boston & Maine 4-6-2 3710.

Courtesy of California State Railroad Museum. Philip Ross Hastings, MD, Collection, [Negative 10504].

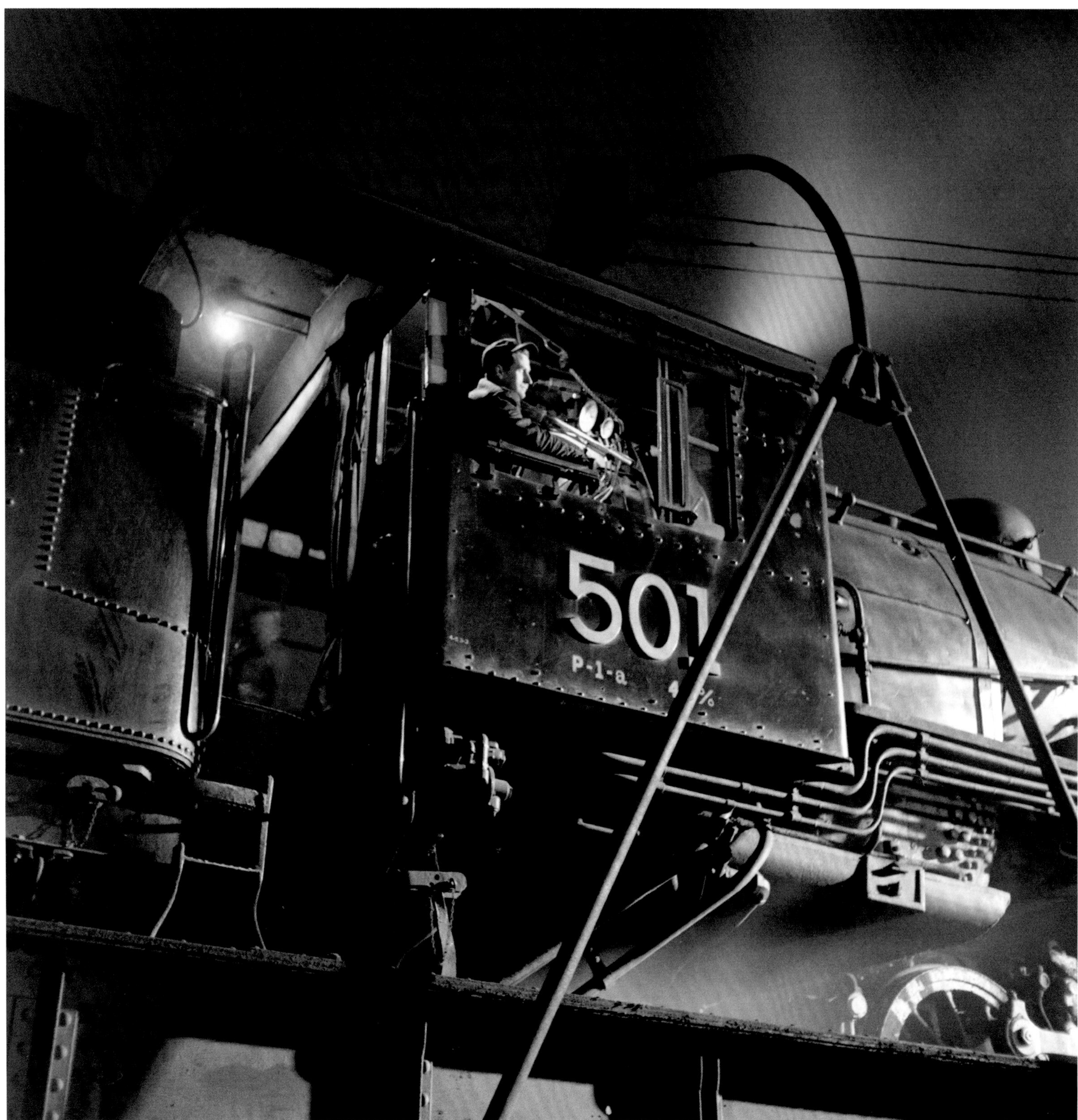
501
P-1-a

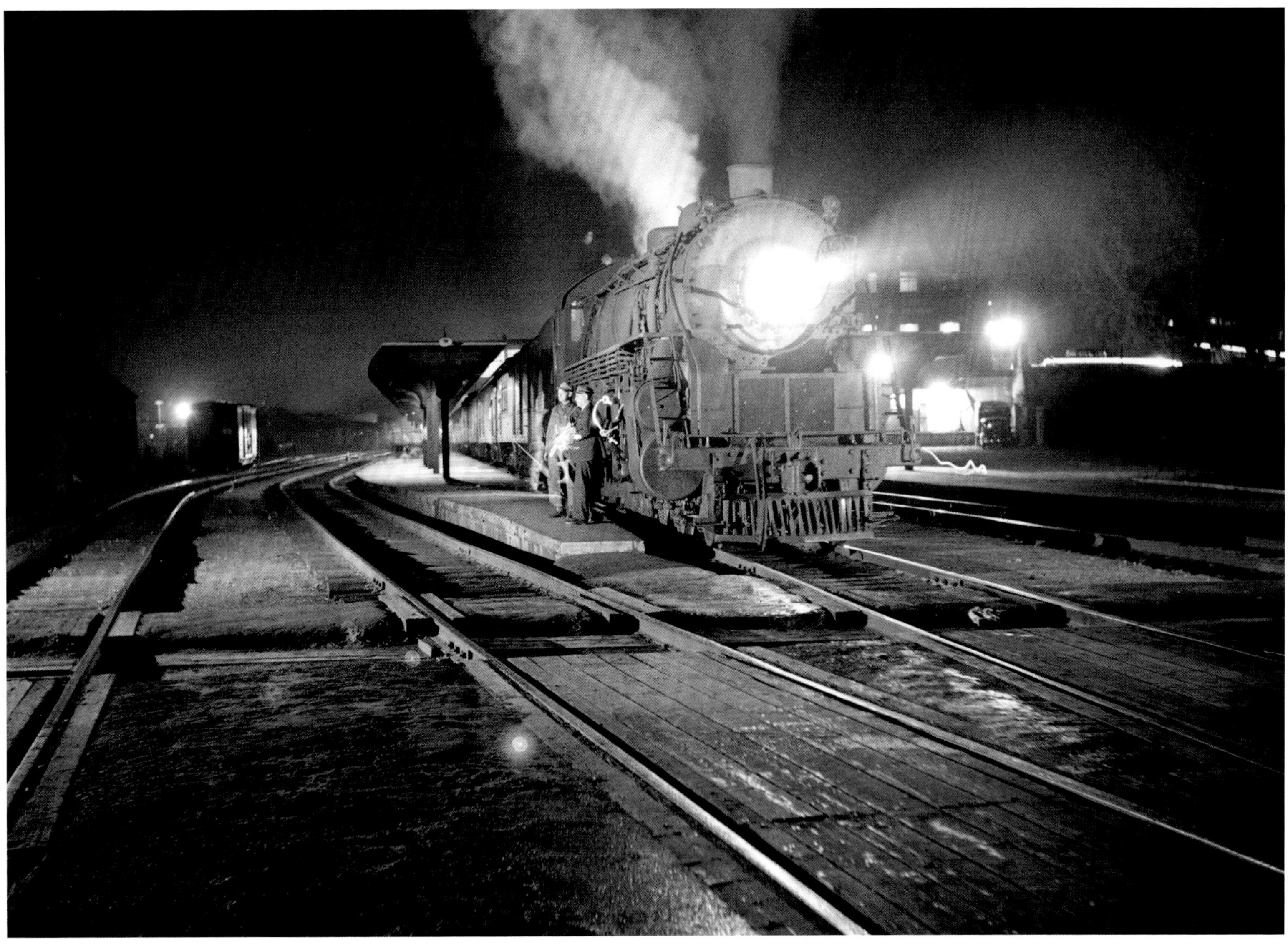

***Facing*, Plate 129.** In another excellent posed view, a Central Vermont hostler sits on the engineer's side of the cab of Central Vermont 501. The locomotive is on a turntable, as shown by the frame in the foreground and the wires running to the apex of the turntable frame at the top center of the image. The 501 was a 0-8-0 switcher. The image was taken in Brattleboro, Vermont, on April 21, 1956. Hastings's notes say this image was taken with "available light."

Courtesy of California State Railroad Museum. Philip Ross Hastings, MD, Collection, [Negative 2655].

Plate 130. In this night view of one of Hastings's favorite railroads, the Rutland, the railroad's *Mount Royal*, led by "Pacific" 85, makes a twenty-minute stop at the station in Burlington, Vermont, which survives today. The train's conductor and engineer discuss orders in the foreground while a coal passer trims the coal pile in the locomotive's tender in the background.

Courtesy of California State Railroad Museum. Philip Ross Hastings, MD, Collection, [Negative 2218].

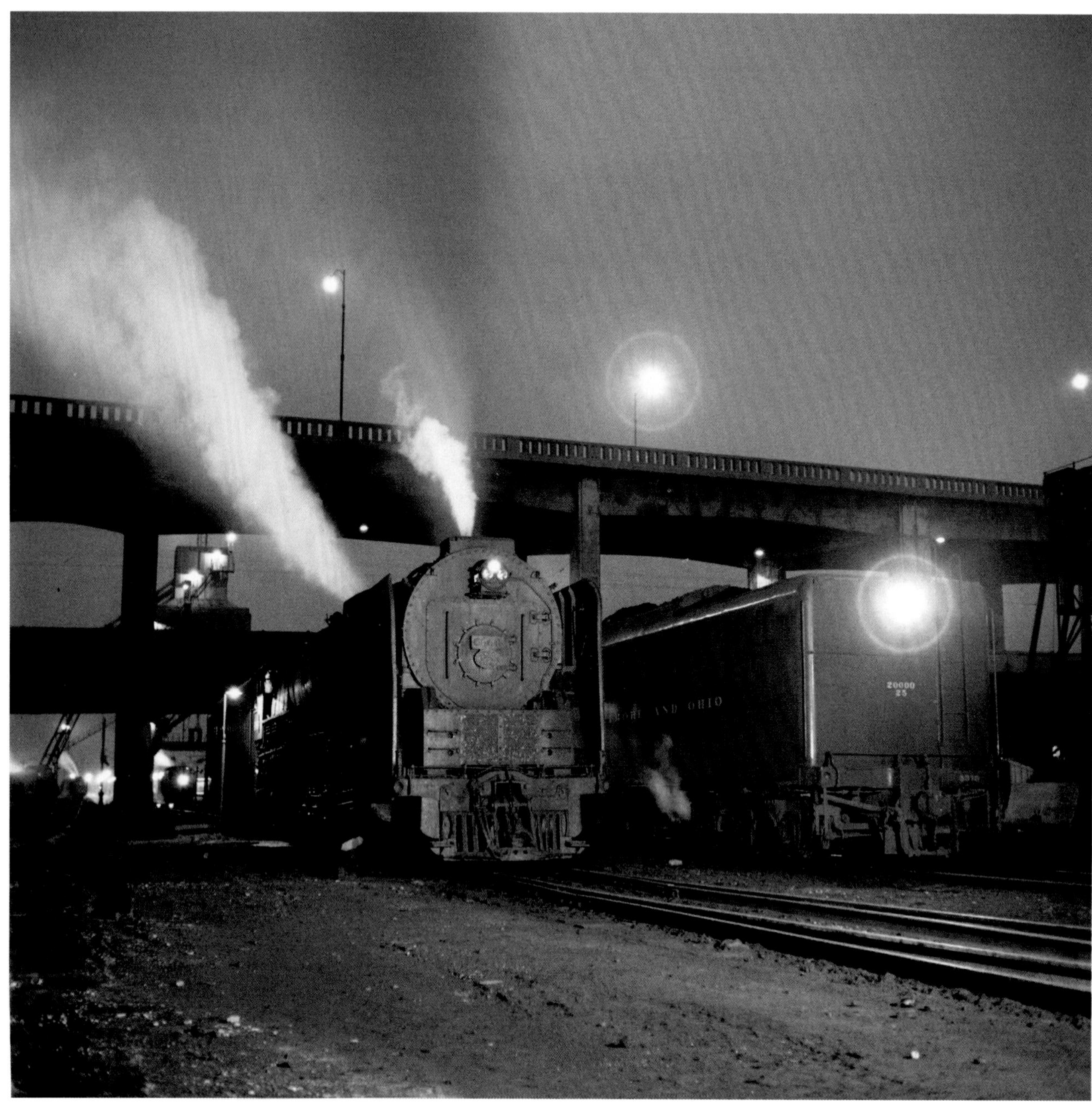

Plate 131. In this nighttime view, magnificent New York Central 6000, the line's first "Niagara" (4-8-4) type, poses beside the tender of a Baltimore & Ohio locomotive ("President" type "Pacific" 5313). Visual interest is added by the light across the Niagara's cab and the locomotives in the background. The location is Cincinnati Union Terminal, Cincinnati, Ohio.

Courtesy of California State Railroad Museum. Philip Ross Hastings, MD, Collection, [Negative 9517].

***Facing*, Plate 132.** In this stunning nighttime view taken from a helper locomotive in the rain, Hastings shows the cab end and cab window of a westbound passenger train. The location is Altoona, and the train is bound up the hill to Gallitzin, Pennsylvania, and beyond. The distorted face of the engineer in 5867, a classic E-7A unit, gives the image a sobering appeal. The image was taken in September 1956. It presages similar work by photographers such as Richard Steinheimer.

Courtesy of California State Railroad Museum. Philip Ross Hastings, MD, Collection, [Negative 3911].

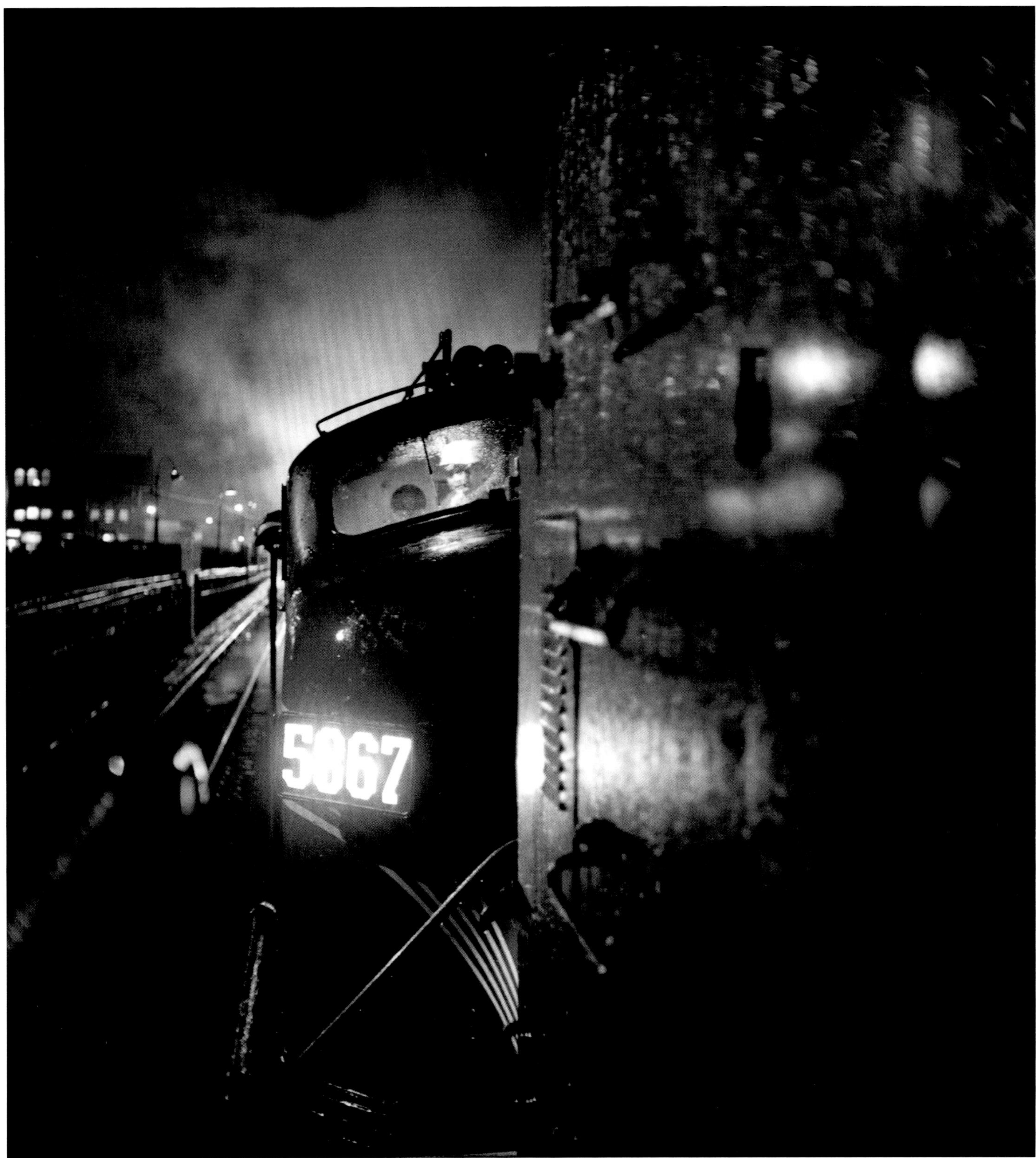
5867

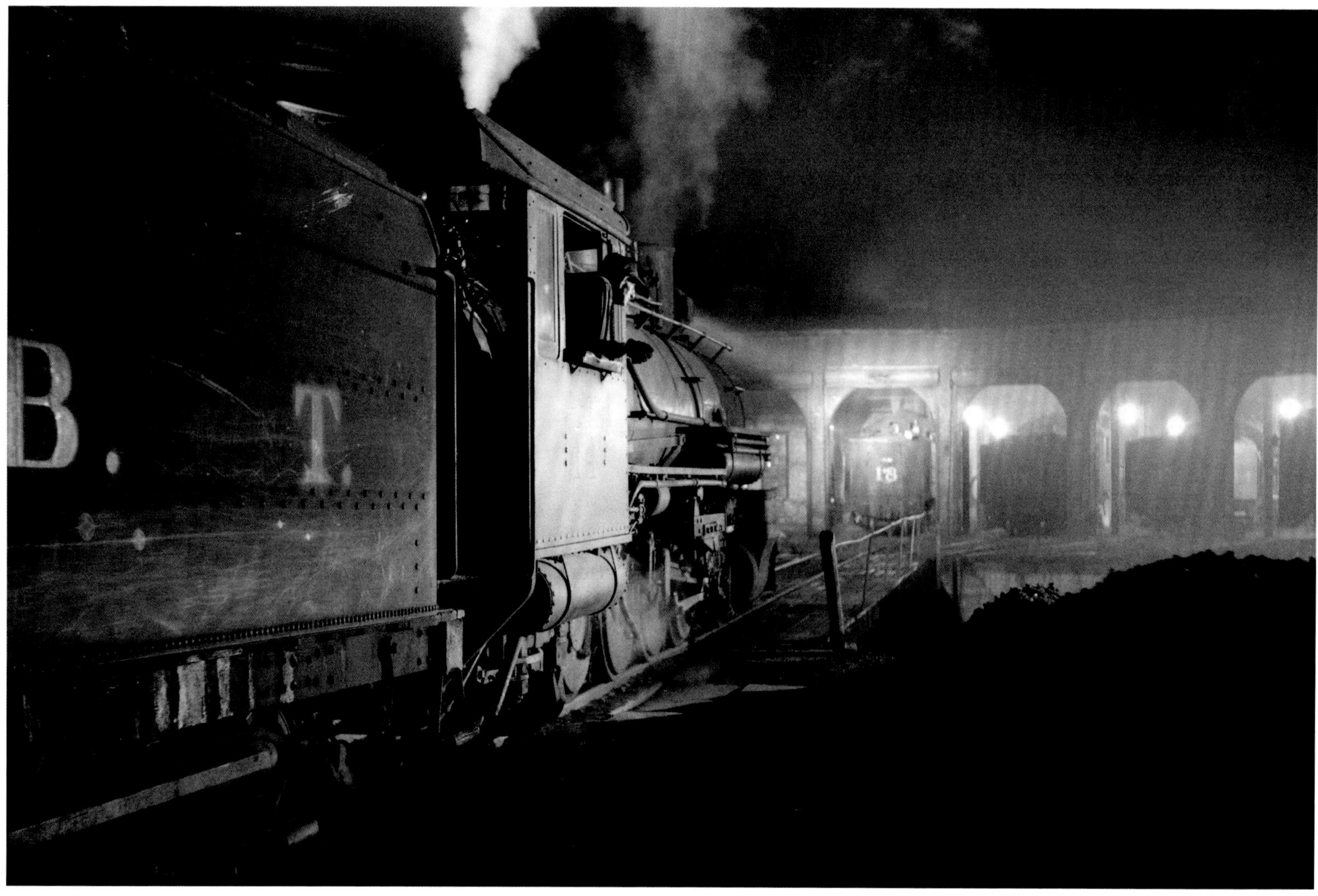

Plate 133. An East Broad Top "Mikado" approaches the turntable and roundhouse at Orbisonia, Pennsylvania, in this Hastings night image. The engineer or hostler is profiled in the middle of the image. The tender end of "Mikado" 18 is visible inside the roundhouse. This image can be repeated today—the East Broad Top reopened in 2021 after ten years of inactivity. The roundhouse, turntable, and six East Broad Top narrow-gauge "Mikados" survive.

Courtesy of California State Railroad Museum. Philip Ross Hastings, MD, Collection, [Negative 7641].

***Facing*, Plate 134.** In this later Hastings night image, a Railway Express Agency (REA) clerk on the Burlington (Chicago, Burlington & Quincy Railroad) looks out of his car as his buddies talk. The train's conductor, at the right, looks over his paperwork. The train is the Burlington's *Ak-Sar-Ben Zephyr* at Omaha, Nebraska, in the 1960s. Hastings's many views of mail, express, and baggage service on American railroads and his station views demonstrate the importance of the railroad to American society during the "Golden Age of Railroading."

Courtesy of California State Railroad Museum. Philip Ross Hastings, MD, Collection, [Negative 6239].

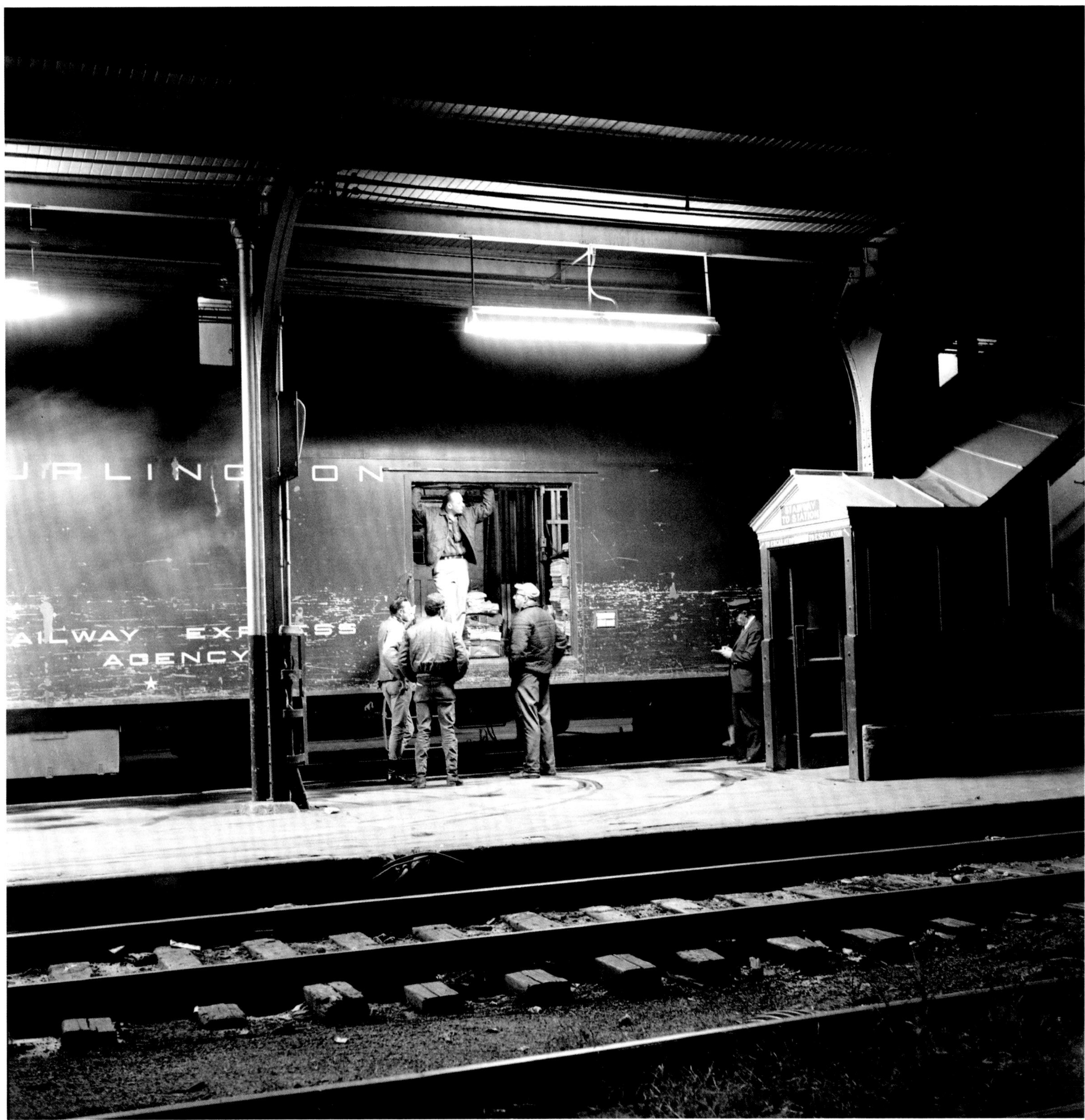
AILWAY
AGENCY

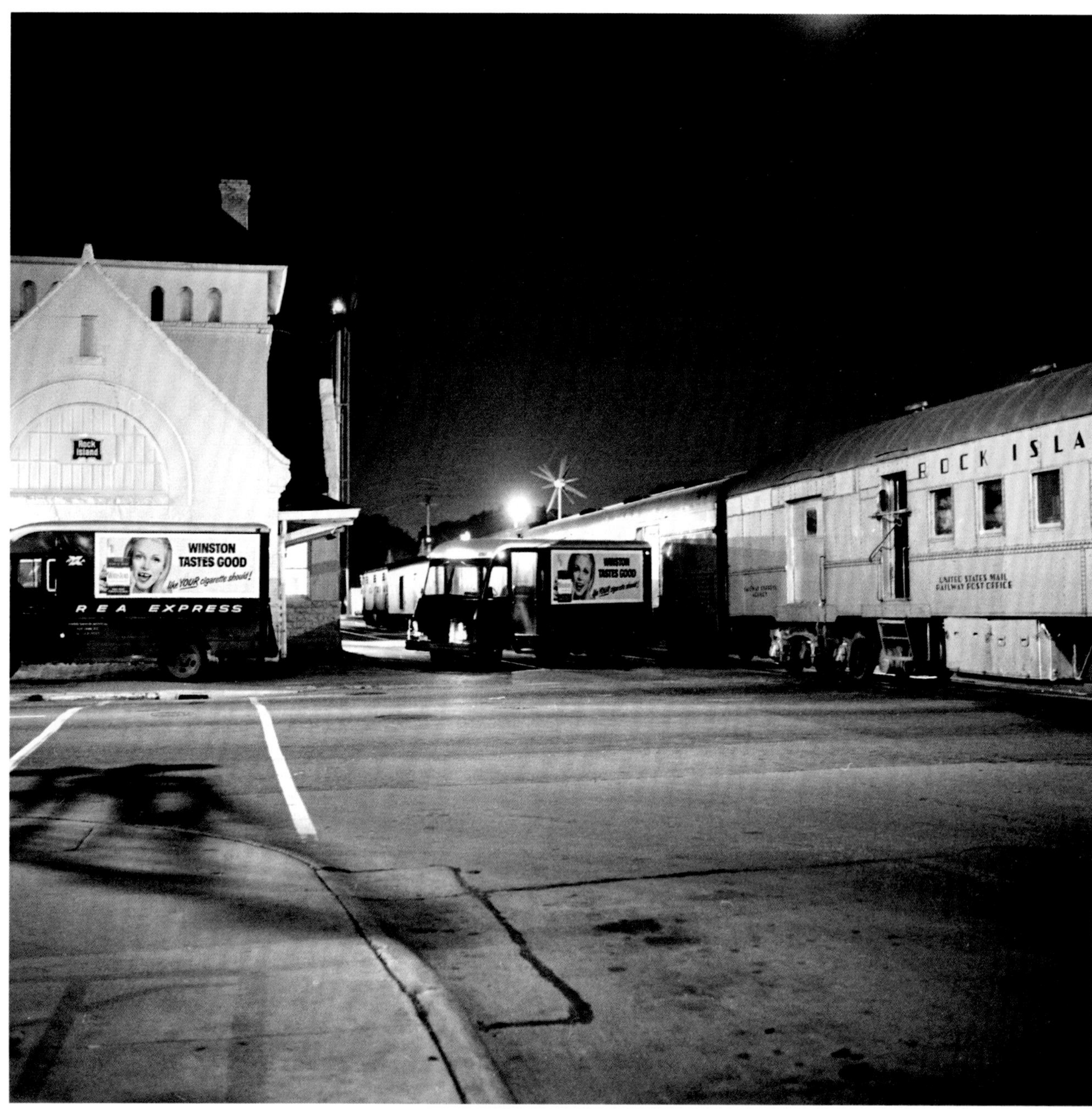

Plate 135. In this later Hastings night view, a Chicago, Rock Island & Pacific Railroad train is stopped at the Waterloo, Iowa, station. Some Railway Express Agency (REA) items are being loaded, and the train's RPO car sits in the foreground. The two REA trucks with "Winston tastes good" advertising—one with the model's front tooth blacked out—both enhance the photo and indicate the time period of the image. The absence of passengers presages the end of "The Rock," which was liquidated in 1980.

Courtesy of California State Railroad Museum. Philip Ross Hastings, MD, Collection, [Negative 4229].

***Facing*, Plate 136.** In this noted and memorable Hastings night photo, Denver & Rio Grande narrow-gauge "Mikado" K-37 499 waits at Toltec siding, its headlight piercing the darkness. The locomotive and its crew—the fireman is captured in his cab window—are waiting for an eastbound freight descending Cumbres Pass. It is the winter of 1955 and 1956. The 499 survives today at the Royal Gorge Park in Colorado.

Courtesy of California State Railroad Museum. Philip Ross Hastings, MD, Collection, [Negative 231].

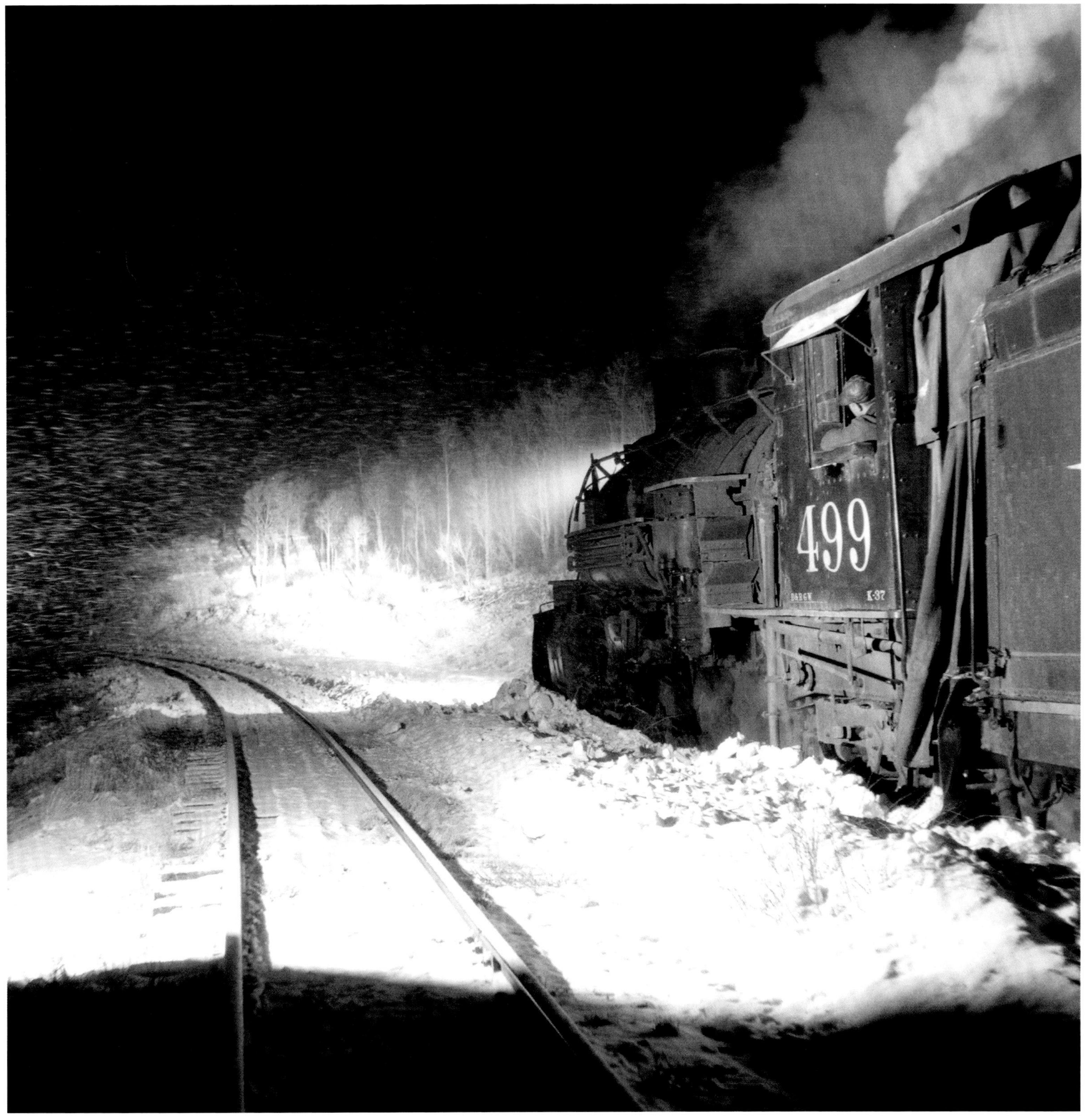
499
K-37

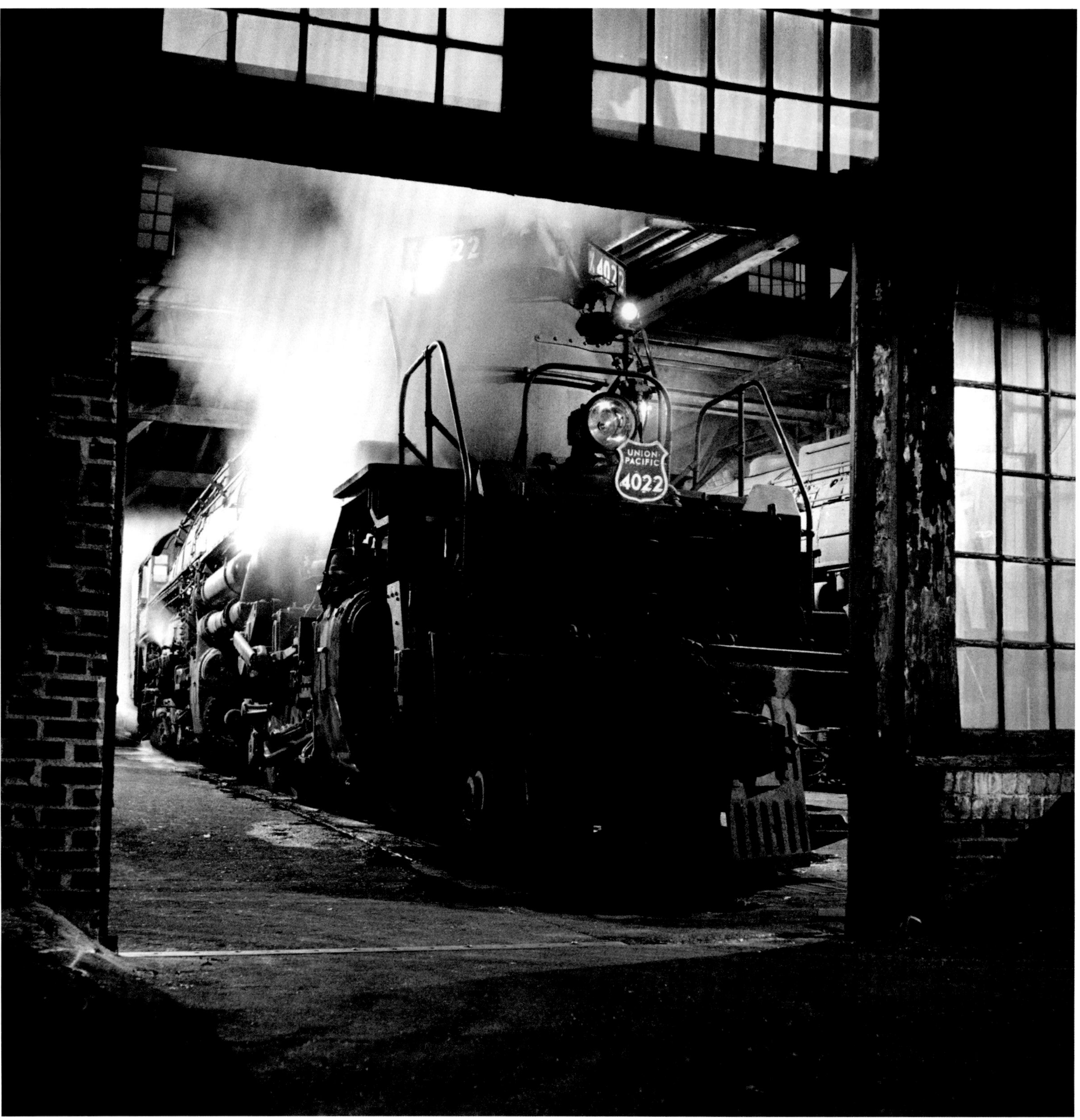
UNION PACIFIC
4022

***Facing,* Plate 137.** Roundhouse / engine house views are a staple of railroad-subject night/darkness photography. In this 1957 image, Union Pacific "Big Boy" 4022 pokes out of a stall during a Wyoming night.

Courtesy of California State Railroad Museum. Philip Ross Hastings, MD, Collection, [Negative 3717].

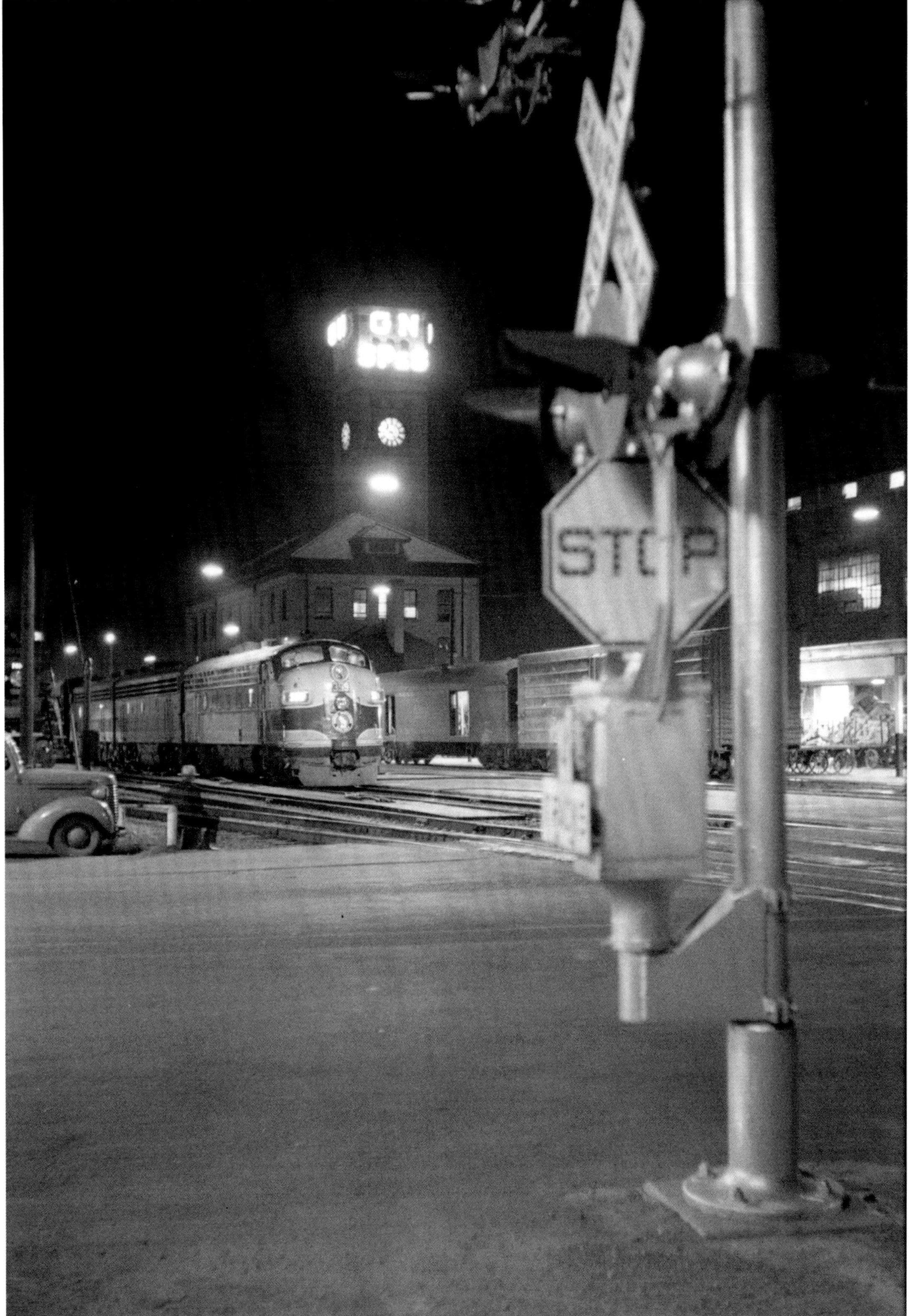

Plate 138. Great Northern train 3, the westbound *Western Star,* sets out cars at the Spokane, Washington, passenger station. Visual interest is added by the seated man and vehicle framing the train at the left, the crossing sign and stop signs at the right, and the Spokane station tower overhead. The locomotive in the middle of the image is Great Northern 359, an F-3A.

Courtesy of California State Railroad Museum. Philip Ross Hastings, MD, Collection, [Negative 9605].

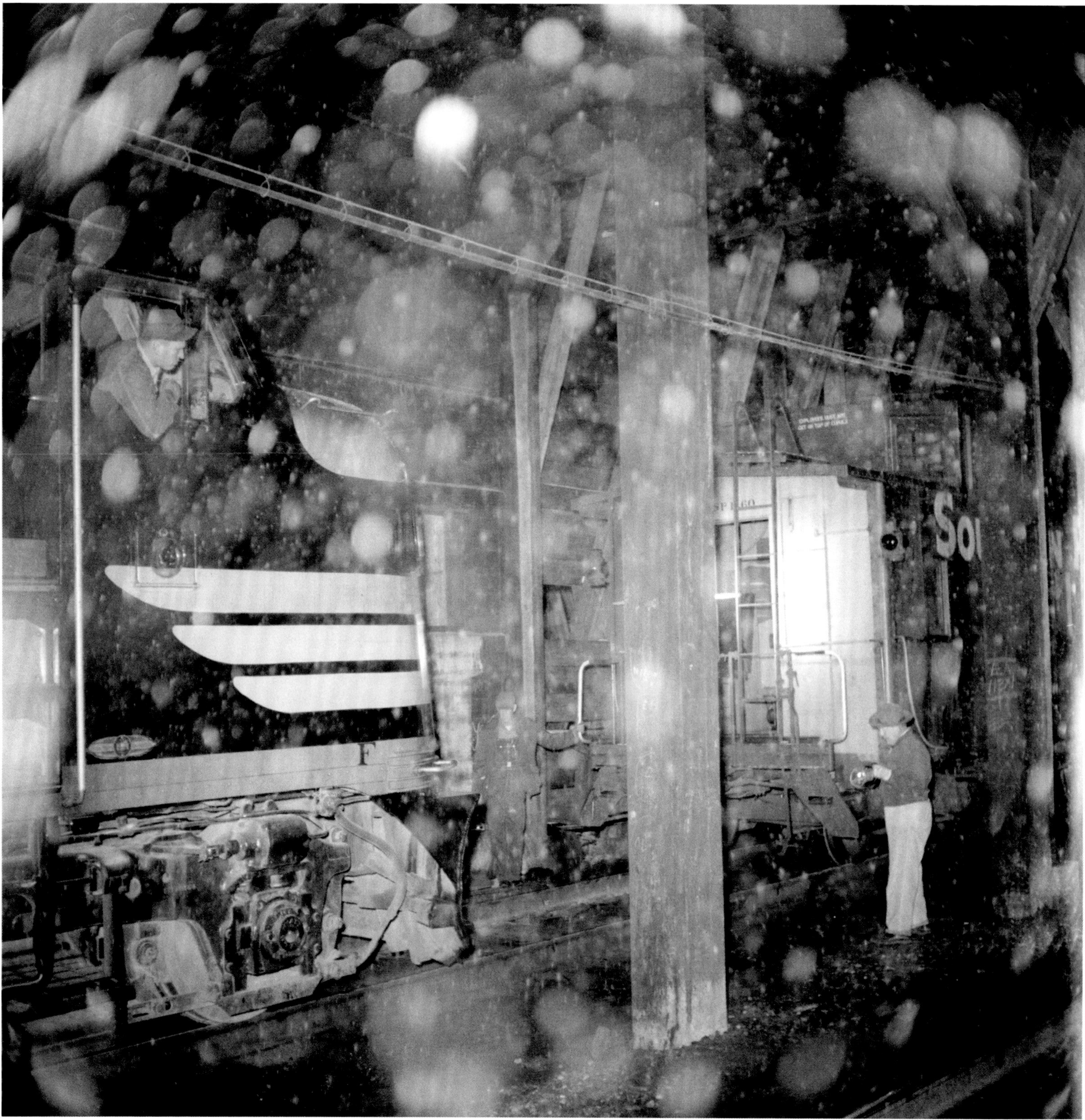

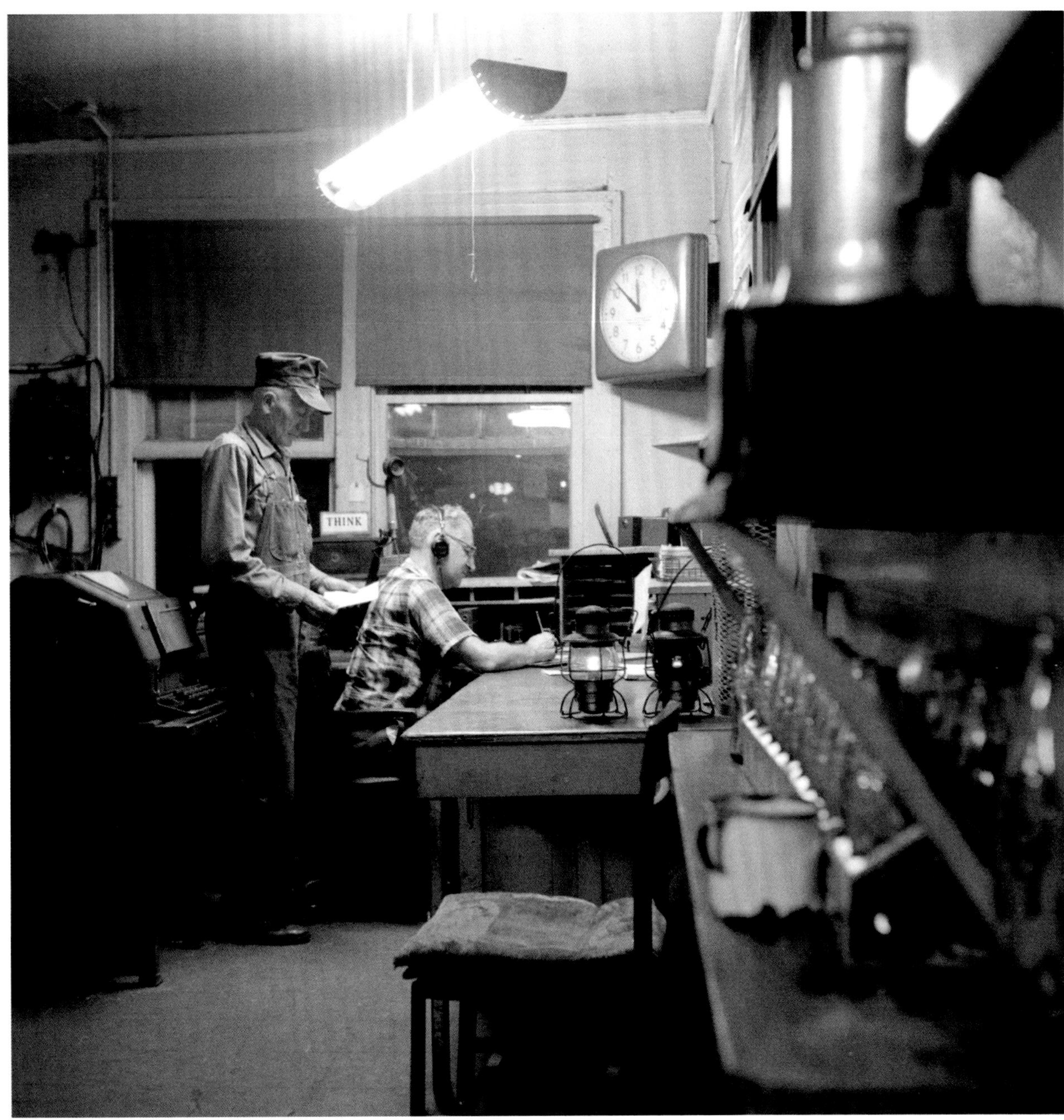

***Facing,* Plate 139.** In another blurred snowflake image by Hastings, a helper engine reassembles a train after cutting out at Norden Summit. The train the helper assisted up the mountain is Extra 6311E. The photo was taken under the snow sheds at Donner Pass. Hastings's flashbulb reflected off the snowflakes filtering through the snow shed.

Courtesy of California State Railroad Museum. Philip Ross Hastings, MD, Collection, [Negative 10322].

Plate 140. The final image in this portfolio of night/darkness Phil Hastings photographs is an operator at work on the Winston-Salem Southbound in Winston-Salem, North Carolina (right). Conductor S. M. Surratt (left) has picked up the waybills and train orders for his train, time freight *209*, due out of Winston Yard at 12:01 a.m. The photo was taken in 1955, the same year as O. Winston Link's similar nighttime view of Troy Humphries and Bernie Cliff at the railroad station in Waynesboro, Virginia.

Courtesy of California State Railroad Museum. Philip Ross Hastings, MD, Collection, [Negative 5677].

NOTES

INTRODUCTION

1. "If Anyone Has Left a Living Legacy to Railroad History, It Is Phil Hastings," *Mid-Continent Railway Gazette*, 10.

2. Philip R. Hastings, "Questionnaire for Railroad Magazine re: Philip R. Hastings, MD," October 13, 1969.

3. Hastings, "O. S. Bradford," 5, 6, 8, 13.

4. Hubbard, "Interesting Railfan No. 85: Philip R. Hastings, MD," 17.

5. Hastings, *The Boston & Maine: A Photographic Essay*, 10.

6. Hastings, "O. S. Bradford," 8.

7. In later years, Hastings also used a 35 mm camera, especially for color transparencies. This book does not reflect this part of his oeuvre. A book focusing on Hastings's color photography would be an interesting and worthwhile addition to our understanding of his work—and of railroad-subject photography in general. Also, Hastings never mentioned using any cameras except a Rolleiflex or 35 mm ones after his juvenile years. However, a substantial minority of the negatives for the images reviewed for this book were in an approximate 2 × 3 format, rather than the Rollei's approximate 2 × 2 format. (None of Hastings's photos used in this book are from 35 mm negatives.) One possible explanation for this is that Hastings might also have used a common camera of the era, the 2 × 3 "Baby" Graphic, the smallest Graphic camera. These cameras could use sheet film or roll film, if they were equipped with a roll film back. Another possibility is that Hastings continued to use his Kodak Vigilant camera. (See introduction text.) The Vigilant that used 620 film produced a 2¼ × 3¼ inch negative, approximately 2 × 3 inches.

8. Hastings, "O. S. Bradford," 8, 12.

9. Hastings, "O. S. Bradford," 5, 8, 10. In Hastings, *The Boston & Maine: A Photographic Essay*, 13, the date of the switch stand photo is given as 1948, but the 1940 date, from photographic evidence, seems more likely to be correct.

10. Hubbard, "Interesting Railfan No. 85: Philip R. Hastings, MD," 19.

11. Hastings, "Questionnaire." However, Hastings states in several sources that his "only railroad pay check" was from the New York, New Haven, and Hartford Railroad for a night of shoveling snow.

12. Hastings interned in Spokane, Washington, and then in the army, he was based at Fort Bragg, North Carolina; Fort Devens, Massachusetts; and Fort George Meade, Maryland. Hastings, "Questionnaire."

13. Hastings, "O. S. Bradford," 12; California State Railroad Museum Library and Archives, *MS 413 Philip Ross Hastings, MD Collection*, "Historical Information," accessed September 5, 2022, https://csrm.andornot.com/media/oac-findingaid/413.pdf; Morgan, "Philip R. Hastings, 1925–1987," 4; Hubbard, "Interesting Railfan No. 85: Philip R. Hastings, MD," 19; Nelson, *Philip R. Hastings: Portrait of the Pennsylvania Railroad*, 124–125; Hastings, "Questionnaire." Hastings was based at the VA Hospital at Canandaigua, New York, during his stint with the Veterans Administration.

14. Many sources misspell her name as Marion Hastings.

15. Hastings, *Remember the Rock*, 48; "If Anyone Has Left a Living Legacy to Railroad History, It Is Phil Hastings," *Mid-Continent Railway Gazette*, 10; Hubbard, "Interesting Railfan No. 85: Philip R. Hastings, MD," 21, 23.

16. Hastings, *Remember the Rock*, 48.

17. Morgan, "Philip R. Hastings, 1925–1987," 4.

18. According to John Gruber, Hastings was first published in *Railroad* in 1946; see his *Focus on Rails*, 22. David P. Morgan states *Trains* published Hastings's first photo (Morgan, "Photo Section," 37). Hastings, in his questionnaire to *Railroad* magazine, states, "My first photo was published in *Trains* in 1946." However, in another source, an undated self-bio in the collections of the California State Railroad Museum Library and Archives, he states his first photo was in *Railroad*.

19. Hastings, "O. S. Bradford," 13.

20. Gruber, *Focus on Rails*, 22, states that Hastings was published "beginning in *Railroad* in 1946." It is unclear whether he meant a photographic or article publication. A search of *Railroad* magazine for 1946 did not locate any Hastings articles. The first publication Hastings mentions is the May 1947 *Trains* article on St. Johnsbury & Lake Champlain Railroad (Hastings, "O. S. Bradford," 13).

21. Hastings, "St. Johnsbury & Lake Champlain," 50.

22. Morgan, "Philip R. Hastings, 1925–1987," 4.

23. Hastings, letter to books editor, Carstens, July 15, 1982. Carstens was the publisher of many railroad-subject books and magazines such as *Railfan*. See also Hastings, letter to Ed and Sally Kochanek, November 17, 1972; Hastings, letter to Mike Schafer, June 14, 1985; Hastings, letter to Jay Stoy, March 22, 1986.

24. H. W. Pontin, letter to Philip R. Hastings, June 3, 1949.

25. Freeman Hubbard, letter to Philip R. Hastings, February 9, 1954. In the letter, Hubbard mentions photos of "good-looking" women twice more. Hubbard's fascination with photos of young women was well known and would be viewed very differently today.

26. Hastings, "Questionnaire."

27. Frank P. Donovan Jr., letter to Hastings, August 21, 1947.

28. To date, the articles have been issued by Kalmbach three times. The first was the original publication in *Trains* magazine, the second in the book *The Mohawk That Refused to Abdicate, and Other Tales*, and the third in three special issues of *Classic Trains*. The text in these various issues is largely the same, but the book has additional images, and the *Classic Trains* articles include a number of previously unpublished images chosen by series editor Greg McDonnell. It is difficult to accumulate the entire original *Trains* series, while the book is easily available on the used-book market and the *Classic Trains* reprints are often offered on eBay. The original *Trains* articles were three in the series "In Search of Steam" (April, May, and June 1954); thirteen in the series "Smoke over the Prairies" (January 1955–February 1956); and fourteen in the series "Steam in Indian Summer" (October 1956–August 1957). The book includes three additional items: "Camelback to Dunellen," "The 2-10-0's That Thought They Could—and Did!," and "Big Boy." Hastings's first article in *Railroad* was "The East Branch and Lincoln," which appeared in the January 1948 issue.

29. *Railroad* magazine, during this period, was printed on pulp stock and extant copies are rapidly degrading. It is not widely held, and there is no readily available index. It would be most helpful to authors focusing on American railroading if an institution with sufficient resources undertook scanning and electronic archiving of this magazine. It would also be helpful to have a comprehensive index for *Railroad*.

30. Hastings, "Questionnaire."

31. Hastings, letter to Mike Schafer, June 14, 1985.

32. Morgan, *The Mohawk That Refused to Abdicate, and Other Tales*, 298.

33. Ibid., 300.

34. Ibid.

35. David P. Morgan, letter to Philip R. Hastings, July 25, 1973.

36. Philip R. Hastings, letter to David P. Morgan, November 17, 1982.

37. Morgan (attributed), "Photo Section," 37.

38. Hastings, "Questionnaire."

39. Nelson, *Philip R. Hastings: Portrait of the Pennsylvania Railroad*, 124–125.

40. Jim Shaughnessy, postcards to Philip R. Hastings, May 15, 1958; June 3, 1958; September 30, 1958.

41. Hastings, "Questionnaire."

42. Nelson, *Philip R. Hastings: Portrait of the Pennsylvania Railroad*, 125; California State Railroad Museum Library and Archives, *MS 413 Philip Ross Hastings, MD Collection*, "Historical Information," accessed September 5, 2022, https://csrm.andornot.com/media/oac-findingaid/413.pdf.

43. "If Anyone Has Left a Living Legacy to Railroad History, It Is Phil Hastings," *Mid-Continent Railway Gazette*, 10–11.

44. Nelson, *Philip R. Hastings: Portrait of the Pennsylvania Railroad*, 10.

45. Hastings's correspondence during this time shows him as the frugal New Englander still—he expected unsolicited correspondents to enclose a self-addressed stamped envelope for a reply.

46. Philip R. Hastings, letter to Kevin P. Keefe, September 13, 1976.

47. "If Anyone Has Left a Living Legacy to Railroad History, It Is Phil Hastings," *Mid-Continent Railway Gazette*, 9.

48. Hastings, *Remember the Rock*, 2.

49. Philip R. Hastings, letter to Donald B. Valentine, Jr., June 2, 1978.

50. "The 1985 Railroad History Awards," *Railroad History*, 8–9.

51. Philip R. Hastings, letter to Jim Boyd, February 6, 1987.

52. Marian B. Hastings, letter to Drew, December 8, 1995.

53. Interview by author with Greg McDonnell, May 29, 2020.

54. Interview by author with Kevin P. Keefe, April 11, 2020.

55. Interview by author with Jim Shaughnessy, September 10, 2006.

56. Brouws and Delvers, *Starlight on the Rails*, 12.

57. See Kyper, "The Boston & Maine's Branch-Line Blues," 28; William B. Stewart's comments in Hastings, *The Boston & Maine: A Photographic Essay*, 12; and Bill Withuhn's comments in Gruber, *Focus on Rails*, 3. See also Gruber's comments on page 21 of *Focus on Rails* and Shaughnessy's comments on page 22.

58. Link always denied that he had artistic intent in taking his famed posed nighttime railroad-subject tableaux, but this claim seems disingenuous. Link also claimed to have no influences on his photography other than Currier and Ives prints. For more on Link, see this author's *O. Winston Link: Life along the Line*.

59. Morgan, "Philip R. Hastings, 1925–1987," 4.

60. Morgan, *The Mohawk That Refused to Abdicate, and Other Tales*, 298.

61. Hastings, "Questionnaire."

62. Mark Smith, letter to Philip R. Hastings, July 11, 1985.

63. A. C. Kalmbach, letter to Hastings, February 25, 1948. The image mentioned in this letter was also a favorite of Lucius Beebe's: See Lucius Beebe, letter to Philip R. Hastings, July 26, 1961.

64. For early examples, see the portraits of railroaders, numbers 13 (by H. W. Pontin) and 39 (by Lucius Beebe) in Beebe's 1940 book, *Highliners: A Railroad Album*.

65. Interview by author with Greg McDonnell, May 29, 2020.

66. Interview by author with Kevin P. Keefe, April 11, 2020.

67. Philip R. Hastings, letter to Mark Smith, December 29, 1985.

68. Philip R. Hastings, letter to Don Ball, July 18, 1979. See note seven for a discussion of the cameras Hastings may have used to take 2½ × 3½ negatives.

69. Also, according to Freeman Hubbard's profile of Hastings, "Interesting Railfans No. 85: Philip R. Hastings, MD," Hastings owned all of Lucius Beebe's books.

70. Gruber, *Focus on Rails*, 21.

71. Hastings and Morgan started discussing the possibility of doing the book that became *The Mohawk That Refused to Abdicate, and Other Tales* soon after their steam safaris started. See David P. Morgan, letter to Philip R. Hastings, April 23, 1957.

72. Shaughnessy's *The Rutland Road* includes a large number of Hastings images.

73. Kyper, "The Boston & Maine's Branch Line Blues," 28.

74. Philip R. Hastings, letter to David P. Morgan, March 20, 1982. See also Hastings, letter to Morgan, November 23, 1981 and Morgan's reply letter of December 17, 1981. At this point, Hastings's working title for the proposed book was *Epic Steam*. Hastings also suggested a book of his photographs to photographer, author, and publisher Donald "Duke" Duke in a letter dated November 26, 1985. In the letter, Hastings suggested it be titled *Fifty Years of Fotographing Trains in the Foggy Bottoms*. In the letter Hastings also mentioned his first railroad photograph was taken in 1937 and that he became involved with the Mid-Continent Railway Museum in 1962 so that a Hastings photography book published in 1987 would honor a fiftieth and a twenty-fifth anniversary. This project was also not realized. Hastings and Krause had many plans for books that were not to be, most notably Hastings profiles of the Milwaukee Road, the Chicago & North Western, the Soo Line, the Illinois Central, Rutland, Canadian Pacific in Vermont, Central Vermont, and Vermont short lines. See Philip R. Hastings, letters to John Krause, October 8, 1978, and February 7, 1980. They also discussed books on the Duluth & Northeastern, the Camas Prairie, and the railroads of the Spokane, Washington, area. See Hastings, letter to Krause, October 12, 1978.

75. Philip R. Hastings, letter to Mark Smith, December 26, 1986.

76. Hastings also envisioned a full book of his photos of the East Broad Top Railroad. See Philip R. Hastings, letter to

Thomas E. O'Neil, July 15, 1972. In a letter to John Krause, December 24, 1977, Hastings outlined his "complete coverages" of railroad subjects: Montreal area; MeC "Mountain Subdivision"; Grand Trunk in New England; CPR in Vermont and Maine; StJ&LC; M&WR, B&C; Central Vermont system; Northern New York steam; San Antonio, Texas; Camas Prairie RR; P-RSL, Camden and Ocean City; and Schlitz "Circus Specials."

77. Mark Smith, letter to Philip R. Hastings, April 28, 1986. This author wishes to note here that he outlined, proposed, and then wrote most of this book before reading this letter.

78. David P. Morgan to Philip R. Hastings, July 3, 1957. This author wishes to note here that he made photo selections for this book before reading this letter.

79. Hubbard, "Interesting Railfans No. 85: Philip R. Hastings, MD," 25.

80. California State Railroad Museum Library and Archives, *MS 413 Philip Ross Hastings, MD Collection*, "Provenance," accessed September 5, 2022, https://csrm.andornot.com/media/oac-findingaid/413.pdf.

1. PORTFOLIO ONE: THE BOSTON AND MAINE

1. For a contemporary view of the B&M as it was during Hastings's young adulthood, see R. M. Neal, *High Green and the Bark Peelers* (New York: Duell, Sloan and Pearce, 1950).

2. Mellon is Andrew Mellon's grandson and an heir to the Mellon banking fortune. Andrew Mellon was treasury secretary from 1921 to 1932 and is best known for opposing government intervention to offset the effects of the Great Depression, which led to his attempted impeachment by Congress.

3. A number of the town spellings mentioned here differ in railroad and nonrailroad use and with time—sometimes the "ugh" ending is included, and sometimes it is not.

4. See plate 112.

2. PORTFOLIO TWO: THE RUTLAND

1. Or railway, depending on the time period.

2. Hastings, "O. S. Bradford," 12.

3. Much of the former Rutland was reunified when the Vermont Railway acquired the Green Mountain Railroad in 1997. The Vermont Rail System also operates the other survivor of the Rutland, the New York & Ogdensburg Railway in New York State.

4. Hastings, "Questionnaire," October 13, 1969.

3. PORTFOLIO THREE: ACROSS NEW ENGLAND

1. With Ed Crist.

2. Today the Maine Central is part of Pan Am Railways, recently purchased by CSX.

3. The Central Vermont has a close historic connection with the Rutland Railroad/Railway—see portfolio 2.

4. Also known during this time as the St. Johnsbury & Lamoille County.

5. See also plate 112, which depicts a well-known New Hampshire short line, the Suncook Valley Railroad.

4. PORTFOLIO FOUR: O CANADA

1. The Quebec Central Railway was a subsidiary of the Canadian Pacific.

5. PORTFOLIO FIVE: NORTHEAST/MID-ATLANTIC

1. By Douglas M. Nelson.

2. Charles Clegg was a master of this type of view.

3. The PRSL's owners leased locomotives to the railroad.

4. Or the Central Railroad of New Jersey (CNJ), owned by the Reading Company, which was in turn owned by the Baltimore & Ohio.

5. The "Camelback" had an engineer's cab located ahead of the locomotive's firebox and a fireman's cab located in the traditional location at the rear of the locomotive.

6. A railway velocipede is a three- or four-wheeled rail vehicle that the rider propels along the track using his or her arms and legs. For a number of period images of Black US railroaders, see the work of Jack Delano.

6. PORTFOLIO SIX: MIDWEST

1. *Passenger Train Journal* was edited by Kevin P. Keefe at the time.

2. New York, Chicago and St. Louis Railroad.

3. Railroad maintenance of way workers are underrepresented in the photographic coverage of American railroads. For excellent period views, see the work of Lewis Hine.

7. Portfolio Seven: West

1. There are also a few images of western short lines and night images taken in the West in Portfolios Eight and Nine.

2. Steam locomotive types usually had names and are also classified using the Whyte system, which has a set of numbers as follows: leading truck-drivers-trailing truck. So in the Whyte system, the "American" type is a 4-4-0. If a locomotive has separately powered sets of drivers, these are separated in the Whyte system, as in this locomotive, a 2-8-8-2. This large locomotive had sixteen driving wheels.

8. Portfolio Eight: Not as Long, but Just as Wide

1. Page 298.

2. Morgan, *The Mohawk That Refused to Abdicate, and Other Tales*, 298.

3. Page 204.

4. See Robertson's *Slow Train to Yesterday* and Beebe, with Charles Clegg's, *Mixed Train Daily*.

9. Portfolio Nine: In the Nighttime

1. Hubbard, "Interesting Railfans No. 85: Philip R. Hastings, MD," 23.

2. These books would not exist without the efforts of photographer and author Jeff Brouws and his wife, agent Wendy Burton. Those who are interested in Shaughnessy's work, and in railroad-subject photography, owe them a great debt.

3. Hastings, "O.S. Bradford," 13.

4. Brouws and Delvers, *Starlight on the Rails*, 12.

5. Hastings moved to Waterloo, Iowa, in 1959. He and his wife, Marian, had five children.

6. Rutland Railroad during part of this time period and Rutland Railway during another part of this time period.

7. See also Lee Rainey and Frank Kyper, *East Broad Top*, 210. Hastings took a number of EBT views for his superb 1953 *Trains and Travel* portfolio about the railroad. He revisited the EBT with David P. Morgan for *Trains* in 1955.

APPENDIX

PHIL HASTINGS'S BIOGRAPHIC TIME LINE AND DESCRIPTION OF HIS PHOTOGRAPHY

From a Letter to Mark Smith, editor, *Locomotive & Railway Preservation*, December 29, 1985:

> Mark, I will herewith attempt my biography with respect to writing, photography and railroad activity.
>
> **April 26, 1925** Born, Bradford, VT
>
> **Summer, 1937** My first decent negative, B&M #1007 by train shed, Concord, NH
>
> **Summer, 1939** First decent camera, Kodak Vigilant f4.5 and 1/200, received from George Norcross
>
> **Jan., 1942** First published photo, cover of Bradford, VT, "Annual Report"
>
> **Jan., 1943** Drew only railroad paycheck, from NYNH&H RR, for one night shoveling snow in Boston, MA, freight yard, after severe blizzard
>
> **Feb., 1946** Print "Saps Running" hung, 5th All-Vermont Camera Club Exhibit, Burlington, VT
>
> **July, 1946** Taught photography course, Camp Tee-la-Wooket, Northfield, VT
>
> **May, 1947** First article published in *Trains* Magazine, "St. Johnsbury and Lake Champlain R.R."
>
> **Jan., 1948** First article published in *Railroad* Magazine, "East Branch and Lincoln R.R."
>
> **1953–1957** Accompanied David P. Morgan, Editor, *Trains*, on annual safari, "In Search of Steam"
>
> **1957** Several prints published in "The Age of Steam" by Lucius Beebe; I think this the first of dozens of subsequent books by various authors which have used my photographs
>
> **1962** Joined the Mid-Continent Railway Historical Society, starting a continuous affiliation leading to my present service on the Board of Directors, and as President of the Society. Also am a qualified Conductor in train service on the Mid-Continent Museum Railway
>
> **1975** Book, *The Mohawk That Refused to Abdicate*, with David P. Morgan, Kalmbach Pub. Co., Milwaukee
>
> **1978** Book, *Grand Trunk Heritage*, Railroad Heritage Press, New York, NY
>
> **1981** Book, *Chicago Great Western*, Carstens Pub., Newton, NJ
>
> **1985** Recipient of the 3rd Annual Achievement Award in photography, Railway and Locomotive Historical Society

From a Letter to Mark Smith, editor of *Locomotive & Railway Preservation*, December 26, 1986:

Highlights of Photographic Coverage

1937–1942 (residing at Bradford, VT)
northern Vermont and New Hampshire
a little of northeastern New York

1946–1950 (Burlington, VT)
northern New England
southern Quebec
northern New York

1948 (six weeks in San Antonio, TX)
San Antonio area, Houston, Brownsville (T&NO, ATSF, MOP, MKT)

1950–1951 (Spokane, WA)
eastern Washington, northern Idaho, western Montana, southern British Columbia (NP, GN, SP&S, MIL, UP, CP, CPR, WI&M)

1951–1952 (Fort Devens, MA)
eastern Massachusetts, southern New Hampshire
North Carolina (A&R, A&W, D&S)

1952–1953 (Fort Geo. Meade, MD)
middle Atlantic and Appalachia (CNJ, PRR, EBT, H&BTM, WMd, B&O, MRLCo, NF&G, C&O, N&W)
1st Colorado expedition (Gunnison, Monarch Branch, Salida)
2nd Colorado expedition (Alamosa to Chama, Raton Pass)

1953–1954 (Albany, NY)
eastern Canada trip with David P. Morgan
another trip to New Brunswick
southeastern New York and eastern PA (PRR, B&O, NYC, UV)
last run of MeC 4-6-2 #470
P-RSL in New Jersey

1954–1955 (Northampton, MA)
"In Search of Steam" with D. P. M. in upper Midwest
more eastern Canada and upper New England

1955–1956 (Albany, NY)
"Steam in Indian Summer" with D. P. M. in eastern U. S.

1956–1959 (Canandaigua, NY)
western New York and southern Ontario (PRR, NKP, CPR, CNR, etc.)
brief visit to Chicago 4/56 (C&NW, GTW, B&O, NKP steam)
1956 trip with D. P. M. (PRR Pbgh. Div., GM, WSSB, SOU Norris Yard)
1957 trip with D. P. M. (GN "Empire Builder," Sierra R. R., SP Sacramento Div., UP "Big Boys")

1959–1986 (Waterloo, IA)

early 1960's
last of mid-west steam (D&NE, B&SO, CB&Q)
trips to Colo. for fall color specials on D&RGW narrow gauge
exploring upper mid-west railroads (CGW, CRI&P, MIL, C&NW, SOO, GB&W,
CB&Q, N&W, IC, WAB, etc.)
starting involvement with Mid-Continent Railway Museum

late 1960's
annual steam-powered "Circus Specials" from Baraboo to Milwaukee
covering the last passenger trains ("Cal. Zephyr," "Yampa Valley," "Lake Cities," "Copper Country Ltd," "Flying Crow," etc.)
taking parents to Arizona on ATSF for three winters (ATSF in northern AZ)
last days of CGW

early 1970s
expanding family trips to include more R. R. photography as the children get older (LV and E-L around Buffalo, NY)
taking the younger kids to Disneyland (FeC and SCL)
Cass Scenic R. R. and environs (WMd, B&O, C&O)
Ontario Northland and Algoma Central
continuing trips to Colorado

late 1970s and early 1980s

a devotion to developing coverage of all railroads in Iowa and Wisconsin, and most railroading in the upper Midwest

final days of the CRI&P, and the MIL in Iowa

covering the entire SOO system

attending Canadian Psychiatric Ass'n. annual conference, and incidentally increasing coverage of railroading in Canada (1978—Halifax, 1979—Vancouver, 1981—Winnipeg, 1982—Montreal)

using visits to emancipated children to increase coverage of the northwest and western Canada (returning from Seattle via British Columbia, Alberta and Saskatchewan)

re-incarnated steam in service (UP 3985 and 8444, N&W 611, NKP 765, RDG 2101, C&NW 1385, NP 328, etc.)

increasing my coverage in the South:

to and from a medical meeting in New Orleans, 12/84

to and from a R&LHS meeting in El Paso, 5/85

to and from a Lexington Group meeting in Memphis, 9/85

a week covering the M-K-T from Kansas City to Houston and back

late 1980s

who knows?

BIBLIOGRAPHY

PHILIP R. HASTINGS—BOOKS—A CHRONOLOGICAL BIBLIOGRAPHY

Morgan, David Page, photography by Philip R. Hastings. *The Mohawk That Refused to Abdicate, and Other Tales.* Milwaukee: Kalmbach, 1975.

Hastings, Philip Ross, edited and designed by John Krause and Ed Crist. *Grand Trunk Heritage: Steam in New England.* New York: Railroad Heritage, 1978.

Hastings, Philip Ross. *Chicago Great Western Railway: Iowa in the Merger Decade.* Newton, NJ: Carstens, ca. 1980.

———. *Remember the Rock.* Andover, NJ: Andover Junction, 1987.

Hastings, Philip Ross, introduction by William B. Stewart, text by Frank Kyper. *The Boston & Maine: A Photographic Essay.* Richmond, VT: Locomotive & Railway Preservation, 1989.

Nelson, Douglas M. *Philip R. Hastings: Portrait of the Pennsylvania Railroad.* Los Angeles: Pine Tree, 2002.

Hastings photos are featured in many other books, including *The Age of Steam, The Rutland Road, Delaware & Hudson,* and *Starlight on the Rails.*

GENERAL BIBLIOGRAPHY

Beebe, Lucius. *Highliners: A Railroad Album.* New York: D. Appleton Century, 1940.

Beebe, Lucius, and Charles Clegg. *Mixed Train Daily: A Book of Short Line Railroads.* New York: Dutton, 1947.

———. *When Beauty Rode the Rails.* Garden City, NY: Doubleday, 1962.

———. *Great Railroad Photographs USA.* Berkeley, CA: Howell-North, 1964.

———. *The Age of Steam.* New York: Promontory, 1990.

Brouws, Jeff, and Ed Delvers. *Starlight on the Rails.* New York: Abrams, 2000.

Fischer, Frederic, director. *Northern Railroads: Vermont and Her Neighbors.* Vermont ETV, 1995, color, 56 minutes.

Gruber, John. *Focus on Rails.* North Freedom, WI: Mid-Continent Railway Historical Society, 1989.

———. *Classic Steam.* New York: Fall River, 2009.

Hastings, Philip R. “St. Johnsbury & Lake Champlain.” *Trains,* May 1947, 50–59.

———. “The East Branch and Lincoln.” *Railroad,* January 1948, 118–125.

———. “Canadian Pacific in New England.” *Trains,* December 1948, 12–15.

———. “Mountain Subdivision.” *Trains,* January 1950, 10–15.

———. “Pacifics to Placid.” *Trains,* September 1950, 22–26.

———. “St. Albans: Home of the C.V.” *Railroad,* May 1951, 18–23.

———. “T&NO Junction.” *Railroad,* February 1952, 34–45.

———. “The Trains That Cost Too Much.” *Trains and Travel,* July 1953, 14–17.

———. "Railroad Town." *Railroad*, August 1953, 10–29.
———. "12,000 Cars a Day." *Trains and Travel*, September 1953, 22–27.
———. "East Broad Top: A Photo Story." *Trains and Travel*, November 1953, 31–49.
———. "Mogul Country Farewell." *Railroad*, March 1954, 32–59.
———. "Into the Freezing Darkness." *Trains*, April 1956, 48–56.
———. "Once in a Timetable: Twilight Flight of the *Crow*." *Passenger Train Journal*, September 1977, 18–22.
———. "Once in a Timetable: Lonely Nights on the *Copper Country*." *Passenger Train Journal*, October 1977, 18–23.
———. "Once in a Timetable: Winter on the *Yampa Valley*." *Passenger Train Journal*, February 1978, 18–24.
———. "Once in a Timetable: *Lake Cities* Legacy." *Passenger Train Journal*, March 1978, 15–20.
———. "Once in a Timetable: Hymn to the *Hawkeye*." *Passenger Train Journal*, July 1978, 13–19.
———. "Once in a Timetable: Lean Times on the *Mainstreeter*." *Passenger Train Journal*, January 1979, 24–29.
———. "Once in a Timetable: GN's *Prairie Ambassador*." *Passenger Train Journal*, June 1979, 18–23.
———. "Once in a Timetable: *The Plainsman*." *Passenger Train Journal*, November 1979, 18–23.
———. "O.S. Bradford." *Locomotive & Railway Preservation*, March 1986, 3–13.
———. "Jack Haley and His Chicago Central Crew." *Trains*, August 1986, 20–24.
———. "Fantrip, 1953-style." *Classic Trains*, Winter 2012, 68–75.
Hubbard, Freeman. "Interesting Railfans No. 85: Philip R. Hastings, M.D." *Railroad*, January 1970, 19–25.
"If Anyone Has Left a Living Legacy to Railroad History, It Is Phil Hastings." *Mid-Continent Railway Gazette*, March 1987, 9–14.
Jessup, Steve. "Marshall Canyon Revisited." *Railfan and Railroad*, February 2022, 52–59.
Knapke, William F., with Freeman Hubbard. *The Railroad Caboose*. San Marino, CA: Golden West, 1968.
Kyper, Frank. "The Boston & Maine's Branch Line Blues." *Locomotive & Railway Preservation*, May–June 1989, 12–29.
Lewis, Robert G. *Handbook of American Railroads*. New York: Simmons-Boardman, 1956.
Link, O. Winston. *Night Trick on the Norfolk & Western Railway*. Roanoke, VA: Norfolk & Western Railway, 1957.
Link, O. Winston, with text by Tim Hensley. *Steam Steel & Stars*. New York: Abrams, 1987.
Mead, Edgar T., Jr. *Through Covered Bridges to Concord*. Brattleboro, VT: Stephen Greene, 1970.
Morgan, David P. "Missouri Pacific's Kingsville Division. *Trains*, June 1949, 16–25.
———. (attributed). "Photo Section." *Trains*, November 1955, 30–45.
———. "Philip R. Hastings, 1925–1987." *Trains*, May 1987, 4.
Morgan, David P, and Philip R. Hastings. "In Search of Steam: Volume I (1953–1954)." *Classic Trains* (Special Collector's Edition), 2007.
———. "In Search of Steam: Volume II (1954–1955)." *Classic Trains* (Special Collector's Edition), 2009.
———. "In Search of Steam: Volume III (1955)." *Classic Trains* (Special Collector's Edition), 2011.
Neal, R. M. *High Green and the Bark Peelers*. New York: Duell, Sloan and Pearce, 1950.
"The 1985 Railroad History Awards." *Railroad History* 153 (Autumn 1985): 6–10.
Plowden, David. *A Time of Trains*. New York: Norton, 1987.
Rainey, Lee, and Frank Kyper. *East Broad Top*. San Marino, CA: Golden West, 1982.
Reevy, Tony. "Artist of the Rail: Phil Hastings." *Railroad History* 198 (Spring–Summer 2008): 66–78.
———. *O. Winston Link: Life along the Line*. New York: Abrams, 2012.
———. *The Railroad Photography of Jack Delano*. Bloomington: Indiana University Press, 2015.
———. *The Railroad Photography of Lucius Beebe and Charles Clegg*. Bloomington: Indiana University Press, 2019.
Robertson, Archie. *Slow Train to Yesterday*. Boston: Houghton Mifflin, 1945.
Shaughnessy, Jim. *Delaware & Hudson*. Berkeley, CA: Howell-North, 1967.
———. *The Rutland Road*. La Jolla, California: Howell-North, 1981.
———. *Jim Shaughnessy: Essential Witness*. London: Thames and Hudson, 2017.
Shaughnessy, Jim, with Jeff Brouws. *The Call of Trains: Railroad Photographs by Jim Shaughnessy*. New York: Norton, 2008.
Steinheimer, Richard, with Jeff Brouws. *A Passion for Trains: The Railroad Photography of Richard Steinheimer*. New York: Norton. 2004.

INDEX

Note: Italicized page numbers indicate illustrations.

TONY REEVY is assistant vice provost for university interdisciplinary initiatives development at North Carolina State University. He is a graduate of North Carolina State University, UNC–Chapel Hill, and Miami University. His previous publications include poetry, nonfiction, and short fiction. He resides in Durham, North Carolina, with wife, Caroline Weaver, and children, Lindley and Ian.

KEVIN P. KEEFE is a Milwaukee-based journalist and a member of the board of directors of the Center for Railroad Photography & Art.